W9-CFI-215

LEARN THE DAYS OF THE WEEK ~ MONTHS ~ SEASONS

with the

MUNCH BUNCH

Library of Congress in Publication Data

Reed, Giles.
   Learn the days of the week, months,
seasons with the Munch Bunch.

   Summary: The members of the Munch Bunch
take part in an activity for each day of the
week and each month and season of the year.
   1. Calendar—Juvenile literature. 2. Months
—Juvenile literature. 3. Days—Juvenile
literature. 4. Seasons—Juvenile literature.
[1. Calendar. 2. Months. 3. Days. 4. Seasons]
I. Mitson, Angela, ill. II. Title.
CE13.R43   1981   529'.2   81-12148
ISBN 0-86625-077-8   AACR2

Rourke Publications, Inc.
Windermere, FL   32786

MONDAY
Monday's child is fair of face

TUESDAY
Tuesday's child is full of grace

WEDNESDAY

Wednesday's child is full of woe

THURSDAY
Thursday's child has far to go

FRIDAY

Friday's child is loving and giving

SATURDAY

Saturday's **child works hard for a living**

SUNDAY

But the child that is born on the Sabbath

day is bonny and blithe and good and gay

Thirty days hath September,

April, June and November

All the rest have thirty one

Excepting February alone

Which has twenty eight days clear

And twenty nine in each Leap Year.

JANUARY

There are 31 days in January

We sometimes have snow in January

FEBRUARY

There are 28 days in February
In a Leap year, there are 29 days in February

MARCH

There are 31 days in March
March can be a windy month

APRIL

There are 30 days in April
In April we have showers of rain

MAY

There are 31 days in May
In May you can see lots of flowers

JUNE

There are 30 days in June

It is nice to have a picnic in June

JULY

There are 31 days in July
There is no school in July

AUGUST

There are 31 days in August
August can be a very sunny month

SEPTEMBER
There are 30 days in September
September is a harvest month

OCTOBER

There are 31 days in October
October **can be a foggy month**

NOVEMBER

There are 30 days in November
Leaves fall from the trees in November

DECEMBER

There are 31 days in December
We get Christmas presents in December

THE SEASONS

SPRING
Spring is the first
season of the year

SUMMER
Summer is the warmest
season of the year

AUTUMN
Autumn is the season when trees shed their leaves

WINTER
Winter is the coldest season of the year

THE DAYS OF THE WEEK

THE MONTHS OF THE YEAR

THE SEASONS

SPRING   SUMMER   AUTUMN   WINTER

· At-A-Glance Phone Numbers ·

Veterinarian _____

Back-up Veterinarian _____

Closest Surgery Center _____

Farrier _____

Insurance Company _____

Policy Number(s) _____

_____

_____

_____

HANDS-ON
SENIOR
HORSE CARE

THE COMPLETE BOOK OF SENIOR EQUINE
MANAGEMENT AND FIRST AID

By Karen E.N. Hayes, DVM, MS
& Sue M. Copeland

PRIMEDIA Enthusiast Group

Group V.P./Group Publishing Director: Susan Harding

Authors: Karen E.N. Hayes, DVM, MS and Sue M. Copeland
Art Director: Lauryl Suire Eddlemon
Director of Product Marketing: Julie Beaulieu
Photography: Kevin McGowan, how-to shots; cover, Arnd Bronkhorst;
Atlas of Aging photos (2), Cappy Jackson.
Illustrations: Kip Carter, MS, CMI
Proofreading: Marilee B. Nudo

Primedia Equine Group
656 Quince Orchard Road, #600
Gaithersburg, MD 20878
301.977.3900
To order call 800.952.5813

On the cover: Friesian foundation stallion Laes, age 26. Owned by
Leyendekker Friesians, 9001 Ave. 360, Visalia, CA 93291.

Library of Congress Cataloging-in-Publication Data

Hayes, Karen E. N.
    Hands on senior horse care : the complete book of senior equine
management and first aid / by Karen E.N. Hayes & Sue M. Copeland.
        p. cm.
Includes bibliographical references (p.   ).
  ISBN 1-929164-11-4
  1. Horses. 2. Horses--Aging. 3. Horses--Diseases. 4. Veterinary
geriatrics. 5. First aid for animals. I. Copeland, Sue M. II. Title.
    SF285.3 .H39 2001
    636.1'089897--dc21
                        2001006161

OTHER BOOKS IN THE HANDS-ON SERIES

• HANDS-ON HORSE CARE, The Complete Book of Equine First Aid. In cooperation with the American
Association of Equine Practitioners. By Karen E.N. Hayes, DVM, MS, edited by Thomas C Bohanon, DVM, MS;
created and edited by Sue M. Copeland. Flow-chart formatted signposts and action plans for a wide range of equine
injuries and disease, plus photographic, step-by-step instructions for such skills as wrapping legs, giving shots, and
identifying toxic plants. 400 pages. $29.95. **Call 800.952.5813, item # ZB28.**

• HANDS-ON DOG CARE, The Complete Book of Canine First Aid. By Sue M. Copeland and John A. Hamil,
DVM. Flow-chart formatted signposts and action plans for a wide range of canine injuries and disease, plus photographic, step-by-step instructions for such skills as wrapping wounds, transporting an injured dog, and giving shots.
400 pages. $29.95. **Call 800.952.5813, item #ZBDB.**

A Special Thanks to:

• Julie Beaulieu, PRIMEDIA Equine Group, for her efforts and perseverance in this project.
• Susan M. Harding, VP, Group Publishing Director, PRIMEDIA Equine Group, for her wisdom and continued support.
• Lauryl Suire Eddlemon, art director for HANDS-ON HORSE CARE, HANDS-ON DOG CARE, and this book, for her excellent, efficient work and professionalism.
• Currie Equine Clinic, Hempstead, Texas, for its terrific help with photography. Dr. Andrew Currie (in the photo on page 385), his wife, Sandy, Cathy Cribbs (the human model in this book), Sabra Zock (horse stylist and handler), and Whit and Granny (our late 20s equine models). We couldn't have done it without you!
• E. W. "Buff" Hildreth, Richmond, Texas, for her assistance with the Top Priority—Tooth Care and Alternative Medicine chapters.
• Kevin McGowan, our terrific how-to photographer, for his can-do, professional attitude and high-quality work.
• Kip Carter, MS, CMI, master medical illustrator, for his wonderful work.
• Marilee B. Nudo, for her eagle-eye proofreading and enthusiastic support.
• Dr. Gary Potter, Texas A&M University, for allowing us to use Dr. Gary Henneke's condition grading chart (page 301). And Dr. Henneke, for his help on that chart.
• Dan Hayes and Rick Copeland, husbands and best friends of the authors, for their endless patience and support of all things horse, including this project.

About the Authors:

KAREN E. N. HAYES, DVM, MS

A 1979 graduate of the University of Illinois' veterinary school and the first woman in that program to win the Up-john Award for Large Animal Clinical Medicine, Dr. Hayes practiced small animal medicine for 3 years, then focused her skills on the horse, earning a specialty degree in equine reproductive physiology and operating equine-exclusive veterinary practices in Wisconsin, Arkansas, then Idaho, where she raises Friesian horses with her psychologist husband, Dan. The award-winning author of HANDS-ON HORSE CARE as well as two other equine-care books and hundreds of horse-related magazine articles, Dr. Hayes has dedicated her love of the horse and her years of veterinary experience to the betterment of horse care through education.

CAPPY JACKSON

SUE M. COPELAND

An award-winning journalist in the equine field, Sue is a lifelong horse owner. She was an editor at *Horse & Rider* Magazine for 11 years. There she garnered numerous writing and editing awards, including the American Horse Publications coveted General Excellence award for the magazine and its team. She is creator and editor of this book's sister publication, HANDS-ON HORSE CARE, which won the AHP's Best Equine-Related Book honor. She is co-author, with Dr. John Hamil, of HANDS-ON DOG CARE (Doral Publications). That book was nominated for excellence by the Dog Writers Association of America, and won a Glyph award for Best How-To Book from the Arizona Book Publishing Association. Sue is a contributing editor to *Horse & Rider* and *Practical Horseman*. She and her husband, Rick, share their Richmond, Texas, farm with three dogs and four horses.

Table of Contents

NOTICE TO READERS
This book provides useful instructions, but we can't anticipate all of your working conditions or the characteristics of your horse, or his injury/illness. For safety, you should use caution, care, and good judgment when following the procedures described in this book. Consider your own skill level and the instructions and safety precautions provided. Neither the publisher nor the authors shall assume responsibility for any injury to persons or horses as a result of the use or misuse of the information provided. Consult your veterinarian whenever you have a question about the care of your horse.

Foreword

Fabo

This book epitomizes and restores all that was missing in the care of senior horses a mere 20 years ago. The magnificent old Arabian stallion Fabo, shown here in 1986 at age 23 (right), was toothless and unable to eat the commonly available premium feeds of the time. He was shedding pounds—and muscle—at an alarming rate.

After much hand-wringing and failed attempts at finding readily available, nutritious substitutes for the hay and grain he could no longer eat, his owner and I discovered that the old boy loved white Wonder Bread. Ripped up, crusts on. Though woefully lacking in fiber and other equine-specific nutrients (which we supplemented in other ways), Wonder Bread slowed down his weight loss, put some shine back in his coat, and allowed him to sire his way through 6 more productive years.

As a scientist, that unconventional diet made me shudder. It solved some of Fabo's problems, and created some others, and I wouldn't recommend it today. But it extended the life of a horse that would have faded away if his owner had refused to think "outside the box."

Volkert

In contrast, my beloved Friesian gelding Volkert, shown at left, was a vigorous 21 in this photo taken in August 2001. At the age of 16 he'd begun losing weight and muscle just as Fabo had, as aging teeth and a slowing digestive tract made it more difficult to get needed nutrition from standard horse rations. Along with the diligent care outlined in this book, Volkert got a new ration: a senior-formulated complete feed, which wasn't available in Fabo's day. Within 3 months of getting the new ration, he looked 3 years younger. This year, the gelding returned to the local show circuit and performed with more verve than horses half his age.

We are blessed today with a wealth of new information and tools in the care of our aging horses, tools that will help your senior not only live longer, but younger. Use this book and adopt those tools as your own. Then, enjoy every precious year of comfort and vitality you'll have with your equine friend.

I dedicate this book to Fabo, Volkert, and my dad—my three favorite old men in all the world.

—Karen E.N. Hayes, DVM, MS

How to Use this Book

HANDS-ON SENIOR HORSE CARE is like having an equine geriatric specialist in your barn, someone who can tell you what to watch for in the care of your senior horse (which we'll define as any horse aged 15 years or older), ask the right questions, and give you an action plan NOW. Your horse will benefit because you'll know how to help preserve his youthful vigor as long as possible. You'll benefit from the help in formulating a premium maintenance program and catching early warning signs of age-related problems, giving you the best shot at a positive outcome. And your veterinarian will benefit because he or she will have fewer after-hours calls and a stronger, healthier, more resilient patient.

This book is organized into four sections.

1 SENIOR SIGNPOSTS AND ACTION PLANS contains the most common age-related signs your horse might display as he passes his prime and enters the realm of senior citizenship—even if he doesn't yet look old. Each is listed as you'd describe it: If his hair looks long, dull, or in any way abnormal, look up "Abnormal Skin Or Coat" in the Table of Contents on page 6. If you notice any other signs—a cough, the beginnings of a swayback, weight loss or gain—go to the appropriate page. There you'll be asked a series of yes-or-no questions based on your observations. Your answers will lead you to an action plan, along with a brief explanation of what the problem might be. You'll be told whether (and when) to call your veterinarian, and given how-to specifics on any first aid to administer while you wait. If home treatment is recommended, it's described in clear, step-by-step fashion.

2 AGE EVENTS highlights 8 common health problems that can occur in the aging equine, from arthritis and loss of social standing, to colic and cancer. Wherever possible, we'll tell you how and why these problems occur, and how you can use this information to protect your horse. We'll provide a list of subtle signposts that will help with early detection, plus what to expect as the conditions progress, and an up-to-date summary of what's being done, in research and in practice, to slow, stop, and in some cases reverse the process.

3 HANDS-ON SENIOR HORSEKEEPING is a road map to preventive, youth-preserving care in your senior horse. Does he need a special ration now that he's getting long in the tooth? Yes he does. Check out our Stay-Young Diet Solutions, where you'll get specific information on when, why, and how to boost your senior's ration to keep his slowing digestive tract working optimally. In Top Priority—Tooth Care, you'll find a detailed dental plan to help ensure your senior gets the most from that ration. All this and more, in step-by-step form. For fun as well as feedback on how your horse is aging, check out our "Virtual Birthday" formula on page 288. There, you can add up the scores for each checkpoint and determine whether your horse's condition makes him younger or older than his actual age. Then, use this book to help adjust your management and melt off the years.

4 REFERENCE INFORMATION includes a combination glossary and index, for an at-a-glance guide to veterinary terms you hear around the barn or from your veterinarian. When you see terms marked with a (G), turn to this section for a definition.

1

FIRST-AID
ACTION PLANS

CHAPTER 1

Changes in
BODY SHAPE/
CONDITION

Weight Loss

SENIOR SIGNPOST: Your senior horse is losing weight despite eating the same amount of food.

What this might mean: It can mean one of a full spectrum of problems, ranging from something as simple as inadequate quantity or quality of food, to cancer.

ACTION PLAN:

Does your horse seem to drool or slobber a lot? Is he leaving food uneaten in his feeder, even though he seems to spend a lot of time working at it? **YES** Call your veterinarian *NOW*—there could be a problem with the nerves supplying the muscles of your horse's tongue, jaw, and/or throat, making it difficult for him to pick up, chew, and/or swallow his feed.

 NO

Is your senior horse medicated with "bute" (phenylbutazone^G) or other pain-killing medication, regularly or more than twice a year, for at least a week at a time? **YES** Call your veterinarian *NOW*—it could be ulcerative colitis^G, a common side effect of phenylbutazone medication.

 NO

Does your senior horse's breath smell like soured or rotted food? Have there been any recent changes in the color, frequency, amount, consistency, shape, or smell of his manure? Does he seem to prefer coarse grass or hay more than his grain? **YES** Call your veterinarian *TODAY* if you answered yes to any query—it could be a digestive problem due to an ulcer^G, infection, inflammation, or cancer.

 NO

Do you see swelling in one or more legs, in the sheath (male) or udder (female)? Does he have a thickened/swollen lower belly wall? Do his withers, neck, shoulders, and/or croup area seem more bony, as though there's less soft tissue covering his bones? Has he developed a swaybacked appearance? **YES** Call your veterinarian *TODAY* if you answered yes to any query—these signs can indicate hypoproteinemia^G and, in severe cases, muscle loss, and can occur in response to malnutrition, chronic underlying health problems such as kidney or liver disease, intestinal tract inflammation, or cancer. For more information about muscle loss while you wait, go to "Muscle Loss," **page 17.**

 NO

ACTION PLAN (CONTINUED):

Is your senior horse's coat rough, abnormally long, thick, and/or overdue to shed? Is he moving stiffly, or walking as though his feet are tender? Has he ever been diagnosed with laminitis^G? Does he seem listless, tired, less "in tune" with his surroundings?

 YES Call your veterinarian *TODAY* if you answered yes to any query—your horse could have Equine Cushing's Disease^G (ECD, also known as pituitary adenoma).

 NO

Does he seem to take longer than usual to eat his feed? Does he tilt his head to one side when he chews? Does he drop unchewed feed, or glops of partially chewed feed on the ground or in his feeder? Do you see more unchewed grains than usual in his manure? Have you seen him pull back from water when first starting to drink? Does his breath smell strongly of mothballs?

 YES Call your veterinarian *TODAY* if you answered yes to any query—your horse could have a dental problem that's interfering with his ability to chew. See "Top Priority—Tooth Care," **page 332**.

 NO

Is your senior horse on a purge-deworming program^G (as opposed to a daily deworming^G program)? Is his appetite normal, but he's less active and has a dull coat? Since his last purge-deworming treatment, has he spent any time in a paddock or pasture where other horses have been, particularly horses whose deworming history is unknown to you?

 YES Call your veterinarian *TODAY* if you answered yes to any query. Arrange for examination of a fresh manure sample, and see "Senior Deworming & Vaccination Program," **page 322**. (For how to collect a fresh manure sample, see page 16.)

 NO

Can you agree to all these statements?
• Your horse's diet is the same as it was last year at this time, and his weight was fine then.
• His activity level is the same as it was last year at this time, and his weight was fine then.
• Other horses eating the same diet look fine.
• He has access to all the fresh water he wants.

 YES Consult with your vet to have your horse and his ration evaluated and adjusted, based on his current activity level, nutritional needs, condition, and dental health. Continue this chart.

 NO

ACTION PLAN (CONTINUED):

Do you feed multiple horses in the same location?

 Observe your horse closely at feed time. Other horses may be eating his food. If that's the case, feed him separately, and go to "The Age Event: Loss of Social Status," **page 279**—he may have lost his position in the herd.

 NO

Is your feed storage accessible to rodents? Does the feed smell foul, and/or are mold, rodent droppings, or bugs visible in it?

 Your feed is likely unpalatable to your horse. Replace it with fresh feed, and update your storage to prevent fouling and spoilage.

 NO

Call your veterinarian for an appointment.

How to Get a Fecal Egg Count^G

Seal two fresh (preferably still warm) manure "muffins" in a Zip-lock® plastic bag and submit within 1 hour to a laboratory-equipped veterinary facility for a fecal egg count.

TIP: Take the sample directly to the clinic, rather than handing it to your on-the-road veterinarian, who might not get back to the lab for several hours. The test likely will be run by a technician at the facility right away. Results will be given in "eggs per gram" (epg). On an effective purge program, your horse's count should be below 100 epg. On a daily program, his count should be 0 to 50. *(Tip: For best accuracy, have your horse's fecal egg count done daily for 3 to 5 days and average the results.)*

Weight loss can happen fast—and be serious—in your senior horse. Keep these guidelines in mind so you can monitor his weight, then take fast action should you note a loss.

• Perform a monthly weight check. Use our weight-check formula on page 330 to calculate your horse's weight. Record your findings on a desk calendar or other handy source, so you can easily compare results. Call your vet if you notice a steady or rapid decline.

• Check your horse's feed bucket daily. Dribbled or unfinished feed could indicate a dental problem, inappetence, or spoiled feed—especially if your horse usually cleans up his feed. The earlier you discover such signs, the more quickly you and your vet can get to—and fix—the root of the problem.

• During winter months, let your fingers do the walking—a long winter coat can mask weight loss. Run your hands along your horse's rib cage on a weekly basis. If his ribs begin to feel more prominent than normal, consult your vet.

• If there's the slightest doubt about your horse's social position and unchallenged access to feed and water, don't wait until signs are obvious—step in now. Either move your horse to a new living situation where he can have companionship without competition for feed, or isolate him at feeding time so he can eat in peace.

Muscle Loss

SENIOR SIGNPOST: Your senior horse's normally broad, well-muscled chest appears somewhat deflated. His withers, neck, shoulders, and/or croup seem more prominent, maybe even bony, as though there's less tissue covering the bone. You may recently have reached for an extra saddle pad to improve saddle fit. You also may have noticed that his back appears to have fallen, giving him the beginnings of a swaybacked appearance.

What this might mean: His muscles aren't getting the nourishment they need. The four most common reasons for muscle malnutrition in an older horse are:

• A downturn in the quality or quantity of feed available to him, or in his ability to eat, digest, and absorb it.

• Less efficient delivery of nutrients to his muscles via circulation.

• Leakage of nutrients (especially protein) out of his body via urine and/or manure, before he has a chance to utilize them.

• An underlying "energy sink"—that's any condition that burns up a lot of energy, such as recovery from a significant trauma (e.g., major surgery or injury), or cancer.

ACTION PLAN:

Does your senior horse have a fever? (see "Senior Vital Signs," **page 292**.)   **YES** ➤ Call your veterinarian *NOW*—your horse could have an infectious disease. Go to **While You Wait**, page 19.

 NO

Does your horse act hungry, but quickly lose interest in food before finishing it? Does he spend a lot of time with his muzzle in the feed, but doesn't clean it up? Does he slobber a lot, and/or drop wads of partially chewed food? Have you seen him pull back from the water bucket, as though startled?   **YES** ➤ Call your veterinarian *NOW* if you answered yes to any query—it could be malnutrition due to a painful dental problem, or injury or disease involving the nerves that supply the tongue, jaw muscles, and/or throat muscles, making it difficult for your horse to pick up, chew, and/or swallow his feed. He's at risk of malnutrition and dehydration.

 NO

➤

ACTION PLAN (CONTINUED):

Is your senior horse's appetite decreased? Does he appear listless, or detached from his surroundings?

 Call your veterinarian *TODAY* if you answered yes to any query. There may be a serious underlying health problem, such as chronic kidney or liver disease, leading to decreased ability to eliminate the natural (and toxic) by-products of normal digestion. Or, there may be widespread inflammation in your senior horse's intestinal tract, allowing nutrients—especially protein—to be wasted, rather than assimilated for use in maintaining body condition and strength.

Is there any swelling (edema^G) in one or more legs, in the sheath or udder, or in the lower belly wall?

 Call your veterinarian *TODAY*—your senior horse may have hypo-proteinemia^G, which can be due to kidney disease, or a disease in the intestinal tract. For more information about edema, go to "Swollen Leg(s)," **page 146** and "Swelling in Belly Wall," **page 22**.

Have there been any changes in your horse's manure (its color, consistency, amount, frequency, "messiness," or smell)?

 Call your veterinarian *TODAY*—your senior horse may have a disorder in his digestive tract, interfering with its ability to digest, move, and/or absorb nutrients.

Is your horse's muscle loss asymmetrical, limited to one or two specific areas of his body (for example, one leg, one shoulder, one hip), rather than generalized to his entire body and affecting right and left sides equally?

 Call your veterinarian *TODAY*—it could be atrophy^G of specific muscle groups due to chronic pain, or due to nerve injury in an isolated part of your horse's body.

Is your horse confined to a stall?

 Go to "Age-Adjusted Exercise," **page 340**. Although gradual muscle loss can be a natural facet of the aging process, it'll be accelerated in a horse that rarely uses his muscles.

ACTION PLAN (CONTINUED):

Is your horse on a diet that was formulated for older horses?

 Go to "Stay-Young Diet Solutions," **page 376.** As your horse ages, his dietary needs change significantly. If you're not adjusting his diet adequately to keep up with them, he could be aging faster than necessary, which includes loss of muscle mass.

Call your veterinarian *THIS WEEK* and set up a general checkup for your horse, with emphasis on aging, to have his diet evaluated and to examine him for any evidence of identifiable and treatable problems contributing to muscle loss. For more information, see "Senior Vet Checks," **page 386**.

WHILE YOU WAIT

Isolate your horse from other horses in case he's contagious. To prevent spread of possible infectious disease, confine your horse to an open-air paddock or stall with a separate water supply, apart from other horses by at least 20 feet. Wash your hands and disinfect your boots (see page 41) after handling your horse and before handling other horses.

Did You Know?

An idle horse's poor circulation makes it difficult for digested nutrients to reach his muscles. Coupled with lack of use, those muscles will shrink. If your senior horse has a problem that makes exercise difficult or painful, there may be special exercise methods, such as swimming, hand-walking/ponying, passive muscle flexion, and other methods of physical therapy that can improve circulation without compounding an existing problem. Consult your veterinarian to find out.

Swayback

SENIOR SIGNPOST: Your horse's back appears sunken. You may also notice that his withers looks more prominent, and his croup seems tilted, bringing his tailhead upward and adding overall to the sway in his back. He may or may not seem to be in any pain from this anatomical change.

What it could mean: Your senior horse may be developing a "swayback," known as *lordosis*G. He's lost muscle mass and/or strength along his topline, and along the sides and underside of his belly, making his back/spine appear to sag. (It's his belly muscles that actually support the weight of his torso, thereby helping to keep his spine from sinking.)

ACTION PLAN:

Does your horse seem to have lost flexibility, moving stiffly or refusing certain cues? Does he flinch, hunch, or flex his back when you touch, groom, or place tack on it?

YES Call your veterinarian *TODAY*—your horse may have a sore back, which can be a clue to the cause of his swayback. For more information, see "Senior Back Check," **page 314**.

Does he appear to have lost weight?

YES There may be an underlying health problem, such as malnutrition, or hypoproteinemiaG. Go to "Senior Condition Check," **page 300**; "Weight Loss," **page 14**, "Muscle Loss," **page 17**.

Is he overweight? If your horse is a mare, is she pregnant?

YES If you answered yes to either query, your senior horse may need adjustments in diet and/or exercise to reduce stress on his back, and improve strength in the muscles that support it. Go to "Age-Adjusted Exercise," "Alternative Medicine," and "Stay-Young Diet Solutions," **pages 340, 388,** and **376**, respectively.

ACTION PLAN (CONTINUED):

Is your horse on a diet specifically formulated for seniors?

For optimal muscle strength, he needs a diet customized for his special needs as a senior. See "Stay-Young Diet Solutions," **page 376**.

Call your veterinarian *THIS WEEK* and arrange for your horse to have a senior-horse checkup to see if there are any identifiable and treatable reasons for his swayback. See "Senior Vet Checks", **page 386**.

the Science of Swaybacks

Just about every aged horse exhibits some degree of sag in his topline and a sharpening of the withers due to thinning muscle mass. But, it's estimated that fewer than one in every four senior horses develops a true swayback—the downward deviation of the spine known as lordosis[G]. Whether your senior horse develops a swayback and at what age depends on many factors. These include:

• *Overall conformation.* Horses with long backs and prominent withers are reported to be at greater risk.

• *Muscle tone.* Strong abdominal muscles are believed to be key to a level back.

• *General health and nutritional status.* These affect bone, joint, and spine health, as well as the muscles and connective tissues that keep everything aligned.

• *Exercise.* When done properly, it can optimize circulation and strengthen muscles that support your horse's back.

Did You Know?

* It may look painful, but in many cases the swaybacked horse does not have back pain.

* Weight gain can place additional stress on muscles that support your senior horse's back and torso. Since packing on pounds often is preceded by decreased activity and loss of condition, weakened abdominal and back muscles may exacerbate his sinking spine.

Swelling in Belly Wall

SENIOR SIGNPOST: The underside of your senior horse's belly wall appears swollen. You might also see a similar swelling in the brisket area between his forelegs, in the sheath area (if your horse is a male), and/or in the udder area (if your horse is female).

What it might mean: It could signal a serious underlying health problem.

ACTION PLAN:

Does your horse have a fever? Has he been off his feed, listless, and/or seemed detached from his surroundings? Has he recently had a cold or other respiratory infection? If your senior horse is a mare, has she foaled within the past 3 days?

YES ▶ Call your veterinarian *NOW* if you answered yes to any query—it could be a blood vessel abnormality (vasculitis^G or purpura^G); dangerously low blood protein levels (hypoproteinemia^G); or a symptom of acute endometritis^G and/or toxemia^G, all of which are potentially life threatening.

 NO

If your senior horse is a mare, is she heavily pregnant?

YES ▶ Call your veterinarian *TODAY*—older, pregnant mares can have a relatively innocent case of ventral edema^G, due to weight gain, general discomfort, and decreased activity, all of which impair circulation. Or, she could be developing a more serious condition, such as a ruptured prepubic tendon^G or ventral hernia^G, either of which can be life threatening if it progresses. Go to **While You Wait**, opposite page. For more information, go to "The Age Event: Declining Fertility," **page 263**.

 NO

Does your senior horse seem to breathe heavily after even the mildest exercise, and take longer than usual to recover? Do you see evidence of labored breathing—flared nostrils, exaggerated movement of his chest or flank with each breath, and possibly an elevated respiratory rate—even when he's been standing idle? Do his gums look abnormally pale?

YES ▶ Call your veterinarian *TODAY*—it could be a heart problem. For more information, go to "Labored Breathing," **page 63** and "Easily Winded," **page 68**.

 NO

ACTION PLAN (CONTINUED):

Is the swelling uneven or lumpy looking and limited to your horse's groin area?

 Call your veterinarian *TODAY*—it could be an inguinal hernia^G, leaving your horse at risk for severe colic^G if a loop of intestine becomes entrapped in the hernia.

 NO

Is your senior horse on a purge-deworming program, rather than a daily deworming^G program, and overdue for a treatment?

 Call your veterinarian *TODAY*—it could be hypoproteinemia^G from a heavy parasite infestation and a resultant severe intestinal inflammation, which can lead to a protein-losing enteropathy^G—loss of valuable protein via manure.

 NO

Does your horse have sores, raw patches, or otherwise unhealthy-looking skin?

 Call your veterinarian *THIS WEEK*. The swelling could be due to a generalized skin disease.

 NO

Call your veterinarian for an appointment.

WHILE YOU WAIT

Confine your pregnant mare to a stall or small paddock with a companion, if necessary, to prevent fretting. If her belly swelling is due simply to poor circulation, confinement can make the condition slightly worse, but if it's due to a developing ruptured prepubic tendon^G or ventral hernia^G, movement can escalate the condition's progress.

NOTES

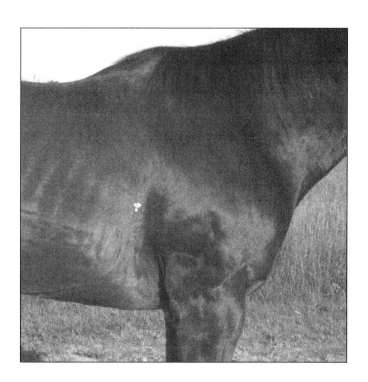

CHAPTER 2

Changes in

SKIN, COAT, SWEATING

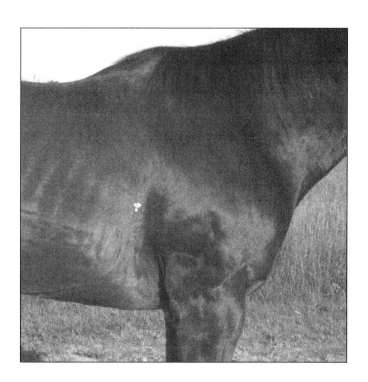

Sores, Scurf, &/Or Crusts

SENIOR SIGNPOST: You see or feel sores or crusts on your horse's skin. When you curry his coat, dandruff emerges. **What this might mean:** It could be a skin problem, such as a minor dermatitis^G or fungus. Or, it could indicate a serious underlying problem.

ACTION PLAN:

Is the affected area(s) limited to pink/hairless skin, or areas on his body where the hair is white?

 YES Call your veterinarian *TODAY*—it could be photosensitization^G, which can result from an underlying liver disease or poisoning. See "Sun-Beater Tips," **page 29**.

 NO

Are there nodules, pimples and/or blisters at various sites on his body, as well as broad areas of crust?

 YES Call your veterinarian *TODAY*—it could be an autoimmune disease such as pemphigus^G or lupus^G, or it could be habronemiasis^G (also known as summer sores).

 NO

Does your horse scratch or rub the affected area(s)?

 YES Go to "Itchy Skin," **page 33**.

 NO

If your senior horse is still ridden, is the saddle and/or girth area affected (with or without involvement of other areas of the body)? Do any of the lesions appear reddened and hairless? Are any other horses affected?

 YES It could be ringworm^G. Go to **Home Treatment #1**, opposite page. Take precautions to prevent spread of this contagious condition to yourself and other animals. If you're queasy about dealing with it, call your veterinarian *TODAY*.

 NO

Do tufts of hair in the crusted areas pull out easily, leaving a tender raw spot?

 YES It sounds like rainrot, also known as dermatophilosis^G. Apply **Home Treatment #1**.

 NO

Are the affected areas located exclusively on the fronts of your horse's hind cannon bones?

 YES Sounds like cannon keratosis^G. Apply **Home Treatment #2**, opposite page.

NO

ACTION PLAN (CONTINUED):

Is the problem limited to the fet-lock, pastern, or heel regions of his lower legs? It could be scratches^G. Go to **Home Treatment #3**, next page.

Call your veterinarian for an appointment.

HOME TREATMENT #1

*(See **Action Plan** to determine whether home treatment is appropriate for your horse's skin condition. If at any time during home treatment, your answers on the **Action Plan** change for the worse, call your vet.)*

Step 1. *Soften and loosen scabs.* Apply a medicated scab softener (see box at right) generously to affected skin areas. Leave on for 1 to 2 hours.

Step 2. *Apply a medicated bath.* Wet your horse. Lather him with a povidine iodine shampoo or scrub (not the surgical solution, which doesn't lather), or Nolvasan scrub (obtain it from your veterinarian or a vet supply catalog). Let the lather stand for 10 minutes, then rinse thorough-ly, gently removing as many of the scabs/loose tufts of hair as possible. (If it's too cold to bathe your horse, spot-treat affected areas.)

SCAB SOFTENER RECIPE:

• 1-16 oz. bottle mineral oil (baby oil is okay)
• 1-16 oz. bottle 3% USP hydrogen peroxide
• 1-12 oz. bottle tincture of iodine

Combine all in a large container. Do not close tightly. Mixture will bub-ble slowly and expand, and can cause a messy explosion.

Step 3. *Dry, fresh air and sunshine.* Keep the skin as dry as conditions permit, avoid blanketing your horse, and maximize his exposure to fresh air and sunshine's ultraviolet rays. These measures can help control infectious organisms in the skin.

Step 4. *Keep it up, and reevaluate.* Repeat Step 2 daily for 7 days, then continue twice a week until lesions are healed. If significant improvement is not seen in 3 days, call your veterinarian for an appointment.

HOME TREATMENT #2

*(See **Action Plan** to determine whether home treatment is appropriate for your horse's hind-limb skin condition. If at any time during home treatment, your answers on the **Action Plan** change for the worse, call your vet.)* ➤

HOME TREATMENT #2 - CONTINUED

Step 1. *Soak affected areas with medication to remove excess keratin.* Clean legs by hosing with cool water. Pat dry, then apply a human acne cream or gel containing 10 percent benzoyl peroxide. Cover with a track wrap and confine your horse for 2 hours.

Step 2. *Wash affected areas with medicated shampoo.* Unwrap the legs, wet them, then lather affected areas with a povidone-iodine-based shampoo or surgical scrub, such as Betadine®. Rinse thoroughly.

Step 3. *Soothe the inflamed tissue.* Daub freshly cleaned tissues with a witch hazel-soaked cotton pad.

Step 4. *Change your horse's living situation, if necessary.* Move your horse to an environment that doesn't irritate the skin of his legs, if necessary. For example, if your pasture grass is tall or infested with weeds, move him to a clean, mowed pasture.

Step 5. *Keep it up.* Repeat Steps 1 through 3 once or twice daily as needed to maintain crust-free legs. If this condition truly is cannon keratosis^G, the cause is unknown and affected skin tends to overreact to simple irritation, so you won't cure it—only manage it and minimize its effects.

HOME TREATMENT #3

*(See **Action Plan** to determine whether home treatment is appropriate for your horse's heel sores. If at any time during home treatment, your answers on the **Action Plan** change for the worse, call your vet.)*

Step 1. *Soften and clean the thickened skin, crusts, and scabs.* Apply an emollient dressing (such as zinc oxide or A&D Ointment®) or poultice, leaving it on overnight. Then wash the area thoroughly with a foaming human acne cleanser containing 10 percent benzoyl peroxide. Leave the lather in contact with affected skin for 10 minutes before rinsing thoroughly. Towel dry, then allow to air dry completely before moving to Step 2.

Step 2. *Clip the site.* Clip hair from the affected area and 1/2-inch beyond it using electric clippers and a sharp, clean, No. 40 blade. Be careful not to nick the skin or allow the blade to become hot.

Step 3. *Dress the site.* Coat all affected surfaces with a thin layer of povidone iodine ointment. Don't bandage unless absolutely necessary to keep tissues clean. The condition will respond better if left open to air.

Step 4. *Confine your horse.* For the next 2 to 3 weeks, keep your horse in an area that's clean and dry. A mowed, grassy paddock is ideal in dry weather; a scrupulously cleaned rubber-floored stall with no bedding, or bedded with shredded office paper (not newspaper, which contains ink) is ideal if indoor confinement is necessary. Stay away from wood shavings, sawdust, and straw or hay, which contain bacteria, and can poke and adhere to sensitive skin.

Step 5. *Keep it up.* Repeat Steps 1 and 3 once or twice daily (depending on how crusty, oozy, and/or scabby the area gets between cleanings). Expect to see an improvement within 3 days. Healing should be complete within 2 to 4 weeks, or longer in severe cases.

Step 6. *Re-evaluate every 3 days.* If the skin isn't improving steadily, the inflammation and/or infection might be too deep to reach with external treatments. Call your veterinarian for confirmation of your diagnosis and to help in treatment, possibly with a systemic (bodywide) medication.

Sun-Beater Tips

Does your horse's pink skin rebel when exposed to the sun? Use these tips to help:

• Limit his exposure to sunlight, by keeping him in during the day, and putting him out at night.

• If you can't control his sun exposure, apply a light coat of a gentle SPF 15 or higher sunscreen to his pink-skinned areas, such as his nose. Use a sensitive-skin formula (such as one designed for children), or one specifically designed for horses.

• Use mechanical sun blockers, such as fly masks and fly sheets, that are designed specifically to help block UV rays.

Hair Loss

SENIOR SIGNPOST: Hair is missing from your senior horse's coat, in a single location, in broad patches, or in a moth-eaten pattern disseminated over his entire body. On closer inspection, individual hairs may or may not be broken, and skin in the hairless area may or may not appear irritated or injured.

What this might mean: It could indicate an underlying general health problem causing symptoms in the skin, or a problem that's limited to the skin.

ACTION PLAN:

Is your senior horse's hair loss non-itchy and primarily at the crest of his neck and tailhead? Is his coat rough-looking overall? Does he have dry, cracked coronary bands? Does he receive supplemental selenium^G, in a selenium-fortified feed product, and/or in a mineral supplement? Do you live in an area that's known to have high levels of selenium^G in the soil and/or water?

 YES Call your veterinarian *TODAY* if you answered yes to any query—it could be selenium toxicosis^G, a.k.a. alkali disease^G. Go to **While You Wait**, page 32.

 NO

Are there distinct, relatively circular areas of hair loss? Are some of the hairless areas crusty and scaly around the edges, but cleaner in the centers?

 YES If you answered yes to both queries, it sounds like ringworm^G, a.k.a. Dermatophytosis^G. If the approximate total of your senior horse's lesions is no larger than your hand, apply **Home Treatment**, page 32, taking precautions to prevent spread of this condition to yourself and other animals. If you're queasy about dealing with it, or the total area is larger than your hand, call your veterinarian *TODAY*—a wider area of ringworm infection suggests that your senior horse's immune system may be run down, indicating an underlying health problem.

 NO

ACTION PLAN (CONTINUED):

Is your senior horse's hair loss in a general, moth-eaten pattern across his torso, without crusts? And/or, does it involve an area around his head and poll, especially where the skin runs over prominent bone structure? Has he been acting lethargic and somewhat depressed? Has he had previous bouts with sore muscles, tying-up syndrome[G], or laminitis[G]? Does he seem to shiver with cold, even on days when other horses in the same environment are comfortable? Does he sweat less than expected on warm or active days? Does he frequently have swollen lower legs?

 YES Call your veterinarian *TODAY* if you answered yes to any query—it could be a thyroid disorder[G].

 NO

Are there multiple hairless areas, especially around your senior horse's head, face, and ears, that are reddened, scaly, crusty, and ulcerated, and/or lacking the pigment that gives your senior horse's skin its normal color? Does he have sores in his mouth? Does he move stiffly, especially before he's warmed up? Is his lower belly wall thickened or swollen with edema? Are his gums abnormally pale?

 YES Call your veterinarian *TODAY* if you answered yes to any query—it could be an autoimmune disease[G], such as pemphigus foliaceus[G] or lupus erythematosus[G].

 NO

Have you seen your horse rubbing or scratching the affected skin? Are there broken-off hairs there?

 YES If you answered yes to either query, hair loss may be the result of excessive scratching and/or rubbing. Go to "Itchy Skin," **page 33**.

 NO

Is the hair loss largely along your horse's topline? Do small tufts of hair in this area pull out easily, with a plaque of crust adhered to the root, leaving a raw sore that's tender to the touch?

 YES If you answered yes to both queries, it sounds like rainrot[G], a.k.a. Dermatophilosis[G] or dew poisoning[G]. Apply **Home Treatment**, next page.

 NO

➤

ACTION PLAN (CONTINUED):

Is the hair loss in distinct, individual areas on his body, with no sign of scurf or crust? Have you seen other horses behaving aggressively against him? Have you seen your senior horse acting afraid of, or deferential to, other horses that he used to dominate socially?

 YES The hairless areas could be bite wounds, due to your senior horse's loss of social status within the herd. Go to "The Age Event: Loss of Social Status," **page 279**.

 NO

Call your vet for an appointment.

WHILE YOU WAIT

Stop feeding all products containing selenium supplementation. Do not give, or permit others to give, your horse any selenium injections.

SCAB SOFTENER RECIPE:

• 1-16 oz. bottle mineral oil (baby oil is okay)
• 1-16 oz. bottle 3% USP hydrogen peroxide
• 1-12 oz. bottle tincture of iodine

Combine all in a large container. Do not close tightly. Mixture will bubble slowly and expand, and can cause a messy explosion.

HOME TREATMENT

*(See **Action Plan** to determine whether home treatment is appropriate for your horse's skin condition. If at any time during home treatment, your answers on the **Action Plan** change for the worse, call your vet.)*

Step 1. *Soften and loosen scabs.* Apply a medicated scab softener (see box at left) generously to affected skin areas. Leave on for 1 to 2 hours.

Step 2. *Apply a medicated bath.* Wet your horse. Lather him with a povidone iodine shampoo or scrub (not the surgical solution, which doesn't lather), or Nolvasan scrub (obtain it from your veterinarian or a vet supply catalog). Let the lather stand for 10 minutes, then rinse thoroughly, gently removing as many of the scabs/loose tufts of hair as possible. (If it's too cold to bathe your horse, spot-treat affected areas.)

Step 3. *Dry, fresh air and sunshine.* Keep the skin as dry as conditions permit, avoid blanketing your horse, and maximize his exposure to fresh air and sunshine's ultraviolet rays. These measures can help control infectious organisms in the skin.

Step 4. *Keep it up, and re-evaluate.* Repeat Step 2 daily for 7 days, then continue twice a week until lesions are healed. If significant improvement is not seen in 3 days, call your veterinarian for an appointment.

Itchy Skin

SENIOR SIGNPOST: Your senior horse is repeatedly rubbing and scratching.

What this might mean: It could be a contagious, itchy, and/or painful skin condition, or it might be a sign of an underlying health problem. No matter what's causing the discomfort, your horse's response can be intense enough to damage his skin and coat, as well as any structures near the itchy spots (such as his eyes).

ACTION PLAN:

Did the itchiness come on suddenly? Does your horse have welts or hives on his skin? Has he been given any medications or vaccines within the past 24 hours? Is he showing any signs of labored breathing, unexplained agitation, or anxiety?

 Call your veterinarian *NOW* if you answered yes to any query—it could be an allergic reaction, including anaphylaxis[G], which can be life-threatening. Go to **While You Wait**, page 35.

Does the itch appear to be on your horse's face, near his eye(s)? Is either eye red, squinted, or watering? Do the tissues around the eye look swollen or traumatized?

 Call your veterinarian *NOW* if you answered yes to either query—it could be a mild to severe eye injury, irritation, or infection, with risk of serious eye damage due to rubbing. Or, it could be a problem elsewhere on your horse's face that's inadvertently caused an eye problem due to rubbing—he can cause serious, even permanent, eye damage unless the underlying discomfort is relieved. For more information while you wait, go to "Squinting &/Or Tearing," **page 105**.

Are the itchy areas mostly where your senior horse's coat is light colored or naturally hairless? Are the whites of his eyes and/or his gums yellow-tinged?

 Call your veterinarian *NOW*—hepatitis[G] and/or cholangitis[G] are serious liver disorders that can cause itchy skin and jaundice[G].

➤

ACTION PLAN (CONTINUED):

Does your senior horse seem to be under attack by biting/sucking insects, more so than other horses in the neighborhood?

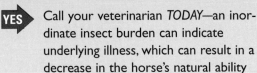 **YES** ▶ Call your veterinarian *TODAY*—an inordinate insect burden can indicate underlying illness, which can result in a decrease in the horse's natural ability to repel pests.

 NO ▼

Is the itchy area mostly on the face and legs, with thickened skin and hair loss?

YES ▶ Call your veterinarian *THIS WEEK*—it could be generalized granulomatous disease, a.k.a. equine sarcoidosis^G.

 NO ▼

Are there hard, raised, nodules in the itchy areas? Is it too early/cool in the season for biting insects? Do you see "moving dandruff" when you examine his skin with a magnifying glass? Does your horse straddle bushes and rock back and forth to relieve an itchy belly?

YES ▶ If you answered yes to any query, it could be lice^G or *Onchocerca cervicalis*^G. Apply **Home Treatment** steps **#3** and **5** (opposite page) as soon as weather permits.

 NO ▼

Is your senior horse rubbing or scratching the skin on the crest and/or side of his neck, or on his shoulders, torso, or tailhead?

YES ▶ It could be an allergic-type overreaction to fly or gnat bites (such as sweet itch^G, an allergy to the bite of the *Culicoides*^G gnat). Apply **Home Treatment** steps **#1, 2, 5,** and **6**.

 NO ▼

Does he stomp his feet and/or rub his lower legs together or on available surfaces, such as tree stumps, bushes, or rocks?

YES ▶ It sounds like leg mange^G. Apply **Home Treatment** steps **#4, 5,** and **6**.

 NO ▼

Is the itch limited to an area that's been treated within the past 24 hours with a topical liniment or medication, such as a blister, leg paint, leg sweat, or any product—especially one containing tea tree oil (melaleuca), pine tar, iodine, or DMSO^G (dimethylsulfoxide)?

YES ▶ It could be a contact dermatitis^G. Apply **Home Treatment** steps **#5** and **6**.

 NO ▼

Is he rubbing only at the base of his tail?

YES ▶ It could be pinworms^G. Or, it could mean a dirty sheath or udder. Apply **Home Treatment** steps **#3, 5,** and **6**, and go to "Down & Dirty Maintenance...," **page 360**.

 NO ▼

Call your vet for an appointment.

WHILE YOU WAIT

1. *Protect yourself.* If your horse is displaying anxious behavior—pacing, whinnying, eyes open wide, nostrils flared—his judgment is impaired and he might inadvertently hurt you. Don't go near him unless you must, and if you must, be especially cautious.

2. *Improve ventilation.* If your horse is having difficulty breathing, make fresh air available. Much of the anxiety displayed in horses with anaphylaxis^G is the result of panic due to difficulty breathing.

3. *Recall all potential allergens.* Think back: Can you recall anything that might have brought on this allergic response? A change in feed source? A change to a different pasture? Any medications, dewormers, vaccinations, or vitamin products given? Any topical cosmetic or therapeutic substances applied to his skin? Any biting or stinging bugs noticed? Report all suspicions to your veterinarian.

HOME TREATMENT

*(See **Action Plan** to determine whether home treatment is appropriate for your horse's itchy skin. If at any time during home treatment, your answers on the **Action Plan** change for the worse, call your vet.)*

Step 1. *Minimize biting insects in your horse's environment.* If biting insects are a problem, choose one or more of the following:
- Compost manure and soiled/wet bedding at least 500 feet from your horses' living environment.
- Eliminate chronically moist areas where some insects breed.
- Use premise insecticides or pest predators to decrease pest insect population.
- Install fine screens in your barn to help keep insects out.
- Install fans to evaporate sweat and physically blow away weak-flying pests.

Step 2. *Minimize biting insects on your horse's body.*
- Apply horse-safe insecticides, following label instructions, daily for 3 days, then twice per week for 3 weeks to kill juvenile parasites as they mature (most insecticides kill only the adult skin parasites).
- Use horse-safe insect repellents on days between insecticide treatments.
- Scrape sweat and keep your horse clean (sweat and dirt attract pests).
- Outfit your horse in a fly mask and fly sheet.
- Bring him indoors during the day, and turn him out at night, when biting flies are less prevalent.

Step 3. *Eliminate external parasites that feed on blood.* Administer ivermectin or moxidectin dewormer according to your horse's body weight (see page 330) at the deworming dose indicated on the label.

➤

Step 4. *Eliminate skin parasites from the affected area.* If mites are a problem (as in leg mange[G]), apply an equine insecticide directly to the affected area, following label instructions, daily for 3 days, then twice per week for 3 weeks to kill juvenile parasites as they mature. Use repellents on days between insecticide treatments.

Step 5. *Soothe irritated skin.* Bathe affected areas with a mild horse shampoo (such as Hylyt-EFA®) to remove irritating scurf/bacteria and cool inflamed skin. After bathing, apply a topical anti-itch, anti-sting preparation, such as colloidal oatmeal (Aveeno®, 1 tablespoon per gallon of water), witch hazel (alone or in commercial preparations such as Allerderm®), calamine lotion, or zinc oxide paste. If your horse's skin is dry and flaky, top that layer with an emollient product such as a solution of Avon Skin-So-Soft® (diluted 1-to-3 in water, and spritzed from a spray bottle), Hylyt-EFA®, or Humilac®.

Step 6. *Remove scale and scurf.* For crusty, scaly, flaky skin conditions, clip hair from the affected areas, extending well into healthy skin around the lesion's perimeter. This will eliminate bacteria residing in the hair, and prevent the accumulation of serum or crust, which would attract more bacteria and insects.

Abnormal Skin or Coat

SENIOR SIGNPOST: Your senior horse's skin and/or coat looks different. Instead of its usual smoothness, it may look unkempt. There may be patches of hair loss or hair breakage, with or without associated skin changes. Or, you may find that no matter how much you groom him, his coat looks dull and dandruff-y. Perhaps his coat appears too long, thick, and/or wavy, while neighboring horses have sleek summer coats.

What this might mean: It could be dermatitis^G, a nutritional deficiency, or a systemic illness. If the underlying problem causes itching or pain, your horse may traumatize himself trying to get relief. (If your horse is scratching his skin, go to "Itchy Skin," page 33.)

ACTION PLAN:

Are there several distinct, smooth bumps that look like welts or hives under unbroken skin, causing some of his hair to stick out and look messy? Is your senior horse acting anxious, breathing rapidly, or wheezing?

 YES Call your veterinarian *NOW* if you answered yes to either query—it could be a severe allergic reaction such as anaphylaxis^G. Go to **While You Wait #1**, page 39.

 NO

Does your senior horse have a fever? (See "Senior Vital Signs," **page 292**.) Has he failed to break a sweat despite warm, humid conditions? Is his hair sticking up abnormally, making it look like velvet, particularly over his rump?

 YES Call your veterinarian *NOW* if you answered yes to any query—it could be anhidrosis^G. Go to **While You Wait #2**, page 39.

 NO

➤

37

ACTION PLAN (CONTINUED):

Is your senior horse's coat abnormally long, thick, and/or wavy? Does he sweat more than usual? Does he look potbellied or fat, but when you touch him, his ribs are actually quite prominent? Has he had recent or intermittent bouts of lameness involving the front feet? Is he drinking more water than usual, and/or causing larger than usual wet spots in the stall? Does he seem to get sick more often than neighboring horses?

 Call your veterinarian *TODAY* if you answered yes to any query—it could be Equine Cushing's Disease[G] (ECD, also known as pituitary adenoma).

Has your horse lost weight? Is his manure dotted with unchewed grain? Has it been more than 6 months since his teeth were examined by an equine veterinary dental specialist? Has it been more than 6 months since his manure was examined for worm eggs?

 Call your veterinarian *TODAY* if you answered yes to any query—it could be malnutrition due to a diet that's not senior-appropriate, or due to a dental problem, excessive parasite load, or an underlying catabolic[G] disease process.

Is his coat oily-looking, even after a recent bath? Does he have dandruff that makes him look worse after a vigorous brushing because flakes come to the surface?

 Call your veterinarian *TODAY* if you answered yes to either query—it could be seborrhea[G].

Is the abnormality present all over his body, rather than just one or two spots? Have you seen him shivering when other horses seem comfortable? Does he seem dull, easily tired, or somewhat detached from his surroundings? Do his eyes appear to bulge? If your senior horse is a broodmare, has there been any doubt about whether she produces adequate milk?

 Call your veterinarian *TODAY* if you answered yes to any query—it could be a thyroid disorder[G].

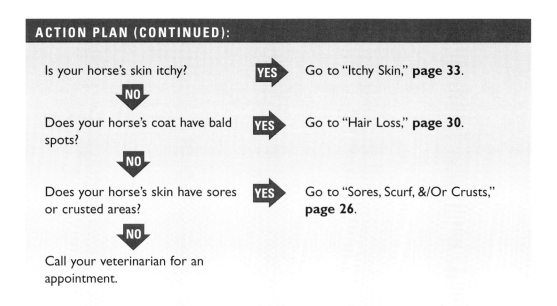

ACTION PLAN (CONTINUED):

Is your horse's skin itchy? **YES** → Go to "Itchy Skin," **page 33**.

NO ↓

Does your horse's coat have bald spots? **YES** → Go to "Hair Loss," **page 30**.

NO ↓

Does your horse's skin have sores or crusted areas? **YES** → Go to "Sores, Scurf, &/Or Crusts," **page 26**.

NO ↓

Call your veterinarian for an appointment.

WHILE YOU WAIT #1

1. *Protect yourself.* If your horse is displaying anxious behavior—pacing, whinnying, eyes open wide, nostrils flared—his judgment is impaired and he might inadvertently hurt you. Don't go near him unless you must, and if you must, be especially cautious.

2. *Improve ventilation.* If your horse is having difficulty breathing, make fresh air available. Much of the anxiety displayed in horses with anaphylaxis is the result of panic due to difficulty breathing.

3. *Recall all potential allergens.* Think back: Can you recall anything that might have brought on this allergic response? A change in feed source? A change to a different pasture? Any medications, dewormers, vaccinations, or vitamin products given? Any topical cosmetic or therapeutic substances applied to his skin? Any biting or stinging bugs noticed? Report all suspicions to your veterinarian.

WHILE YOU WAIT #2

Cool him. If your horse has failed to sweat despite hot, humid conditions, cool him by hosing or swabbing him with a washcloth drenched in cool water. Concentrate on the areas behind and between his ears, on his forehead, the underside of his neck along the jugular vein, in his armpits, and on his groin and underbelly. Place him in the shade where there's a natural breeze, or in front of a fan to encourage evaporation. Re-wet him every 5 minutes or sooner if he dries off. Continue until your vet arrives, or until your horse's temperature drops to 101° F, whichever happens first.

Change in Sweating

SENIOR SIGNPOST: Your horse is sweating more than usual, or less than you think he should under the circumstances. Or, he's sweating only in certain areas of his body, even when he hasn't been exercising and the weather is fairly cool.

What this might mean: It could indicate a problem in his sweat glands or in their nerve supply. Or, it could suggest a systemic illness.

ACTION PLAN:

Does your senior horse have a fever (see "Senior Vital Signs," **page 292**)? Is he off his feed? Does he seem to be listless or detached from his surroundings, or experiencing colic^G-like discomfort? Is your senior horse a pregnant mare?

 YES Call your veterinarian *NOW* if you answered yes to any query—it could be a systemic condition, such as infectious disease, colic^G, or labor pains. Go to **While You Wait #1**, opposite page.

 NO

Is your senior horse being treated with medication for heaves^G (a.k.a. chronic obstructive pulmonary disease, or COPD)?

 NO

 YES Call your veterinarian *TODAY*, before you give the next dose—some heaves medications can cause sweating and heart symptoms. Your horse may require a dosage adjustment.

Is your senior horse sweating more in general? Is his coat overly long, thick, curly, and/or overdue to shed? Does he look potbellied? Has he lost weight? Have you noticed him drinking more than usual, and/or making larger-than-usual urine spots in his stall?

 NO

 YES Call your veterinarian *TODAY* if you answered yes to any query—it could be Equine Cushing's Disease^G (ECD, also known as pituitary adenoma).

Is your senior horse sweating less than usual, remaining essentially dry even on hot days or during strenuous exercise, when you'd expect him to break a sweat? Does his hair stand on end when he's worked in the hot sun? Does he seem easily chilled, shivering when neighboring horses appear comfortable?

 NO

 YES Call your veterinarian *TODAY* if you answered yes to any query—it could be a thyroid disorder^G, and/or anhidrosis^G. Go to **While You Wait #2**, opposite page.

ACTION PLAN (CONTINUED):

Have you noticed patches of sweat in distinct locations on your senior horse, such as in one flank, around his poll, or on the side of his face, without any apparent reason for sweating (it's not hot and he hasn't been exercising)? **YES** Call your veterinarian *TODAY*—patchy, inappropriate sweating can be a sign-post of inflammation, irritation, trauma, and/or sweat-gland damage, or damage to nerve fibers of the cervicosympathetic trunk^G that innervates them.

 NO

Call your veterinarian for an appointment.

WHILE YOU WAIT #1

1. *Isolate your horse from other horses in case it's contagious.* To prevent the spread of possible infectious disease, confine your horse to an open-air paddock or stall with a separate water supply, apart from other horses by at least 20 feet. Wash your hands and disinfect your boots (see box at right) after handling your horse and before handling other horses.

2. *Be alert.* If he's showing colic-type symptoms, go to "Colic," page 221.

WHILE YOU WAIT #2

Cool him. If your horse has failed to sweat despite hot, humid conditions, cool him by hosing or swabbing him with a washcloth drenched in cool water. Concentrate on the areas behind and between his ears, on his forehead, the underside of his neck along the jugular vein, in his armpits, and on his groin and underbelly. Place him in the shade where there's a natural breeze, or in front of a fan to encourage evaporation. Re-wet him every 5 minutes or sooner if he dries off. Continue until your vet arrives, or until your horse's temperature drops to 101° F, whichever happens first.

DISINFECTION DETAIL

Use these tips to help prevent carrying a contagious disease on your skin or clothing after handling a sick horse.

1. When entering the horse's stall or paddock: Wear rubber boots and close-weave fabric coveralls with long sleeves. Confine your hair in a hat. Use disposable latex or rubber examination gloves whenever working with/around the sick horse. Leave these garments at the stall door or paddock gate, where they can be donned before entering and taken off when you leave.

2. Upon leaving the horse's stall or paddock: Discard the used disposable gloves in a closed receptacle outside the enclosure. Disinfect your boots with a plastic scrub brush and Lysol® Disinfectant Concentrate (2 1/2 tablespoons per gallon of water) in a dishpan or bucket. Leave boots outside the enclosure to dry. Cover or discard the Lysol® solution for safety. (It's toxic if swallowed.)

3. When tending to more than one horse, take care of the sick one last.

NOTES

CHAPTER 3

Changes in
GAIT/
MOVEMENT

Moves Stiffly &/Or Slowly

SENIOR SIGNPOST: Your senior horse moves as though he's stiff, sore, or walking on eggshells (especially with his front feet). He may "weathervane" when he turns, reluctant to bend his spine. Or, he may balk or refuse to take a certain path, such as up (or down) an incline, or across a gravel road.

What this might mean: It signals a serious underlying problem. He may be in pain, either in an isolated area of his body, or all over. For instance, a severe headache can be an underlying cause. Or, he may be afraid to move because mental or physical changes make his environment seem less safe.

ACTION PLAN:

Does your senior horse have a fever? (See "Senior Vital Signs," **page 292**.)

 NO

YES Call your veterinarian *NOW*—it could be an oncoming general illness, such as painful pleuritis^G or pleuropneumonia^G, which can cause symptoms of stiffness before the classic signs of the disease appear. Early, aggressive treatment may be necessary for recovery. Go to **While You Wait #1**, page 46.

Has your senior horse recently had diarrhea^G, colitis^G, strangles^G, or any other serious illness?

 NO

YES Call your veterinarian *NOW*—it could be laminitis^G, which sometimes occurs in the aftermath of significant illness. Go to **While You Wait #2,** page 46, and "The Age Event: Laminitis," **page 273**.

Has your senior horse been exercised, either by you or at liberty, within recent hours? Did he exercise strenuously yesterday? Is his urine tinted brown, like coffee?

 NO

YES Call your veterinarian *NOW* if you answered yes to any query—it could be acute myositis^G or exertional rhabdomyolysis. Go to **While You Wait #1**.

Does he seem more prone to stumble, stagger, slip, or fall than he did before? Does he hold his head, or one ear, tilted to one side? Have you seen him lean against a solid object when at rest? Have you recently seen even a small amount of blood coming from either nostril?

 NO

YES Call your veterinarian *NOW* if you answered yes to any query—your senior horse could have a problem with his equilibrium or balance, due to a neurological problem such as Equine Protozoal Myeloencephalitis^G (EPM), or an inner-ear disorder. Go to **While You Wait #3**, page 47.

ACTION PLAN (CONTINUED):

Does your senior horse seem stiff or tender-footed when traveling over hard, uneven, or gravel footing? When at rest, does he seem to shift his weight from leg to leg, and/or hold his forelegs farther in front of him than usual, like a sawhorse?

 Call your veterinarian *NOW* if you answered yes to either query. It could be laminitis^G. Go to **While You Wait #2,** page 46. For more information, see "The Age Event: Laminitis," **page 273**.

 NO

Is there any evidence of trauma? Has your senior horse had conflicts with another horse? Has he recently over-exerted himself (for example, running a long distance, being chased by dogs, or panicking after becoming separated from herdmates)?

 Call your veterinarian *TODAY* if you answered yes to any query. Your senior horse may have injured himself.

 NO

Have you been feeding hay that's been stored for more than a year? Do you live in an area in which the trees are mostly needle-bearing and evergreen, rather than leafy and deciduous? Are the soil and forage in your area known or rumored to be lower than normal in selenium? Do you add fat to your horse's diet, in the form of unsaturated fat?

 Call your veterinarian *TODAY* if you answered yes to any query—it could be a health-threatening selenium deficiency^G, which can be exacerbated by any of these circumstances.

 NO

At dusk or after dark, does he seem spookier than usual and/or afraid to pass through familiar gates or passages?

 Call your veterinarian *TODAY* if you answered yes to either query. Your senior horse could have a vision problem. For more information, see "Vision Problems," **page 112**.

 NO

Do your senior horse's flexibility and willingness to move improve with movement, or during a pre-exercise warm-up session? Is he worse after a period of confinement?

 Call your veterinarian *TODAY* if you answered yes to either query—It could be arthritis^G. While you wait, go to "The Age Event: Arthritis," **page 227**.

 NO

Call your veterinarian for an appointment.

➤

Bute: Resist The Urge

What's the first thing you reach for when your oldster acts stiff and sore? Is it "bute" (phenylbutazone^G)? Think before you do so again. With advancing age, your senior horse's body is less able to tolerate medications' side effects. Decreases in appetite, fiber intake, water intake, activity level, and gut motility all can contribute to an exaggerated toxic response to bute, whose side effects include:

- Stomach ulcers^G
- Ulcerative colitis^G
- Aplastic anemia^G in you (from handling it).

Use bute sparingly, under your veterinarian's guidance. Opt for commercially prepared bute paste or gel, rather than tablets. Wear rubber gloves and avoid contact with the medication. The more you handle it, the greater your own risk of side effects.
Finally, ask your vet for a safer alternative. One reason bute's so popular is that it's cheap. In the long run, though, its side effects can make it quite expensive.

WHILE YOU WAIT #1

1. *Isolate your horse from other horses in case it's contagious.* To prevent the spread of possible infectious disease, confine your horse to an open-air paddock or stall with a separate water supply, apart from other horses by at least 20 feet. Wash your hands and disinfect your boots (see page 41) after handling your horse and before handling other horses.

2. *Restrict movement.* Until a definitive diagnosis can be made, assume your horse has a disorder that can be worsened by movement. Don't move him unless absolutely necessary.

WHILE YOU WAIT #2

1. *Confine your horse.* Confine your horse to a small (12 x 12) stall or paddock with soft footing. If he moves stiffly, is reluctant to move, rocks back on his hind legs, or has an exaggerated digital pulse (see page 295), don't move him. Rather, confine him where he stands, using portable corral panels or a makeshift enclosure. Or, simply stay with him until your vet arrives.

2. *Don't feed him.* Offer water only. Your horse should have no feed of any kind until your vet's ruled out laminitis^G, which might be the result of, or worsened by, certain kinds of feeds.

3. *Chill his feet.* Draw out excess heat in the affected feet by applying flexible ice packs (such as frozen bags of peas or corn) to his hoof walls for 5 minutes every half hour.

WHILE YOU WAIT #3

1. *Protect yourself.* With this kind of gait anomaly, your horse is likely to move in unexpected ways. Be alert, and don't put yourself in a position where you could be stepped on, knocked over, or conked on the head.

2. *Protect your horse.* Your horse can do serious damage to himself if he feels compelled to move. If it can be done safely, halter and hold him where he is while you wait for your vet. Or, if possible, have a helper hold your horse while you set up portable corral panels around him, to protect him from other horses.

Did You Know?

Inflammation of the pleura (the Saran Wrap-like lining of your horse's chest cavity), as is seen with pleuritisᴳ and pleuropneumoniaᴳ, is extremely painful and can cause your horse to resist flexing, bending, moving, or being touched over his rib cage. Often preceded by significant stress (such as a long road trip or an upper-respiratory infection), stiffness and soreness may be the first symptoms you see in your senior horse.

Lameness

SENIOR SIGNPOST: Your senior horse is limping, shifting his weight frequently, holding up a leg, or otherwise displaying signs of lameness.

What this might mean: It could be a "standard" lameness due to injury, or it could be an age-related condition.

ACTION PLAN:

Does your senior horse have a fever? (See "Senior Vital Signs," **page 292**.)

 YES Call your veterinarian *NOW*—signs of lameness, with fever, can indicate a developing infection or severe inflammatory process with laminitis^G. Go to **While You Wait #1**, opposite page.

 NO

Is he shifting his weight from one front leg to the other? Does he stand with his front legs farther forward than usual? Is he tender-footed when walking across gravel or hard and/or uneven surfaces? Do the walls of any of his hooves feel colder or warmer than usual? Do any of his feet have a more prominent digital pulse? (See "Senior Vital Signs," **page 295**.)

 YES Call your veterinarian *NOW* if you answered yes to any query—it could be laminitis^G. Go to **While You Wait #1**, opposite page.

 NO

Has his feed recently changed? Did he eat a larger-than-usual volume of grain within the past 3 days?

 YES Call your veterinarian *NOW*—it could be laminitis^G due to endotoxemia^G. Go to **While You Wait #1**, opposite page.

 NO

Is he fatter or thinner than he should be? (See "Senior Condition Check," **page 300**.) Does he have an unusually long, wavy, scruffy coat that's overdue to shed? Does he sweat more than usual? Does he shiver on cool days when other horses are perfectly comfortable?

YES Call your veterinarian *NOW*—it could be laminitis^G due to a hormonal imbalance such as Equine Cushing's Disease^G (ECD, also known as pituitary adenoma; see "The Age Event: Cushing's Disease," **page 257**) or thyroid disease^G. Go to **While You Wait #1**, opposite page.

 NO

ACTION PLAN (CONTINUED):

Is he holding up one leg and reluctant to bear weight on it, or walking with a severe head-bobbing limp?

 YES Call your veterinarian *NOW*—it could be a serious injury of the supporting structures, such as a sprained or ruptured tendon (bowed flexor tendon, or a ruptured extensor tendon), sprained ligament (such as carpal or check ligament), injured joint, or a fracture, all of which are more common in older horses due to loss of soft tissue elasticity and decreased bone density. Go to **While You Wait #2**, below.

 NO

Is the affected leg(s) swollen, unusually warm, or unusually cold?

 YES Call your veterinarian *NOW*—there could be a serious underlying illness or injury, including venous thrombosis^G, vasculitis^G, folliculitis^G, or deep-tissue injury. Go to **While You Wait #2**.

 NO

Does the lameness appear after your senior horse has been idle for several hours, getting better as he moves?

YES Call your veterinarian *TODAY*—arthritis^G is a likelihood. Thanks to new treatment and management tools, it need not be permanent or crippling. For more information, go to "The Age Event: Arthritis," **page 227**.

NO

Call your veterinarian *TODAY* for a soundness examination.

WHILE YOU WAIT #1

1. *Confine your horse.* Movement might make things worse. Until proven otherwise, confine him to a box stall or small paddock and provide a companion, if necessary, to discourage fretful movement.

2. *Chill any warm feet.* Select a flexible ice pack large enough to wrap around the entire hoof wall. (This might take two packs.) Apply the pack(s) and secure with a wrap. Leave on for 5 minutes. Repeat every half hour, or until your vet arrives, whichever happens first.

3. *Avoid feeding him.* Give no feed—only water—until your vet arrives and can confirm or dismiss laminitis^G as a cause of lameness.

WHILE YOU WAIT #2

1. *Confine your horse.* Movement might make things worse. Confine him to a box stall or small paddock and provide a companion, if necessary, to discourage fretful movement. ➤

Which Leg is Lame?

In most cases, pinpointing a lameness isn't difficult if you follow these steps. *Caveat:* If your horse's lameness is obvious and he's reluctant to bear weight on the leg(s), skip these steps and immediately call your vet. These diagnostics could cause further damage.

WHAT YOU'RE LOOKING FOR

• **Head-bob:** Your horse's head bobs UP when a sore forelimb hits the ground. His head bobs DOWN when a sore hind limb hits the ground. *(Tip: A head-bob is easiest to see when your horse is trotted toward you. As a general rule, the more pronounced the bob, the more severe the pain.)*

• **Hip-hike or hip-drop:** The hip on one side raises HIGHER and/or sinks LOWER than the other side. *(Tip: This is easiest to see when your horse is trotted away from you. Make it more visible by sticking a piece of white adhesive tape on each hip, to give your eye a reference point.)*

• **Toe-drag:** The toe of the affected hind limb drags the ground on the forward swing.

• **Shortened stride** The stride on one leg is shorter than the stride on the other legs.

NOW LOCATE THE LAME LEG

Follow these steps. Call your veterinarian if you observe any sign of injury or lameness in Steps 1, 2, or 3. If you still can't ferret out the lameness, call your vet for help.

Step 1. Examine your horse's legs and feet for external evidence of injury.

• Stand him squarely on solid, level ground, then visually examine each leg and coronary band for bumps, swellings, wounds, discharges, or other such problems.

• Feel each hoof for excess heat, then check your horse's digital pulse. (For how to do so, see page 295.)

• Pick up, clean, and examine each foot for nails, cracks, bruises, or other abnormalities. Note any resistance, which could indicate pain in another foot/feet, hence his reluctance to increase the load there.

Step 2. Watch your horse trot a straight line. Lameness that's barely perceptible at the walk can become more evident at the trot.

• Find a flat, smooth surface with solid footing.

• Recruit a helper. Give her a crop or whip, if necessary, to help get your horse trotting in hand.

• Have your helper trot the horse on a straight line away from you, for about 50 feet, loosely holding the lead so as not to inhibit a head-bob. Then have the pair trot toward you, then past you, so you can view the horse from the front and side.

Repeat the exercise 2 to 3 times. If you still can't identify the lame leg(s), one of three things could be happening:

1. Your horse may be too lame, fresh, or uncomfortable to cooperate.

2. The lameness is bilateral or too subtle to show up on a straight line.

3. There is no lameness.

Step 3. Longe your horse. Have your helper longe the horse in both directions, gradually tightening the circle. Or, have your helper trot him in circles in hand. As a general rule, the tighter the circle, the more pronounced the lameness. Still can't see the problem's origin? Call your vet.

WHILE YOU WAIT #2 - CONTINUED

2. *Cool the foot, tendon, or joint suspected of being the problem.* Select an ice pack large enough to extend at least 2 inches beyond the affected area's margins. Slip it between layers of a clean cloth, center it over the area, and hold it there. Ice on: 5 minutes. Ice off: 15 minutes. Repeat this cycle 3 more times or until your vet arrives, whichever happens first.

3. *Apply a support wrap.* If you're reasonably sure where the problem is, apply a support wrap appropriate to the area being bandaged, adding an extra layer of padding and being especially careful to apply the elastic layer evenly and firmly enough to prevent slippage.

How Lame is Your Horse?

There are many different methods of defining and grading lameness. We've adopted the classification of the American Association of Equine Practitioners, as defined in their Guide to Horse Shows:

Definition: Lameness is a deviation from the normal gait or posture due to pain or mechanical dysfunction.

Classification:

Grade 1: Difficult to observe; not consistently apparent regardless of circumstances (i.e., weight carrying, circling, inclines, hard surfaces, etc.).
Grade 2: Difficult to observe at a walk or trotting a straight line; consistently apparent under certain circumstances (i.e., weight carrying, circling, inclines, hard surfaces, etc.).
Grade 3: Consistently observable at a trot under all circumstances.
Grade 4: Obvious lameness; marked nodding, hitching, or shortened stride.
Grade 5: Minimal weight bearing in motion and/or at rest; inability to move.

Bizarre Gait &/Or Behavior

SENIOR SIGNPOST: Your horse is moving and/or behaving in an abnormal manner, doing things that seem illogical, or having difficulty performing certain tasks he normally does without a problem. He may aimlessly wander or circle, "star gaze" (stare up at the sky), or press his head against a solid object. Or, he may be lie down and have difficulty getting up.

What this might mean: It could be a problem involving your horse's nervous system, or an underlying problem involving his muscles, tendons, bones, joints, etc.

ACTION PLAN:

Does your senior horse have a fever? (See "Senior Vital Signs," **page 292**.)

 Call your veterinarian *NOW*—it could be one of several infections that can affect your horse's nervous system, including but not limited to EPM^G (Equine Protozoal Myeloencephalitis), Lyme disease^G, bastard strangles^G, and rabies^G. (See "Rabies Caution," **page 76**.) Isolate him from other horses until your vet arrives.

 NO

Are his gums and/or the whites of his eyes yellow-tinged? Does he have crusty, scabby skin in areas of his body that are light-colored?

 Call your veterinarian *NOW* if you answered yes to either query—it could be a liver problem called hepatoencephalopathy^G, resulting in a buildup of natural toxins that affect brain function. Go to **While You Wait #1**, page 54.

 NO

Did the abnormal symptoms appear within 24 hours of purge deworming^G your horse?

 Call your veterinarian *NOW*—migrating parasite larvae in your horse's brain may have been activated by the treatment.

 NO

Is it possible your horse is overdue for deworming?

 Call your veterinarian *NOW*—it could be a parasite-related problem in the nervous system, such as verminous encephalitis^G or stroke due to parasitic thromboembolism^G.

NO

ACTION PLAN (CONTINUED):

Has there been any evidence of injury anywhere on his body that appeared around the time his symptoms did? **YES** Call your veterinarian *NOW*—it could be head trauma, or a blood clot, mass, or hemorrhage in the nervous system.

 NO

Does your senior horse have episodes in which he suddenly collapses, or almost collapses because his knees have buckled? Has he had any seizures that you know of or suspect, or had brief periods when he acts depressed, confused, or afraid? Does he have unexplained skin calluses (hairless, thickened areas) or wounds on the fronts of his knees (carpal joints) and/or forelimb fetlocks? **YES** Call your veterinarian *NOW* if you answered yes to any query—it could be syncope^G from a heart problem, narcolepsy^G, or a seizure disorder in the brain.

 NO

Does he stumble, stagger, or sway when he walks? Have you seen him leaning on a solid object, as though needing help standing? Does he lift his legs higher than usual, or keep them abnormally stiff and straight? Does he knuckle over, or drag a toe as he moves and bears weight? **YES** Call your veterinarian *NOW* if you answered yes to any query—there could be a degenerative or inflammatory problem in your horse's nervous system or inner ear.

 NO

Are his gums abnormally pale? Does he seem more harassed by insects than other horses in the same environment? Has it been longer than 6 months since he's had a negative Coggins test? **YES** Call your veterinarian *NOW* if you answered yes to any query—it could be a brain condition associated with advanced EIA^G (Equine Infectious Anemia, a.k.a. Coggins disease). Go to **While You Wait #2**, page 54.

 NO

Has he tested negative for HYPP^G (Hyperkalemic Periodic Paralysis), which has been linked to having the Quarter Horse stallion Impressive in the pedigree? **NO** Call your veterinarian *TODAY*—it could be HYPP.

 YES

Call your veterinarian for an appointment.

WHILE YOU WAIT #1

Confine your senior horse to a stall or other enclosure out of direct sunlight. If he has a liver problem, he is at increased risk of photosensitization^G, a skin condition that causes severe sunburn and scabby sores in hairless and/or pink-skinned areas of his body. Be alert when working around a horse that's showing signs of abnormal mental state. He's more likely to perceive danger even when there is none, and hurt you in the process of trying to protect himself.

WHILE YOU WAIT #2

Isolate your horse from other horses, to help prevent spread of possible infectious disease. Since EIA^G is spread by biting/sucking insects, bring him indoors if possible and apply a fly sheet and insect repellent. Do the same for other horses on the premises.

CAUTION

1. *Handle with care.* If your horse's mental state is altered, his behavior can be unpredictable. He may suddenly bolt, strike, bite, or collapse and seize, injuring you and bystanders. Be especially alert when working around him, leaving yourself a safety "space cushion" in case you need to make a quick get away.

2. *Be riding smart.* A horse that has any health problem affecting his gait or general behavior, including narcolepsy^G or epilepsy^G, is at increased risk of taking missteps and losing his balance, or having sudden "spells," any of which can cause him to fall, possibly hurting himself—and you. For this reason, if your horse is suspected of having any of these problems, don't ride him unless your veterinarian is able to rule these diagnoses out and/or resolve the problem and give your horse a clean bill of health neurologically.

Down, Can't (or Struggles to) Get Up

SENIOR SIGNPOST: Your senior horse is lying down and stays there, even in the face of stimuli, such as your approach, that usually would cause him to spring to his feet.

What this might mean: He's cast, injured, exhausted, ill, or has a neurological problem that's preventing him from rising.

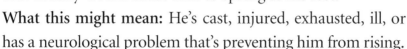

ACTION PLAN:

Does your senior horse have a fever (see "Senior Vital Signs," **page 292**), or feel abnormally warm and/or moist with sweat? Does he occasionally roll or thrash? Are you able to coax him to get up, but he goes down again?

 NO

YES Call your veterinarian *NOW* if you answered yes to any query—it could be a serious infection, a painful condition such as colic[G] or peritonitis[G], or hemorrhage into the abdominal cavity. Go to **While You Wait #1**, next page.

Does your horse seem mentally off—weak, or depressed, and apparently unconcerned about being down?

 NO

YES Call your veterinarian *NOW*—it could be a severe injury or illness causing weakness or an altered mental state. Go to **While You Wait #2**, next page.

Is your senior horse a mare that's foaled within the past 24 hours?

 NO

YES Call your veterinarian *NOW*—it could be exhaustion and weakness from birthing, internal bleeding from a ruptured uterine artery[G], or damage to nerves supplying one or both hind limbs, paralyzing the associated muscles. Go to **While You Wait #3**, next page.

Does he appear physically traumatized and/or injured?

 NO

YES Call your veterinarian *NOW* if you answered yes to either query—it's possible your horse is injured. Go to **While You Wait #2**.

➤

ACTION PLAN (CONTINUED):

Is your horse alert, his legs obviously cast (stuck) against a barrier or fence? Does he appear relatively unscathed physically? Can you approach him without causing him to thrash?

 Apply **Home Treatment**, opposite page. If this fails for any reason, call your veterinarian *NOW*.

Call your veterinarian *NOW*—the longer your senior horse is down, the more damage may occur to his head, legs, and muscles, as well as to his lungs.

WHILE YOU WAIT #1

1. *Isolate your horse from other horses in case it's contagious.* To prevent the spread of possible infectious disease, confine your horse to an open-air paddock or stall with a separate water supply, apart from other horses by at least 20 feet. Wash your hands and disinfect your boots (see page 41) after handling your horse and before handling other horses.

2. *If he's showing colic-type symptoms, go to "Colic," page 221.* For more information, see "The Age Event: Colic," page 251.

WHILE YOU WAIT #2

1. *Protect your horse from self-inflicted injury.* The most common injury resulting from being down is head/eye injury from swinging the head and slamming it against the ground or wall in repeated attempts to rise. Pad the environment: Add thick, soft bedding and strategically placed bales of hay or straw around him.

2. *Keep him warm.* If your horse's mental state is depressed, he'll make little if any effort to rise and could become hypothermic^G, particularly if it's cold outside. Surround him with bedding, and cover him with a blanket.

WHILE YOU WAIT #3

1. *Move the foal.* If you can do so without putting yourself at risk, move the foal to an adjacent enclosure so he won't be injured.

2. *Protect the mare.* Pad the area around her with bales of hay or straw. Remove all obstacles to prevent her from colliding with them, and to make it safer for personnel to move around her.

3. *Keep it quiet.* Encourage her to lie quietly by leaving her alone. Her chance of forming a durable blood clot and halting the bleeding will be better if she remains still.

HOME TREATMENT

*(See **Action Plan** to determine whether home treatment is appropriate for your cast horse. If at any time during home treatment, your answers on the **Action Plan** change for the worse, call your vet.)*

Step 1. *Get help.* Enlist the aid of two or more strong helpers.

Step 2. *Test your strength.* If you and your helpers collectively are strong enough to do so without hurting your backs or knees, grab handfuls of mane and tail and try to pull your horse away from the wall, then quickly get out of the way to avoid injury when he rises.

Step 3. *Get ropes.* If you can't find enough muscle power for Step 2, or if you've executed that step and your horse still can't get up (and you see no visible reason why), it could be that he's been cast so long that his down legs have "gone to sleep," and you'll have to turn him over. Get two strong, soft ropes that are each at least 20 feet long (tie non-clip ends of two soft lead ropes together to make one rope).

Definition:
THE CAST HORSE

A horse is cast when he has the physical ability to rise, but there's external interference. Because of the way his weight is distributed, a horse must follow a routine in order to get to his feet.

1: Position himself on his chest, with hind limbs drawn up beneath him.

2: Extend his forelimbs in front of him.

3: Swing his head and neck as ballast, while simultaneously pushing with his hind limbs to raise his hindquarters, and bracing himself with his forefeet.

In the typical cast-horse scenario, the stall is freshly bedded, just begging your horse to roll. He lowers himself, rolls up onto his back for a brisk scratch...and rolls over onto his other side, his legs bunched up against the wall. He can't get positioned to stand up.

Step 4. *Position the ropes.* Stand behind your horse's spine, away from the danger of struggling legs. Lean over his torso and loop one rope under each of the two bottom legs, then work each rope up the leg until it's well above his hock (hind leg) and knee (front leg).

Step 5. *Pull him over.* With one or two people at each rope, pull both legs simultaneously to turn him over. This will be difficult, but one strong person or two people with average strength can do it. *Caution*: Don't let his hooves hit you on their way over. To help avoid risk of injury, be alert and ready to move out of his way as he rises.

NOTES

CHAPTER 4

RESPIRATORY CHANGES

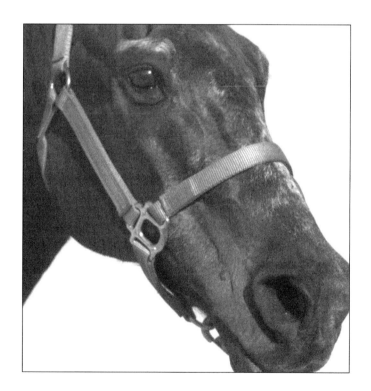

Coughing

SENIOR SIGNPOST: Your horse has developed a cough.
What it might mean: A viral or bacterial infection, an allergy, foreign body, or obstruction in his throat or lungs.

ACTION PLAN:

Is there a watery or thick nasal discharge with bits of feed in it? Was your senior horse treated by stomach tube within the last week? Has he had one or more bouts of choke^G within the past year?

 YES Call your veterinarian *NOW* if you answered yes to any query—it could be choke^G, a ruptured esophagus^G, and/or aspiration pneumonia^G. Go to **While You Wait #1**, opposite page.

NO

Does your horse have a fever? Is he off his feed? Does he appear dull, depressed, or detached from his surroundings? Are his eyes bloodshot?

 YES Call your veterinarian *NOW* if you answered yes to any query—it could be a respiratory-tract infection such as pneumonia^G or rhinotracheitis^G (a "cold"). Go to **While You Wait #2**, opposite page, and see "Why Call Your Vet For A Common Cold?" **page 62**.

NO

Is your horse having recurring coughing fits?

 YES Call your veterinarian *NOW*—it could be bronchitis^G or foreign material stuck in your senior horse's airways.

NO

Is there a rotted or mothball-like smell to his breath?

 YES Call your veterinarian *TODAY*—there could be an obstruction in your senior horse's throat, such as a growth, abscess, or foreign body in or near his respiratory tract.

NO

Does your senior horse exhibit decreased exercise tolerance? Does he become winded more easily than usual, breathing heavily and flaring his nostrils? Does he take longer than usual to recover after exercise?

 YES Call your veterinarian *TODAY* if you answered yes to any query—it could be a chronic lung or airway infection, heaves^G (see "The Age Event: Heaves," **page 267**), or congestive heart failure^G. While you wait, see "Labored Breathing," **page 63**.

NO

ACTION PLAN (CONTINUED):

Does the cough occur mostly when your senior horse exerts himself, resulting in faster and deeper breathing? Has he recently recovered from a "cold?"

 NO

 YES If you answered yes to both queries, it could be airway hyperresponsiveness^G. **Apply Home Treatment #1**, next page.

Is the cough present mostly when he first starts exerting himself, getting somewhat better as he continues exercising? **YES**

 NO

It could be pharyngitis^G or tracheitis^G—inflammation of the tissues in the throat and upper-neck portion of his trachea (windpipe). Apply **Home Treatment #1**.

Does your senior horse share his living space with donkeys or mules, or with any other horses that have commingled with donkeys or mules? **YES**

It could be lungworms^G. Apply **Home Treatment #2**, next page.

 NO

Call your veterinarian for an appointment.

WHILE YOU WAIT #1

1. *Remove all feed and water, as well as bedding if your horse appears interested in eating it. (Or, stay with him until your vet arrives.)* That way he won't add bulk to the feed caught in his esophagus, which would increase his risk that it'll spill into his lungs and cause aspiration pneumonia^G.

2. *Keep him calm and quiet, preferably with his head held relaxed and low, so the material that's overflowing will spill onto the ground, instead of down his trachea (windpipe) and lungs.*

WHILE YOU WAIT #2

Isolate your horse in a quiet paddock or well-ventilated (but not drafty) stall with plenty of fresh water and plain salt. This is more for the patient's well-being than to protect the other horses—pneumonia rarely is contagious in horses but your sick horse is at risk of catching other conditions due to his weakened state. He's also less capable of meeting social challenges, so confining him will reduce stress. If he's shivering, blanket him.

HOME TREATMENT #1

Minimize deep breathing and dust. Give your senior horse 3 weeks off before allowing him to run, roll in dust, or do anything that gets him breathing heavily or coughing. That's because a cough that appears under these circumstances is due, at least in part, to pharyngitis[G], tracheitis[G], and/or what's called airway hyperresponsiveness[G]. It takes a minimum of 3 weeks for the irritated and hypersensitive tissues to calm down. Every time your horse's airways get irritated during that time, the 3-week clock gets "reset," meaning he'll stay hypersensitive longer. Repeat this scenario too many times, and his irritated cough can become long-term, maybe even permanent.

HOME TREATMENT #2

Deworm him. If there's a chance your senior horse has lungworms[G], treat him with a purge dewormer[G] labeled effective against the *Dictyocaulus*[G] family of worms. Ivermectin is a good choice. Follow the label instructions. If he shows signs of general illness (fever, depression, inappetance), call your vet.

> ## Why Call Your Vet for a Common Cold?
>
> Your older horse has decreased reserves, increased vulnerability to serious infections, and increased risk of dehydration and impaction colic.
>
> So, don't treat colds lightly. The money you spend treating one early could save you big bucks down the road—and save your horse from serious health problems.

Labored Breathing

SENIOR SIGNPOST: Your senior horse seems to get winded more quickly than usual with very little exertion, leading to flared nostrils, heavy breathing, and possible sweating. Once he's winded, it seems to take longer for him to catch his breath. In fact, you may have noticed that he breathes harder than usual even when he's at rest.

What this might mean: It could mean a problem in his lungs, in the airways leading to the lungs, or in his cardiovascular system.

ACTION PLAN:

Has the labored breathing appeared suddenly, within a couple hours of giving your senior horse some kind of medication, such as penicillin or a vaccine? Have hives appeared anywhere on his body? **YES** Call your veterinarian *NOW* if you answered yes to either query—it could be a severe allergic reaction such as anaphylaxis^G. Go to **While You Wait #2**, page 111.

 NO

Does your horse have a fever? (See "Senior Vital Signs," **page 292**.) Has he been trailered within the past 2 weeks, and/or introduced to unfamiliar horses? Does he resent having his chest touched? **YES** Call your veterinarian *NOW* if you answered yes to any query—it could be anhidrosis^G, or it could be pneumonia^G or pleuropneumonia^G (also known as shipping fever), which requires prompt treatment for best outcome. Go to **While You Wait #1**, page 65.

 NO

Has he been medicated by stomach tube within the past 3 days? Has he had an episode of choke^G within the past 3 days? **YES** Call your veterinarian *NOW* if you answered yes to either query—it could be aspiration pneumonia^G due to medication and/or stomach contents spilling into the lungs.

 NO

Has he been sick with respiratory signs (fever, cough, nasal discharge) within the past 3 weeks? **YES** Call your veterinarian *NOW*—it could be that the recent respiratory tract infection has caused abscesses to form in your horse's lungs or has spread to his heart valves. Or, he could have a heart arrhythmia^G or congestive heart failure^G.

 NO

➤

ACTION PLAN (CONTINUED):

Are there any wounds, swellings, or tender areas, or any other evidence of trauma to your senior horse's rib cage or abdominal/flank region? Has he been housed with aggressive horses?

 YES Call your veterinarian *NOW* if you answered yes to either query—trauma may have led to lung damage and/or damage to tissues near the lungs, resulting in such conditions as pneumothoraxG, hemothoraxG, or diaphragmatic herniaG, which require prompt treatment for best outcome.

 NO

Does your senior horse make a noise (e.g., snoring, roaring, honking, whistling, etc.) when he inhales and/or exhales?

 YES Call your veterinarian *TODAY*—it sounds like a problem in the nerves that supply the muscles that hold your horse's upper throat open, resulting in a partial blockage of airflow to his lungs.

 NO

Have you noticed a foul smelling and/or blood-tinged discharge from either nostril? Is his breath foul-smelling? Do any of his facial features seem to droop or look asymmetrical when viewed from the front?

 YES Call your veterinarian *TODAY* if you answered yes to any query—it could be a mass in your horse's nasal passage(s) or upper throat region, either of which can partially block the flow of air into his chest.

 NO

Is your horse's coat bone dry despite the fact that it's hot, and neighboring horses are sweating freely?

 YES Call your veterinarian *TODAY*—it could be anhidrosisG. See **While You Wait**, step **#2**, opposite page.

 NO

Does his breathing get worse when he's stall-confined and/or has just eaten hay, and better when he's out in pasture? Does he have a ridge or ditchlike line in his body wall, just behind his rib cage on both sides, where muscles seem to lift his torso when he exhales?

 YES Call your veterinarian *TODAY*—it could be heavesG (a.k.a. chronic obstructive pulmonary diseaseG, or COPD). For more information, see "The Age Event: Heaves," **page 267**.

 NO

Call your veterinarian *TODAY*.

WHILE YOU WAIT

1. *Isolate your horse from other horses in case it's contagious.* To prevent spread of possible infectious disease, confine your horse to an open-air paddock or stall with a separate water supply, apart from other horses by at least 20 feet. Wash your hands and disinfect your boots (see page 41) after handling your horse and before handling other horses.

2. *Cool him.* If your senior horse is panting, and/or if the hair over his rump area is standing up (common signs of anhidrosis^G), grab a bucket of cool water and a sponge, or a garden hose, and wet him down, then stand him in a shaded area with a light breeze or fan. (If you don't have access to water, swab his poll, shoulders, rump, and neck with a cloth soaked in isopropyl alcohol.)

Breathe-Right Travel Tips

When hauling your senior horse—especially on trips over several hours—keep the following suggestions in mind, to help minimize the risk of a travel-related respiratory infection.

• **Maximize trailer ventilation.** When possible, haul your horse in a stock or modified-stock-type trailer. The open-air configuration ensures maximum airflow. (If the weather is cold and/or wet, you can blanket your horse with clothing appropriate for the conditions, such as a waterproof, breathable turnout sheet or blanket.) Enclosed trailers are respiratory disasters waiting to strike. Stagnant air encourages mold and germ growth. Every breath your horse takes in such an environment puts him at risk for infection.

• **Avoid tying his head too high.** Tie your horse such that he can hold his ears slightly below withers level, but not so low that he can get a leg over the tie. If you can do so safely, don't tie him at all, so he can lower his head to his knees when he wants to for proper drainage of debris and mucus from his upper respiratory tract. If your horse is unable to lower his head even slightly, that material will have no choice but to trickle into his lungs, increasing his risk of shipping fever^G (a.k.a. pleuropneumonia^G).

• **Ask your vet about administering an immune stimulant.** Injectable immune stimulants, such as EqStim® (ImmunoVet) and Equimune® (Vetrepharm), administered before your horse's trip, can help boost his immune system, making him less susceptible to respiratory tract infections from travel-related stress and exposure to germs.

Noisy Breathing

SENIOR SIGNPOST: Your senior horse makes a sound when he breathes, such as a wheezing, rasping, snoring, or gurgling noise.

What this might mean: There's something interfering with the flow of air through his respiratory tract.

ACTION PLAN:

Does your senior horse seem to be in respiratory distress? Are his nostrils flared? Is his breathing more rapid and/or labored than usual, even when he hasn't undergone strenuous exercise?

 Call your veterinarian *NOW* if you answered yes to any query—it could be a blockage in or near the respiratory tract, or an asthmalike spasm in the muscles of the bronchial tree that's making it difficult for your horse to get enough air. For more information, go to "Easily Winded," **page 68**.

Is there any drooping, sagging, grimacing, or asymmetry of your senior horse's facial features? Is he drooling excessively or dropping chewed feed from his mouth instead of swallowing it?

 Call your veterinarian *TODAY* if you answered yes to either query—there may be damage, pressure, or inflammation to one or more nerves in your senior horse's throat or upper neck, causing paralysis of muscles that hold the upper part of the throat open.

Is there any nasal discharge?

 Call your veterinarian *TODAY*—there may be a foreign body, cyst[G], abscess[G], blood clot, or tumor in your senior horse's nostril, blocking the airflow.

Does your horse make a gurgling or fluttering noise as he exhales, especially when you work him hard and/or he's flexed at the poll? Does he seem to tire more quickly than normal when you work him?

Call your veterinarian *TODAY* if you answered yes to any query—it could be a dorsal displacement of the soft palate (DDSP)[G], which is partially blocking your senior horse's nasal passages as he exhales.

ACTION PLAN (CONTINUED):

Do you hear a high-pitched, wheezy, "roaring" noise when your horse canters or gallops, and then only when he inhales? Is he a large (over 16-hand) male with a long neck?

 YES Call your veterinarian *THIS WEEK* if you answered yes to either query—it could be laryngeal hemiplegia[G].

 NO

Is your horse making a rasping noise, like heavy breathing or the intake of a snore when he inhales?

 YES Call your veterinarian *TODAY*—it could be a collapsed pharynx[G].

 NO

Call your veterinarian for an appointment.

Noise Makers

Here are some general conditions that can cause respiratory noise in your senior horse.

- Alar fold, excessive
- Botulism poisoning
- DDSP
- EEE
- Encephalitis
- Entrapped epiglottis
- EPM
- Laryngeal hemiplegia
- Lead poisoning
- Pharyngeal cyst
- Rabies
- Russian Knapweed poisoning
- VEE
- WEE
- Yellow star thistle poisoning

(See Glossary for detailed descriptions.)

Easily Winded

SENIOR SIGNPOST: Your senior horse seems to run out of air more easily than usual, breathing heavily, flaring his nostrils, and taking longer than usual to recover after getting winded.

What this might mean: A problem in his respiratory tract or lungs, a cardiovascular problem, or an underlying illness.

ACTION PLAN:

Does your senior horse have a fever? (Go to "Senior Vital Signs," **page 292**.)

 YES ▶ Call your veterinarian *NOW*—there's likely to be an infectious disease involving the respiratory tract, leaving your senior horse at risk for complications, including dehydration. Or, it could be anhidrosis^G. Go to **While You Wait #1,** opposite page.

 NO

Are his gums very pale, or blue-tinged?

 YES ▶ Call your veterinarian *NOW*—it could be severe anemia^G, and/or a cardiovascular problem, either of which can leave your horse oxygen-starved.

 NO

Does your senior horse breathe heavily all the time, even when not exerting himself?

 YES ▶ Call your veterinarian *TODAY*—this isn't a case of being winded, it is persistent heavy breathing, which can suggest different, or more advanced, underlying problems. For more information, go to "Labored Breathing," **page 63**.

 NO

Is your senior horse's coat bone dry while his neighbors are sweating? Is the hair over his rump standing up, resembling velvet?

 YES ▶ Call your veterinarian TODAY if you answered yes to either query—it could be early Equine Cushing's Disease^G (ECD, also known as pituitary adenoma), or a mild to moderate case of anhidrosis^G (a more severe case would be accompanied by elevated body temperature). Go to **While You Wait #2,** opposite page. For more information about Cushing's disease, go to "The Age Event: Equine Cushing's Disease," **page 257**.

 NO

Call your veterinarian *TODAY*—it could be an early case of heaves^G, or congestive heart failure^G.

WHILE YOU WAIT #1

Isolate your horse from other horses in case it's contagious. To prevent spread of possible infectious disease, confine your horse to an open-air paddock or stall with a separate water supply, apart from other horses by at least 20 feet. Wash your hands and disinfect your boots (see page 41) after handling your horse and before handling other horses.

WHILE YOU WAIT #2

Cool him. If your horse has failed to sweat despite hot, humid conditions, cool him by hosing or swabbing him with a washcloth drenched in cool water. Concentrate on the areas behind and between his ears, on his forehead, the underside of his neck along the jugular vein, in his armpits, and on his groin and underbelly. Place him in the shade where there's a natural breeze, or in front of a fan to encourage evaporation. Re-wet him every 5 minutes or sooner if he dries off. Continue until your vet arrives, or until your horse's temperature drops to 101° F, whichever happens first.

Did You Know...?

Most life-threatening bacterial respiratory infections, such as pleuropneumoniaG or "shipping fever," are caused by bacteria that live normally in your horse's mouth. What causes them to move into the respiratory tract and wreak havoc? An impaired immune system, say most researchers, often the result of stress.

NOTES

CHAPTER 5

Changes in
EATING/
DRINKING

Increased Water Intake

SENIOR SIGNPOST: Your senior horse is drinking more water than usual, and doing so on a regular basis—even when he hasn't exercised.

What this could mean: It could be a normal reaction to hot, humid weather, a side-effect of medication, or evidence of a serious problem, such as a kidney disorder or Equine Cushing's Disease^G (ECD, also known as pituitary adenoma).

ACTION PLAN:

Is your senior horse's coat shaggy, dull, and overdue to shed? Does he move stiffly, especially when traveling over hard, rocky, or uneven footing? Does he seem to sweat excessively?

 Call your veterinarian *NOW* if you answered yes to any query—it could be a disorder in your senior horse's brain, such as a pituitary adenoma, resulting in Equine Cushing's Disease^G and/or laminitis^G, and/or diabetes mellitus^G.

 NO

Does your senior horse act listless? Is his appetite decreased? Has he lost weight over the past couple months? Does he have sores inside his mouth? Is there any puffiness or swelling in his lower legs, or under his belly?

 Call your veterinarian *TODAY* if you answered yes to any query—it could be a kidney disorder.

 NO

Is your senior horse confined to a stall most of the time? Has he been going through his salt block faster than usual?

 Call your veterinarian *TODAY* if you answered yes to either query—it could be psychogenic polydipsia^G and/or excessive salt consumption^G, either of which can be due to boredom. Go to "Did You Know," **opposite page**.

NO

Is the weather unusually warm or humid? Are many of the horses in the stable or neighborhood sweaty, including your horse?

 Observe your horse closely. It may be a normal reaction to the heat. Call your vet if your horse develops any other signs outlined in this chart.

NO

Call your veterinarian for an appointment.

Did You Know?

Psychogenic polydipsia^G almost always results from boredom, so your job (after your veterinarian has addressed the kidney disorder called medullary washout^G that can result from polydipsia^G) is to make your horse's life more interesting. Add toys, activities, and pasture turn-out. Above all, don't take matters into your own hands and withhold salt and/or water if you suspect this may be your horse's problem. Medullary washout^G as a result of this abnormal behavior must first be addressed.

Did You Also Know?

The average, 1,000-pound horse drinks 10 to 15 gallons of water in an idle day. On days when he sweats, from high ambient temperature or exercise, his water intake might double or even triple.

Jerks Back from Water

SENIOR SIGNPOST: Your senior horse clearly wants water, but he jerks his head out of the water source before drinking, or acts like he's afraid to approach it.

What this might mean: Something is making it unpleasant, painful, or frightening to drink. That's dangerous—within a day or two of decreased water intake, your senior horse can become dangerously dehydrated.

ACTION PLAN:

If you offer your senior horse a fresh, individual bucket of water in a location that's not near the usual water source, does he drink it? Do other horses act afraid to drink from the old water source? Is the old water source electrified (with a tank heater, for example)? Are there any electrical devices wired and/or grounded near it?

 Call an electrician *NOW* if you answered yes to any query, to search for stray voltage or a damaged, shorted, or improperly grounded electrical device. Shut off all electrical devices and power sources in the vicinity, and immediately provide safe water in an alternate location, preferably in a new container so the horses' fear of the old container won't cause additional delay in drinking.

Did your senior horse receive an injection in the neck muscles within the last 3 or 4 days? Are there any areas of heat, swelling, or discharge on his neck?

 Call your veterinarian *TODAY* if you answered yes to either query. Neck pain might be discouraging your horse from lowering his head to drink. While you wait, offer him a fresh bucket of water in a location that allows him to use a different neck position (e.g., higher).

Call your veterinarian *TODAY*—it could be a painful dental condition that causes sensitivity to cold. Offer body-temperature (98.5 to 100.5° F) water in the meantime, alongside your senior horse's usual water source.

"Plays" in the Water

SENIOR SIGNPOST: Your senior horse has been observed dunking his muzzle in the water source, without actually drinking, or lingering there after he's finished drinking. He may swish his mouth back and forth as though washing it out, or he may simply hold it there without moving.

What this might mean: It can be a sign of pain or discomfort that's relieved when submerged in the cool water. Although more commonly seen in young foals with ulcers^G in their mouths, throats, or stomachs, muzzle-dunking can also signal ulcers in older horses as well as other serious problems.

ACTION PLAN:

Have there been any recent changes in your senior horse's mental attitude, such as unprovoked excitement, depression, staggering, or head-pressing?

 NO

 YES Call your veterinarian *NOW* if you answered yes to any query—it could be as innocent as a headache, or as ominous as illness or injury to your senior horse's nervous system. See **Rabies Caution**, next page.

When he's away from the water, does your senior horse often shake his head or nod it aggressively, as though trying to ward off an invisible swarm of insects?

 NO

 YES Call your veterinarian *TODAY*—it could be a case of head shaking^G, which can be due to irritation of specific nerves in the face that apparently is relieved somewhat by dunking in cool water.

Does he snort excessively? Does he have a constant or intermittent, thickened and/or blood-tinged nasal discharge that never seems to resolve? Does his breath smell rotten or strongly of mothballs?

 NO

 YES Call your veterinarian *TODAY* if you answered yes to any query. Your senior horse could have an infection in his nasal passages, mouth, sinuses, and/or guttural pouch^G(es).

Has your senior horse's feed intake decreased over the past several weeks? Has he been treated recently with "bute" or any other pain-killing medication? Has it been more than 6 months since he's been treated with a boticide^G such as ivermectin?

 NO

 YES Call your veterinarian *TODAY* if you answered yes to any query. Your horse could have ulcers in his mouth, throat, stomach, or colon, and/or a heavy infestation of stomach bots.

Call your vet for an appointment.

CAUTION

Among the possible causes of drooling, an inability to swallow, mental changes, and/or gait abnormalities is a rare but notorious one: Rabies[G]. If rabies is a consideration in your horse's case, don't take chances—take precautions.

1. **Call for help!** This is a veterinary 9-1-1. Call your veterinarian and/or animal control. Such professionals can advise you of how to confine the horse. Rabies is always fatal in horses—your goal now will be to minimize exposure to yourself, your family, and other pets/animals.

2. **Isolate!** Immediately isolate the horse from all other animals and humans in your household. A rabid horse's saliva is teaming with rabies virus, which is highly contagious to humans/animals. Avoid any contact with the horse. If you must handle him, don intact, waterproof gloves (such as household rubber gloves), and protect all other body parts (especially broken skin) from contact with his saliva. Shower immediately after exposure to the horse.

3. **Be alert** for unexpected behavior. Rabies can cause aggression and/or a lack of coordination. Stay out of harm's way.

4. **If you or anyone in your family is bitten** or licked by a suspected rabies carrier, immediately wash the area with warm, soapy water—and call your doctor for advice.

5. **Clean up!** Ask your vet and/or animal control official how to properly disinfect any areas the horse has been.

6. **Think back.** Has your horse had any contact/exposure with wildlife, such as skunks, bats, racoons, or foxes? Familiarize yourself with those animals that are known rabies carriers in your area, and protect your pets—and children—from them.

7. **Alert animal control officials** if you see an odd-behaving critter in your area. (For instance, if you see a nocturnal animal such as a skunk or raccoon moseying around during daylight, that's a red-alert.)

8. **Save it.** If a pet kills a wild animal, use the above clothing precautions, then bag the carcass and call your vet or the health department. They can test the animal for the rabies virus, so you'll know whether your horse, pet,—and family—have been exposed.

Hungry, But Doesn't Finish Meal

SENIOR SIGNPOST: Your senior horse digs into his feed as though very hungry, but pushes away from it before he finishes, then can't be coaxed to eat anything for several hours. **What this might mean:** It usually means there's pain associated with eating, which is severe enough to override your horse's hunger. Painful tooth problems, inadequate moistening and/or chewing, choke^G, and/or lesions in the soft tissues of the mouth are common causes.

ACTION PLAN:

When your senior horse refuses food, have you seen a nasal discharge containing bits of feed? Does he stretch his neck, work his jaw, and/or retch? Can you see or feel a thickening or fistlike lump anywhere along the front of his neck, where his esophagus lies? Is there a smooth indentation in his neck over the jugular vein on either side? Has your senior horse ever received intravenous injections in the jugular vein?

 YES Call your veterinarian *NOW* if you answered yes to any query—it could be choke^G, which occurs when swallowed feed fails to go all the way to the stomach, instead becoming lodged in the esophagus. See "Anatomy of a Choke," **next page**.

 NO

Does your senior horse tilt his head while chewing? Does his breath smell rotten, or strongly like mothballs? Has he been observed eating unusual things instead of his regular feed (such as wood, dirt, bedding)? Does he pull back suddenly from the water source, or act as though he's afraid to approach and drink?

 YES Call your veterinarian *TODAY* if you answered yes to any query—it could be tooth pain, tooth-induced injuries to the soft tissues of your horse's mouth, or he could have a twig or thick-walled stem wedged in the gaps between his teeth.

 NO

➤

ACTION PLAN (CONTINUED):

Does one or more feature of your senior horse's face droop or sag? Does his tongue loll outside his mouth? Was he under general anesthesia within the past week? Does he wear a halter all the time?

 YES Call your veterinarian *TODAY* if you answered yes to any query—it could be damage to nerve(s) of your senior horse's face and jaw, due to injury or disease.

 NO

Do you give your senior horse a special diet formulated and prepared especially for older horses?

 NO Go to "Stay-Young Diet Solutions," **page 376**, for feed suggestions that are easier for an older horse to chew, resulting in relief from dental and/or jaw pain due to increased (and less effective) chew time.

YES

Call your veterinarian for an appointment.

Anatomy of a Choke

A common cause of failure to finish a meal in older horses is painful wadding of food in the esophagus, known as choke^G. It most often is due to incomplete chewing and wetting of the feed due to old, inadequate, or missing teeth, a diet not designed for older horses, inadequate dental care, and/or an abnormal narrowing of the esophagus due to prior injuries and resultant scar tissue.

To help prevent this from happening to your horse, use these tips:
• Consult your veterinarian to design a ration that will be easily chewed and digested by your horse, to minimize wadding. This could include a senior feed specifically designed for this purpose, and/or wetting the feed before feeding, to further help with chewing and digestion.

• Schedule twice-yearly dental exams for your senior citizen. See "Top Priority—Tooth Care," page 332.

• Feed your senior horse in isolation, so he doesn't feel the need to eat quickly in order to get his share. If he gobbles or bolts his feed, use a large feeder, spreading the grain around so he'll have to pick up individual pieces and won't be able to gulp big mouthfuls. And/or, place large, smooth rocks (no smaller than the size of an adult fist) in his grain bucket, so he'll have to work around them.

• If at all possible, turn him out to pasture so he can eat fresh grass the way he was designed to: in a constant trickle, rather than in a few large meals. Or, find a way to feed him in 3 to 4 small meals. Either way, he won't get voraciously hungry and may eat more slowly.

• Ask your veterinarian to administer and/or prescribe medications that don't require jugular-vein injections. Even when the needle is properly placed, medication can leak out of the vein's injection site, causing inflammation and scarring of adjacent tissues—including your horse's esophagus. If intravenous injections must be given, ask that they be given in the right jugular vein rather than the left. In most horses, the esophagus lies on the left side.

Off Feed (lacks appetite)

SENIOR SIGNPOST: Your senior horse isn't eating his ration with his usual gusto. He may leave grain and the leafy parts of his hay, but eat stemmy hay and straw bedding. Perhaps he's eating less of everything—or nothing at all.

What this might mean: It could be something as simple as spoiled or tainted feed. It could mean there's a problem in his ability to pick up, chew, and/or swallow his feed. Or, it could mean he's not feeling well—loss of appetite often is the first outward sign of an internal problem.

ACTION PLAN:

Does your senior horse have a fever? (See "Senior Vital Signs," **page 292**.)

 NO

 YES Call your veterinarian *NOW*—it could be the early stages of an infectious disease. Go to **While You Wait #1**, next page.

Does he seem dull, listless, less responsive than usual, and/or detached from his surroundings? Does he lie down repeatedly, look at his flank, possibly roll? Have you applied fertilizer to your senior horse's pasture, or to adjacent fields, within the past month? Did he have access to land that has seen many horses over the past 30 years, such as fairgrounds or roadside rest corrals?

 NO

 YES Call your veterinarian *NOW* if you answered yes to any query—it could be colic^G, due to a variety of underlying problems including (but not limited to) fertilizer poisoning^G, impaction^G, or severe intestinal parasite infestation (especially small strongyles^G). Go to **While You Wait #2**, next page.

Has he been medicated within the past month with "bute" or any other pain-killing medication? Has he had recent bouts of loose manure that smells metallic or like dog feces? Has it been longer than 6 months since he was treated with ivermectin or moxidectin, to kill stomach bots?

 NO

 YES Call your veterinarian *NOW* if you answered yes to any query—it could be ulcers^G.

➤

ACTION PLAN (CONTINUED):

Does his face appear asymmetrical when you look at it from the front? Are there any swellings visible? Is there any foul-smelling discharge coming from either nostril? Does his breath smell rotten, or strongly of mothballs? Does he tilt his head to one side while eating?

 Call your veterinarian TODAY if you answered yes to any query—it could be a painful dental problem, such as an abscess^G, a fractured tooth, or soft-tissue injury in his mouth (a common problem in older horses with missing teeth).

 NO

Does he approach his feed as though he intends to eat, but fails to get it successfully into his mouth? Does he spill a large percentage of his feed? Does he slobber excessively and leave much of the feed in the feeder?

 Call your veterinarian TODAY if you answered yes to any query—it could be a problem in his jaw, or in the nerves controlling his tongue, his jaw, and/or the swallowing muscles of his throat.

 NO

Call your veterinarian for an appointment.

WHILE YOU WAIT #1

Isolate your horse from other horses in case it's contagious. To prevent spread of possible infectious disease, confine your horse to an open-air paddock or stall with a separate water supply, apart from other horses by at least 20 feet. Wash your hands and disinfect your boots (see page 41) after handling your horse and before handling other horses.

WHILE YOU WAIT #2

1. *Remove all feed.* Remove grain and hay from stall feeders; remove bedding if your horse eats it (it's not unusual for a horse with mild intestinal upset to eat straw or shavings). Leave his water.

2. *If your horse wants to roll or thrash, protect him (and his human attendants).*
• To keep your horse from hurting himself, and to make it easier for human attendants to stay out of harm's way: Re-bed his stall with extra-deep bedding; line stall walls with 1 or 2 layers of hay or straw bales; and remove all movable protrusions (movable feeders, buckets).
• Or, remove him to an arena or paddock with obstacles removed.

• Replace his standard halter with a padded one (such as a fleece-lined travel halter), so the halter's hardware won't damage facial nerves if he falls.

• Unless your horse is thrashing (which would make this too dangerous for you), apply padded shipping bandages to his legs, and a padded crash helmet to his head, if he's accustomed to them.

• If it can be done safely, check and record baseline vital signs every 5 minutes and provide the data to your veterinarian. (For how to do so, see page 292.)

• If your horse is insured (mortality or major medical), call your insurance agent and report that he's colicking. Be sure to familiarize yourself with the policy before a crisis, so you know what's required to comply.

MYTH: Keep your colicky horse walking.

FACT: In a mild to moderate colic, walking your horse might help move bubbles of gas and/or jostle loops of bowel back into their correct positions. But if your horse is intent on lying down, you're not going to be helping the situation by slapping, whipping, kicking, or shouting at him to get up and keep moving. You'll only be adding stress on an already stressful situation, and forcing him to expend energy he'll need to get well. If walking seems to help your horse feel better, walk on. If it's a struggle to keep him on his feet, let him lie down. If he'll lie quietly, all the better. If he's intent on thrashing, no amount of physical abuse is going to stop him, and you might get yourself hurt trying. Instead, do what you can to protect him (without getting hurt yourself): Go to **While You Wait #2**, previous page.

NOTES

CHAPTER 6

Changes in
HEAD, FACE, &/Or MOUTH

Sunken Spot above Eyes

SENIOR SIGNPOST: Your senior horse has a sunken spot or depression just above his eyes, covered by undamaged skin. As far as you know, it wasn't there when he was younger.
What this might mean: It could be a sign of injury. Or, it could be a normal, age-related change.

ACTION PLAN:

Does your senior horse have a fever? (See "Senior Vital Signs," **page 292**.)

 YES Call your veterinarian *NOW*—there could be an underlying illness causing your senior horse to be dehydrated, which could cause the facial depressions as his skin and soft tissue become dried and thinned. If the illness is chronic, it could cause muscle loss, which can further contribute to facial depressions. Go to **While You Wait**, opposite page.

NO

Is there a similar depression on both sides, symmetrical, one above each eye?

 NO Call your veterinarian *NOW*—it could be an injury, such as a skull fracture, either a fresh one or an earlier, healed one.

YES

Is your senior horse off his feed? Is his body-condition score 4 or less? (See "Senior Condition Check," **page 300**.)

 YES Call your veterinarian *NOW* if you answered yes to either query—there could be an underlying degenerative condition that's interfering with your senior horse's protein levels, leading to muscle loss and dehydration. Either can result in facial depressions.

 NO

When your senior horse chews, does something under the depressions move, so the overlying skin moves in and out?

 YES It's a normal anatomical change that occurred as your senior horse aged. See "The Aging Face of Equines," **opposite page**.

 NO

Call your veterinarian *THIS WEEK* for an appointment to find out what's causing the sunken spots.

WHILE YOU WAIT

Isolate your horse from other horses in case it's contagious. To prevent the spread of possible infectious disease, confine your horse to an open-air paddock or stall with a separate water supply, apart from other horses by at least 20 feet. Wash your hands and disinfect your boots (see page 41) after handling your horse and before handling other horses.

The Aging Face of Equines

Those depressions above your senior horse's eyes mark his aging face just as sags and wrinkles will eventually mark yours. Here's why.

Your horse's skull forms a protective socket around his eyeball, made of several skull bones that fused as he developed. Just to the outside of that socket, the *zygomatic* bone forms a bridge, called the *zygomatic arch*, which extends backward from the outer corner of his eye to just beneath the base of his ear. This bone corresponds to your cheekbone. The upright portion of your senior horse's lower jaw bone slips underneath that arch when he opens his mouth, then slips back down when his mouth closes.

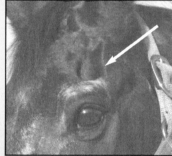

When your senior was younger, the space above the arch was covered by muscle, connective tissue, and "baby fat." As he ages, the baby fat disappears and his muscle and connective tissues thin. With nothing supporting the skin over the arch, it sags, forming what looks like a socket above his eye.

Watch that depression when your horse eats. As he opens his mouth, you'll see movement there due to his lower jawbone protruding into its space.

Sunken Face

SENIOR SIGNPOST: The bone structure of your horse's face looks unusually prominent, as though the tissue beneath his skin has shrunken/dried up. There are deep depressions just above his eyes, and the skin covering these depressions moves in and out when he chews (something you won't see in your younger horses).

What this might mean: Your senior horse may have an underlying health problem that's caused dehydration and/or muscle breakdown.

ACTION PLAN:

Does your senior horse have a fever? (See "Senior Vital Signs," **page 292.**) Is he off his feed? Is he drinking less water than usual?

 YES Call your veterinarian *NOW* if you answered yes to any query—it could be dehydration from a general illness. Go to **While You Wait**, opposite page.

 NO

Has your senior horse lost weight in the past 6 months? Is he drinking more water than usual? Is his stall bedding wetter than usual?

 YES Call your veterinarian *TODAY* if you answered yes to any query—it could be an underlying condition causing dehydration and muscle loss, such as a chronic kidney problem. For more information, go to "Weight Loss," **page 14.**

 NO

Has there been a change in your horse's manure over the past several weeks, such as looser consistency, lighter or darker color, or an increase or decrease in frequency and amount? Has your horse been given "bute" (phenylbutazone^G) or any other pain-killing medication within the past several weeks?

 YES Call your veterinarian *TODAY*—it could be protein loss due to an intestinal condition such as granulomatous enteritis^G or ulcerative colitis^G, which can interfere with digestion and absorption of nutrients. For more information, go to "Changes in Manure," **page 169.**

 NO

ACTION PLAN (CONTINUED):

Does your senior horse have strong- or foul-smelling breath or a nasal discharge? Does he tilt his head while eating, or spit out wads of partially chewed feed? Does he object to a bit he used to accept? Has it been longer than 6 months since his teeth were checked by an equine veterinary dental specialist?

 NO

Call your veterinarian for an appointment. It might be a "normal" age-related decline in your senior horse's condition, but a general examination, with a comprehensive blood screening and possibly additional tests, might reveal something that can be remedied entirely or in part.

 YES

Call your veterinarian *TODAY* if you answered yes to any query—it could be a painful dental problem. Or, it could be periodontal disease[G], causing chronic infection and loosened teeth. Any dental problem can make your horse reluctant to eat and/or drink, or make it difficult or impossible for him to grasp and/or chew his feed properly, resulting in muscle loss and/or dehydration.

WHILE YOU WAIT

Isolate your horse from other horses in case it's contagious. To prevent the spread of possible infectious disease, confine your horse to an open-air paddock or stall with a separate water supply, apart from other horses by at least 20 feet. Wash your hands and disinfect your boots (see page 41) after handling your horse and before handling other horses.

Head Shaking

SENIOR SIGNPOST: Your senior horse is shaking his head from side to side, up and down, or rocker-fashion, like a dog. He doesn't do it all the time, but he does seem to do it at times when there's no obvious explanation. You don't see any bites or sores on his face or ears, nor do you see bugs buzzing around him.

What this might mean: There could be an internal problem, such as neuritis^G (nerve-tissue inflammation), causing irritating sensations in or around his ears, eyes, muzzle, or facial skin. Or, irritation in one or more of those areas could be due to an external influence, such as insects, mites, or dermatitis^G. It could mean he's uncomfortable with his bit, due perhaps to a painful tooth problem. Or, it could be a behavior problem.

ACTION PLAN:

Does your horse stagger, stumble, or appear dizzy? Has there been a change in his gait? Does he hold his head tilted to one side? Does he hold his tail pulled over to one side? Is there a droop or grimace in his facial features?

 YES Call your veterinarian *NOW* if you answered yes to any query—it could be a brain injury, encephalitis^G such as Equine Protozoal Myeloencephalitis^G (EPM), or inflammation deep in the inner ear. See "Caution," **at right**.

 NO

Is one or both ears held in an abnormal position?

 YES Call your veterinarian *TODAY*—your horse could have a mite or tick infestation in one or both ears, or he could have a middle- or outer-ear infection.

 NO

Has your horse recently recovered from a respiratory infection or other illness? Does his head shaking seem to start when you bring him out of the barn and into the sunlight?

 YES Call your veterinarian *TODAY* if you answered yes to either query—it could be a post-viral inflammatory condition (neuritis^G, or vasomotor rhinitis^G). See "Head Shaking: The Disorder," **page 90**, and go to **While You Wait**, opposite.

 NO

Does the head shaking occur only when your horse is wearing a bit? Does he behave normally when you work him with a different bit, or with no bit?

 YES Call your veterinarian *THIS WEEK*. It could be a dental problem.

 NO

ACTION PLAN (CONTINUED):

Does the head shaking occur only when your horse is being asked to work? Does it stop when he's in the same environment, wearing the same tack, but at rest?

 Call your veterinarian *THIS WEEK.* It could be a behavior or training problem, for which your vet can suggest an equine behavior specialist or trainer.

Call your veterinarian for an appointment.

WHILE YOU WAIT

Avoid triggers. If you've identified the conditions that trigger your horse's head-shaking behavior, such as direct sunlight or wind, avoid those conditions. They'll only aggravate already irritated nerves and make his problem more severe, longer-lasting, and resistant.

CAUTION

1. *Handle with care.* **If your horse's mental state is altered, his behavior can be unpredictable. He may suddenly bolt, strike, bite, or collapse and seize, injuring you and bystanders. Be especially alert when working around him, leaving yourself a safety "space cushion" in case you need to make a quick getaway.**

2. *Be riding smart.* **A horse that has any health problem affecting his gait or general behaviors, including narcolepsy[G] or epilepsy[G], is at increased risk of taking missteps and losing his balance, or having sudden "spells," any of which can cause him to fall, possibly hurting himself—and you. For this reason, if your horse is suspected of having any of these problems, don't ride him unless your veterinarian is able to rule out these diagnoses and/or resolve the problem and give your horse a clean bill of health neurologically.**

➤

I f your horse shakes his head as though being swarmed by invisible insects, he's entering a diagnostic Twilight Zone. The behavior could be:

• A sterotypy^G, putting it in the same category as cribbing^G, wood chewing, and other such behaviors.

Head Shaking: The Disorder

• A "work avoidance" training problem.

• A reaction to mouth pain when the bit contacts a sore spot.

• A condition that causes a buzzing, stinging, or burning sensation somewhere on the face, due to nerve-supply inflammation.

Most common is the nerve-supply condition. When triggered by bright or direct sunlight, it's called photic head shaking^G. When triggered by wind, it's called vasomotor rhinitis^G. Other triggers include tack, dust, or flies touching the affected area. Treatment includes avoidance of triggers plus medications and patience. In time, most cases become less severe, and eventually resolve.

Bad Breath

SENIOR SIGNPOST: Your horse's breath has a strong, unnatural odor, perhaps reminiscent of decay or mothballs.

What this might mean: He could have a dental problem, or an underlying disease process.

ACTION PLAN:

Does your horse have a fever? (See "Senior Vital Signs," **page 292.**) **YES** Call your veterinarian *NOW*—there's an underlying infectious disease, which places your senior horse at risk for complications, including dehydration. Go to **While You Wait,** below.

 NO

Is your horse working his mouth even when he's not eating? Does he tilt his head when he chews? **YES** Call your veterinarian *TODAY* if you answered yes to either query—it could indicate a lodged foreign body in your senior horse's mouth, a painful injury, or an infection.

 NO

Have you noticed a discharge from one or both nostrils? Are there any swellings or draining sores on your senior horse's face? **YES** Call your veterinarian *TODAY* if you answered yes to either query—your senior horse could have an infected or abscessed tooth, or an infected guttural pouch[G].

 NO

Can you see feed packed in the spaces between your senior horse's teeth, or any sores or lesions on his gums, tongue, or cheeks? Is his saliva blood-tinged, or dark-colored? **YES** Call your veterinarian *TODAY* if you answered yes to either query—your senior horse may have periodontal disease[G] (see "Top Priority—Tooth Care," **page 332**) and/or lesions in his mouth due to sharp, fractured, or displaced teeth. Or, there may be a tumor in his mouth.

 NO

Call your veterinarian for an appointment.

WHILE YOU WAIT

Isolate your senior horse in an open-air paddock or stall with a separate water supply, apart from other horses by at least 20 feet. Wash your hands and disinfect your boots (see page 41) after handling him and before handling other horses. Offer him his usual feed for this time of day, plus salt and plenty of fresh water.

Loose/Floppy Lower Lip

SENIOR SIGNPOST: Your horse's lower lip frequently hangs loosely, sometimes actually swinging or flopping around when he moves his head.

What this might mean: Slack facial muscles, which can be a sign of general weakness or damage to nerves of the face. It also can be as simple as a relaxed and/or sleepy horse who doesn't have a care in the world.

ACTION PLAN:

Does your senior horse have a fever? (See "Senior Vital Signs," **page 292**.)

 NO

 YES Call your veterinarian *NOW*—it could be an infectious disease. Go to **While You Wait #1**, opposite page.

Is your horse having difficulty picking up, chewing, or swallowing his feed? Does he drool? Does he have access to a weed called yellow star thistle^G? Does his feed include raw corn?

 NO

 YES Call your veterinarian *NOW* if you answered yes to any query—it could be infection or injury to the brain, to nerve tissue in the neck, or a brain condition such as nigropalladial encephalomalacia^G (caused by poisoning from eating yellow star thistle^G), or leukoencephalomalacia^G (due to ingestion of corn mold). Go to **While You Wait #2**, opposite page.

Has there been a change in his behavior? Does he stagger, or lean on solid objects, or otherwise act dizzy?

 NO

 YES Call your veterinarian *NOW* if you answered yes to either query—it could be an underlying condition affecting his brain function, such as encephalitis^G. See "Caution," **page 94**.

Is he off his feed? Has he lost weight in the past 6 weeks? Does he seem easily fatigued and slow to recover from exertion?

 YES Call your veterinarian *TODAY*—it could be an underlying illness or degenerative condition that's robbing your senior horse of energy.

NO

ACTION PLAN (CONTINUED):

When you look at your horse's face from the front, does it look asymmetrical or lopsided? Does one side of the lower lip droop lower than the other side? Is there any sag, droop, or grimace in other facial features, such as an eye, or nostril? Has your horse had general anesthesia within the past few weeks, or been cast in a stall or trailer? Has he been kicked, or collided with a solid object such as a tree? Did he recently struggle while tied? Does he always wear a halter?

 Call your veterinarian *TODAY* if you answered yes to any query—it could be a jaw injury, or damage to one or more of the nerves supplying the face.

 NO

Does your senior horse's lower lip ever close and look normal, for example if he's startled, or if he's anxious about being fed? Does he appear to notice if you touch his chin or pull one of its whiskers?

 NO Call your veterinarian *TODAY* if you answered no to either query—the nerves and/or muscles of the lower lip are not functioning properly, and a general examination and nerve function tests should yield clues as to why.

 YES

Call your veterinarian for a senior vet check (**page 386**), to confirm that this is just a "normal" floppy lip rather than a symptom of an underlying problem.

WHILE YOU WAIT #1

Isolate your horse from other horses in case it's contagious. To prevent the spread of possible infectious disease, confine your horse to an open-air paddock or stall with a separate water supply, apart from other horses by at least 20 feet. Wash your hands and disinfect your boots (see page 41) after handling your horse and before handling other horses.

WHILE YOU WAIT #2

Protect your senior horse. Remove protruding objects from your horse's enclosure that could result in collisions or spills, and keep stress and noise to a minimum to avoid exciting him.

CAUTION

1. *Handle with care.* If your horse's mental state is altered, his behavior can be unpredictable. He may suddenly bolt, strike, bite, or collapse and seize, injuring you and bystanders. Be especially alert when working around him, leaving yourself a safety "space cushion" in case you need to make a quick getaway.

2. *Be riding smart.* A horse that has any health problem affecting his gait or general behaviors, including narcolepsy[G] or epilepsy[G], is at increased risk of taking missteps and losing his balance, or having sudden "spells," any of which can cause him to fall, possibly hurting himself—and you. For this reason, if your horse is suspected of having any of these problems, don't ride him unless your veterinarian is able to rule out these diagnoses and/or resolve the problem and give your horse a clean bill of health neurologically.

Abnormal Gum Color

SENIOR SIGNPOST: Your horse's normally pink gums are abnormally pale, are brighter than usual, or have a purplish or yellowish tint.

What this might mean: A systemic illness. Many conditions that are otherwise invisible can produce changes in gum color, providing a valuable early warning sign.

ACTION PLAN:

Does your senior horse have a fever? (See "Senior Vital Signs," **page 292**.)

 NO

 YES Call your veterinarian *NOW*—your horse has an underlying infectious disease. Go to **While You Wait**, next page.

Are his gums yellow-tinged? Has he lost weight in recent weeks? Have there been changes in his overall demeanor, such as skittishness, depression, anxiety, or aggression? Has he shown any signs of colic-type pain (see **page 221**)?

 NO

YES Call your veterinarian *NOW* if you answered yes to any query—it could be liver disease and/or cholelithiasis^G (gallstones). Or, it could be evidence that your horse hasn't been eating for several days.

Are his gums brick-red or muddy-looking?

 NO

YES Call your veterinarian *NOW*—it could be shock^G, a serious problem in your senior horse's cardiovascular system, or blood poisoning (endotoxemia^G).

Are his gums a deep red or raspberry pink? Is your senior horse breathing rapidly or acting as though he's having trouble breathing? Is he anxious or weak?

 NO

YES Call your veterinarian *NOW* if you answered yes to any query—unless your horse has just been very physically active, intensely pink gums can be a sign of shock^G or poisoning.

Are your horse's gums white, or so pale they're just barely pink?

 NO

 YES Call your veterinarian *TODAY*—your senior horse could be anemic due to internal blood loss, nutritional deficiency, or an underlying disease process. ➤

ACTION PLAN (CONTINUED):

Do his gums have a purple or blue tint? Is your horse's capillary refill time delayed (see "Senior Vital Signs," **page 292**)? Does he seem to tire easily or have less energy than usual?

 Call your veterinarian *TODAY* if you answered yes to any query—it could be a cardiovascular problem.

Call your veterinarian and schedule an appointment for a senior vet check **(page 386)**.

WHILE YOU WAIT

Isolate your senior horse in an open-air paddock or stall with a separate water supply, apart from other horses by at least 20 feet. Wash your hands and disinfect your boots (see page 41) after handling him and before handling other horses. Offer him his usual feed for this time of day, plus salt and plenty of fresh water.

Pasture Toxins

Here are some toxic plants and weeds that can cause bright or deep pink gums.

- **Arrowgrass**
- **Beets**
- **Corn stalks (in certain soils)**
- **Leaves and twigs of fruit trees**
- **Leaves, berries, flowers, and roots of Elderberry**
- **Pigweed**
- **Sorghum (Sudan grass, Johnson grass)**

Sores &/Or Growths on Face

SENIOR SIGNPOST: One or more sores, lumps, or growths on your senior horse's face.

What this might mean: An underlying health problem, or it could mean there's an infection, parasite infestation, or tumor on or within his face or head.

ACTION PLAN:

Is there any evidence the lesion(s) is interfering with normal function, such as closing an eye, picking up feed, swallowing, or breathing?

 YES Call your veterinarian *NOW*—regardless of its cause, the lesion's presence may pose a serious health risk due to its location.

 NO

Is the skin swollen, reddened, raw, ulcerated, and/or crusty in one or more of the pink, white, or hairless areas around your horse's lips, nostrils, and/or eyes?

 YES Call your veterinarian *TODAY*—it could be photosensitization^G, (which can be caused by liver disease, or by eating the toxic weed St. John's Wort) or a sun-sensitive skin cancer such as squamous cell carcinoma^G (SCC).

 NO

Are there similar, nodular lesions elsewhere on your horse's body?

YES Call your veterinarian *TODAY*—it could be a serious underlying condition, such as granulomatous enteritis^G, sarcoid^G, pemphigus foliaceus^G, cutaneous lymphoma^G, habronemiasis^G, or collagenolytic granuloma^G.

 NO

Is the lesion(s) smooth and dark-colored? Is it covered with normal skin? Is your horse entirely or partially gray in color?

 YES Call your veterinarian *THIS WEEK* if you answered yes to any query—it could be melanoma^G, for which there may be several treatment options.

 NO

Call your veterinarian for an appointment to determine the nature of the lesion(s) and discuss treatment options.

➤

Did You Know ?

Studies show that by the time your black-skinned gray, white, or partially white horse is 15 years of age, his odds of having a melanomaG are a sobering 80%, due to the amount of melaninG in his skin. Although you'll see them in his skin, they can spread internally—a "benign" melanoma can become malignant over time. For more information about melanoma and other types of skin cancer, go to "The Age Event: Cancer," page 241.

Nix the Sun

Limit your horse's exposure to ultraviolet rays. Squamous Cell CarcinomaG (SCC) has been linked to sun exposure. Horses with little or no sun protection have a significantly higher incidence of SCC, especially if they have any light-colored hair and/or skin.

• Apply sun block or mechanical protection (fly masks, fly sheets labeled to provide UV protection). Do so daily during warm months, when the sun is closest to the earth—even on overcast days. If you live near the equator, where weather is warm most of the time, do it year-round.
• Keep your horse indoors during peak UV times. (From 10 a.m. to 3 p.m. in most areas.) Turn him out only when the sun's rays are less direct. Or, provide sun shelter, such as a walk-in shed, making it appealing by keeping a salt lick and water inside.
• Re-seed and water grassless areas. The sun's rays are absorbed by live forage, but reflected by bald ground, giving your horse a double dose of UV. If he lives on a dry lot, arrange alternate living quarters.

CHAPTER 7

Changes in
THE EYES

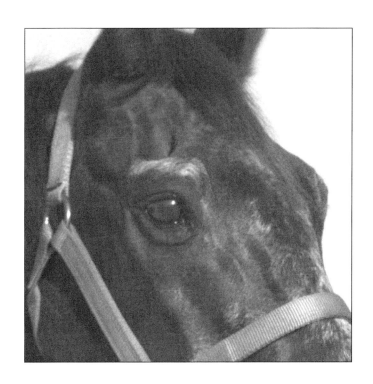

Foggy or Cloudy Eye

SENIOR SIGNPOST: Instead of a normal, clear appearance, your horse's eye looks cloudy—either there's a distinct white spot, or the whole eye looks foggy.

What this might mean: A serious problem within or beside the eyeball that threatens to impair your horse's vision.

ACTION PLAN:

Is your horse's eye reddened or squinting?

 YES Call your veterinarian *NOW*—redness or squinting can indicate eye pain, which coupled with cloudiness suggests a serious eye condition (e.g., corneal ulcer[G], corneal abscess[G], uveitis[G], or trauma). For more information, see "Squinting &/or Tearing," **page 105**. Go to **While You Wait #1**, opposite page.

 NO

Is your senior horse in poor overall health? Does he have a rough, shaggy haircoat? Has he lost weight in recent months? Does he drink more water than usual? Is his appetite poor? Has he been ill, or suffered any accidents or injuries in the past several weeks?

 YES Call your veterinarian *NOW* if you answered yes to any query—it could be an acute cataract[G], a dislocated lens[G], a detached retina[G], or a degenerative eye disorder[G], all of which can be an aftermath of significant illnesses or injuries.

 NO

Is there any indication that your senior horse's vision might be affected? (See "Quick Vision Test," **page 113**.) Is it possible he's suffered trauma to the head, for example from rearing up in a trailer, or flipping over backward?

 YES Call your veterinarian *NOW* if you answered yes to either query—it could be an early, severe case of acute uveitis[G], which can cause temporary or permanent blindness. A blow to the head, or to the eye itself, also can cause brief or lasting vision problems and eye cloudiness. For more information, see "Vision Problems," **page 112**. Go to **While You Wait #2**, opposite page.

NO

ACTION PLAN (CONTINUED):

Do you see red, vein-like structures extending onto the eyeball from its outer margins? Does the involved eye appear enlarged when compared to the other eye? Or, if both eyes are involved, do they look larger than normal? Has the involved eye been watery at any time in the past 2 weeks?

 Call your veterinarian *TODAY* if you answered yes to any query—the cloudiness could be due to edema^G or scar tissue from a previous or ongoing injury, infection, or inflammatory eye condition, such as uveitis^G (a. k. a. Moon Blindness). Or, it could be a symptom of glaucoma^G. (For more information, see "Bulging Eye," **page 110**.)

Call your veterinarian for an appointment. It's probably a senile cataract^G, which usually is left untreated, but it's a good idea to make sure.

WHILE YOU WAIT #1

1. *Ice the eye.* Slip a flexible ice pack (such as a bag of frozen peas or corn) between layers of a clean, folded cloth. Gently place it over your horse's eye, holding it there without applying pressure. This will reduce inflammation, discomfort, and swelling, and relax surrounding muscles. Keep the ice on for 5 minutes; off for 15 minutes. Repeat until your vet arrives.

2. *Bandage the eye.* If your horse has been squinting or attempting to rub his eye, use the bandaging technique outlined on page 109. This will keep his eyelid closed and help protect the eye from self-trauma.

3. *Bring your horse indoors; stop him if he rubs.* If the eye isn't bandaged, confine your horse to a dark stall or otherwise protect him from wind, dust, and bright light that can further irritate his eye. Place feed below eye-level so dust and chaff don't drift into his eye. Assign someone to watch and stop him if he rubs.

WHILE YOU WAIT #2

Confine your senior horse to a familiar enclosure that's free of obstacles he might run into. Provide a companion, if necessary, to prevent fretting. If he's anxious, or if there's any evidence he's been rubbing the eye, such as raw, dirty, or hairless areas on his face, stay with him until your veterinarian arrives so he doesn't further injure the eye (or himself).

Did You Know ?

Cataracts^G, which commonly rob vision in other species, can affect your senior horse. However, they rarely do so to an obstructive degree. Technically, a cataract refers to any focal opacity in the lens. Some such opacity can be evident in your oldster, but generally will remain insignificant.

Did You Also Know ?

An aging horse's declining immune system can increase his susceptibility to eye problems, such as corneal ulcers^G and Moon Blindness^G (uveitis^G), a recurring immune-mediated inflammation of the eye.

Whites of Eyes are Yellow

SENIOR SIGNPOST: The whites of your senior horse's eyes appear yellow, instead of their usual white.

What this might mean: It could mean there's a serious underlying problem, such as a blood disorder or liver disease.

ACTION PLAN:

Is your senior horse displaying abnormal behavior, such as anxiety or aggression for no apparent reason, dizziness, or acting as though he can't see?

 NO

 YES Call your veterinarian *NOW* if you answered yes to either query—it could be hepatoencephalopathy^G, or poisoning from eating feed contaminated with mold or mycotoxin^G. Go to **While You Wait**, next page.

Does your senior horse have a fever? (See "Senior Vital Signs," **page 292.**)

 NO

YES Call your veterinarian *NOW*—it could be a serious underlying illness such as acute or chronic active liver disease, liver abscess, or an infectious blood disorder such as Equine Infectious Anemia^G (EIA, also known as Coggins Disease), Babesiosis^G, or Piroplasmosis^G. Go to **While You Wait,** next page.

Has he shown any signs of mild or repeating colic?

 NO

YES Call your veterinarian *NOW*—it could be a liver or bile duct problem such as hepatitis^G, cholangitis^G, or cholelithiasis^G.

Does his breath smell of garlic or onions? Are there wild onions within his pasture, or domestic onions in a vegetable garden he can reach into, or in a compost pile he has access to? Are there any red maple trees (or their leaves) within his environment?

YES Call your veterinarian *NOW*—it could be hemolytic anemia^G from onion^G or red maple poisoning^G.

 NO

 ➤

ACTION PLAN (CONTINUED):

Has your senior horse been off his feed over the past day or more?

 Call your veterinarian *NOW*—it's not unusual for a horse that's not eating properly to become temporarily jaundiced[G]. Unless you're intentionally withholding his feed (for example, in preparation for elective surgery), the loss of appetite suggests an underlying health problem that warrants immediate veterinary attention.

Call your veterinarian *TODAY*.

WHILE YOU WAIT

1. *Isolate your horse from other horses in case it's contagious.* To prevent the spread of possible infectious disease, confine your horse to an open-air paddock or stall with a separate water supply, apart from other horses by at least 20 feet. Wash your hands and disinfect your boots (see page 41) after handling your horse and before handling other horses.

2. *Protect your horse.* Remove protruding objects from your horse's enclosure that could result in collisions or spills, and keep stress and noise to a minimum to avoid exciting him.

3. *Protect yourself.* If your horse is displaying anxious behavior—pacing, whinnying, eyes open wide, nostrils flared—his judgment is impaired and he might inadvertently hurt you. Don't go near him unless you must, and if you must, be especially cautious.

RABIES CAUTION: Among the possible causes of drooling, an inability to swallow, mental changes, and/or gait abnormalities, is a rare but notorious one: Rabies. If rabies is a consideration in your horse's case, don't take chances—take precautions.
1. Don't handle your horse unless it's absolutely necessary.
2. If you must handle him, wash your hands thoroughly, then don intact waterproof gloves (such as exam gloves or household rubber gloves) and protect all other body parts from contact with his saliva.
3. Be alert for unexpected behavior (rabies can cause aggression and/or lack of coordination), and stay out of harm's way.

Squinting &/Or Tearing

SENIOR SIGNPOST: Your senior horse is holding an eye partially or completely closed, and/or there may be watery tears, possibly mixed with a thicker discharge, running from the affected eye. You may see a dried crust on his face, depending on how long his eye has been weeping. He may squint more when in bright sunlight.

What this might mean: His eye either hurts or itches, due to an external problem (such as trauma, dust, or other foreign material), or a problem within the eyeball itself (such as infection or acute inflammation). Whatever's causing it, the discomfort may tempt your horse to rub or scratch the eye, which could result in permanent damage.

ACTION PLAN:

Do you see any redness (blood or otherwise) in or around your senior horse's eye and/or in or near its tears? Are the eyelids or skin around the eye swollen or abraded? Does he seem sensitive to light?

 NO

 YES Call your veterinarian *NOW* if you answered yes to any query—squinting, redness, and/or tearing indicate eye pain. It could be due to injury, infection, or foreign body, or there could be an acute inflammatory problem. Your horse is at risk of serious and possibly permanent damage to the eye from the ongoing cause as well as rubbing or scratching.

Does the normally clear part of his eye (the cornea^G) look foggy (steamy) or cloudy?

 NO

YES Call your veterinarian *NOW*—cloudiness indicates injury and/or infection that's serious enough to result in swelling and loss of clarity within the cornea^G. This can be due to such problems as corneal injury or uveitis^G.

Do you see a foreign body in or around his eye?

 NO

YES Call your veterinarian *NOW*—immediate medical treatment will be necessary to avoid further damage.
See "Avoid Pulling Foreign Bodies," **next page.**

➤

ACTION PLAN (CONTINUED):

Is the eye tearing, but not squinting, with no evidence of redness, rubbing, swelling, or discomfort? Call your veterinarian for an appointment. It could be a plugged tear duct^G.

 NO

Will your horse allow you to open the eyelid and treat the eye? Apply **Home Treatment**, below.

 NO

Call your veterinarian *NOW*—prompt treatment may be needed to prevent further eye injury.

WHILE YOU WAIT

1. *Ice the eye.* Slip a flexible ice pack (such as a bag of frozen peas or corn) between layers of a clean, folded cloth. Gently place it over your horse's eye, holding it there without applying pressure. This will reduce inflammation, discomfort, and swelling, and relax surrounding muscles. Keep the ice on for 5 minutes; off for 15 minutes. Repeat until your vet arrives.

2. *Bandage the eye.* If your horse has been squinting or attempting to rub his eye, use the bandaging technique outlined on page 109. This will keep his eyelid closed and help protect the eye from self-trauma.

> **AVOID PULLING FOREIGN BODIES!**
> If you pull foreign matter (such as long hairs or grass stems) that are protruding from beneath your horse's eyelids, they could slice the cornea^G. Instead, bandage the eye and call your veterinarian, who can sedate your horse if necessary, block his blink reflex if necessary, and safely lift any foreign matter off the cornea.

> **AVOID FORCING AN EYE OPEN!**
> Some eye injuries are so severe that the eyeball is at risk of rupturing, either because of direct damage from the injury or because the injured eye's layers are weakened from infection. Your horse's defense against further eye injury—his blink reflex—is too powerful to overwhelm if it's fully activated. If you were to persist, your efforts could cause a fragile eye to rupture.

3. *Bring your horse indoors; stop him if he rubs.* If the eye isn't bandaged, confine your horse to a dark stall or otherwise protect him from wind, dust, and bright light that can further irritate his eye. Place feed below eye level so dust and chaff don't drift into his eye. Assign someone to watch and stop him if he rubs.

HOME TREATMENT

*(See **Action Plan** to determine whether home treatment is appropriate for your horse's weeping eye. If at any time during home treatment, your answers on the **Action Plan** change for the worse, call your vet.)*

Step 1. *Clean dried discharge from around eye.* Wet a clean gauze sponge with room-temperature saline solution (1 tsp. salt dissolved in 1 quart water) until saturated but not dripping. Lay the gauze over the trail of discharge. Hold for several seconds or as needed to soften, then wipe clean. This will prevent skin irritation from developing beneath the crust, and eliminate the risk of attracting face flies, which can further irritate the eyes.

Step 2. *Soothe and protect the eye and surrounding tissues.* Apply a thin film of boric acid or Lacri-lube™ ophthalmic ointment to soothe and lubricate your horse's eye.

Step 3. *Re-evaluate.* Five minutes after completing treatment, look at the eye: Is it still weeping? If so, call your vet NOW.

Step 4. *Apply a fly mask to keep flies away from his eyes.* They'll be attracted by the moisture and can make the problem worse. Or, the eye irritation may have been caused by flies in the first place.

TIP: To get an enhanced look at your horse's uncomfortable eye without touching it or otherwise activating his blink reflex, stand 3 feet away, just to the bad eye's side. Make a sound that'll arouse his interest (whistle, cluck, or rustle oats in a bucket). Unless the eye pain is extreme, he'll widen his eye to see what you've got.

How to Lock Out Flies

Use one or more of these methods to keep flies away from your senior horse's eyes:

• Apply a fly face mask.

• Make an artificial forelock. Attach knotted strips of low-lint, close-weave fabric to the poll strap on your horse's halter.

• Apply chemical insect repellents. Away from your horse, spray a horse-safe fly repellent (such as permethrin) onto the artificial forelock, let dry completely, then affix to your horse's halter. *Note:* Be careful when spraying, wiping, or dabbing repellents directly onto your horse's face. Most contain chemicals that can irritate his eyes. Thick water- and sweat-proof ointments such as Swat® are less likely to drip into your horse's eyes and would be a safer choice of repellent for around them than thin solutions.

Sores, Lump or Growth in or around the Eye(s)

SENIOR SIGNPOST: Your senior horse has a growth, swelling, lump, or sore spot around his eye(s), and/or inside the eyeball itself.

What this might mean: It could indicate an injury, infection, foreign body, parasite infestation, or sarcoid^G. Or, it could be a type of eye cancer.

ACTION PLAN:

Has your horse been rubbing or scratching the affected eye?

 NO

 YES Call your veterinarian *NOW*—even minor eye irritations can result in permanent eye damage if your horse is rubbing or scratching the area. Go to **While You Wait**, opposite page.

Do you see a foreign body in or around his eye?

 NO

 YES Call your veterinarian *NOW*—immediate medical treatment will be necessary to avoid further damage. See warning, "Avoid Pulling Foreign Bodies," **page 106**.

Is the involved eye squinting, tearing, or cloudy?

 NO

 YES See "Squinting &/or Tearing," **page 105**, and "Foggy or Cloudy Eye," **page 100**.

Do you see a raw, ulcerated lesion that's mostly affecting the white or pink skin around your horse's eye? Do you see similar lesions in/on the other eye, or elsewhere on your senior horse's body? Is he being given any medications, including antibiotics? Does he have access to the weed known as goat weed (a.k.a. St. Johns Wort, or Klamath weed)?

 NO

 YES Call your veterinarian *TODAY* if you answered yes to any query. It could be a specific type of skin cancer known as squamous cell carcinoma^G. Or, it could be an erosive skin condition called photosensitization^G, which can occur as a side effect to the use of certain drugs, as a symptom of poisoning with goat weed, or as a symptom of internal disease such as liver or kidney problems.

ACTION PLAN (CONTINUED):

Is the growth raised and lumpy, located in the inner corner of your senior horse's eye, where upper and lower lids meet? Does it appear to have invaded the eyeball itself? Do you see any similar looking lumps elsewhere on his body?

 YES ▶ Call your veterinarian *TODAY* if you answered yes to any query—it could be a sarcoidᴳ, or one of a number of different kinds of cancer. Or, it could be due to a skin-invading parasite called *Habronema*ᴳ.

 NO

Call your veterinarian for an appointment.

WHILE YOU WAIT

Protect your horse's eye from self-trauma. Either bandage the eye (see bandaging box below), or have someone stay with your horse to prevent him from rubbing it.

Quick Eye Bandage

You'll need:
- A stack of gauze sponges, a thick sanitary napkin, or a disposable diaper (any of which must be large enough to completely cover the eye)
- Elastic bandage, such as Vetrap® or an Ace bandage
- Tape (such as bandage or electrical)
- Sterile isotonic eyewash (0.09% saline)

Step 1. Soak the bandage in isotonic solution so it's wet, but not dripping.
Step 2. Center it over the eye.
Step 3. Hold the pad in place temporarily, using tape.
Step 4. Secure the pad by wrapping the elastic bandage between your horse's ears, under his jaw, then over the pad.
Step 5. Anchor the bandage in place using tape.

Did You Know?

Some types of eye cancer grow in the tissues around the eye and, as they spread, can invade the eyeball; some actually start inside the eyeball; others start elsewhere in the body and spread to the eye, or vice versa.

Bulging Eye

SENIOR SIGNPOST: One or both of your senior horse's eyes appears to be bulging, giving him a "startled" appearance. **What this might mean:** There could be a serious underlying problem.

ACTION PLAN:

Is either eye squinted or running? Is there evidence that your senior horse's vision is impaired? (See "Quick Vision Test," **page 113**.) For instance, have you seen him bump into familiar obstacles or other horses as though he doesn't see them, or is he reluctant to walk through familiar areas? Has he recently had a respiratory infection, such as strangles^G?

 YES Call your veterinarian *NOW* if you answered yes to any query—it could be an internal eye problem such as glaucoma^G or acute uveitis^G, which can cause permanent blindness; a problem in the vision area of your senior horse's brain or in his optic nerve^G; orbital cellulitis^G, due to infection in adjacent sinuses; or, an abscess^G or mass behind the affected eye, pushing it outward. Go to **While You Wait #1**, opposite page.

 NO

Has your horse recently had a blow to the head or face, such as from struggling while tied or in a horse trailer? Has he fought or played with another horse? Does the normally clear area of one or both eyes appear cloudy or white?

 YES Call your veterinarian *NOW* if you answered yes to any query—your horse could have suffered head/facial trauma resulting in injury to the eyeball(s) and/or socket(s). This can cause bleeding within or behind the eye and other damage. Prompt treatment can help limit damage and preserve his vision.

 NO

Does he seem anxious or nervous? Is he breathing rapidly, pacing, whinnying, or otherwise appearing agitated, for no apparent reason? Has he been treated with any medication within the past 24 hours? Does he have welts or hives in his skin, particularly on the side of his neck? Has he had access within the past 6 hours to weedy areas in his environment?

 YES Call your veterinarian *NOW* if you answered yes to any query—widened eyes could indicate anxiety from a developing mental problem such as encephalitis^G or hepatoencephalopathy^G, or a serious allergic reaction such as anaphylaxis^G. Or, your horse might have been exposed to toxic or hallucinogenic weeds, such as locoweed, which can cause mental changes. Go to **While You Wait #2**, opposite page.

 NO

ACTION PLAN (CONTINUED):

Does your horse have an abnormally long coat, and/or broad patches of hair loss? Does he sweat more than usual, and/or shiver as though uncomfortably cold even when the weather is balmy and other horses seem fine? Have you noticed him drinking more water than usual, and/or urinating more?

 YES → Call your veterinarian *TODAY*—it could be Equine Cushing's Disease^G and/or a thyroid disorder^G.

 NO

Call your veterinarian today for an appointment.

WHILE YOU WAIT #1

Confine your senior horse to a familiar enclosure that's free of obstacles he might run into. Provide a companion if necessary to prevent fretting. If he's anxious, or if there's any evidence he's been rubbing the eye, such as raw, dirty, or hairless areas on his face, stay with him until your veterinarian arrives, so he doesn't further injure the eye (or himself).

WHILE YOU WAIT #2

Protect yourself. If your horse is displaying anxious behavior—pacing, whinnying, eyes open wide, nostrils flared—his judgment is impaired and he might inadvertently hurt you. Don't go near him unless you must, and if you must, be especially cautious.

Vision Problems

SENIOR SIGNPOST: You suspect that your senior horse is having difficulty seeing. He may snort and hesitate to enter familiar places, especially if they're darkened. He may step on things he'd normally avoid or move more slowly and cautiously than usual. His eyes may appear wider than usual, and/or his ears may move more than usual. You may observe him colliding with things or spooking more than usual.

What this might mean: It could be a problem in your horse's brain, affecting his ability to process information, or causing him to feel off-balance and affecting his ability to navigate. Or, it could be a vision problem. *(Note: If possible, confirm your suspicions with the Quick Vision Test on page 113. If your horse's vision is not impaired, turn to the Action Plan that best describes his symptoms.)*

ACTION PLAN:

Does your senior horse have a fever? (See "Senior Vital Signs," **page 292.**) Is he off his feed? Is he leaning his body or pressing his head against solid objects, wandering aimlessly, or walking in circles? Do you see any clear or blood-tinged discharge coming from one or both ears or nostrils? Has he recently flipped over backward, or otherwise received a blow to the poll?

 YES Call your veterinarian *NOW* if you answered yes to any query—it could be traumatic injury, inflammation, or infection in your senior horse's brain and/or optic nerve[G]. Go to **While You Wait #1**, opposite page.

 NO

Has your senior horse been dull, listless, off his feed, feverish, or diagnosed with an illness within the past week?

 YES Call your veterinarian *NOW*—several illnesses can cause blindness. Prompt treatment might restore your horse's vision.

 NO

Is either eye red, cloudy, runny, or squinted?

 YES Call your veterinarian *NOW*—it could be acute uveitis[G] (a.k.a. Moon Blindness), or injury and/or infection in the eye. Go to **While You Wait #2**, page 114.

 NO

ACTION PLAN (CONTINUED):

Does your horse's vision impairment seem most pronounced at night? At dusk or in the dark, does he act nervous and reluctant to walk through a familiar doorway or gate that's no problem during the day? Call your veterinarian *THIS WEEK*—horses normally have better night vision than we do, so decreased night vision could mean your senior horse is developing cataracts^G.

Call your veterinarian for an appointment.

WHILE YOU WAIT #1

Isolate your horse from other horses in case it's contagious. To prevent the spread of possible infectious disease, confine your horse to an open-air paddock or stall with a separate water supply, apart from other horses by at least 20 feet. Wash your hands and disinfect your boots (see page 41) after handling your horse and before handling other horses.

QUICK VISION TEST

USE THIS TEST TO HELP DECIDE WHETHER YOUR HORSE IS TRULY VISION-IMPAIRED, AND WHETHER THE PROBLEM HAS AFFECTED ONE OR BOTH EYES.

1. Blindfold one eye by laying a thick pad, such as a disposable diaper folded in half, across the eye (absorbent side against the skin). Tape it to your horse's halter.

2. Wear clothing that doesn't "swish." In a well-lit area with minimal distractions, have a helper loosely hold your horse. Stand 3 feet away, to the side of the uncovered eye, and lob 3 cotton balls toward him, one after the other, so they bounce gently off the top of his face between his eye and muzzle. Did he flinch when the first one approached, before it touched him? Did he try to avoid the second? Did he watch the third one? If your answers are no, no, and no, he probably can't see. Repeat with the other eye.

3. If you're still unsure, in a well-lit area and with one of his eyes covered, lead your horse on a loose lead rope toward a bale of hay set 15 feet ahead. Walk purposefully—don't go so slowly that he has time to lower his head and smell it. Does he try to avoid hitting the bale? If not, he probably can't see it. Cover the other eye, and repeat.

WHILE YOU WAIT #2

1. *Ice the eye.* Slip a flexible ice pack (such as a bag of frozen peas or corn) between layers of a clean, folded cloth. Gently place it over your horse's eye, holding it there without applying pressure. This will reduce inflammation, discomfort, and swelling, and relax surrounding muscles. Keep the bag on for 5 minutes; off for 15 minutes. Repeat until your vet arrives.

2. *Bandage the eye.* If your horse has been squinting or attempting to rub the eye, use the bandaging technique outlined on page 109. This will keep his eyelid closed and help protect the eye from self-trauma.

3. *Bring your horse indoors; stop him if he rubs.* If the eye isn't bandaged, confine your horse to a dark stall or otherwise protect him from wind, dust, and bright light that can further irritate his eye. Place feed below eye level so dust and chaff don't drift into his eye. Assign someone to watch and stop him if he rubs.

Did You Know?

Vision problems are relatively uncommon in older horses—
at least noticeable ones. That's because horses often mask any vision
problem, by clinging to the familiar in their environment and their
routine. However, if you were to change a vision-impaired horse's
pasture or stall, his problem could reveal itself. He might bang
a hip walking through an unfamiliar stall door, or even
walk into an unfamiliar wall or fence.

CHAPTER 8

Changes in
THE EARS

Droopy Ears

SENIOR SIGNPOST: Your senior horse seems to be holding both ears at "half mast," angled out to the sides instead of upright. **What this might mean:** It could mean general weakness, as can occur with an underlying illness. Or, it could mean the nerves controlling your horse's ears and other facial features have been damaged.

ACTION PLAN:

Is your horse off his feed, depressed, and/or feverish? (Go to "Senior Vital Signs," **page 292**.)

 YES Call your veterinarian *NOW*—it could be fatigue and/or general malaise due to an underlying illness, including encephalitis^G. Go to **While You Wait #1**, opposite page.

 NO

Has your horse recently had general anesthesia or mechanical restraint? Does he wear a halter most of the time? Is it possible he recently banged his head, such as during a trailer ride or while cast in a stall? Has he recently set back while tied? Is there evidence of head trauma, such as raw, hairless, or swollen spots on his face and poll? Have you seen blood or a clear liquid draining from one or both ears or nostrils?

 YES Call your veterinarian *NOW* if you answered yes to any query—it could be head trauma, and/or there could be damage to the nerves that supply your horse's head and/or ears. Early treatment often is successful in resolving or minimizing the damage. Go to **While You Wait #2**, opposite page.

 NO

Does he have feed packed in one cheek? Are any of his other facial features droopy, grimaced, or asymmetrical?

YES Call your veterinarian *NOW* if you answered yes to any query—it sounds like neurological damage due to injury or disease. Go to **While You Wait #3**, page 118.

 NO

Does your horse stagger, stumble, or otherwise indicate loss of balance? Has his gait changed? Does he hold his head at a tilt?

  YES Call your veterinarian *NOW* if you answered yes to any query—it could be a brain injury, encephalitis^G, an infection deep in the inner ear, or an infestation with ear mites^G or ticks^G. Go to **While You Wait #2**, opposite page.

NO

ACTION PLAN (CONTINUED):

Does he seem tenderfooted? Has he recently been diagnosed with laminitis^G?

 YES Call your veterinarian *NOW* if you answered yes to either query—there may be a serious underlying problem.

Has your horse lost weight? Is his coat shaggy and/or dull, possibly overdue to shed? Does he seem to sweat excessively?

 YES Call your veterinarian *TODAY* if you answered yes to any query—there may be a serious underlying problem, such as pituitary adenoma (a.k.a. Equine Cushing's Disease^G, or ECD).

Has your horse been shaking his head?

 YES Go to "Head Shaking," **page 88**.

Is there a brownish wax in or near the entrance to your horse's affected ear(s)? Does either ear smell sour?

 YES Call your veterinarian *TODAY*—it could be an infestation with ear mites^G, or an infection in the ear canal.

Is there a crusty accumulation anywhere on the upright portion of the affected ear, or on the skin around its base? Does the crust melt into a dark brown liquid when moistened? Will your horse allow you to treat his ear?

 YES If you answered yes to all these queries, apply **Home Treatment**, next page. It could be inflammation and irritation from flies or gnat bites.

Call your veterinarian for an appointment.

WHILE YOU WAIT #1

Isolate your horse from other horses in case it's contagious. To prevent the spread of possible infectious disease, confine your horse to an open-air paddock or stall with a separate water supply, apart from other horses by at least 20 feet. Wash your hands and disinfect your boots (see page 41) after handling your horse and before handling other horses.

WHILE YOU WAIT #2

1. *Avoid moving your horse (unless your veterinarian instructs you to do so).* If he's weak, dizzy, or in pain, forced movement might do significant harm. If at all possible, provide confinement by erecting portable corral panels around him, or stay with him until the vet arrives. Bring fresh water to him, as he might not have been able to get to a water source on his own. ➤

Screen Bugs OUT! If insects are attacking your senior horse's ears (and eyes), you have nonchemical options for blocking access to that tender skin. Outfit your old friend in a combination fly mask/ear guard. (Available through such catalogs as KV Vet Supply, 800.423.8211; www.kvvet.com.) These provide a highly effective mechanical barrier against biting pests, such as flies and gnats. As a bonus, they provide protection against the sun's destructive UV rays, which can cause such cancers as squamous cell carcinoma[G]. Be sure, though, to remove the fly mask at night. (Separate ear guards are available.) The mask's screening can impede vision after dark.

2. *Protect yourself.* A weak or dizzy horse can stagger or fall without warning. Stay alert and out of harm's way.

WHILE YOU WAIT #3

If your senior horse is wearing a halter, take it off so its hardware doesn't press on superficial nerves. Use a larger halter while your veterinarian examines him, so the headstall portion can be pulled behind his poll, where it's less likely to interfere with the exam or further traumatize already injured nerves.

HOME TREATMENT

STEP 1: *Clean out the crud.*

Why: Because that crud is attracting more bugs. Cleaning the ears also helps prevent infection, and soothes irritated tissues.

What you'll need:
- A bucket of clean, bath-warm water; add 1 teaspoon table salt per quart of water. (The salt helps loosen scurf, scabs, and crust.)
- 3 or 4 clean, soft cloths or a stack of disposable 4 x 4 gauze sponges.
- Earplugs, so nothing trickles or falls into the ear canal. Thick wads of cotton work well, as do 1-inch yarn balls available at art-supply stores.

How to do it:
- Gently insert the earplugs.
- Dunk one of the cloths, squeeze it so it doesn't drip, and gently press it over the inner surface of your horse's ear for half a minute or so, to melt crust, loosen scurf, and soften and moisturize the top layer of skin.
- Repeat as necessary, using a clean cloth each time, until you can wipe the ear clean. *(Note: Unless you must, don't clip your horse's ears. Hair makes it more diffi-*

cult for bugs to get in, and protects skin from sunburn, windburn, and foreign objects such as grass seeds.)

STEP 2: *Apply an emollient/insect repellent.*

Why: To keep bugs out and moisture in, resulting in supple, healthy skin.

What you'll need: If your horse's ears are clipped—

• An opaque cream with the consistency of cake frosting, such as Gold Nugget Gnat-Away® (by Neogen, 800.477.8201) or Farnam's Swat®. This will help protect his ear skin from sun, wind, bugs, and drying.

How to do it:

• Apply about a tablespoon, in a thin layer, directly onto the smooth inner surface of each ear. Don't massage it in—let it remain a mechanical barrier between skin and bug. If you rub it around, you'll thin that barrier.

• Remove the earplugs.

What you'll need: If your horse's ears are unclipped—

• A thinner product that'll penetrate to the skin, such as a 50-50 mixture of Avon's Skin-So-Soft® bath oil and water, or a gentle insect repellent gel made for use on human infants.

How to do it:

• Apply about 1/4 teaspoon to the tip of your finger and rub it through the hair onto the ear surface to coat the skin. In the process, the hair will get coated as well, helping to fortify this natural, mechanical barrier.

• Remove the earplugs.

Repeat steps 1 and 2 daily or every other day as needed, depending on the condition of your horse's ears and the severity of biting insects in your area.

Did You Know?

Older horses are more attractive targets for biting insects than younger ones. It's not uncommon for senior herd members to be virtually covered with mosquitoes and flies, while younger ones are only marginally bothered. Veterinarians believe this is due to a combination of factors, including declining immunity, thinning and increasingly dehydrated skin (easier to penetrate and less sensitive, thus eliciting less defensive tail-swishing and skin-jigging by the horse), and less overall activity, making an older horse easier for bugs to find, land on—and bite.

Flesh Wound or Growth on the Ear

SENIOR SIGNPOST: The upright portion of your horse's ear is injured, misshapen, or has one or more growths or lumps on/in it.

What this might mean: No matter what caused it—injury, infection, or some type of tumor—if the inner cartilage is affected, his ear could become permanently misshapen.

ACTION PLAN:

Has your senior horse's ear been lacerated, mangled, bitten, or otherwise injured? For instance, has he recently pulled his head from between two fence boards?

 YES Call your veterinarian *NOW* if you answered yes to either query—the injured ear might need stitches or surgical reconstruction to prevent infection, curling, or puckering of cartilage.

 NO

Has the ear tip been blunted or become dark, hardened, or leathery after a subzero cold spell?

 YES Call your veterinarian *TODAY*—it's probably frostbite. Frostbitten ears can be reshaped surgically to look more normal.

 NO

Do you see and/or feel a growth, lump, or multiple pimple-like lesions on or near the ear?

 YES Call your veterinarian for an appointment. It could be a type of skin cancer, or an underlying general health problem such as pemphigus foliaceus[G]. Or, it could be a parasite infestation such as onchocerciasis[G] or habronemiasis[G].

 NO

Are there chalky, whitish, or brownish plaques on the inside of the upper portion of the ear?

 YES It sounds like benign aural plaques[G], which are believed to be caused by a virus. (See "Aural Plaques at a Glance," **opposite page**.) Go to **Home Treatment**, opposite page.

 NO

Call your veterinarian for an appointment.

HOME TREATMENT

STEP 1: *Clean out the crud.*

Why: Because that crud is attracting more bugs. Cleaning the ears also helps prevent infection, and soothes irritated tissues.

What you'll need:
- A bucket of clean, bath-warm water; add 1 teaspoon table salt per quart of water. (The salt helps loosen scurf, scabs, and crust.)
- 3 or 4 clean, soft cloths or a stack of disposable 4 x 4 gauze sponges.
- Earplugs, so nothing trickles or falls into the ear canal. Thick wads of cotton work well, as do 1-inch yarn balls available at art-supply stores.

How to do it:
- Gently insert the earplugs.
- Dunk one of the cloths, squeeze it so it doesn't drip, and gently press it over the inner surface of your horse's ear for half a minute or so, to melt crust, loosen scurf, and soften and moisturize the top layer of skin.
- Repeat as necessary, using a clean cloth each time, until you can wipe the ear clean. (*Note:* Unless you must, don't clip your horse's ears. Hair makes it more difficult for bugs to get in, and protects skin from sunburn, windburn, and foreign objects (such as grass seeds*).*

STEP 2: *Apply an emollient/insect repellent.*

Why: To keep bugs out and moisture in, resulting in supple, healthy skin.

What you'll need: If your horse's ears are clipped—
- An opaque cream with the consistency of cake frosting, such as Gold Nugget Gnat-Away® (by Neogen, 800.477.8201) or Farnam's Swat®. This will help protect his ear skin from sun, wind, bugs, and drying.

AURAL PLAQUES at a GLANCE

Aural plaques are flat, raised, irregular lesions that can be quite visible because the involved skin lacks its usual pigmentation, making it white. They're believed to be caused by a virus carried by biting flies. Prevention is your best defense, using diligent bug protection as described in "Home Treatment," at left. If your horse's ears are already stricken, there are a few things you need to know.

- No treatment has proven effective in regressing them.
- Although the plaques themselves don't bother your horse, there's evidence that they do get bigger, uglier, and sore if irritated by flies. Keep your horse's ears soothed and protected to minimize the plaques' size.
- If you're going to a show, camouflage plaques with a nontoxic marking pen or an appropriately colored makeup concealer. Experiment ahead of time to find the shade that blends best with your horse's natural color.

➤

How to do it:

- Apply about a tablespoon, in a thin layer, directly onto the smooth inner surface of each ear. Don't massage it in—let it remain a mechanical barrier between skin and bug. If you rub it around, you'll thin that barrier.
- Remove the earplugs.
- Consider also using a mechanical barrier, such as mesh ear guards. See "Screen Bugs Out!," page 118.

What you'll need: If your horse's ears are unclipped—

- A thinner product that'll penetrate to the skin, such as a 50-50 mixture of Avon's Skin-So-Soft® bath oil and water, or a gentle insect repellent gel made for use on human infants.

How to do it:

- Apply about 1/4 teaspoon to the tip of your finger and rub it through the hair onto the ear surface to coat the skin. In the process, the hair will get coated as well, helping to fortify this natural, mechanical barrier.
- Remove the earplugs.

Repeat steps 1 and 2 daily or every other day as needed, depending on the condition of your horse's ears and the severity of biting insects in your area.

Excessive Ear Movement

SENIOR SIGNPOST: Your horse's ears seem to be moving more often than usual.

What this might mean: He's straining to hear, as one might do when feeling anxious or vulnerable. Or, it could mean he's lost some degree of muscle control over his ear movement.

ACTION PLAN:

Is your senior horse reluctant to move? Is he exhibiting atypical (for him) social behavior, such as aggression, or does he seem fearful, depressed, anxious, or frightened? Does the abnormal ear movement continue constantly, even when he's not appearing to pay attention to his surroundings?

 YES Call your veterinarian *NOW* if you answered yes to any query—it could be chorea^G, a symptom of encephalitis^G or other central nervous system (CNS) illness, or brain injury. (See "Rabies Caution," **page 104**.)

 NO

Are the whites of his eyes yellow-tinged?

 YES Call your veterinarian *NOW*—your horse could have a liver problem that has caused a toxin buildup resulting in abnormal CNS function.

 NO

Can your horse pass the "Quick Vision Test" (**page 113**)?

 NO Call your veterinarian *NOW*—your senior horse's excessive ear movement may mean he's paying extra attention to sounds, in an attempt to compensate for suddenly impaired vision.

 YES

Does your senior horse shake his head more often than neighboring horses, and/or more often than usual?

 YES Call your veterinarian *TODAY*—there could be a problem in your senior horse's ear canal, or in the nerve supply to his ears and/or poll area.

 NO

Can your horse pass the "Quick Hearing Test," **next page**?

 NO Call your veterinarian *TODAY*—your senior horse could have a problem in his ears or in the nerve tissue involved in hearing.

 YES

Call your veterinarian for an appointment.

➤

Quick Hearing Test

If your horse has perfect hearing, he probably can perceive all the same sounds you can (if your hearing is normal), plus higher-frequency (ultrasonic) sounds that to the human ear are imperceptible, such as some of the highest wavelengths of an urgent whinny.

If your senior horse is hearing impaired, his ability to hear high-frequency sounds will be the first to suffer, particularly if they're soft. Here's a test you can use to screen your horse for high-frequency, low-amplitude hearing loss.

What you'll need:
• A variety of noisemakers: a plastic grocery bag, several twigs to snap, and a "silent" (to you) dog-training whistle. The bag and breaking twigs will emit a wide range of sounds, including high-frequency ones. The dog whistle emits only high-frequency sounds that you can't hear.
• A familiar-to-your-horse stall, or other small enclosure, that's free of wind noise, traffic noise, and other such audio distractions. Remove any feed—chewing hay or grain will adversely affect your horse's ability to hear. (Just as chewing potato chips affects yours.)

Put your horse in the stall or enclosure.
Stand at least 10 feet behind him (out of kicking range). Remain there until he ignores you. Then, with minimal movement (so you don't evoke a visual response instead of an auditory one), make some soft stimulus sounds: Crinkle the bag, snap the twigs, blow several blasts on the dog whistle. Wait a minute or so between each, so he won't figure out the sounds are all coming from you and ignore them.

Evaluate your horse's reactions. You'll know he's heard the sound if he flicks an ear toward you (or spooks). If he fails to react to the bags and twigs, he could have a profound hearing loss. (Or, he may have chosen to ignore the noise!) If he doesn't react to the dog whistle, he could have some high-frequency hearing loss.

Consult your vet if you suspect any degree of hearing loss.

CAUTION

If your horse's mental state is altered, his behavior can be unpredictable. He may suddenly bolt, strike, bite, or collapse and seize, injuring you and bystanders. Be especially alert when working around him, leaving yourself a safety "space cushion" in case you need to make a quick getaway.

Hearing Loss

SENIOR SIGNPOST: Sometimes when you (or another horse, or dog/cat) approach your horse, he doesn't seem aware and reacts as though startled. He may be spooking more than usual, even in familiar surroundings. And, one or both ears may move more than normal—or not at all.

What this might mean: He may have suffered a hearing loss, either through age-related changes and/or damage from a lifetime of loud-noise exposure. It also could be something as innocent as debris clogging his outer ear, or as serious as injury or disease to the inner ear and/or brain.

Note: To avoid missing or misinterpreting signposts, give your horse the Quick Hearing Test (page 124) to check him for profound hearing loss. If results indicate his hearing is not impaired, reassess the signs you've observed and turn to a more appropriate **Action Plan.**

ACTION PLAN:

Does your horse have a fever? (See "Senior Vital Signs," **page 292**.) Does he seem depressed, or detached from his surroundings? Is his appetite decreased?

YES ▶ Call your veterinarian *NOW* if you answered yes to any query—what seems like hearing loss may simply be detachment or lethargy due to underlying discomfort or illness. Go to **While You Wait**, next page.

 NO

Is your horse being treated, or has he recently been treated, with antibiotics or any other medication?

YES ▶ Call your veterinarian *NOW*—your horse may be suffering an ototoxic[G] reaction, which can cause permanent hearing loss due to sensitivity to a particular medication.

 NO

Is either ear drooping, as though limp? Do you see any evidence of drooping, grimacing, or asymmetry elsewhere in your horse's face or lips?

YES ▶ Call your veterinarian *NOW* if you answered yes to either query—there may be illness- or injury-related damage to the head's nerve supply.

 NO

Has your horse's hearing loss seemed to come on suddenly?

YES ▶ Call your veterinarian *NOW*—there may be a serious underlying problem.

 NO

▶

ACTION PLAN (CONTINUED):

Are there hairless, rubbed, raw, scabby, or scurfy areas on or around either of your horse's ears? Does either ear feel abnormally warm? Does he hold one or both ears in an abnormal, tilted position? Have you seen him rubbing or scratching one or both of his ears? Is there a brownish, waxy substance accumulated inside the upright portion of either ear? Does either ear smell sour?

 YES Call your veterinarian *TODAY* if you answered yes to any query—your horse could have inflammation in, on, or around his ears caused by infection, insect bites, a foreign body (such as a grass awn), or infestation with ear mites^G. Or, he could have an ear tick^G in the outer ear canal of one or both ears.

 NO

Are both ears swollen?

 YES Call your veterinarian *TODAY*—your horse may have injured his ears, resulting in ear-canal swelling.

 NO

Has your senior horse ever traveled in a horse trailer? Has he ever attended horse shows or parades? Has he been exposed often to the sound of gunfire, or loud machinery? Has he been in environments where there was a lot of wind or smoke?

 YES Call your veterinarian *THIS WEEK*—it could be an accumulation of ear wax in the outer ear canal. Wax-producing glands can become overactive when ears are irritated by loud noise, cold wind, smoke, and fumes. Or, it could be age-related hearing loss. For more information, see "Senior Hearing Check," **page 310**.

 NO

Call your veterinarian for an appointment.

WHILE YOU WAIT

Isolate your horse from other horses in a quiet, well-ventilated (but not drafty) stall or paddock. Provide fresh water and plain salt. If he's shivering, blanket him. Disinfect your hands (or wear disposable gloves) and boots after handling him and before handling other horses, using a solution of 2 1/2 tablespoons of Lysol® Disinfectant Concentrate per gallon of water.

Did You Know?

Ototoxicity^G (hearing loss as a permanent side effect) is rare from some medications, while for others it's fairly common. Included in the latter category are the antibiotics gentamicin and amikacin. If a drug reaction is the culprit in your horse's hearing loss, switching medications early may preserve some of his hearing.

9

Changes in the
NECK, BACK, TORSO

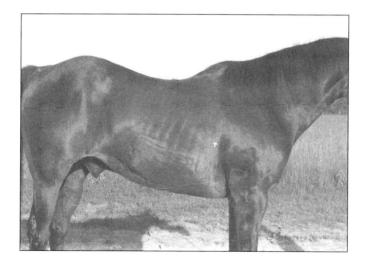

Back Pain

SENIOR SIGNPOST: Your senior horse drops (sinks) his back when finger pressure is applied along his spine.

What this might mean: Pain in the nerves, muscles, or bone in the area of the spine, or it could be kidney pain.

ACTION PLAN:

Does your senior horse have a fever? (See "Senior Vital Signs," **page 292**.) Does he act dull, depressed, or detached from his surroundings? Is he off his feed?

 YES Call your veterinarian *NOW* if you answered yes to any query—it could be general myositis^G, an infectious disease, a kidney infection (pyelonephritis^G), or osteomyelitis^G (bone infection) in or near the spine. Go to **While You Wait**, opposite page.

 NO

Do you feel a squishy or a snap-crackle-pop sensation, like lightweight "bubble wrap," under your senior horse's skin when you run your fingers over his spine? Has he taken a fall, or flipped over backward, within the past couple of weeks?

 YES Call your veterinarian *NOW* if you answered yes to either query—it could be injury to the dorsal spinous process^G(es) of the vertebrae in the chest portion of your horse's spine. Go to **While You Wait**, opposite page.

 NO

Is your senior mare pregnant? Is her belly larger than expected? Is her lower belly wall swollen with edema^G, and/or tender?

 YES Go to "Abnormally Large Pregnant Belly," **page 215**.

 NO

Has your senior horse ever had myositis^G (tying-up syndrome)? Do the muscles of his rump, shoulders, neck, and/or back feel hard or overly tense? Is he reluctant to move? Does he flinch, tighten his torso, and/or hunch up or sink his back when you apply pressure to the muscles alongside his neck, or along his spine? (For how to check your horse's back for pain, see "Senior Back Check," **page 314**.)

 YES Call your veterinarian *NOW* if you answered yes to any query—it could be myositis^G, or it could be injury and soreness in your senior horse's back muscles.

 NO

ACTION PLAN (CONTINUED):

Has your senior horse had an injection in his neck muscles within a week before these symptoms appeared? Does the injection site look swollen and/or feel abnormally warm? It could be a local inflammatory reaction at the site, causing stiffness and pain in the neck, making your senior horse reluctant to move. Apply **Home Treatment**, below.

It could be back pain. Go to "Senior Back Check," **page 314**, and call your veterinarian for an appointment.

WHILE YOU WAIT

Isolate your senior horse in an open-air paddock or stall with a separate water supply, apart from other horses by at least 20 feet. Wash your hands and disinfect your boots after handling him and before handling other horses (see page 41). Offer him his usual feed for this time of day, plus salt and plenty of fresh water.

HOME TREATMENT

Because you already indicated, in your answers to the **Action Plan** queries, that your senior horse isn't feverish or off his feed, you've helped rule out the possibility that an infection at the injection site has spread and become a dangerous, body-wide problem. Check his rectal temperature twice daily, and keep a close eye on his appetite while you're treating his inflamed shot site. Call your veterinarian NOW if a change occurs in either.

Step 1: *Ice the area.* Select an ice pack large enough to extend at least 2 inches beyond the swelling's margins. Slip it between layers of a clean cloth, center it over the area, and hold it there for 5 minutes. Repeat every 15 minutes for a total of 6 treatments.

Step 2: *Massage; light exercise.* Massage the area gently with your fingertips, rubbing in the direction of the muscle fibers. Hand walk your horse to increase circulation.

Step 3: *Reevaluate often.* At least every 4 hours, reassess your horse's condition: Has the swelling increased in size, heat, or tenderness? Is he becoming generally ill—losing his appetite, becoming depressed, spiking a fever? If you observe any of these signs, call your veterinarian NOW.

Swayback

SENIOR SIGNPOST: Your horse's back appears sunken. You may also notice that his withers look more prominent, and his croup seems tilted, bringing his tailhead upward and adding overall to the sway in his back. He may or may not seem to be in any pain from this anatomical change.

What it could mean: Your senior horse may be developing a "swayback," known as lordosis[G]. He's lost muscle mass and/or strength along his topline, and along the sides and underside of his belly, making his back/spine appear to sag. (It's his belly muscles that actually support the weight of his torso, thereby helping to keep his spine from sinking.)

ACTION PLAN:

Does your horse seem to have lost flexibility, moving stiffly or refusing certain cues? Does he flinch, hunch, or flex his back when you touch, groom, or place tack on it?

 YES Call your veterinarian *TODAY*—your horse may have a sore back, which can be a clue to the cause of his swayback. For more information, see "Senior Back Check," **page 314**.

 NO

Does he appear to have lost weight?

 YES There may be an underlying health problem, such as malnutrition, or hypoproteinemia[G]. Go to "Weight Loss" and "Muscle Loss," **pages 14** and **17**, respectively.

 NO

Is he overweight? If your horse is a mare, is she pregnant?

 YES If you answered yes to either query, your senior horse may need adjustments in diet and/or exercise to reduce stress on his back, and improve strength in the muscles that support it. Go to "Age-Adjusted Exercise," "Alternative Medicine," and "Stay-Young Diet Solutions," **pages 340, 388**, and **376**, respectively.

 NO

ACTION PLAN (CONTINUED):

Is your horse on a diet specifically formulated for seniors?

 NO For optimal muscle strength, he needs a diet formulated to meet his special needs as a senior. See "Stay-Young Diet Solutions," **page 376**.

 YES

Call your veterinarian *THIS WEEK* and arrange for your horse to have a senior-horse checkup to see if there are any identifiable and treatable reasons for his swayback. See "Senior Vet Checks," **page 386**.

The Science of Swaybacks

Just about every aged horse exhibits some degree of sag in his topline and a sharpening of the withers due to thinning muscle mass. But, it's estimated that fewer than one in every four senior horses develops a true swayback—the downward deviation of the spine known as lordosis[G]. Whether your senior horse develops a swayback and at what age depends on many factors. These include:
- *Overall conformation.* Horses with long backs and prominent withers are reported to be at greater risk.
- *Muscle tone.* Strong abdominal muscles are believed to be key to a level back.
- *General health and nutritional status.* These affect bone, joint, and spine health, as well as the muscles and connective tissues that keep everything aligned.
- *Exercise.* When done properly, it can optimize circulation and strengthen muscles that support your horse's back.

Did You Know?

It may look painful, but in most cases the swayback horse does not seem to have back pain.

Did You Also Know?

Weight gain can place additional stress on muscles that support your senior horse's back and torso. Since packing on pounds often is preceded by decreased activity and loss of condition, weakened abdominal and back muscles may exacerbate his sinking spine.

Swelling in Belly Wall

SENIOR SIGNPOST: The underside of your senior horse's belly wall appears swollen. You might also see a similar swelling in the brisket area between his forelegs, in the sheath area (if your horse is a male), and/or in the udder area (if your horse is female).

What it might mean: It could signal a serious underlying health problem.

ACTION PLAN:

Does your horse have a fever? (See "Senior Vital Signs," **page 292**.) Has he been off his feed, listless, and/or seemed detached from his surroundings? Has he recently had a cold or other respiratory infection? If your senior horse is a mare, has she foaled within the past three days?

 YES ▶ Call your veterinarian *NOW* if you answered yes to any query—it could be a blood-vessel abnormality (vasculitis^G or purpura^G); dangerously low blood protein levels (hypoproteinemia^G); or a symptom of acute endometritis^G and/or toxemia^G, all of which are potentially life threatening.

 NO

If your senior horse is a mare, is she heavily pregnant?

 YES ▶ Call your veterinarian *TODAY*—older, pregnant mares can have a relatively innocent case of ventral edema^G, due to weight gain, general discomfort, and decreased activity, all of which impair circulation. Or, she could be developing a more serious condition such as a ruptured prepubic tendon^G or ventral hernia^G, either of which can be life threatening if it progresses. Go to **While You Wait**, opposite page. For more information, go to "The Age Event: Declining Fertility (in mares)," **page 263**.

 NO

Does your horse seem to breathe heavily after even mild exercise, and take longer than usual to recover? Is his breathing labored—flared nostrils, exaggerated chest/flank movement with each breath, and possibly an elevated respiratory rate—even when he's been standing idle? Do his gums look abnormally pale?

 YES ▶ Call your veterinarian *TODAY*—it could be a heart problem. For more information go to "Labored Breathing," **page 63**.

 NO

ACTION PLAN (CONTINUED):

Is the swelling uneven or lumpy looking and limited to your horse's groin area?

 YES → Call your veterinarian *TODAY*—it could be an inguinal hernia^G, leaving your horse at risk for severe colic if a loop of intestine becomes entrapped in the hernia.

 NO

Is your senior horse on a purge-deworming^G program, rather than a daily deworming^G program, and overdue for a treatment?

 YES → Call your veterinarian *TODAY*—it could be hypoproteinemia^G from a heavy parasite infestation and a resultant severe intestinal inflammation, which can lead to a protein-losing enteropathy^G—loss of valuable protein via manure.

 NO

Does your horse have sores, raw patches, or otherwise unhealthy-looking skin?

 YES → Call your veterinarian *THIS WEEK*. The swelling could be due to a generalized skin disease.

 NO

Call your veterinarian for an appointment.

WHILE YOU WAIT

Confine your pregnant mare to a stall or small paddock with a companion, if necessary, to prevent fretting. If her belly swelling is due simply to poor circulation, confinement can make the condition slightly worse, but if it's due to a developing ruptured prepubic tendon^G or ventral hernia^G, movement can escalate the condition's progress.

Swelling or Dent in Front/Upper Neck

SENIOR SIGNPOST: In the normally smooth, shallow jugular groove area—just to either side of the trachea (windpipe) at the front of your horse's upper neck—there's a swelling and/or an irregular depression under his skin.

What this might mean: Tissue there is currently, or has been, inflamed or traumatized.

ACTION PLAN:

Has your horse had an intravenous injection in this area within the past week? Does he seem to have difficulty swallowing, as evidenced by leftover feed in his feeder, chewed feed on the ground, or slobbering?

YES Call your veterinarian *NOW* if you answered yes to either query—it could be an inflammatory reaction at the injection site, resulting in damage to the vein and/or the tissues around it. Prompt action can minimize the damage and the potential for nerve injury and scar tissue. (See "The IV Injection and its Risks," **at right.**)

 NO

Within the past several weeks, has your horse had a nasal discharge containing bits of partially chewed feed? Has he started to eat enthusiastically, then apparently lost interest before his meal was finished? Is there a swelling under his neck that seems to change size from time to time? Has your senior horse ever been diagnosed with choke^G?

YES Call your veterinarian *NOW* if you answered yes to any query—your horse could be suffering from choke^G, or is at high risk of choking on his next meal. Go to **While You Wait**, page 136.

 NO

Do you feel hard lumps on both sides of your senior horse's windpipe, in the throatlatch area? Does he seem to tire easily? Does he seem less able to tolerate cold weather?

YES Call your veterinarian *THIS WEEK* if you answered yes to any query—it could be a goiter^G due to a thyroid disorder^G.

 NO

ACTION PLAN (CONTINUED):

Call your veterinarian for an appointment. It's likely there's been prior damage to the tissues in this deformed area of your senior horse's neck, possibly from an IV injection. Scar tissue may have caused shrinkage and sinking of the tissues there. Your horse is at increased risk for choke^G as a result. Your veterinarian can discuss feeding and management changes that can help decrease that risk.

The IV Injection and its Risks

Most IV (intravenous) injections are given in your horse's jugular vein, due to ease of access. But there are drawbacks to the routine use of the jugular vein: Repeated injections into the vein can cause damage to its wall. It'll scar as it heals, becoming narrower, or might even scar shut. (Your senior horse can tolerate this if his other jugular vein is healthy.)

Important structures adjacent to the vein can get poked or injected with medication meant to go IV. These include—

• *The carotid artery*, which carries blood to the head. Your senior horse will flip over backward and have a seizure if medication is injected here.

• *Vital nerves* that provide branches to the throat, tongue, head and face. Those nerves can be damaged if medication meant for the vein leaks onto their fibers.

• *The esophagus*, which is sensitive to injury and tends to scar and shrink, resulting in a tendency to choke frequently when eating.

Horses that routinely get phenylbutazone^G ("bute") injections commonly develop dents in their necks, due to leakage of that medication into the adjacent tissues. Of all the equine medications, bute is by far one of the most caustic and tissue-damaging.

The solution? Avoid allowing anyone who's inexperienced to give IV injections to your horse. If bute is prescribed, ask whether an oral version is acceptable.

➤

WHILE YOU WAIT

1. Confine your horse to a quiet enclosure.

2. Withhold food and water, which would make the choke worse and increase risk of aspiration pneumonia.

3. Keep him calm, so he'll keep his head somewhat lowered. This will help prevent backed-up food and liquid from draining down into his lungs, rather than onto the ground.

CHOKE & YOUR SENIOR HORSE

Choke[G] can occur with increasing frequency in your senior horse. The culprit often is underlying tooth pain and incomplete chewing of feed, possibly coupled with prior damage to the esophagus due to rough or frequent stomach tubing, previous chokes, and/or jugular vein injection attempts.

If the blockage is severe, some swallowed feed may back up through your horse's nostrils. Otherwise it remains an uncomfortable lump in his throat, until it breaks up and goes down, or gets bigger and harder, resulting in an emergency. Each time this happens, damage is done to the esophagus. The more often it's damaged—and the more severely—the more likely your senior horse will choke in the future.

Lump/Bump on Neck

SENIOR SIGNPOST: There's a swelling or enlargement on the side of your horse's neck.

What this might mean: Infection, inflammation, or injury in the swollen tissues, due to a recent injection or trauma.

ACTION PLAN:

Has your senior horse had an IM (intramuscular) injection in his neck within the past week? Does he have a fever? Is he off his feed?

 YES Call your veterinarian *NOW* if you answered yes to either query—it could be an underlying illness, or Clostridial myositis^G due to infection at the injection site.

 NO

When you press on the swollen area, does it feel crackly, as though there's air bubbling within soft tissues?

 YES Call your veterinarian *NOW*—it could be subcutaneous emphysema^G, due to injury to the trachea (windpipe), allowing air to leak into the soft tissues under the skin, or an infection involving dangerous, gas-producing bacteria.

 NO

If your horse had an injection, is the site abnormally warm to the touch? Does he object to your touch there? Is he reluctant or slow to lower his head (e.g., to eat or drink)?

 YES If you answered yes to any query, it's likely a local inflammatory reaction to the injected medication. Apply **Home Treatment #1**, next page.

 NO

Does the swollen area feel fluid-filled, like a water balloon? Is there any evidence the area has been traumatized, such as from a kick or bite?

 YES If you answered yes to either query, it's likely to be a hematoma^G. Apply **Home Treatment #2**, next page.

 NO

Call your veterinarian for an appointment.

➤

HOME TREATMENT #1

*(See **Action Plan** to determine whether home treatment is appropriate for your horse's hot swelling. If at any time during home treatment, your answers on the **Action Plan** change for the worse, call your vet.)*

Step 1: *Ice the area.* Select an ice pack large enough to extend at least 2 inches beyond the swelling's margins. Slip it between layers of a clean cloth, center it over the area, and hold it there for 5 minutes. Repeat every 15 minutes for a total of 6 treatments.

Step 2: *Massage; light exercise.* Massage the area gently with your fingertips, rubbing in the direction of the muscle fibers. Hand-walk your horse to increase circulation.

Step 3: *Re-evaluate often.* At least every 4 hours, reassess your horse's condition: Has the swelling increased in size, heat, or tenderness? Is he becoming generally ill—losing his appetite, becoming depressed, spiking a fever? If so, call your vet NOW.

HOME TREATMENT #2

*(See **Action Plan** to determine whether home treatment is appropriate for your horse's neck. If at any time during home treatment, your answers change for the worse, call your vet.)*

Step 1: *Apply ice and pressure to stop bleeding under the skin.* Select an ice pack large enough to overlap the hematoma's margins. Place it directly on the skin and press almost hard enough to push your horse off-balance. (Ask a helper to press on the opposite side, to steady him). Ice on: 20 minutes; off: 5 minutes. Repeat twice more, with fresh packs.

Step 2: *Confine your horse, to protect blood clots that have formed to stop the bleeding.* For the next 12 hours, confine your horse to a box stall or paddock, with fresh grass or hay and a companion, if necessary, to prevent fretful movement.

Step 3: *Stimulate the area to encourage uptake of accumulated blood/serum.* The following day:
- Place a hot water bottle filled with hot (but tolerable on your hand) water over the swelling; hold it there for 5 minutes.
- Follow immediately with an ice pack for 5 minutes.
- Follow with 2 minutes of brisk stimulation with a rubber curry, to increase circulation.
- Repeat the cycle twice more, for a total of 3 cycles per session, 2 sessions per day.

Step 4: *Three or more days after the injury, exercise to improve circulation and discourage scarring.* Immediately following Step 3, exercise your horse. For an idle horse, walk 5 minutes, intersperse walking and jogging for 15 minutes, then walk 10 minutes for a cool-down. For a horse on regular exercise, perform a 50 percent easier version of his usual daily routine.

Step 5: *Keep it up.* Repeat Steps 1 through 4 until the area looks normal. This might take as long as 6 weeks, depending on the severity and age of the hematoma/seroma[G] when you started treatment. (The older it is, the longer it'll take to resolve.)

Visible Jugular Vein

SENIOR SIGNPOST: Your horse's jugular vein appears like a garden hose under the skin in his jugular groove area. You may or may not see the vein pulsing with his heartbeat. And, you may or may not see other veins on his body looking prominent and distended.

What this might mean: A serious underlying heart problem. Or, it could mean there's a problem in your senior horse's liver or lungs, causing elevation in his veins' pressure.

ACTION PLAN:

Do your senior horse's jugular veins show on both sides of his neck, rather than just one side? Is he off his feed, depressed, dull, and/or acting anxious or preoccupied? Are small veins distended elsewhere on his body?

 YES Call your veterinarian *NOW* if you answered yes to any query—it could be a serious heart problem and/or a mass or growth in your senior horse's chest and/or abdomen. Go to **While You Wait #1**, next page.

 NO

Does your senior horse have a fever? (See "Senior Vital Signs," **page 292**.) Is there edema in his lower legs or along his lower belly wall? Does he seem to tire easily, breathing heavily with only slight exercise? Does he suddenly resent it when you tighten his girth? Are his gums unusually pale, or even slightly blue-tinged? Is his capillary refill time (CRT, see "Senior Vital Signs," **page 292**) longer than 2 seconds?

 YES Call your veterinarian *NOW* if you answered yes to any query—it could be an underlying infectious or degenerative disease, an accumulation of fluid in the sac around your senior horse's heart (pericarditis^G), or an arrhythmia^G. Go to **While You Wait #1** and **#2**, next page.

 NO

Is there a yellow tinge to your horse's gums and/or the whites of his eyes? Has he lost weight in the last few months? Have there been any changes in his appetite, and/or in the color, volume, or consistency of his manure? Do you see a rhythmic pulse in his distended jugular veins?

 YES Call your veterinarian *TODAY* if you answered yes to any query—it could be a liver problem.

 NO

ACTION PLAN (CONTINUED):

Is only one jugular vein distended, without pulsation?

 YES

It's probably an obstruction in that individual vein, without an underlying disease process or body-wide consequences. (The vein on the opposite side can do the work of both veins.) The most likely cause is scar tissue from damage to the vein at some point in the past, due to intravenous injection(s). Make a note of it in your horse's medical records, and bring it to your veterinarian's attention the next time you speak to him/her.

NO

Call your veterinarian for a senior-horse checkup (see **page 386**) *TODAY.*

WHILE YOU WAIT #1

1. Confine your horse to a quiet enclosure with shelter from weather and other horses, both of which can be stressful.

2. If he's shivering, blanket him.

3. If he's sweating, hose him off or sponge him with cool water.

4. Provide a compatible companion, if necessary, to prevent separation anxiety.

WHILE YOU WAIT #2

Isolate your horse from other horses in case it's contagious. To prevent the spread of possible infectious disease, confine your horse to an open-air paddock or stall with a separate water supply, apart from other horses by at least 20 feet. Wash your hands and disinfect your boots (see page 41) after handling your horse and before handling other horses.

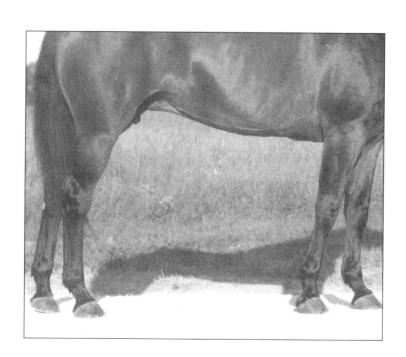

CHAPTER 10

Changes in
LEGS &
HOOVES

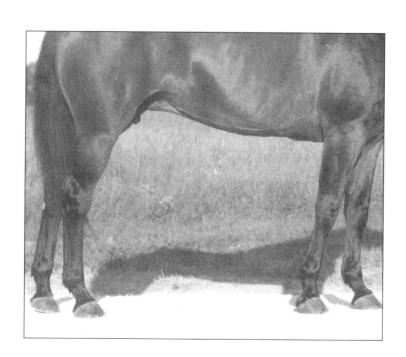

Lameness

SENIOR SIGNPOST: Your senior horse is limping, shifting his weight frequently, holding up a leg, or otherwise displaying signs of lameness.

What this might mean: It could be a "standard" lameness due to injury, or it could be an age-related condition.

ACTION PLAN:

Does your senior horse have a fever? (See "Senior Vital Signs," **page 292.**)

 YES Call your veterinarian *NOW*—signs of lameness, with fever, can indicate a developing infection or severe inflammatory process with laminitis^G. Go to **While You Wait #1**, opposite page.

 NO

Is he shifting his weight from one front leg to the other? Does he stand with his front legs farther forward than usual? Is he tender-footed when walking across gravel or hard and/or uneven surfaces? Do the walls of any of his hooves feel colder or warmer than usual? Do any of his feet have a more prominent digital pulse? (See "Senior Vital Signs," **page 292.**)

 YES Call your veterinarian *NOW* if you answered yes to any query—it could be laminitis^G. Go to **While You Wait #1,** opposite page.

 NO

Has his feed recently changed? Did he eat a larger-than-usual volume of grain within the past 3 days?

 YES Call your veterinarian *NOW*—it could be laminitis^G due to endotoxemia^G. Go to **While You Wait #1**, opposite page.

 NO

Is he fatter or thinner than he should be? (See "Senior Condition Check," **page 300.**) Does he have an unusually long, wavy, scruffy coat that's overdue to shed? Does he sweat more than usual? Does he shiver on cool days when other horses are perfectly comfortable?

YES Call your veterinarian *NOW*—it could be laminitis^G due to a hormonal imbalance such as Equine Cushing's Disease^G (ECD, also known as pituitary adenoma; see **page 257**) or thyroid disease^G. Go to **While You Wait #1**.

 NO

ACTION PLAN (CONTINUED):

Is he holding up one leg and reluctant to bear weight on it, or walking with a severe head-bobbing limp?

 YES ▶ Call your veterinarian *NOW*—it could be a serious injury of the supporting structures, such as a sprained or ruptured tendon (bowed flexor tendon, or a ruptured extensor tendon), sprained ligament (such as carpal or check ligament), injured joint, or a fracture, all of which are more common in older horses due to loss of soft tissue elasticity and decreased bone density. Go to **While You Wait #2**, page 145.

NO ▼

Is the affected leg(s) swollen, unusually warm, or unusually cold?

 YES ▶ Call your veterinarian *NOW*—there could be a serious underlying illness or injury, including venous thrombosis^G, vasculitis^G, folliculitis^G, or deep-tissue injury. Go to **While You Wait #2**, page 145.

NO ▼

Does the lameness appear after your senior horse has been idle for several hours, getting better as he moves?

 YES ▶ Call your veterinarian *TODAY*— arthritis^G is a likelihood. Thanks to new treatment and management tools, it need not be permanent or crippling. For more information, go to "The Age Event: Arthritis," **page 227**.

 NO ▼

Call your veterinarian *TODAY* for a soundness examination.

WHILE YOU WAIT #1

1. *Confine your horse.* Movement might make things worse. Until proven otherwise, confine him to a box stall or small paddock and provide a companion, if necessary, to discourage fretful movement.

2. *Chill any warm feet.* Select a flexible ice pack large enough to wrap around the entire hoof wall. (This might take two packs.) Apply the pack(s) and secure with a wrap. Leave on for 5 minutes. Repeat every half hour, or until your vet arrives, whichever happens first.

3. *Avoid feeding him.* Give no feed—only water—until your vet arrives and can confirm or dismiss laminitis^G as a cause of lameness.

Which Leg is Lame?

In most cases, pinpointing a lameness isn't difficult if you follow these steps. *Caveat:* If your horse's lameness is obvious and he's reluctant to bear weight on the leg(s), skip these steps and immediately call your vet. These diagnostics could cause further damage.

WHAT YOU'RE LOOKING FOR

• **Head-bob:** Your horse's head bobs UP when a sore forelimb hits the ground. His head bobs DOWN when a sore hind limb hits the ground. (*Tip:* A head-bob is easiest to see when your horse is trotted toward you. As a general rule, the more pronounced the bob, the more severe the pain.)

• **Hip-hike or hip-drop:** The hip on one side raises HIGHER and/or sinks LOWER than the other side. (*Tip:* This is easiest to see when your horse is trotted away from you. Make it more visible by sticking a piece of white adhesive tape on each hip, to give your eye a reference point.)

• **Toe-drag:** The toe of the affected hind limb drags the ground on the forward swing.

• **Shortened stride:** The stride on one leg is shorter than the stride on the other legs.

NOW LOCATE THE LAME LEG

Follow these steps. Call your veterinarian if you observe any sign of injury or lameness in Steps 1, 2, or 3. If you still can't ferret out the lameness, call your vet for help.

Step 1. Examine your horse's legs and feet for external evidence of injury.

• Stand him squarely on solid, level ground, then visually examine each leg and coronary band for bumps, swellings, wounds, discharges, or other such problems.

• Feel each hoof for excess heat, then check your horse's digital pulse. (For how to do so, see page 295.)

• Pick up, clean, and examine each foot for nails, cracks, bruises, or other abnormalities. Note any resistance, which could indicate pain in another foot/feet, hence his reluctance to increase the load there.

Step 2. Watch your horse trot a straight line. Lameness that's barely perceptible at the walk can become more evident at the trot.

• Find a flat, smooth surface with solid footing.

• Recruit a helper. Give her a crop or whip, if necessary, to help get your horse trotting in hand.

• Have your helper trot the horse on a straight line away from you, for about 50 feet, loosely holding the lead so as not to inhibit a head-bob. Then have the pair trot toward you, then past you, so you can view the horse from the front and side.

Repeat the exercise 2 to 3 times. If you still can't identify the lame leg(s), one of three things could be happening:

1. Your horse may be too lame, fresh, or uncomfortable to cooperate.

2. The lameness is bilateral or too subtle to show up on a straight line.

3. There is no lameness.

Step 3. Longe your horse. Have your helper longe the horse in both directions, gradually tightening the circle. Or, have your helper trot him in circles in hand. As a general rule, the tighter the circle, the more pronounced the lameness. Still can't see the problem's origin? Call your vet.

WHILE YOU WAIT #2

1. *Confine your horse.* Movement might make things worse. Until proven otherwise, confine him to a box stall or small paddock and provide a companion, if necessary, to discourage fretful movement.

2. *Cool the foot, tendon, or joint suspected of being the problem.* Select an ice pack large enough to extend at least 2 inches beyond the area's margins. Slip it between layers of a clean cloth, center it over the area, and hold it there. Ice on: 5 minutes. Ice off: 15 minutes. Repeat this cycle 3 more times or until your vet arrives, whichever happens first.

3. *Apply a support wrap.* If you're reasonably sure where the problem is, apply a support wrap appropriate to the area being bandaged, adding an extra layer of padding and being especially careful to apply the elastic layer evenly and firmly enough to prevent slippage.

How Lame is Your Horse?

There are many different methods of defining and grading lameness. We've adopted the classification of the American Association of Equine Practitioners, as defined in their Guide to Horse Shows:

Definition: Lameness is a deviation from the normal gait or posture due to pain or mechanical dysfunction.

Classification:

   Grade 1: Difficult to observe; not consistently apparent regardless of circumstances (i.e., weight carrying, circling, inclines, hard surfaces, etc.).
   Grade 2: Difficult to observe at a walk or trotting a straight line; consistently apparent under certain circumstances (i.e., weight carrying, circling, inclines, hard surfaces, etc.).
   Grade 3: Consistently observable at a trot under all circumstances.
   Grade 4: Obvious lameness; marked nodding, hitching, or shortened stride.
   Grade 5: Minimal weight bearing in motion and/or at rest; inability to move.

Swollen Leg(s)

SENIOR SIGNPOST: One or more of your senior horse's legs and/or leg joints appears swollen or enlarged. There may or may not be any associated lameness.

What this might mean: Generalized illness, some of which can cause edema^G of the lower legs. Or, it could mean there's been an injury in or near the swollen area.

ACTION PLAN:

Is the swelling limited to one leg?

 YES Call your veterinarian *NOW*—it's likely to be injury or infection in the supportive structures and/or joint(s) of the affected leg. Or, it could be snakebite, cellulitis^G, or folliculitis^G in the skin. Go to **While You Wait #1**, opposite page.

 NO

Does your senior horse have a fever? (See "Senior Vital Signs," **page 292.**) Has he recently shown symptoms of respiratory infection (runny nose, bloodshot eyes, increased respiratory rate, cough)? Is your horse a mare who was bred, within the past 2 weeks, by natural cover or artificial insemination?

 YES Call your veterinarian *NOW* if you answered yes to any query—it could be purpura hemorrhagica^G, or vasculitis^G (e.g., from infection with Equine Viral Arteritis^G, a.k.a. EVA). Go to **While You Wait #2,** opposite page.

 NO

Has your senior horse seemed dull, listless, or detached from his surroundings within the last 6 months? Has he lost weight? Does he tire more easily than usual, breathe heavily with only mild exertion, and/or take longer than usual to recover after exercise? Are his gums paler pink than usual, or slightly blue-tinged?

 YES Call your veterinarian *TODAY* if you answered yes to any query—your senior horse's edema may be the result of hypoproteinemia^G due to malnutrition or an underlying health problem (such as kidney disease, chronic inflammatory bowel disease^G, heavy parasite load, or hepatitis^G). Or, he could have a heart problem.

NO

ACTION PLAN (CONTINUED):

Is the swelling limited to both hind legs?

 YES Call your veterinarian *TODAY*—it could be degenerative suspensory ligament desmitis^G. Or, it could be stocking up^G due to sluggish circulation. (For more information on stocking up, see "Taking Stock of Stocking Up," **next page**.)

 NO

Does the swelling in the affected legs significantly improve within 20 minutes of exercise?

 YES It's likely stocking up. Go to **Home Treatment**, next page. For more information, see "Taking Stock of Stocking Up," **next page**.

 NO

Call your veterinarian *TODAY*—there may be a serious underlying problem such as hypoproteinemia^G, a kidney problem, or an infection such as folliculitis^G or cellulitis^G.

WHILE YOU WAIT #1

1. *Keep your horse still.* Further movement could worsen whatever's causing his swollen leg(s). Get him out of harm's way as best you can, then confine him. Provide a companion, if necessary, to discourage fretful movement.

2. *Ice the leg.* Chill the area to limit pain and swelling. Select an ice pack large enough to overlap the swollen area by at least 2 inches all around its margins. Slip it between the layers of a clean cloth, center it over the area, and hold it manually or secure with a wrap. Ice on: 5 minutes. Ice off: 15 minutes. Repeat this cycle 3 more times or until your vet arrives, whichever happens first.

WHILE YOU WAIT #2

Isolate your horse from other horses in case it's contagious. To prevent spread of possible infectious disease, confine your horse to an open-air paddock or stall with a separate water supply, apart from other horses by at least 20 feet. Wash your hands and boots (see page 41) after handling your horse and before handling other horses.

HOME TREATMENT

Movement is the most effective treatment for stocking up.

1. *Turn him out.* If your horse is stallbound, provide pasture time. If pasture is not available, a paddock is preferable to a stall, as he'll have more room to move around.

2. *Put hay, salt, and water* at separate corners of the enclosure, so your senior horse will be compelled to move.

3. *Exercise him.* Initiate an exercise program suitable to his condition. (See "Age-Adjusted Exercise," page 340.)

4. *Get creative.* If a pre-existing and untreatable unsoundness makes exercise too painful, try passively flexing and extending his legs, to improve lymph flow and resolve the stocking up. (See "Senior Stretches," page 348.)

5. *Gently massage* the affected limbs, from just above the coronary band to the top of the leg, to help facilitate lymph drainage.

Taking Stock of Stocking Up

What it is: In most cases, stocking up in an elderly horse is the result of lymph fluid accumulating in his lower extremities.

Why it happens: "Poor circulation" from inactivity is the most common explanation. Lymph fluid, which is part of your senior horse's immune system, circulates through his body in lymph vessels (much like blood vessels) that connect lymph nodes. Unlike blood, lymph isn't pumped by your horse's heart. Instead, upward movement from lower extremities happens when muscles adjacent to the lymph vessels press on them, squeezing the fluid upward. If your senior horse stands idle for long periods of time, his lymph won't circulate. You see evidence of that when his lower legs swell, particularly his hind legs, as it accumulates. Within 20 minutes of even mild walking, stocked-up legs will look significantly trimmer.

How to help and/or prevent it: See "Home Treatment," above.

Moves Stiffly &/Or Slowly

SENIOR SIGNPOST: Your senior horse moves as though he's stiff, sore, or walking on eggshells (especially with his front feet). He may "weathervane" when he turns, reluctant to bend his spine. Or, he may balk or refuse to take a certain path, such as up (or down) an incline, or across a gravel road.

What this might mean: It signals a serious underlying problem. He may be in pain, either in an isolated area of his body, or all over. For instance, a severe headache can be an underlying cause. Or, he may be afraid to move because mental or physical changes make his environment seem less safe.

ACTION PLAN:

Does your senior horse have a fever? (See "Senior Vital Signs," **page 292.**)

 YES Call your veterinarian *NOW*—it could be an oncoming general illness, such as painful pleuritis^G or pleuropneumonia^G, which can cause symptoms of stiffness before the classic signs of the disease appear. Early, aggressive treatment may be necessary for recovery. Go to **While You Wait #1**, page 151.

 NO

Has your senior horse recently had diarrhea^G, colitis^G, strangles^G, or any other serious illness?

 YES Call your veterinarian *NOW*—it could be laminitis^G, which sometimes occurs in the aftermath of significant illness. Go to **While You Wait #2,** page 151, and "The Age Event: Laminitis (Founder)," **page 273.**

 NO

Has your senior horse been exercised, either by you or at liberty, within recent hours? Did he exercise strenuously yesterday? Is his urine tinted brown, like coffee?

 YES Call your veterinarian *NOW* if you answered yes to any query—it could be acute myositis^G or exertional rhabdomyolysis. Go to **While You Wait #1**.

 NO

Does he seem more prone to stumble, stagger, slip, or fall than he did before? Does he hold his head, or one ear, tilted to one side? Have you seen him lean against a solid object when at rest? Have you recently seen even a small amount of blood coming from either nostril?

 YES Call your veterinarian *NOW* if you answered yes to any query—your senior horse could have a problem with his equilibrium or balance, due to a neurological problem such as Equine Protozoal Myeloencephalitis^G (EPM), or an inner-ear disorder. Go to **While You Wait #3,** page 152. ➤

 NO

ACTION PLAN (CONTINUED):

Does your senior horse seem stiff or tender-footed when traveling over hard, uneven, or gravel footing? When at rest, does he seem to shift his weight from leg to leg, and/or hold his forelegs farther in front of him than usual, like a sawhorse?

 NO

 YES Call your veterinarian *NOW* if you answered yes to either query. It could be laminitis^G. Go to **While You Wait #2.** For more information, see "The Age Event: Laminitis (Founder)," **page 273.**

Is there any evidence of trauma? Has your senior horse had conflicts with another horse? Has he recently over-exerted himself (for example, running a long distance, being chased by dogs, or panicking after becoming separated from herdmates)?

 NO

 YES Call your veterinarian *TODAY* if you answered yes to any query—your senior horse may have injured himself.

Have you been feeding hay that's been stored for more than a year? Do you live in an area in which the trees are mostly needle-bearing and evergreen, rather than leafy and deciduous? Are the soil and forage in your area known or rumored to be lower than normal in selenium? Do you add fat to your horse's diet, in the form of unsaturated fat?

 NO

YES Call your veterinarian *TODAY* if you answered yes to any query—it could be a health-threatening selenium deficiency^G, which can be exacerbated by any of these circumstances.

At dusk or after dark, does he seem spookier than usual and/or afraid to pass through familiar gates or passages?

 NO

 YES Call your veterinarian *TODAY* if you answered yes to either query—your senior horse could have a vision problem. For more information, see "Vision Problems," **page 112.**

Do your senior horse's flexibility and willingness to move improve with movement, or during a pre-exercise warm-up session? Is he worse after a period of confinement?

 NO

 YES Call your veterinarian *TODAY* if you answered yes to either query—it could be arthritis^G. While you wait, go to "The Age Event: Arthritis," **page 227.**

Call your vet for an appointment.

WHILE YOU WAIT #1

1. *Isolate your horse from other horses in case it's contagious.* To prevent spread of possible infectious disease, confine your horse to an open-air paddock or stall with a separate water supply, apart from other horses by at least 20 feet. Wash your hands and boots (see page 41) after handling your horse and before handling other horses.

2. *Restrict Movement.* Until a definitive diagnosis can be made, assume your horse has a disorder that can be worsened by movement. Don't move him unless absolutely necessary.

WHILE YOU WAIT #2

1. *Confine your horse.* Confine your horse to a small (12 x 12) stall or paddock with soft footing. If he moves stiffly, is reluctant to move, rocks back on his hind legs, or has an exaggerated digital pulse (see page 295), don't move him. Rather, confine him where he stands, using portable corral panels or a makeshift enclosure. Or simply stay with him until your vet arrives.

2. *Don't feed him.* Offer water only. Your horse should have no feed of any kind until your vet's ruled out laminitis^G, which might be the result of, or be worsened by, certain kinds of feeds.

➤

Bute: Resist The Urge

What's the first thing you reach for when your oldster acts stiff and sore? Is it "bute" (phenylbutazone^G)? Think before you do so again. With advancing age, your senior horse's body is less able to tolerate medication side effects. Decreases in appetite, fiber intake, water intake, activity level, and gut motility all can contribute to an exaggerated toxic response to bute, whose side effects include:

- Stomach ulcers^G
- Ulcerative colitis^G
- Aplastic anemia^G in you (from handling it).

Use bute sparingly, under your veterinarian's guidance. Opt for commercially prepared bute paste or gel, rather than tablets. Wear rubber gloves and avoid contact with the medication. The more you handle it, the greater your own risk of side effects. Finally, ask your vet for a safer alternative. One reason bute's so popular is that it's cheap. In the long run, though, its side effects can make it quite expensive.

WHILE YOU WAIT #2 - CONTINUED

3. *Chill his feet.* Draw out excess heat in the affected area by applying flexible ice packs (such as frozen bags of peas or corn) to his hoof walls for 5 minutes every half hour, until your vet arrives.

WHILE YOU WAIT #3

1. *Protect yourself.* With this kind of gait anomaly, your horse is likely to move in unexpected ways. Be alert, and don't put yourself in a position where you could be stepped on, knocked over, or conked on the head.

2. *Protect your horse.* Your horse can do serious damage to himself if he feels compelled to move. If it can be done so safely, halter and hold him where he is while you wait for your vet. Or, if possible, have a helper hold him while you set up portable corral panels around the horse, to protect him from other horses.

Did You Know?

Inflammation of the pleura (the Saran Wrap-like lining of your horse's chest cavity), as is seen with pleuritis^G and pleuropneumonia^G, is extremely painful and can cause your horse to resist flexing, bending, moving, or being touched over his rib cage. Often preceded by significant stress (such as a long road trip or an upper-respiratory infection), stiffness and soreness may be the first symptoms you see in your senior horse.

Down, Can't (or Struggles to) Get Up

SENIOR SIGNPOST: Your senior horse is lying down and stays there, even in the face of stimuli that usually would cause him to spring to his feet, such as your approach.

What this might mean: He's cast, injured, exhausted, ill, or has a neurological problem that's preventing him from rising.

ACTION PLAN:

Does your senior horse have a fever (see "Senior Vital Signs," **page 292**), or feel abnormally warm and/or moist with sweat? Does he occasionally roll or thrash? Are you able to coax him to get up, but he goes down again?

 YES Call your veterinarian *NOW* if you answered yes to any query—it could be a serious infection, a painful condition such as colic^G or peritonitis^G, or hemorrhage into the abdominal cavity. Go to **While You Wait #1,** next page.

 NO

Does your horse seem mentally off—weak, or depressed, and apparently unconcerned about being down?

 YES Call your veterinarian *NOW*—it could be a severe injury or illness causing weakness or an altered mental state. Go to **While You Wait #2,** next page.

 NO

Is your senior horse a mare that's foaled within the past 24 hours?

 YES Call your veterinarian *NOW*—it could be exhaustion and weakness from birthing, internal bleeding from a ruptured uterine artery^G, or damage to nerves supplying one or both hind limbs, paralyzing the associated muscles. Go to **While You Wait #3,** next page.

 NO

Does he appear physically traumatized and/or injured?

 YES Call your veterinarian *NOW* if you answered yes to either query—it's possible your horse is injured. Go to **While You Wait #2.**

 NO

➤

153

ACTION PLAN (CONTINUED):

Is your horse alert, his legs obviously cast (stuck) against a barrier or fence? Does he appear relatively unscathed physically? Can you approach him without causing him to thrash?

 Apply **Home Treatment**, opposite page. If this fails for any reason, call your veterinarian *NOW*.

Call your veterinarian *NOW*—the longer your senior horse is down, the more damage may occur to his head, legs, and muscles, as well as to his lungs.

WHILE YOU WAIT #1

1. *Isolate your horse from other horses in case it's contagious.* To prevent the spread of possible infectious disease, confine your horse to an open-air paddock or stall with a separate water supply, apart from other horses by at least 20 feet. Wash your hands and disinfect your boots (see page 41) after handling your horse and before handling other horses.

2. *Watch him.* If he's showing colic-type symptoms, go to "Colic," page 221.

WHILE YOU WAIT #2

1. *Protect yourself from self-inflicted injury.* The most common injury resulting from being down is head/eye injury from swinging the head and slamming it against the ground or a wall in repeated attempts to rise. Pad the environment. Add thick, soft bedding and strategically placed bales of hay or straw around him.

2. *Keep him warm.* If your horse's mental state is depressed, he'll make little effort to rise and could become hypothermic^G, particularly if it's cold outside. Surround him with thick bedding, and cover him with a blanket.

WHILE YOU WAIT #3

1. *Move the foal.* If you can do so without putting yourself at risk, move the foal to an adjacent enclosure so he won't be injured.

2. *Protect the mare.* Pad the area around her with bales of hay or straw. Remove all obstacles to prevent her from colliding with them, and to make it safer for personnel to move around her.

3. *Keep it quiet.* Encourage her to lie quietly by leaving her alone. Her chance of forming a durable blood clot and halting the bleeding will be better if she remains still.

HOME TREATMENT:

*(See **Action Plan** to determine whether home treatment is appropriate for your cast horse. If at any time during home treatment, your answers on the **Action Plan** change for the worse, call your vet.)*

Step 1. *Get help.* Enlist the aid of two or more strong helpers.

Step 2. *Test your strength.* If you and your helpers collectively are strong enough to do so without hurting your backs or knees, grab handfuls of mane and tail and try to pull your horse away from the wall, then quickly get out of the way to avoid injury when he rises.

Step 3. *Get ropes.* If you can't find enough muscle power for Step 2, or if you've executed that step and your horse still can't get up (and you see no visible reason why), it could be that he's been cast so long that his down legs have "gone to sleep," and you'll have to turn him over. Get two strong, soft ropes that are at least 20 feet long (tie the nonclip ends of two soft lead ropes together to make one rope).

Step 4. *Position the ropes.* Stand behind your horse's spine, away from the danger of struggling legs. Lean over his torso and loop one rope under each of the two bottom legs, then work each rope up the leg until it's well above his hock (hind leg) and knee (front leg).

Definition: THE CAST HORSE

A horse is cast when he has the physical ability to rise, but there's external interference. Because of the way his weight is distributed, a horse must follow a routine in order to get to his feet.

1. Position himself on his chest, with hind limbs drawn up beneath him.

2. Extend his forelimbs in front of him.

3. Swing his head and neck as ballast, while simultaneously pushing with his hind limbs to raise his hindquarters, and bracing himself with his forefeet.

In the typical cast-horse scenario, the stall is freshly bedded, just begging your horse to roll. He lowers himself, rolls up onto his back for a brisk scratch...and rolls over onto his other side, his legs bunched up against the wall. He can't get positioned to stand up.

Step 5. *Pull him over.* With one or two people at each rope, pull both legs simultaneously to turn him over. This will be difficult, but one strong person or two people with average strength can do it. *Caution:* Don't let his hooves hit you on their way over. To help avoid risk of injury, be alert and ready to move out of his way as he rises.

Crumbly or Cracked Hooves, Won't Hold Shoes

SENIOR SIGNPOST: Your senior horse's hooves have become more brittle or crumbly than they were, and now are prone to breaking apart. When you have him shod, he frequently loses a shoe; the damage from clinched nails pulling through his hoof wall results in even more cracking and crumbling.

What this might mean: It could mean there's an underlying health and/or nutritional problem, and/or a degenerative condition in the hoof horn itself.

ACTION PLAN:

Does your senior horse exhibit any signs of lameness, ranging from subtle (a stiff, stilted gait, particularly when on hard or rocky terrain, or in a tight circle) to the obvious (a pronounced limp, or weight-shifting while at rest)? Is he reluctant to pick up a foot for you? Does the hoof wall on one or more feet feel stone cold, or abnormally warm? Has he ever shown similar symptoms before, or been diagnosed with laminitis[G]?

 YES Call your veterinarian *NOW* if you answered yes to any query—underlying metabolic and/or circulatory abnormalities may have set up your horse for poor-quality hoof horn and recurring laminitis[G], or founder[G]. Go to **While You Wait #1,** opposite page. For more information on laminitis, see "The Age Event: Laminitis (Founder)," **page 273**.

 NO

Does your senior horse tire more easily than usual, and/or take longer than usual to recover after a workout? Do his lower legs stock up[G] when he's inactive (for example, when confined to a stall for 24 hours)? Is he exercised and/or turned out to pasture less often than 2 days per week? Do his gums appear paler pink than usual, or blue-tinged? Do his lower legs often feel cold to the touch, particularly when compared to other horses in the barn?

 YES Call your veterinarian *TODAY* if you answered yes to any query—it could be a cardiovascular problem causing poor circulation to your senior horse's extremities.

 NO

ACTION PLAN (CONTINUED):

Has your senior horse lost weight over the past 6 months? Has there been a change (increase or decrease) in his appetite in that period of time? Does his ration consist of basically the same components as 2 years ago? Have you seen other horses in his group behaving aggressively toward him?

 YES Call your veterinarian *TODAY* if you answered yes to any query—it could be an underlying health problem, including but not limited to a nutritional deficiency due to a diet that's not senior-appropriate, or inadequate feed intake because of social pressure from dominant herd members.

 NO

Is the footing damp where your senior horse feeds, drinks, or rests? Have you noticed an offensive odor when inspecting and/or cleaning his hooves? Are there any areas of the coronary band that are swollen, abnormally warm, painful to the touch, deformed, or sunken-in?

 YES Call your veterinarian *TODAY* if you answered yes to any query—your senior horse may have a fungal or bacterial infection in the hoof horn, or hoof horn degeneration due to excessive moisture. Or, there may be an abnormality in hoof-horn production due to an underlying problem in your horse's feet, or in his general health. Go to **While You Wait #2,** next page.

 NO

Is your senior horse's coat dry and dull? Is his mane broken off? Is his tail thin and ratty? Are his coronary bands cracked and raw? Does his diet include a selenium supplement? Has he been given one or more injections of selenium?

 YES Call your veterinarian *TODAY* if you answered yes to any query—it could be selenium poisoning[G].

 NO

Call your veterinarian for an appointment.

WHILE YOU WAIT #1

1. *Isolate your horse from other horses in case it's contagious.* To prevent the spread of possible infectious disease, confine your horse to an open-air paddock or stall with a separate water supply, apart from other horses by at least 20 feet. Wash your hands and disinfect your boots (see page 41) after handling your horse and before handling other horses.

2. *Confine your horse.* Movement might make things worse. Until proven otherwise, confine him to a box stall or small paddock and provide a companion, if necessary, to discourage fretful movement.

3. *Avoid feeding him.* Give no feed—only water—until your vet arrives and can confirm or dismiss laminitis[G] as a cause of lameness.

WHILE YOU WAIT #2

1. *Evaluate, and, if necessary, change your horse's living situation.* If your horse's current environment is unhealthy for his hooves—lots of rocks, or low-lying and wet—move him to an enclosed location that's smooth, dry, and soft. A clean, mowed, grassy paddock would be ideal.

2. *Limit strenuous exercise that can stress feet.* Rather, keep your horse limbered up and his circulation flowing with daily controlled walks on good footing.

3. *Seek expert, and frequent, farriery.* Have your horse's hooves tended to as often as every 3 weeks by a competent farrier who can trim, balance, and if necessary, shoe your horse in a manner that helps hold his hooves together.

Selenium: Lifesaving Poison

Selenium is a powerful antioxidant mineral that works with Vitamin E to combat toxic free radicals in your senior horse's body. Most unsupplemented horses get all the selenium they need in pasture and hays. However, many regions—especially those with pine-type (needle-bearing) trees, indicating acidic soil—are selenium-deficient. Horses that eat selenium-deficient forage are at increased risk for a variety of health problems, mostly degenerative ones and cancers from an overload of toxic free radicals.

Trouble is, there's a fine line between getting enough selenium and getting too much. An excess causes problems including dry, brittle coat and hooves, breakage of mane and tail hairs, birth defects, and sudden death. Some regions contain soil with toxic selenium levels, which can produce toxic forage. Even without selenium supplements, these horses are at risk for selenium poisoning[G].

Does your senior horse need a selenium supplement? Ask your veterinarian to submit a blood sample to a state or commercial laboratory to test your oldster's selenium levels. If the report indicates he needs supplementation, proceed with your veterinarian's guidance. For added safety, use oral supplements, not injectable ones. They're less likely to result in overdose. To help ensure your horse gets precisely what he needs, mineralwise, try to find a locally formulated feed designed by equine nutrition experts to complement your regional soil content.

Sinking Fetlock(s)

SENIOR SIGNPOST: When bearing weight, your senior horse's fetlock(s) sinks toward the ground, as though lacking in strength or elasticity.

What this might mean: Injury or illness in the lower leg's supportive soft tissues, most commonly the suspensory ligament, and/or generalized weakness due to an underlying illness.

ACTION PLAN:

Does your senior horse have a fever? (See "Senior Vital Signs," **page 292.**)

 Call your veterinarian *NOW*—it could be weakness from an acute underlying illness. Go to **While You Wait,** next page.

 NO

Is it primarily the hind legs that are affected? Has your senior horse lost weight and/or muscle mass within the past 6 months? Has he been drinking and/or urinating more than usual? Does he spend more time than usual lying down? Is your horse a pregnant older mare?

 Call your veterinarian *TODAY* if you answered yes to any query—it could be muscle weakness due to an underlying chronic, degenerative disease such as EDM^G (equine degenerative myelopathy), polyneuritis equi^G (a.k.a. cauda equina syndrome), or degenerative suspensory ligament desmitis^G (DSLD).

 NO

Are all four limbs affected? Does your senior horse eat hay from a large livestock bale? Does he seem depressed and listless? Are other horses on the premises showing signs of drooling, weakness, droopy eyes, or listlessness?

 Call your veterinarian *NOW* if you answered yes to any query—it could be botulism^G (a.k.a. forage poisoning).

 NO

Is only one leg affected? Is there any heat, lameness, and/or soreness to the touch in the affected leg?

 Call your veterinarian *TODAY*—it could be injury to supportive structures, such as the suspensory ligament or flexor tendon.

 NO

Call your veterinarian for an appointment.

➤

WHILE YOU WAIT

1. *Isolate your horse from other horses in case it's contagious.* To prevent the spread of possible infectious disease, confine your horse to an open-air paddock or stall with a separate water supply, apart from other horses by at least 20 feet. Wash your hands and disinfect your boots (see page 41) after handling your horse and before handling other horses.

2. *Confine your horse.* Movement might make things worse. Until proven otherwise, confine him to a box stall or small paddock and provide a companion, if necessary, to discourage fretful movement.

Did You Know?

To Avoid Sinking Suspensories: WALK

The main job of your horse's suspensory ligamentsᴳ is to keep his fetlocks from sinking too far toward the ground. Overweight seniors and aged broodmares are especially vulnerable to breakdown of the hind-limb suspensory ligaments. Here's why:

Unlike most ligaments, which are semi-elastic straps of tough connective tissue binding bone to bone, the suspensory ligament contains muscle tissue. It actually gets stronger with regular exercise, such as walking. A sedentary horse loses muscle tissue in his suspensories. They must hold up his fetlocks, passively "hanging" them by the ligaments, without muscular support. And, most horses will alternately rest one hind limb, allowing the other to bear extra weight. Like an overburdened rope, the suspensories will begin to fray, resulting in a sinking fetlock. This increases stress on the ligament, damaging it further. The fetlock sinks even more, and a vicious cycle is born.

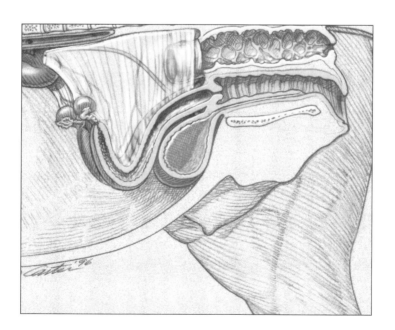

CHAPTER 11

Changes in
GENITALS

Lump, Sore, or Growth on/near Penis/Vulva

SENIOR SIGNPOST: A lump or open sore on or beside your stallion's or gelding's penis or sheath, or your mare's vulva. **What this might mean:** It could be an abnormal growth, a parasite infestation, or a local inflammatory reaction.

ACTION PLAN:

Are there individual nodular, raw sores on the hairless skin around your senior horse's anus, around your mare's vulva, and/or on your stallion's or gelding's penis or sheath?

YES ▶ Call your veterinarian *TODAY*—it could be a parasite infestation, such as habronemiasis^G (also known as summer sores^G), or an erosive skin cancer such as squamous cell carcinoma^G (SCC).

NO ▼

Do you see lumps, ranging from pea-size to golf-ball size and covered smoothly by skin, on or near the genitals of your senior horse, and possibly elsewhere on his body?

YES ▶ Call your veterinarian *TODAY*—it could be an allergic condition, such as drug eruption or granulomatous disease, or a type of cancer, such as lymphosarcoma^G.

NO ▼

If your senior horse is a stallion, do you see blisterlike lesions, hard nodules, and pustules (white, pus-filled "pimples"), and/or depigmented (lacking his usual skin coloration) spots on his penis? Has he been sexually active within the past 2 months?

YES ▶ Call your veterinarian *TODAY*—it could be a venereal disease called coital exanthema^G.

NO ▼

Is there a black lump(s) around your senior horse's anus and/or vulva, and/or on the underside of his tail-head? Is your horse white or gray with black skin?

YES ▶ Call your veterinarian *THIS WEEK*—it could be melanoma^G.

NO ▼

ACTION PLAN (CONTINUED):

Is there a raw, scraped, scabby area around the top of your senior horse's tailhead and/or around his anus, where adjacent hairs have been broken off? Does he rub this area on fence posts, tree trunks, etc.?

 Call your veterinarian *THIS WEEK*—it could be self-trauma due to parasites such as intestinal pinworms^G, or skin parasites such as mites^G, or lice^G. Or, it could be your senior horse has contamination and/or infection in the sheath (if he's a male) or udder area (if a female). Any of these problems can cause severe itching around the anus and tailhead. To rule out a dirty sheath or udder as the culprit, see "Down & Dirty Maintenance...," **page 360**.

Call your veterinarian for an appointment.

Did You Know?

Studies show that by the time your black-skinned gray, white, or partially white horse is 15 years of age, his odds of having a melanoma are a sobering 80%, due to the amount of melanin^G in his skin. Although you'll see them in his skin, they can spread internally— a "benign" melanoma can become malignant over time. For more information about melanoma and other types of skin cancer, go to "The Age Event: Cancer," page 241.

Changes in the Vulva

SENIOR SIGNPOST: The anatomy or position of your senior mare's vulva has changed.

What this might mean: Loss of muscle tone, loss of supporting connective tissue, and/or sagging internal reproductive organs. These can be normal, age-related changes, or they can be premature and severe due to an underlying health problem. Either way, they threaten your senior mare's fertility and general health.

ACTION PLAN:

Is the hairless skin of your senior mare's vulva irregular, distorted, lumpy, or affected with one or more open sores?

 Call your veterinarian *TODAY*—it could be a parasite infestation such as habronemiasis[G], tumor growth such as melanoma[G], self-trauma due to an itchy or painful skin condition such as pinworm[G] infestation or *Culicoides* hypersensitivity[G], skin irritation due to waxy accumulation of cellular debris between the halves of her udder, or a venereal disease[G].

 NO

Is there a moist, milky-colored discharge adhered to the bottom of your mare's vulvar lips, or dried onto her tail hairs and/or the inner surface of her thighs, hocks, and hind fetlocks?

 Call your veterinarian *TODAY*—your senior mare may be urine pooling[G] and/or wind sucking[G], resulting in a vaginal infection. Or, she may have pyometra[G] with an intermittently open cervix, which occasionally permits some pus to drain out through the vulva.

NO

Does the upper half of her vulva seem sunken? Are the vulvar lips partially pulled open? Is she a problem breeder?

 Call your veterinarian *THIS WEEK* if you answered yes to any query—an underlying loss of muscle mass/tone due to an age-related nutritional deficiency and/or an underlying health problem may be interfering with the vulvar lips' ability to seal out contamination. Or, your senior mare may have pyometra[G], with or without an underlying cervicitis[G], causing the cervix to seal closed. The extra weight of the fluid-filled uterus may be pulling on her external genitalia.

 NO

Call your veterinarian for an appointment.

Changes in Penis &/Or Sheath

SENIOR SIGNPOST: Changes in your senior horse's penis and/or sheath—there's swelling or lumps, lesions, abnormal discharge, and/or an abnormal odor.

What this might mean: An underlying problem affecting circulation and/or the flow of urine in the genital area. Or, it could be a parasite infestation, infection, or skin cancer.

ACTION PLAN:

Is your senior horse's penis partially or completely protruding from its sheath, and he's unable to fully retract it?

YES Call your veterinarian *NOW*—it could be penile paralysis^G due to nerve damage, or paraphimosis^G. Whatever the cause, your senior horse's exposed penis is vulnerable to permanent damage from drying and trauma.

 NO

Does your senior horse's sheath appear swollen?

YES Call your veterinarian *NOW*—though it could be edema^G due to a simple chronic infection (balanoposthitis), it could also be from a serious underlying health problem, such as hypoproteinemia^G, polyneuritis equi^G, or envenomation from a snake bite or bee sting. Or, it could be due to direct trauma to the sheath, e.g., from a kick. From the outside, they all can look the same, but the more serious causes require immediate veterinary attention.

 NO

Do you see open sores and/or nodules on your senior horse's penis? Does his penis appear distorted, asymmetrical, and/or not hanging normally when he drops it?

YES Call your veterinarian *TODAY* if you answered yes to either query—it could be a parasite infestation, infection, injury, and/or scar tissue, or tumor growth, such as squamous cell carcinoma^G.

 NO

➤

ACTION PLAN (CONTINUED):

Does the tip of your horse's penis appear distorted and/or swollen? Does he assume the urination position for an abnormally long period of time? Does the urine stream seem smaller than usual, deflected, or split? Has it been longer than a year since you've cleaned his sheath? Does his penis seem to have a lot of waxy buildup (smegma^G)?

 If you answered yes to any query—it could be a bean^G, a.k.a. smegmolith. Go to "Down & Dirty Maintenance...," **page 360**.

Call your veterinarian for an appointment.

Did You Know ?

Common tranquilizers from the *phenothiazine* family, including promazine and acepromazine, should not be used in a stallion, cryptorchid, or gelding that's being treated with the hormone testosterone. That's because testosterone increases the risk of a well-known side effect of phenothiazine use: penile paralysis^G, which is permanent and incurable. The reason for this effect is unknown. Surgery—either amputation of the penis, or attaching it inside the sheath so it can't come out—is the only treatment.

Genital Discharge

SENIOR SIGNPOST: A constant or intermittent discharge coming from your senior horse's genital area.

What this might mean: An infection, a growth, an inflammatory process, or a circulatory problem going on in the urinary and/or reproductive tract.

ACTION PLAN:

Is your senior horse a pregnant mare?   **YES** → Call your veterinarian *NOW*—it could be infection in the vagina, cervix, uterus, and/or fetal membranes, each of which threatens the pregnancy and possibly your mare.

 NO

If your senior horse is a mare, is the discharge milky and/or foul smelling? Do you notice a pattern to when it drains, such as when she postures to urinate, or when she sneezes or stands on an incline? Is there evidence of a milky discharge adhered or dried to her tail, hocks, and/or fetlocks?   **YES** → Call your veterinarian *TODAY*—it could be a vaginal infection, or a uterine infection such as pyometra[G]. (See "Pyo Pointers," **next page**.)

 NO

Does the discharge look like blood? Do you see it most often when your senior horse is urinating, or just afterward? Is there dried blood in the tail hairs, or crusted onto his/her hocks or fetlocks?   **YES** → Call your veterinarian *TODAY*—if your senior horse is a mare, it could be vaginal varicose veins[G] (also known as vaginal varicosities). Or, regardless of gender, it could be a urinary tract infection with or without the formation of bladder stones (a.k.a. uroliths[G]).

NO

➤

ACTION PLAN (CONTINUED):

Are there reddened, raw, hairless, or scalded areas in the skin around the vulva, inner thighs, hocks, and hind fetlocks (mares), or prepuce, adjacent belly wall, and hind fetlocks (geldings/stallions)? Does your senior horse smell of stale urine? Do you sometimes see urine dripping from his/her genital area? Have you observed your senior horse assuming the urinating position for an abnormally long period of time?

 YES Call your veterinarian *TODAY* if you answered yes to any query—your senior horse may have developed urinary incontinence^G, due to infection, injury, growth of an abnormal mass, or nerve dysfunction in or near the urogenital tract.

 NO

Call your veterinarian for an appointment.

PYO Pointers

Here's an at-a-glance look at pyometra.

■ Translated, pyometra means "uterus full of pus."

■ It occurs when a mare has a uterine infection that can't drain because the only natural opening—the cervix—has sealed itself closed, usually due to scarring.

■ While pyometra in dogs and other species can be fatal, in mares the condition can go undetected for months, even years, without noticeable symptoms.

■ A protective coating on the uterine lining prevents bacteria and toxins from entering the mare's bloodstream.

■ A "pyo" mare may live her normal life span without any significant problems aside from infertility.

■ In almost every case, pyo ruins the uterus, which likely was in bad shape already, or the condition would not have become established.

■ Treatment options include opening the scarred cervix and draining out gallons of pus, then finding a way to keep the cervix permanently open, or surgically removing the uterus.

■ Another viable option, depending on the mare's age and condition, is "watchful waiting," which means playing the odds she'll die from old age before the pyo causes health problems. For the vast majority of old mares, this approach works well.

■ The gamble with watchful waiting is that the uterine wall may develop an opening that leaks pus into the abdominal cavity, causing a painful (and usually fatal) infection called peritonitis^G.

CHAPTER 12

Changes in
MANURE

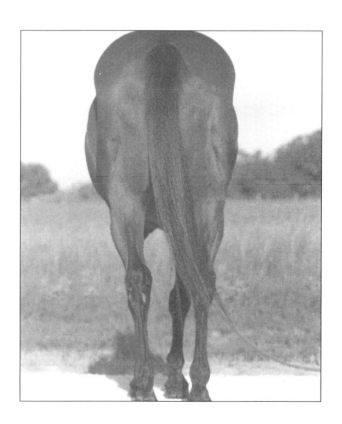

Hard, Small Manure Balls

SENIOR SIGNPOST: Your horse has passed less manure than usual—fewer and smaller piles—and what he does pass consists of manure balls that are individual, not pressed together. Each ball is smaller and harder than usual.

What this might mean: That his manure is too dry, due to dehydration, slowed passage through the intestinal tract, and/or decreased fiber and/or water intake. Whatever the cause, abnormally dry manure leaves your horse at increased risk of constipation and colic, due to impaction.

ACTION PLAN:

Is your senior horse showing signs of colic pain (see **page 222**)?

 YES Call your veterinarian *NOW*—the earlier colic^G is treated, the better your horse's chances of complete recovery. Go to **While You Wait #1,** opposite page.

 NO

Does your senior horse have a fever? (See "Senior Vital Signs," **page 292.**)

 YES Call your veterinarian *NOW*—it may be an infectious disease. Fever, often accompanied by decreased feed and water intake, can accelerate dehydration and its risks. Go to **While You Wait #2,** page 172.

 NO

Has your senior horse lost weight over the past few weeks? Does he have difficulty picking up, chewing, and/or swallowing his feed, as evidenced by leftover, spilled, soggy, and/or half-chewed feed in his feeder and/or on the ground? Has he been drooling?

YES Call your veterinarian *NOW* if you answered yes to any query—it could be injury or illness to your senior horse's brain and/or the nerves that supply his jaw, tongue, and/or throat, resulting in decreased feed and/or water intake, and impaired digestion.

 NO

Do you see white, wormlike strands of mucus on your senior horse's manure?

 YES Call your veterinarian *NOW*—fecal mucus suggests that your senior horse's intestinal tract is irritated and that its motility^G is slowed, either of which can lead directly to colic if not treated promptly. For more information on colic signposts, see "Colic," **page 221**, and "The Age Event: Colic," **page 251**.

NO

ACTION PLAN (CONTINUED):

Have you seen your horse approach a water source anxiously or reluctantly, or dip his muzzle in only to jerk back? Are other horses drinking from the same source with no problem? Does he tilt his head to one side when chewing? Does he dig into his feed as though he's hungry, but quit before he's finished?

Call your veterinarian *TODAY* if you answered yes to any query—it could be a painful tooth problem interfering with adequate fiber and/or water intake. Go to **While You Wait #3,** next page.

Apply **Home Treatment**, next page.

WHILE YOU WAIT #1

1. *Remove all feed.* Remove grain and hay from stall feeders; remove bedding if your horse eats it (it's not unusual for a horse with mild intestinal upset to eat straw or shavings). Leave his water.

2. *If your horse wants to roll or thrash, protect him (and his human attendants).*
• To keep your horse from hurting himself, and to make it easier for human attendants to stay out of harm's way: Re-bed his stall with extra-deep bedding; line stall walls with 1 or 2 layers of hay or straw bales; and remove all movable protrusions (feeders, buckets, etc.).
• Or, remove him to an arena or paddock with obstacles removed.
• Replace his standard halter with a padded one (such as a fleece-lined travel halter), so the halter's hardware won't damage facial nerves if he falls.
• Unless your horse is thrashing (which would make this too dangerous for you), apply padded shipping bandages to his legs, if he's accustomed to them.
• If it can be done safely, check and record baseline vital signs every 5 minutes and provide that information to your veterinarian. (See "Senior Vital Signs," page 292.)
• If your horse is insured (mortality or major medical), call your insurance agent and report that he's colicking. Be sure to familiarize yourself with the policy before a crisis, so you know what's required to comply.

➤

WHILE YOU WAIT #2

Isolate your horse from other horses in case it's contagious. To prevent the spread of possible infectious disease, confine your horse to an open-air paddock or stall with a separate water supply, apart from other horses by at least 20 feet. Wash your hands and disinfect your boots (see page 41) after handling your horse and before handling other horses.

The Big Fallacy: Keep your colicky horse walking.

Fact: In a mild to moderate colic[G], walking your senior horse might help move bubbles of gas and/or jostle loops of bowel back into their correct positions. But if your horse is intent on lying down, you're not going to be helping the situation by slapping, whipping, kicking, or shouting at him to get up and keep moving. You'll only be adding stress on an already stressful situation, and forcing him to expend energy he'll need to get well.

If walking seems to help your senior horse feel better, walk on. If it's a struggle to keep him on his feet, let him lie down. If he'll lie quietly, all the better. If he's intent on thrashing, no amount of physical abuse is going to stop him, and you might get yourself hurt trying. Instead, do what you can to protect him (without getting hurt yourself): Go to While You Wait #1, page 171.

WHILE YOU WAIT #3

Offer your senior horse a fresh bucket of body-temperature water (98.5-100.5°F) alongside his usual source of room-temperature water. If he'll drink it, it might help relieve his dehydration.

HOME TREATMENT:

*(See **Action Plan** to determine whether home treatment is appropriate for your horse's dry manure. If, at any time during home treatment, your answers on the **Action Plan** change for the worse, call your vet.)*

Step 1. *Offer fresh drinking water, in a clean container.* If it's cold outside, or abruptly/significantly colder than it has been, offer a second bucket alongside the first, containing warm water (120° F). Use a cook's thermometer to get the temperature just right.

Step 2. *Encourage your horse to drink.* Offer your senior horse a fresh bucket of body-temperature water (98.5-100.5°F) alongside his usual fresh, clean source of room-temperature water, and provide free-choice table salt or an unmineralized salt block. (Some horses dislike the taste of minerals, so won't partake of the block or loose mineralized salt.)

Step 3. *Provide light exercise.* To stimulate gut motility and drinking, hand-walk your horse, take him for an easy walking trail ride, or provide turnout in a paddock with a companion for at least 20 minutes. Offer room-temperature water every 10 minutes during the workout.

Step 4. *Watch for signs of deterioration.* Inspect consistency and total volume of manure passed. If there's no improvement within 8 to 12 hours, or if at any time you see new evidence of mucus, colic^G, or decreased manure output, call your veterinarian immediately.

Step 5. *If your senior horse shares a water source with other horses, the other horses might be keeping him from drinking.* Observe them and him. If that's the case, reconfigure your horse's living arrangements such that he has free access to his own water source.

TIP: Some Like it Hot— Sometimes!

With advancing age, some horses like their water warmed up, especially when the weather turns chilly. Offer your oldster a bucket of water that's been warmed to 120°F, by mixing hot water into a partial bucket of clean water and checking the temperature with a cook's instant-read thermometer (about $10 at most stores). Offer his usual water too, so he has a choice. Studies show that although most horses choose cooler water more often, they do seem to prefer the warmed water once in a while, and when they do, they drink more than usual.

Step 6. *If your senior horse shares a water source with other horses, are they drinking freely from it?* If not, check it. Something may be rendering it undrinkable, such as electric shock or contamination.

Did You Know?

Your horse's saliva is rich in sodium bicarbonate, a.k.a. baking soda. When he chews, he's not only crushing his feed into smaller pieces, he's also mixing it with sodium bicarbonate, which helps neutralize the powerful acids in his stomach, thereby helping to protect him from stomach ulcers. Feeds that don't require much chewing won't provide that protection.

Diarrhea

SENIOR SIGNPOST: Watery manure, in shapeless puddles on the ground, splattered on walls, and/or dried on your senior horse's tail, buttocks, or hocks.

What this might mean: Whatever the underlying cause, diarrhea leaves your senior horse at risk for dehydration and electrolyte imbalance, which can quickly become serious.

ACTION PLAN:

Is your senior horse breathing rapidly, and/or flaring his nostrils with each breath? Is he acting anxious for no apparent reason? Do you see/feel multiple bumps under his skin?

 YES Call your veterinarian *NOW* if you answered yes to any query—it could be an anaphylactic reaction[G], or a form of shock[G]. Go to **While You Wait,** page 177.

 NO

Is your horse showing any signs of colic (see **page 222**)?

 NO

YES Call your veterinarian *NOW*—it could be enteritis[G], or poisoning. While you wait, go to "Colic," **pages 221** and **251**.

Does your senior horse have a fever? (Go to "Senior Vital Signs," **page 292**.) Are other horses on the premises sick, too?

 YES Call your veterinarian *NOW* if you answered yes to either query—it's likely an infectious disease, such as Potomac Horse Fever[G], salmonellosis[G], or *E. coli* enteritis[G], with associated risks of endotoxemia[G], laminitis[G], dehydration, and/or shock[G]. Go to **While You Wait,** page 177.

 NO

Has your horse been receiving medical treatments with "bute" (phenylbutazone[G]) or other pain-killing NSAID[G] medications within the past month? Has he been treated with any antibiotics within the past 2 weeks?

 YES Call your veterinarian *NOW*—it could be inflammation and/or ulcers in your horse's intestinal tract due to NSAID[G] side effects, or an upset in the normal population of gut bacteria due to antibiotic use.

 NO

ACTION PLAN (CONTINUED):

Has your senior horse had one or more bouts of colic^G within the past 4 months? Has he been under increased stress within that same period of time?

 NO

 YES Call your veterinarian *TODAY*—it could be salmonellosis^G, an infectious and highly contagious intestinal disease. Go to **While You Wait, page 177.**

Is your senior horse on a purge-deworming^G program? Has it been 6 weeks or more since he was last dewormed? Has it been longer than 6 months since he's had a fecal exam to determine if his deworming program has avoided parasite resistance? Has he recently had access to a grassy field or corral where multiple other horses have been within the past 30 years, such as fairgrounds or corrals at roadside rest stops?

 YES It could be clinical cyathostomiasis^G. Call your veterinarian *TODAY* to discuss appropriate treatment, which could be handled by home treatment, depending on your horse's condition.

 NO

Does your senior horse's manure contain recognizable pieces of hay or grain, more so than what you see in the manure of neighboring horses?

 NO

 YES Call your veterinarian *TODAY*—it could mean your senior horse isn't chewing his feed properly, and the resultant larger particles are less well digested, irritating, and tend to move too fast through his colon, making it difficult for the colon to reabsorb normal amounts of water.

Has your horse lost weight over the last 6 months for no apparent reason?

 NO

 YES Call your veterinarian *TODAY*—it could be an underlying illness such as granulomatous enteritis^G, intestinal cancer, inflammatory bowel disease^G, or chronic poisoning (e.g., long-term exposure to lead). Or, it could mean your horse isn't getting enough nutrition from his feed due to changes in his teeth, his ability to digest feed, and/or his metabolism.

➤

ACTION PLAN (CONTINUED):

Has your horse's diarrhea^G been going on, consistently, for more than a week, with no normal manure passed during that period of time? Were there any changes in his diet or management around the time his diarrhea started? Has your horse been getting "stool softeners," bulk laxatives, or cathartic medications in his feed, such as DSS (dioctyl sodium sulfosuccinate), psyllium husks, or sloppy bran mashes? Is his feed formulated at a mill that also mixes feed for non-equine livestock?

 YES Call your veterinarian *TODAY*—it could be an underlying liver problem, poisoning, or feed contamination. Or, it could be sensitivity to or overdose of stool-softening, bulk laxative, or cathartic medications.

 NO

Is your horse fed on the ground? Is the soil in your region sandy?

 YES If you answered yes to either query, it could be grit, gravel, and/or sand ingestion, causing chronic bowel irritation. Go to "Nitty Gritty Sand Test," **page 177**, to test your senior horse's manure for sand and other gritty ingredients. Follow the action plan instructions at the end of the test if the results are positive. If there's no sand in your horse's manure, continue this **Action Plan**.

 NO

Is the diarrhea only occasional, interspersed with the passage of normal manure piles?

 YES It's probably a case of temporary, nervous, loose stool, usually associated with a high-strung personality, a high-stress environment or life style, and/or maladaptive behavior (e.g., the extremely herdbound horse that whinnies, paces, and passes loose stool when separated from herd mates). Work with your vet to make your senior's environment less anxiety-producing. Otherwise, no action is necessary unless the loose stool continues for more than an hour. (If it does, repeat the **Action Plan**.)

 NO

Call your veterinarian *TODAY* for a consultation.

WHILE YOU WAIT

1. *Isolate your horse from other horses in case it's contagious.* To prevent the spread of possible infectious disease, confine your horse to an open-air paddock or stall with a separate water supply, apart from other horses by at least 20 feet. Wash your hands and disinfect your boots (see page 41) after handling your horse and before handling other horses.

2. *Remove his feed.* To avoid worsening an already irritated intestinal tract, remove grain and hay from your horse's stall feeders. Remove bedding if he eats it. (It's not unusual for a horse with intestinal upset to eat straw or shavings.)

3. *Give him the opportunity to replenish some of his fluid/electrolyte deficits voluntarily.* Provide three 5-gallon buckets of fresh, room-temperature water prepared as follows:

- One plain bucket of water.
- One mixed with a commercial electrolyte product made specifically for horses (follow label directions).
- One with 1/3 of a 1-pound box of baking soda mixed in.

CAUTION

Your horse's diarrhea might be contagious to you. Take the following precautions:

1. Wear latex or rubber gloves when handling your horse and his bedding.
2. Wash your hands thoroughly with soap and hot water after handling your horse and/or any materials contaminated with manure (clothing, boots, gloves, stall bedding, etc.).
3. Keep your hands, gloves, and sleeves away from your face.
4. Isolate your horse from children less than 1 year of age, or from any adult with a compromised immune system.
5. Call your doctor if you or a family member shows any evidence of illness, even if it's not diarrhea.
6. Keep your pets locked up. Family members might be infected by contact with a pet that came into contact with infected manure.

Nitty Gritty Sand Test

Find out if your horse is at risk:

1. Into a clean 1-quart, clear glass pickle jar or its equivalent, put 1 cup of your horse's fresh manure balls.
2. With a garden hose, add clean water to fill the jar, and mix thoroughly to a brown slurry.
3. Set the jar on a flat surface and let the contents settle for 5 minutes.
4. Turn the water on again, to a small stream (about the diameter of a #2 pencil lead). Let it run gently into the jar so it overflows, taking the lighter material with it without disturbing any heavier material that might have settled to the bottom.
5. Let the water run until most of the lighter, fibrous material has spilled out.
6. Let the jar stand another 5 minutes.
7. Now look for sand in what's settled to the bottom.

How much sand is significant? The rule of thumb is, 1/4 teaspoon sand per cup of manure means he's eating a dangerous amount and is at risk for sand colic[G]. If your horse's manure contains that amount or more, call your vet.

Abnormal Color Manure

SENIOR SIGNPOST: Your horse's manure is a different color than usual, and different than that of other horses eating a similar diet.

What this might mean: There's been a change in what he's eating, or in the way his body processes his usual diet. There may be a problem in one or more of his digestive organs, which has altered the enzymes and pigments that normally color the manure. Or, there may be blood leaking somewhere within the digestive tract.

ACTION PLAN:

Is your horse's manure a beige or pale gray color? **YES** Call your veterinarian *NOW*—it could be a problem in your horse's pancreas and/or liver.

 NO

Is his manure dark red, or tarry black? **YES** Call your veterinarian *NOW*—there's likely a bleeding lesion in your horse's digestive tract.

 NO

Call your veterinarian *TODAY* and describe the changes you see in your senior horse's manure.

BLOOD SIGNS

Bright red blood in or on your senior horse's manure means there's a bleeding lesion somewhere in the lower part of his intestine or rectum. If the blood is coming from the stomach and/or upper intestinal tract, it'll get digested along with his regular feed, which will change it from red and fluid, to black and tarry. In many cases, however, upper gastrointestinal (GI) bleeding in a horse doesn't show up in his manure, at least not to the naked eye, because the amount of blood is too small relative to the volume of ingesta (material). For a somewhat more reliable indicator of GI bleeding, try a human occult blood test, which you can buy at most pharmacies without a prescription. It's not perfect, but it may reveal blood in otherwise normal looking manure. A positive test result will help steer your veterinarian in his or her diagnostic efforts. A negative result, however, doesn't necessarily rule out a small, bleeding lesion.

Pasty Manure

SENIOR SIGNPOST: The consistency of your senior horse's manure is more like peanut butter than the usual individual "muffins."

What this might mean: That he's not getting enough fiber in his diet, or the fiber he does get isn't being broken down properly.

ACTION PLAN:

Is your senior horse spending more time than usual standing with his tail elevated, passing little or no manure? Are there smears of manure on his buttocks or tail? Is the amount of manure in his enclosure less than he usually passes in a day?

 NO

 YES Call your veterinarian *NOW* if you answered yes to any query—pasty-consistency manure like this (which can result when your senior horse avoids high-fiber foods, for example, if his teeth are bothering him), is likely to become impacted in his intestines and rectum, leading to constipation and colic^G if proper treatment isn't given promptly.

Is the color of your senior horse's manure different than usual, such as unusually pale or gray, or dark red or black?

 NO

 YES Call your veterinarian *NOW*—your senior horse could have a liver problem, or a bleeding disorder within his gut. For more information, see "Abnormal Color Manure," **page 178**.

Does your senior horse's ration include at least 1% of his body weight in roughage (fiber)? Does he leave some of the fiber in favor of soft leaves and grain, possibly due to dental pain?

 NO

 YES If you answered yes to both queries, call your veterinarian today for a general examination and a dental checkup, to help determine why your horse's manure is pasty.

Call your veterinarian for an appointment—your senior horse isn't getting enough insoluble fiber to maintain normal gut function. (Some senior complete feeds lack adequate fiber.) Your vet can help you choose a well-formulated ration and check your horse's mouth. For more information, go to "Stay-Young Diet Solutions," **page 376**, and "Top Priority—Tooth Care," **page 332**.

NOTES

CHAPTER 13

Changes in
URINE/
URINATION

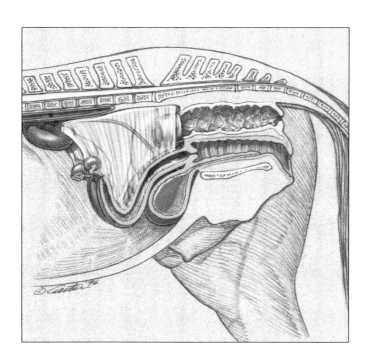

Excessive or Frequent Urination

SENIOR SIGNPOST: Your senior horse's stall is wetter (and smellier) than usual from urine, even though you clean it regularly. Or, you see him assume the urinating position more often than usual. You may also have noticed that your horse is drinking more water than he normally does.

What this might mean: It could be an underlying general health problem. If he's urinating more often, but not necessarily producing more urine, it could mean there's an infection or obstruction in his urinary tract.

ACTION PLAN:

Does your senior horse have a fever? (See "Senior Vital Signs," **page 292**.)

 NO

 YES Call your veterinarian *NOW*—your senior horse likely has an infectious disease that may involve his kidneys or other vital organs. Go to **While You Wait**, opposite page.

Does your senior horse have a shaggy, dull coat that's overdue to shed? Is he eating less? Has he lost weight? Does he seem to sweat excessively? Does he seem stiff, sore, or reluctant to move, especially over rocky, hard, or uneven footing? Are his lower legs puffy or swollen? Is there any swelling under his belly?

 NO

YES Call your veterinarian *NOW* if you answered yes to any query. It could be a problem developing in your horse's metabolism, such as Equine Cushing's Disease[G] (ECD; also known as pituitary adenoma), which can put him at risk of laminitis[G]. See "The Age Event: Laminitis (Founder)," **page 273**. Or, it could be a kidney problem.

Have you noticed your senior horse drinking more water than usual?

 NO

 YES Call your veterinarian *TODAY*—it could be a serious underlying health problem such as Equine Cushing's Disease[G]. For more information about excessive water drinking, go to "Increased Water Intake," **page 72**.

ACTION PLAN (CONTINUED):

Is your senior horse assuming the urinating position more frequently? Does the amount of urine he passes at each session seem smaller than usual? Have you seen him turn and look at his flank more than once in the past couple of weeks? Does he seem especially touchy in the flank area? If your horse is a mare, is there dried blood in the hairs of her tail?

 NO

 YES Call your veterinarian *TODAY* if you answered yes to any query. Your senior horse could have an infection or growth in the bladder or urinary tract, and/or he could have a urolith^G (kidney stone) that's on the move.

Is your senior horse stall-bound, with little or no activity in his life? Has he been wood-chewing, or working excessively at his salt block?

 NO

 YES Call your veterinarian *TODAY* if you answered yes to either query. He could have a condition called medullary washout^G or psychogenic polyuria/polydipsia^G.

If your senior horse is a male, has it been longer than a year since you've cleaned his sheath and the tip of his penis?

 NO

 YES There could be a growth, lesion, or bean^G (a.k.a. smegmolith) obstructing normal urine flow. For information about sheath cleaning, go to "Down & Dirty Maintenance...," **page 360**.

Call your veterinarian for an appointment.

WHILE YOU WAIT

Isolate your horse from other horses in case it's contagious. To prevent the spread of possible infectious disease, confine your horse to an open-air paddock or stall with a separate water supply, apart from other horses by at least 20 feet. Wash your hands and disinfect your boots (see page 41) after handling your horse and before handling other horses.

Abnormal Urine Color

SENIOR SIGNPOST: When your senior horse urinates, the color looks different.

What it could mean: It might not be a significant finding at all. Or, it can indicate a serious underlying problem.

ACTION PLAN:

Does the urine appear brown or pink? **YES** ▶ Call your veterinarian *NOW*—there could be a serious underlying problem, such as poisoning from eating red maple leaves^G or onions^G (domestic or wild), hemolysis^G from internal bleeding somewhere in your horse's body, a urinary tract infection, or myoglobinuria^G from muscle breakdown, injury, or myositis^G (tying-up).

NO ▼

Is the urine a darker yellow than usual? Is your senior horse's capillary refill time longer than 2 seconds (see "Senior Vital Signs," **page 292**)? Do his manure balls seem smaller, drier, and/or harder than usual, and separated into individual balls instead of pressed together? Does he fail the skin pinch test (see "Senior Vital Signs," **page 292**)? Are the whites of his eyes yellow-tinged? **YES** ▶ Call your veterinarian *NOW* if you answered yes to any query—your senior horse could be dehydrated, which suggests a serious underlying health problem and leaves him at increased risk for impaction colic^G. He may also have a liver problem.

NO ▼

Is your senior horse's urine paler yellow than usual, more like clear or only slightly yellow-tinged water? Have you noticed him drinking more water than usual? Have you noticed that his stall is more urine-soaked than usual, and/or have you seen him urinating larger volumes of urine? **YES** ▶ Call your veterinarian *TODAY* if you answered yes to any query—it could be an underlying kidney problem, or a metabolic problem such as Equine Cushing's Disease^G or diabetes^G.

NO ▼

ACTION PLAN (CONTINUED):

Do you see what looks like red blood in the urine? **YES** Call your veterinarian *TODAY*. It could be an infection or growth in the bladder or urinary tract. Or, if your senior horse is a mare, she could have developed vaginal varicose veins^G (also called vaginal varicosities), which occasionally bleed alarming amounts of blood, usually towards the end of a urination.

 NO

Is the urine creamy-looking? **YES** If you see no other abnormalities —e.g., no discomfort, no behavior change, no change in urinary habits, no blood, etc.—occasional creamy-looking urine may be normal, due to changes in the amount of protein added to the urine on its way out of the kidneys. Continue this **Action Plan**.

NO

Have you seen urine spots in the snow that are bright orange or rust in color? **YES** If you see no other "abnormalities" in your senior horse, it's likely to be normal. Pigments called porphyrins^G, naturally present in urine, may turn orange when exposed to air. Although this happens in all seasons, it's most visible when urine is deposited on white snow.

NO

Call your veterinarian for an appointment.

Abnormal Urine Stream

SENIOR SIGNPOST: When your senior horse urinates, it comes out in an abnormal-looking stream.

What this might mean: It might not be significant, or it could indicate a serious underlying problem.

ACTION PLAN:

Is the urine stream scanty, or only trickling?

 NO

YES ➤ Call your veterinarian *NOW*—there could be an obstruction blocking your senior horse's urinary tract, which can cause kidney damage from back-pressure.

Is the urine stream split or diverted (e.g., spraying off to one side)?

 NO

YES ➤ Call your veterinarian *TODAY*—there could be a partial obstruction (such as from a urolith^G, growth, scar tissue, lesion, or a bean^G in a stallion/gelding, in or near the urinary tract) interfering with normal flow. Kidney damage could result if the obstruction moves or enlarges.

Does the urine come out in a gush, or a more powerful stream than you remember?

 NO

YES ➤ Call your veterinarian *TODAY*—your senior horse's urine volume may be increased due to an underlying problem.

Call your veterinarian for an appointment.

CHAPTER 14

14

Changes in

PERFORMANCE/ ATTITUDE

at Work, Play, or Rest

Exercise Intolerance, Shortness of Breath

SENIOR SIGNPOST: Your senior horse tires more easily than usual. He may breathe more heavily than usual, with nostril flare and obvious chest movement after mild exercise; it may take longer for him to recover. You may see evidence of labored breathing—chest movement and nostril flare—even when he's at rest.

What this could mean: A heart problem, generalized weakness due to an underlying health disorder, and/or a problem in his lungs.

ACTION PLAN:

Did your senior horse's shortness of breath come on suddenly?

 YES Call your veterinarian *NOW*—it could be the beginnings of a severe allergic reaction, poisoning, a severe injury such as a pneumothoraxG or ruptured diaphragmG (e.g., from a kick, collision, or fall), or a cardiac arrhythmiaG. While you wait, see "Labored Breathing," **page 63**.

 NO

Does your senior horse have a fever? (Go to "Senior Vital Signs," **page 292**.) Is he acting dull, depressed, or detached from his surroundings? Is he off his feed?

 YES Call your veterinarian *NOW* if you answered yes to any query—there could be an underlying systemic disease, including (but not limited to) pneumoniaG, upper respiratory disease, or anhidrosisG. Go to **While You Wait #1** and **#2**, opposite page.

 NO

Do your senior horse's gums appear abnormally pale, or slightly blue-tinged? Does he seem generally weak?

YES Call your veterinarian *NOW* if you answered yes to either query—it could be a cardiovascular problem or an underlying health problem causing severe anemiaG.

 NO

ACTION PLAN (CONTINUED):

Does he make snoring-like noises when he breathes? **YES** Call your veterinarian *TODAY*—your senior horse could have a growth, cyst^G, hematoma^G, irritation or damage to nerves of the head, laryngeal paralysis^G, or an abscess^G, any of which can block airflow through his nasal passages. While you wait, see "Noisy Breathing," **page 66**.

NO

Does he have a cough? Does he have a constant or occasional thick nasal discharge? Has he recently had a "cold?" Does he drop wads of chewed feed on the ground, or slobber? **YES** Call your veterinarian *TODAY* if you answered yes to any query—it could be heaves^G (a.k.a. chronic obstructive pulmonary disease, or COPD), a guttural pouch infection^G, laryngeal paralysis^G, or airway hyperresponsiveness^G. Go to **While You Wait #2**, below. For more on heaves, see "The Age Event: Heaves," **page 267**. While you wait, see coughing, **page 60**.

NO

Is your horse's coat dry, even when you work him in warm weather, and while horses around him are sweating normally? **YES** Call your veterinarian *TODAY*—it could be anhidrosis^G, meaning a failure to sweat. While you wait, keep your horse in a cool, shaded area, hosing him off as necessary to help prevent overheating.

NO

Call your veterinarian for an appointment.

WHILE YOU WAIT #1

Isolate your horse from other horses in case it's contagious. To prevent the spread of possible infectious disease, confine your horse to an open-air paddock or stall with a separate water supply, apart from other horses by at least 20 feet. Wash your hands and disinfect your boots (see page 41) after handling your horse and before handling other horses.

WHILE YOU WAIT #2

1. *Provide fresh water, plain salt, shelter from the weather (including the hot sun, if applicable), and good ventilation.* Protect him from drafts, dust, and stress. If he's hungry, offer him a fresh, clean flake of his usual hay that you've just dunked in clean water, so it's absolutely dust free.

2. *Cool him.* If he's panting, failing to sweat despite high heat/humidity, and the hair over his rump area is standing up (a common sign of anhidrosis^G), grab a bucket of cool water and a sponge, or a garden hose, and wet him down, then stand him in a light breeze or the airflow from an electric fan. (If you don't have access to water, swab his poll, shoulders, rump, and neck with a cloth soaked in isopropyl alcohol.)

Inactivity

SENIOR SIGNPOST: Your horse seems detached, disinterested, and uninvolved compared to his normal behavior. (See "Baseline Senior Behavior," page 289.) Instead of grazing, for example, he nibbles occasionally but mostly stands idle, hanging his head. Instead of playing with herd mates, he shoos them away. Instead of running with the herd when the dinner bell rings, he brings up the rear at a disinterested walk.

What this might mean: It could mean he's in pain, or that he's got a condition that's robbed him of energy and/or appetite. Or, it could mean a problem in his sensory perception has turned his familiar surroundings into a threatening place.

ACTION PLAN:

Does your senior horse have a fever? (See "Senior Vital Signs," **page 292**.) Has he failed to break a sweat while the others around him are sweating freely?

 YES → Call your veterinarian *NOW* if you answered yes to either query—your senior horse could have an infectious systemic disease, or anhidrosis^G. Go to **While You Wait #1**, opposite page.

 NO

Is he reluctant to move, even when you halter him and ask him to? Is he dull, lethargic, and lacking appetite?

 YES → Call your veterinarian *NOW*—your horse might be in pain, as from colic^G or a severe lameness such as laminitis^G, or he could be feeling off-balance due to a neurologic problem such as Equine Protozoal Myeloencephalitis^G. While you wait, go to "Colic," **pages 221** and **251**, and "The Age Event: Laminitis (Founder)," **page 273**.

 NO

Does your senior horse stand in the "parked out" position—forelimbs farther forward than usual? Does he rock his weight back onto his hind limbs when shifting or moving?

 YES → Call your veterinarian *NOW* if you answered yes to either query—he could be developing a severe lameness, such as laminitis^G, or he could have pain in his back, neck muscles, rump muscles, or the belly muscles that support the weight of his torso, from injury or due to myositis^G (a.k.a. tying-up syndrome). (For more information, see "Senior Back Check," **page 314**.) Go to **While You Wait #2**, page 192.

 NO

ACTION PLAN (CONTINUED):

Does your senior horse frequently stand as though posturing to urinate, raise his or her tail, and (if he's a male) drop his penis, without actually passing much (or any) urine?

 YES

Call your veterinarian *TODAY*—your horse could have a bladder or urinary-tract problem such as infection, a growth, or a urolith^G on the move. Or (if your horse is a male), a bean^G (also known as a smegmolith) might be obstructing normal urine flow.

 NO

Is his breathing labored, even after mild exertion? Are his nostrils flared most of the time, even when he's been standing idly? Are his gums a pale pink or near-white color? Are there mosquitoes and/or biting flies in your area at any time during the year?

 YES

Call your veterinarian TODAY if you answered yes to any two of these queries—your horse may be anemic and/or suffering from a heart problem or other serious illness. While you wait, see "Labored Breathing," **page 63**.

 NO

Does your horse blink or flinch when you bring your hand rapidly towards the side of his face?

 NO

Go to "Vision Problems," **page 112**—he may have suffered a loss of vision, and he's withdrawn from his usual activities because he doesn't feel secure.

 YES

Call your veterinarian for an appointment.

WHILE YOU WAIT #1

1. *Isolate your horse from other horses in case it's contagious.* To prevent the spread of possible infectious disease, confine your horse to an open-air paddock or stall with a separate water supply, apart from other horses by at least 20 feet. Wash your hands and disinfect your boots (see page 41) after handling your horse and before handling other horses.

2. *Cool him.* If your senior horse is panting, failing to sweat despite high heat/humidity, and if the hair over his rump area is standing up (common signs of anhidrosis), grab a bucket of cool water and a sponge, or a garden hose and wet him down. Then stand him in a light breeze or in front of a fan. (If you don't have access to water, swab his poll, shoulders, rump, and neck with a cloth soaked in isopropyl alcohol.)

➤

WHILE YOU WAIT #2

1. *Keep your horse still.* Further movement could worsen whatever's causing his lameness. Get him out of harm's way as best you can, then confine him. Provide a companion, if necessary, to discourage fretful movement.

2. *Ice the leg.* If you can easily determine where the pain is, chill the area to limit pain and swelling. Select an ice pack large enough to overlap the injured area by at least 2 inches all around its margins. Slip it between layers of a clean cloth, center it over the injury, and hold it manually or secure with a wrap. Ice on: 5 minutes. Ice off: 15 minutes. Repeat this cycle 3 more times or until your vet arrives, whichever happens first.

3. *Apply a support wrap.* Again, if you're reasonably sure where the problem is, apply a support wrap appropriate to the area being bandaged, adding an extra layer of padding and being especially careful to apply the elastic layer evenly and firmly enough to prevent slippage.

4. *Avoid feeding him.* Give no feed—only water—until your vet arrives and can confirm or dismiss laminitis[G] as a cause of the lameness, and/or determine that immediate surgery won't be necessary.

Lowered Social Status

SENIOR SIGNPOST: Herd members that used to be beneath your horse in the social hierarchy are showing signs of disrespect: They may squeeze him out at the feeder, or fail to step aside to let him pass. They may even pin their ears, bare their teeth, bite, or kick at him.

What this might mean: Loss of social status can be a normal sign of aging, but it can also indicate a specific health problem that's left your senior citizen less able to assert himself.

ACTION PLAN:

Does your senior horse have a fever? (See "Senior Vital Signs," **page 292**.)

 YES Call your veterinarian *NOW*—your horse likely has an infectious disease that's causing lethargy and making him vulnerable to social challenge. Go to **While You Wait #1**, next page.

Is he listless and detached from his surroundings? Does he fail to respond, or respond in a lackluster manner, when approached by you or another horse?

 YES Call your veterinarian *NOW*—it could be a problem in your senior horse's mental state, interfering with normal stimulus-response patterns. This can be a condition that directly affects his brain function, such as an encephalomyelopathy^G, or an illness or injury that causes depression or mental dulling as a symptom. See **While You Wait #2**, next page.

Does your senior horse breathe heavily even with mild exertion, cough a lot, and take longer than usual to recover from exercise? Does he lack energy? Are his nostrils flared most of the time, even when he's idle? Does he have a worried expression?

YES Call your veterinarian *TODAY* if you answered yes to any query—your horse may have an underlying health problem such as heaves^G, anemia^G, or a heart problem. See **While You Wait #2**, and "Labored Breathing," **page 63**.

ACTION PLAN (CONTINUED):

Does your senior horse seem jumpier than usual, more apt to spook or startle when approached? Does he fail to move away from or chase away horses that would normally cause such a response, seeming to be oblivious to their presence?

 NO

 YES If you answered yes to any query, your horse may have suffered a hearing loss or have vision problems, making him a target for social conflict. Go to "Senior Hearing Check" and "Senior Vision Check," **pages 310** and **306**, respectively, and give your horse the "Quick Vision Test" and "Quick Hearing Test." Then, continue this **Action Plan**.

Has your horse lost weight (see "Senior Condition Check," **page 300**)? At feed time, does he stand back, seeming to await permission to eat?

 NO

 YES Your horse's lowered social status is directly affecting his condition. If you answered yes to either query, go to "The Age Event: Loss of Social Status," **page 279**, for information on how—and why—to change his management.

Have there been any new additions to the herd, or have any horses left? Have there been any changes to the feeding configuration?

 NO

 YES See "The Age Event: Loss of Social Status," **page 279**—your horse could be getting short shrift in the herd's shuffle to re-establish who's above whom.

Call your veterinarian for an appointment. If you administered the Quick Vision and/or Hearing Tests, be sure to share your results with him/her.

WHILE YOU WAIT #1

Isolate your horse from other horses in case it's contagious. To prevent the spread of possible infectious disease, confine your horse to an open-air paddock or stall with a separate water supply, apart from other horses by at least 20 feet. Wash your hands and disinfect your boots (see page 41) after handling your horse and before handling other horses.

WHILE YOU WAIT #2

Remove your horse from a herd situation to avoid conflict-related injury. Provide access to fresh water, plain salt, and forage.

Cold-Weather Intolerance

SENIOR SIGNPOST: Your senior horse used to do fine in cold weather. Now, when the mercury plummets he just stands and shivers.

What this might mean: It could mean he needs more heat-generating feed; he's lost too much weight, leaving his natural layer of insulation (body fat) too thin to keep him warm; there's a problem affecting his internal "thermostat," such as a thyroid disorder or a pituitary condition; or, it could mean he's chilled because of an underlying health problem.

ACTION PLAN:

Does your horse have a body condition score below 4? (See "Senior Condition Check," **page 300**.)

 Go to "Weight Loss," **page 14** and "Muscle Loss," **page 17**. Continue this **Action Plan.**

Does he clean up his feed? Does his diet include less than 2% of his body weight per day in roughage? (For a 1,100-pound horse, that'd be 22 pounds of high-fiber hay.)

 If you answered yes to either query, or you aren't sure how much roughage he gets per day, it's likely he needs more heat-generating fiber in his diet. Weigh the hay he gets per day, and estimate how much of it he actually eats. If it's less than 2% of his body weight, adjust his diet as necessary to meet or exceed that 2% amount, and see "Stay-Young Diet Solutions," **page 376**, for more information. Then, continue this **Action Plan**.

Is your horse's coat dull, shaggy, over-long, or overdue to shed? Does he seem to lack energy? Are his lower legs frequently puffy or swollen looking? Does he have a history of Tying-Up Syndrome[G]?

 Call your veterinarian *TODAY* if you answered yes to any query. It could be a thyroid disorder[G] or Equine Cushing's Disease[G] (ECD, also known as pituitary adenoma).

➤

ACTION PLAN (CONTINUED):

Is your horse's coat thin, but otherwise shiny and healthy? Is he housed in an area where there's no shelter from wind and rain, or not enough shelter for every horse to have a safe and secure place to rest without being hassled?

 YES

If you answered yes to either query, it could be a management problem (needs shelter, needs blankets). Work with your veterinarian to update your management practices so your senior horse's stay-warm needs are met.

 NO

Call your veterinarian for an appointment.

Be Weather Wise

Have you noticed how elderly people bundle up in sweaters while the younger folks around them are in shirt sleeves? Or, how senior citizens may fan themselves while you think the temperature is just right? This difference in temperature regulation has been attributed to a number of factors, including a slowing metabolism and changes in aging skin that make an aged individual more sensitive to heat and cold. Older horses may suffer the same sensitivities. Take the following steps to be sure hot and cold extremes don't stress your senior citizen:

■ **Provide adequate shelter.** Be sure your senior horse has a draft-free shelter to keep him out of wind, cold, and precipitation in winter weather, and to provide shade in the summer. If he's showing signs of a loss of social status (see pages 193 and 279), house him with herd mates that are willing to share shelter space. (Otherwise, the shelter does your oldster no good.)

■ **Blanket him, if necessary.** If you notice that your horse is shivering despite the shelter, blanket him accordingly. A variety of weatherproof materials in various weights are available that will help block wind and precipitation during turnout, while reducing the risk of overheating. (If you stall your senior horse, he may need help during extreme cold. Blanket him accordingly.) Be sure to check your senior horse's clothing at least once a day, to be sure it's securely in place, and that he's not heating up.

■ **Watch him carefully during hot and/or humid days.** If your horse is panting, and/or has ceased to sweat, hose or sponge him off and move him to a shaded, breezy area (or in front of a fan). If you can, keep him inside during the day (with a fan on him, if necessary), and turn him out at night, when temperatures are cooler and sun isn't an issue. Consult your vet.

■ **Feed him right.** Malnutrition is a prime cause of lower body temperatures in an aged horse, due to lack of energy intake. See "Stay-Young Diet Solutions," page 376. Be sure he's getting enough heat-generating fiber during cold-weather months. Work with your veterinarian to craft a ration that provides 2% of your horse's body weight per day in high-quality roughage. If your senior has problems chewing roughage, a number of options exist, including extruded complete feeds (roughage in kibble form, such as Wendlands One 'n Only), and chopped and pelleted hay.

Easily Winded

SENIOR SIGNPOST: Your senior horse seems to run out of air more easily than usual, breathing heavily, flaring his nostrils, and taking longer than usual to recover after getting winded.

What this might mean: A problem in his respiratory tract or lungs; a cardiovascular problem; or an underlying illness.

ACTION PLAN:

Does your senior horse have a fever? (See "Senior Vital Signs," **page 292**.)

 YES Call your veterinarian *NOW*—there's likely to be an infectious disease involving the respiratory tract, leaving your senior horse at risk for complications, including dehydration. Or, it could be anhidrosis^G. Go to **While You Wait**, next page.

 NO

Are his gums very pale, or blue-tinged?

 YES Call your veterinarian *NOW*—it could be severe anemia^G, and/or a cardiovascular problem, either of which can leave your horse oxygen-starved.

 NO

Does your senior horse breathe heavily all the time, even when not exerting himself?

 YES Call your veterinarian *TODAY*—this isn't a case of being winded, it's persistent heavy breathing, which can suggest different, or more advanced, underlying problems. For more information, go to "Labored Breathing," **page 63**.

 NO

➤

ACTION PLAN (CONTINUED):

Is your senior horse's coat bone dry while his neighbors are sweating? Is the hair over his rump standing up, resembling velvet?

 YES

Call your veterinarian *TODAY* if you answered yes to either query—it could be early Equine Cushing's DiseaseG (ECD, also known as pituitary adenoma), or a mild to moderate case of anhidrosisG (a more severe case would be accompanied by elevated body temperature). If the weather is hot and/or humid, hose off your horse, and keep him in a shaded area until the veterinarian arrives, to help avoid the possibility of overheating. For more information about Cushing's disease, go to "The Age Event: Cushing's Disease," **page 257**.

NO

Call your veterinarian *TODAY*—it could be an early case of heavesG, or congestive heart failureG.

WHILE YOU WAIT

Isolate your horse from other horses in case it's contagious. To prevent the spread of possible infectious disease, confine your horse to an open-air paddock or stall with a separate water supply, apart from other horses by at least 20 feet. Wash your hands and disinfect your boots (see page 41) after handling your horse and before handling other horses.

Resistance to Saddling or Mounting

SENIOR SIGNPOST: Your senior horse seems to tense up when a saddle is placed on his back, when the girth is tightened, and/or when you mount.

What this might mean: He's in pain.

ACTION PLAN:

Does your senior horse have a fever? (See "Senior Vital Signs," **page 292**.) Does he act dull, depressed, or detached from his surroundings? Is he off his feed?

 NO

 YES Call your veterinarian *NOW* if you answered yes to any query—it could be general myositis^G, an infectious disease, a kidney infection (pyelonephritis^G), or osteomyelitis^G (bone infection) in or near the spine. Go to **While You Wait**, next page.

Do you feel a squishy or a snap-crackle-pop sensation, like lightweight "bubble wrap" under your senior horse's skin when you run your fingers over his spine? Has he taken a fall, or flipped over backward, within the past couple of weeks?

 NO

 YES Call your veterinarian *NOW* if you answered yes to either query—it could be injury to the dorsal spinous process^G(es) of the vertebrae in the chest portion of your horse's spine. Go to **While You Wait,** next page.

If your senior mare is pregnant, is her belly larger than expected? Is her lower belly wall swollen with edema^G, and/or tender?

 NO

 YES If you answered yes to either query, go to "Abnormally Large Pregnant Belly," **page 215**.

Has your senior horse ever had myositis^G (tying-up syndrome)? Do the muscles of his rump, shoulders, neck, and/or back feel hard or overly tense? Is he reluctant to move? Does he flinch, tighten his torso, and/or hunch up or sink his back when you apply pressure to the muscles along-side his neck, or along his spine? (For how to check your horse's back for pain, see "Senior Back Check," **page 314**.)

 NO

 YES Call your veterinarian *NOW* if you answered yes to any query—it could be myositis^G, or it could be injury and soreness in your senior horse's back muscles.

➤

199

ACTION PLAN (CONTINUED):

Has your senior horse had an injection in his neck muscles within a week before these symptoms appeared? Does the injection site look swollen and/or feel abnormally warm? **YES** It could be a local inflammatory reaction at the site, causing stiffness and pain in the neck, making your senior horse reluctant to move. Apply **Home Treatment**, below.

 NO

It could be back pain. Go to "Senior Back Check," **page 314**, and call your veterinarian for an appointment.

WHILE YOU WAIT

Isolate your senior horse in an open-air paddock or stall with a separate water supply, apart from other horses by at least 20 feet. Wash your hands and disinfect your boots (see page 41) after handling him and before handling other horses. Offer him his usual feed for this time of day, plus salt, and plenty of fresh water.

HOME TREATMENT:

Because you already indicated in your answers to the **Action Plan** queries that your senior horse isn't feverish or off his feed, you've helped rule out the possibility that an infection at the injection site has spread and become a dangerous, body-wide problem. Check his rectal temperature twice daily, and keep a close eye on his appetite while you're treating his inflamed shot site—and call your veterinarian NOW if change occurs in either.

Step 1: *Ice the area.* Select an ice pack large enough to extend at least 2 inches beyond the swollen area's margins. Slip it between layers of a clean cloth, center it over the area, and hold it there for 5 minutes. Repeat every 15 minutes for a total of 6 treatments.

Step 2: *Massage; light exercise.* Massage the area gently with your fingertips, rubbing in the direction of the muscle fibers. Hand-walk your horse to increase circulation.

Step 3: *Re-evaluate often.* At least every 4 hours, reassess your horse's condition: Has the swelling increased in size, heat, or tenderness? Is he becoming generally ill—losing his appetite, becoming depressed, spiking a fever? If you observe any of these signs, call your veterinarian NOW.

Spooking More Than Usual

SENIOR SIGNPOST: Your senior horse seems more easily startled than usual, spooking at things, places, and individuals he's usually comfortable around. He may be worse in low light, such as at dusk or after dark.

What this might mean: He could be vision impaired. Another potential culprit is hearing loss, or a combination of the two. A third possibility is a change in mental state, altering his ability to differentiate friendly, nonthreatening things from potential danger.

ACTION PLAN:

Is your senior horse showing aggressive and/or defensive behaviors when startled, such as kicking, bolting, or biting? Does he have any unexplained wounds? Has he recently suffered a blow to the head?

 Call your veterinarian *NOW* if you answered yes to any query—it could be a neurological disorder. See "Caution," **next page**.

Is he holding one or both ears tilted or splayed out? Is he tilting his head? Does he seem unresponsive to sounds he usually responds to?

 If you answered yes to any of these queries, your senior horse could have a significant hearing impairment. Go to "Quick Hearing Test," **page 124**. Then continue this **Action Plan**.

Is your senior horse stepping on or tripping over things he'd normally avoid? Does he move haltingly, rather than confidently, through closed-in areas or obstacles?

 If you answered yes to either of these queries, it could be a vision problem. Go to "Quick Vision Test," **page 113**. (*Tip:* If your senior horse shows these symptoms more often in low-light conditions, test him under those same conditions.) Then continue this **Action Plan**.

Call your veterinarian for an appointment. Go to "Handle With Care," **next page**.

➤

CAUTION

Among the possible causes of drooling, an inability to swallow, mental changes, and/or gait abnormalities is a rare but notorious one: Rabies. If rabies is a consideration in your horse's case, don't take chances—take precautions.

1. Don't handle your horse unless it's absolutely necessary.

2. If you must handle him, wash your hands thoroughly, then don intact waterproof gloves (such as exam gloves or household rubber gloves) and protect all other body parts from contact with his saliva.

3. Be alert for unexpected behavior (rabies can cause aggression and/or lack of coordination), and stay out of harm's way.

Handle with Care

Take care when approaching or working around any horse, especially a senior one who's been spooking more than usual. Vision or hearing loss can exacerbate a horse's instinctive fight-or-flight response, putting you at risk for injury. As you approach, speak to him and move quietly into his field of vision—but out of kicking or striking distance—until he turns an eye or an ear toward you, signaling that he's aware of your presence. And, make sure you have a handy escape route whenever you work near your senior. Finally, avoid kneeling next to him. Instead, squat or stand, so you can quickly move out of the way, if necessary.

CHAPTER 15

Changes in
REPRODUCTIVE
PERFORMANCE

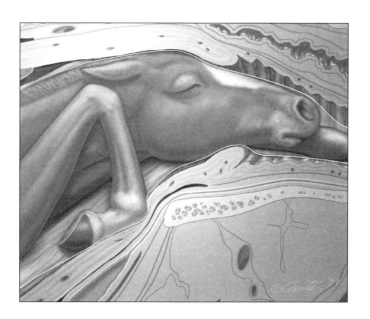

Abnormal "Heat" Behavior

 **SENIOR SIGNPOST:** Your senior mare's estrus behavior has changed. Perhaps she's become a "silent heat" mare. Or, she's in heat more often than she should be. Perhaps she acts like she's in heat, but changes her mind when the stallion gets close.

What this might mean: There could be an underlying health problem, or she might have reached the equine equivalent of menopause.

ACTION PLAN:

Is your senior mare lame or tender-footed? **YES** Call your veterinarian *NOW*—she could have laminitis^G, which along with abnormal heat behavior can be a symptom of hormonal imbalance caused by such conditions as Equine Cushing's Disease^G (ECD; also known as pituitary adenoma) or a thyroid disorder^G. Go to **While You Wait #1**, opposite page.

NO

Does your senior mare have a dull, shaggy coat that appears overdue to shed? Does she sweat excessively? Has she lost weight? **YES** Call your veterinarian *TODAY* if you answered yes to any query—your senior mare may have a hormone imbalance caused by one of the above conditions. Go to **While You Wait #1**.

NO

Does your senior mare act like she's in heat more often than usual? Is her IOI (interovulatory interval^G) shorter than 19 days? (See "Tell-Tale IOI" **at right**.) Does she behave as though she's in heat, then fight the stallion or act afraid when he approaches? Does she have any external evidence of vaginal discharge? (Be sure to check her tail for dried discharge.) **YES** Call your veterinarian *TODAY* if you answered yes to any query—your senior mare could have a uterine infection.

NO

ACTION PLAN (CONTINUED):

Does your senior mare behave stallion-like (arching her neck, prancing, vocalizing, or mounting another horse)? Is she more aggressive in general, with humans as well as horses? Has she lost weight in the last few months?

 YES Call your veterinarian *TODAY* if you answered yes to any query—your senior mare may have a hormone imbalance due to a GCT (granulosa cell tumor[G]) on one of her ovaries. Go to **While You Wait #2**, below.

 NO

Has your senior mare failed to come into heat?

 YES Call your veterinarian for an appointment. A previous heat (estrus) cycle may have produced an anovulatory follicle[G], which has interfered with normal cycling. Often, a simple treatment resolves the problem.

 NO

Call your veterinarian for an appointment.

WHILE YOU WAIT #1

1. *Confine your mare to a small paddock or stall with soft footing.*

2. *Offer fresh water and plain salt*, placing them near enough that she doesn't have to take more than 1 step to reach them.

3. *Keep her cool.* If she's sweaty, clip her coat and sponge water on her, to help prevent overheating.

4. *Remove feed.* Do not offer any grain or sweet feed, which could exacerbate her problem. Instead, offer her usual forage (dried hay or hay cubes).

WHILE YOU WAIT #2

Handle your mare with care. Ovarian tumors often cause serious behavior problems because of the high levels of male hormone they secrete. This can turn your mare into an aggressive "stallion." She could hurt you.

TELL-TALE IOI

Keeping track of your mare's heat cycles can help you keep tabs on her reproductive health. During breeding season, a healthy mare's estrous cycle consists of two phases: estrus (heat), which lasts 7 days on average; and diestrus (out of heat), which lasts 14 days on average. Total those for an overall interovulatory interval (IOI; the number of days from ovulation to ovulation) of 21 days.

When uterine inflammation is present, diestrus will be shortened by at least 2 days, for an IOI of 19 days or less. That means if your mare begins coming into heat more quickly than normal, she could have a uterine infection. Call your veterinarian.

Senior Mare: Keeps Having Miscarriages

SENIOR SIGNPOST: You have no difficulty getting your senior mare pregnant, but she keeps losing the pregnancy.

What this might mean: A physical problem in the uterus, cervix, vagina, or vulva, or a hormonal problem.

ACTION PLAN:

Does your senior mare have irregular, unreliable heat cycles? **Note:** In order to answer this query accurately, you need detailed teasing records, preferably confirmed with veterinary reproductive examinations including rectal palpation and/or ultrasound. If your information is not reliable in this area, continue with this **Action Plan** as best you can, then contact your veterinarian for help in assessing your mare's cycles.

YES ▶ Call your veterinarian *THIS WEEK*—your senior mare could have an underlying general health problem, (including but not limited to nutritional deficiency and Equine Cushing's Disease[G] (ECD, also known as pituitary adenoma), which can interfere with the hormonal balance necessary for regular estrous cycles. For more information on ECD, go to **page 257**. For more information about nutrition, See "Diet and the Older Broodmare" at right.

 NO

Is your mare's Interovulatory Interval (IOI) less than 19 days? (See "Tell-Tale IOI" **page 205**.)

YES ▶ Call your veterinarian *THIS WEEK*—there could be inflammation in the reproductive tract, with or without infection, or there could be moderate to severe pain elsewhere in your mare's body, either of which can cause release of the hormone prostaglandin, which can disrupt your senior mare's estrous cycle.

NO

Has your senior mare been examined by your veterinarian this breeding season and found free of uterine infection and excessive uterine "cysts" (a.k.a. lymphatic lacunae[G])? Has her uterine lining been given a biopsy grade of 2 or less no earlier than last breeding season, and/or did she carry a pregnancy successfully to term last breeding season?

NO ▶ If you can't answer yes to both queries, call your veterinarian *THIS WEEK*—infection, decreased ability to clear out normal uterine debris, uterine "cysts," and scar tissue all can be an increasing problem as your mare ages, even if she's never before been pregnant.

 YES

ACTION PLAN (CONTINUED):

Has your senior mare ever been pregnant successfully? Has her reproductive tract been examined and found to be anatomically normal this breeding season?

 YES

 NO Call your veterinarian *THIS WEEK* if you were unable to answer yes to either query—if your mare's never been pregnant before, it's possible she has a long-standing, undiscovered reproductive-tract abnormality. Or, if she's produced at least one foal, she could have internal injuries to her reproductive tract from foaling, causing adhesions and/or increasing her susceptibility to chronic and/or repeated bouts of vaginal, cervical, uterine, and/or oviduct contamination and infection.

Is your senior mare's vulva tilted or curved, instead of vertical and straight? Is the upper portion of her vulva sunken under her anus? Do the vulvar lips appear stretched and/or pulled partially open? Are they soiled with manure?

 YES Call your veterinarian *THIS WEEK* if you answered yes to any query—age-related changes in the anatomy of the perineum^G can predispose your senior mare to vaginitis^G, urine pooling^G, pneumovagina^G (also known as wind sucking), and cervicitis^G, any of which can interfere with reproductive function.

 NO

Call your veterinarian for an appointment, or for a referral to an equine reproduction specialist.

Diet and the Older Brood Mare

Diet affects reproduction in your older mare. A senior diet formulated for her increased nutritional needs will enable her to have smoother transitions into the breeding season and ovulate more regularly. Older mares fed a diet that's balanced and endowed with at least 6% to 7% supplementary fat have healthier levels of the reproductive hormone progesterone^G, which is necessary to maintain pregnancy. For more information, go to "Stay-Young Diet Solutions," page 376, and "The Age Event: Declining Fertility (in mares)," page 263.

Senior Stallion: Trouble in the Breeding Shed

SENIOR SIGNPOST: Your senior stallion seems interested in mares and seems to know the routine when exposed to a mare in heat, but he seems unable, or unwilling, to follow through all the way to ejaculation.

What this might mean: It could mean he's in pain and his discomfort is sufficient to distract him; there's a problem in his reproductive system; or there's an underlying problem in his general health.

ACTION PLAN:

Has your senior stallion lost weight in recent months? Is he easily tired? When he's not in the company of mares, does he seem depressed, dull, disinterested in his surroundings? Is his coat shaggy, dull, or overdue to shed? Does he seem to sweat excessively?

YES Call your veterinarian *TODAY* if you answered yes to any query—your senior stallion may have an underlying health problem that's contributing to a hormone imbalance. For more information, go to the **Action Plan** for each of your senior stallion's symptoms.

 NO

Since the beginning of this breeding season, has he been evaluated by a veterinarian and determined to be free of any acute or chronic conditions that result in pain and/or restrict his flexibility, with or without obvious lameness (such as arthritis^G, back pain, hock pain, hip pain, or fusion of any previously inflamed joints)? Has your senior stallion been ill and/or injured within the past 6 months?

NO Call your veterinarian *TODAY* and request a full soundness evaluation. Untreated pain and/or restricted range-of-motion—especially in the hock, hip, and lower back joints—can interfere with your senior stallion's ability to breed. See "Studly Duty," **at right** and continue this **Action Plan**.

 YES

Does your senior stallion seem to do everything right in the breeding shed, but simply fails to ejaculate?

YES Call your veterinarian *TODAY*—your senior stallion may have inflammation, infection, and/or blockage (ampullitis^G, seminal vesciculitis^G) in the passageways the semen must flow through during ejaculation.

 NO

ACTION PLAN (CONTINUED):

Is your senior stallion being handled by someone other than his usual handler?

 Try a different handler—your senior stallion may be responding to handling methods that inadvertently interfere with teasing and breeding.

Call your veterinarian for an appointment.

Studly Duty

Contrary to what you might think, life in the breeding shed can be hard work for a stallion. Age-related mental or physical pain can easily put a stud out of work. For instance, a stallion needs full mental acuity, as well as his sense of sight and smell, to make sure a mare will be receptive to his advances. He needs strong, sound, and relatively pain-free hind legs, loins, and back—as well as good balance—in order to mount and dismount the mare—and to dodge any kicks she might aim in his direction. Any condition that affects those areas will make breeding a tough chore for even the most enthusiastic of breeding-shed performers.

Senior Mare: Can't Become, or Stay, Pregnant

SENIOR SIGNPOST: You've bred your senior mare at least twice this season, but she isn't pregnant.

What this might mean: She's not being bred at precisely the right time; there's a problem in her reproductive tract preventing a pregnancy; or she's getting pregnant but not staying that way. Or, it could mean there's a problem with the stallion.

ACTION PLAN:

Has your veterinarian confirmed that your mare became pregnant on at least one of this season's breedings?

 YES Call your veterinarian for an appointment to examine your senior mare's reproductive tract for the presence of infection, inflammation, intraluminal[G] fluid accumulation, and "cysts" (lymphatic lacunae[G]). Any of these can allow a pregnancy to become established, but cause early embryonic death.

 NO

Have you and your veterinarian seen the stallion's breeding records from this and last season, and satisfied yourselves that he's providing your mare with at least 500 million live, healthy sperm cells per breeding?

 NO Call the stallion owner and/or breeding manager *TODAY*, request those records, and share them with your veterinarian—if the stallion's subfertile, repeatedly breeding your senior mare not only might be futile, but also could infect her reproductive tract.

 YES

Have your teasing records, your mare's IOI (interovulatory interval[G]), and/or veterinary examination of your senior mare confirmed that she's having normal heat (estrus) cycles, with normal heat behavior and true ovulations? (For more information, see "Tell-Tale IOI," **opposite page.**)

 NO Call your veterinarian *THIS WEEK*—without this information, you can't know whether your senior mare has an underlying problem causing a hormone imbalance, or whether she might have contamination or infection in her reproductive tract. For more information, see "Abnormal 'Heat' Behavior," **page 204.**

 YES

ACTION PLAN (CONTINUED):

Does the upper half of your senior mare's vulva seem sunken in? Are the vulvar lips partially pulled open, or soiled with manure? Is there a milky discharge at the bottom of the vulvar lips, or dried onto her tail hairs and/or the inner surface of her thighs, hocks, and hind fetlocks?

 YES → Call your veterinarian *THIS WEEK* if you answered yes to any query—your senior mare may be urine poolingG and/or wind suckingG, increasing her susceptibility to inflammation and/or reproductive tract infection and thereby interfering with her fertility.

 NO

On the cycles that were bred, was ovulation confirmed by veterinary examination (preferably ultrasound)? Was it confirmed that your mare did not double-ovulate?

 NO → Call your veterinarian for an appointment. Your mare's next breeding cycle should be monitored by ultrasound examinations to make sure the breedable follicle ovulates, and that your mare does not double-ovulate (which can interfere with pregnancy or cause twin pregnancy).

 YES

Call your veterinarian for an appointment.

TELL-TALE IOI

Keeping track of your mare's heat cycles can help you keep tabs on her reproductive health. During breeding season, a healthy mare's estrous cycle consists of two phases: estrus (heat), which lasts 7 days on average; and diestrus (out of heat), which lasts 14 days on average. Total those for an overall interovulatory interval (IOI; the number of days from ovulation to ovulation) of 21 days.

When uterine inflammation is present, diestrus will be shortened by at least 2 days, for an IOI of 19 days or less. That means if your mare begins coming into heat more quickly than normal, she could have a uterine infection. Call your veterinarian.

 ➤

Should I "Regumate®" her?

Giving an aged mare daily supplemental progesterone[G], in the form of the oral synthetic progestin Regumate®, is a common practice to "keep the old gal pregnant." Studies have shown that this can decrease the number of pregnancies lost by older broodmares when their blood progesterone levels are lower than what's needed to maintain pregnancy, or when no definitive cause for pregnancy loss can be found. Is this a good idea for your mare?

It might be. But if she's harboring a low-grade infection in her reproductive tract, treating her with progesterone could upset the standoff between infectious organisms and immunity—and result in a full-blown infection that'll be tough to beat.

So, don't reach for the Regumate® unless you and your veterinarian have confirmed that your senior mare needs supplemental progesterone and isn't harboring a reproductive tract infection.

Senior Stallion: Declining Pregnancy Rate

SENIOR SIGNPOST: Your senior breeding stallion may be showing normal interest in mares and may be breeding with no apparent difficulty. However, there's been a decline in his pregnancy rate (the percentage of mares that become pregnant) and/or in the laboratory-determined quality of his semen.

What this might mean: A reproductive-tract problem, or an overall health issue.

ACTION PLAN:

Has your senior stallion been ill, even with just a mild "cold," any time within the past 3 months? Has he had any accidents, falls, or fights, or otherwise been injured or lamed within that same time period? Has he been given any medications?

 YES ▶ Call your veterinarian *TODAY* if you answered yes to any query—your senior horse's sperm cells are vulnerable to fever, inflammation, stress, injury to reproductive organs, and/or medication side effects.

 NO

Does his ejaculate ever appear pink or blood-tinged? Yellowish?

 YES ▶ Call your veterinarian *TODAY* if you answered yes to any query—sperm are maimed or killed by blood, urine, inflammatory cells, and other contaminants. The underlying cause needs to be found and resolved.

 NO

Are your senior stallion's testicles smaller than they used to be?

 YES ▶ Call your veterinarian *TODAY*—your senior stallion may have testicular degeneration[G].

 NO

Does your senior stallion breed by artificial insemination (AI)?

 YES ▶ Ask your veterinarian to review the collection techniques, semen processing, semen handling, and equipment to make sure they're not contributing to loss of healthy sperm in the ejaculate. (See, "Sperm Sensitivities," **next page**.)

 NO

 ➤

ACTION PLAN (CONTINUED):

Do you routinely have your senior stallion's ejaculate examined in the laboratory for volume, sperm count, sperm quality, and contaminants?

Call your veterinarian for an appointment.

Call your veterinarian *TODAY* and have a breeding soundness examination done. Many problems revealed in such an examination can be resolved with proper treatment. Any delay in diagnosis and treatment can decrease the odds of full recovery.

Did You Know?

It takes 72 days for your stallion to build new, healthy spermatozoa from the ground up. That means anything that kills mature and near-mature spermatozoa—including a brief low-grade fever— can interfere with his pregnancy rate for weeks to come.

Sperm Sensitivities

Spermatozoa can be quickly incapacitated and/or killed when exposed to:
• Urine • Blood • Pus
They're also vulnerable to:
• Sunlight
• Detergent residues (on reusable collection equipment, glassware, syringes, etc.)
• Rubber (such as the rubber plunger on a syringe, or the rubber adaptor at the end of an AI pipette)
• Lubricants
• Temperature changes
• Time spent outside the reproductive tract
• Seminal fluid.

Seminal fluid? You bet. The very liquid in which spermatozoa reside is toxic if they remain in it for long. In nature, sperm were meant to spend less than a minute in a stallion's semen. That's one reason cooled, shipped semen must be diluted with an extender. Diluting the seminal fluid's toxic effects is a necessity when sperm are shipped across countries or continents, spending up to 24 hours surrounded by semen.

Abnormally Large Pregnant Belly

SENIOR SIGNPOST: You expect your senior mare's belly to get large as her pregnancy develops, but this is over the top—her abdomen seems enormous, and she seems very uncomfortable, reluctant to move, and may be off her feed.

What this might mean: One of several potentially life-threatening problems of near-term pregnancy in older mares, including fetal hydrops^G, ruptured prepubic tendon^G, ventral hernia^G, and/or ruptured abdominal muscles.

ACTION PLAN:

Is your senior mare off her feed? Does she stand with her forelegs stretched out in front, like a sawhorse? Does she have a fever?

 YES Call your veterinarian *NOW* if you answered yes to any query—your senior mare may have fetal hydrops^G or peritonitis^G, either of which can place her and her unborn fetus at grave risk.

 NO

Does your mare object to having her lower belly wall pressed or probed with your fingertips? Is her lower belly wall swollen with edema?

 YES Call your veterinarian *NOW*—there may have been some small ruptures in the abdominal muscles and/or the prepubic tendon^G. The incidence of either condition tends to increase with age.

NO

Was your senior mare examined by ultrasound by Day 40 after her last breeding, to ensure that she's not carrying twins?

 NO Call your veterinarian *TODAY*—she could be carrying twins, which can be life-threatening for both mare and fetuses, is more likely to happen as she gets older, and doubles the weight of the pregnancy on her supportive structures.

 YES

Call your veterinarian *TODAY*—your mare should be examined by rectal palpation and/or ultrasound to make sure she and the fetus are okay.

➤

215

If your mare's near-term pregnancy is in trouble, placing her and/or her fetus at risk, your veterinarian may offer the following choices, depending on the diagnosis:

Watchful Waiting: This means there's a chance the pregnancy could continue to term, and your mare could deliver a normal, healthy foal and live to raise him. Choosing this option usually means you'll need to place your mare in an "intensive management" situation (such as a stall with turnout or a paddock rather than a remote pasture), where she can be watched around the clock for any changes.

Pregnancy Problems
and your choices

Abortion: This means there's a strong possibility the fetus is abnormal, dying, or already dead, and it'd be in your senior mare's best interest to terminate the pregnancy before her condition worsens. In most cases, this is done by a series of hormone injections to soften the cervix and induce labor, with a veterinarian in attendance during the entire procedure. The mare with fetal hydropsG may need intravenous fluids before, during, and after delivery to protect her against shockG.

Induce Labor: This option is logical if your mare is able to assist in vaginal delivery, examination indicates that the fetus is well-developed and likely to survive, milk is available (either from the mare, or an alternate source), and veterinary attendance is desired at birth.

Cesarean Section: This option is logical if the mare's and/or fetus's condition are likely to make vaginal delivery difficult or impossible.

CHAPTER 16

MISCELLANEOUS SIGNPOSTS

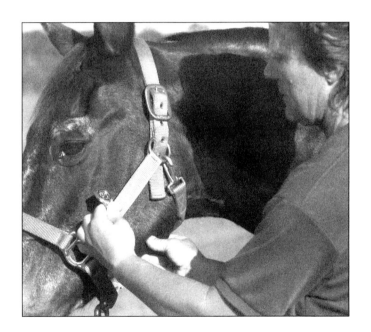

Fever

SENIOR SIGNPOST: You thought your horse felt excessively warm or seemed depressed, so you took his temperature and found that he's got a fever—it's higher than the normal range of 99.5° to 101.5° F. (That's the normal range for the average horse. But, every horse, including your senior, has his own unique "normal range" within that average. See "Reading The Heat" page 220. For how to take his temperature, see "Senior Vital Signs," page 292.)

What this might mean: It can be a sign of infectious disease, drug reaction, heat exhaustion^G, or anhidrosis^G.

ACTION PLAN:

Take your senior horse's temperature again, using a different thermometer. Fever confirmed? **NO** Time for a new thermometer.

 YES

Has your senior horse been exercising, either free or controlled, within the past hour? **YES** Walk your horse for 30 minutes to cool him, then recheck his temperature. Still high? If so, continue this **Action Plan**.

 NO

Is it hot outside? Is your horse in the sun? Are other horses sweating, while your horse is not? Is the sum of ambient temperature + relative humidity greater than 120? **YES** Call your veterinarian *NOW* if you answered yes to 2 or more of these queries—it could be heat exhaustion^G and/or anhidrosis^G. Go to **While You Wait**, opposite page.

 NO

Is your senior horse a mare that foaled within the past 72 hours? Or within the past 2 months? **YES** Call your veterinarian *NOW* if you answered yes to either query—it could be acute endometritis^G or lactation tetany^G, respectively.

 NO

Has your senior horse been vaccinated or treated with any medication within the past 24 hours? **YES** Call your veterinarian *NOW*—it could be a mild reaction to a live vaccine, or a dangerous reaction known as malignant hyperthermia^G.

 NO

ACTION PLAN (CONTINUED):

Within the past 3 weeks, has your horse had contact with a sick horse? **YES** Call your veterinarian *TODAY*—your horse could be coming down with an infection.

NO

Call your veterinarian for advice and an appointment.

WHILE YOU WAIT

Cool your horse. If the ambient temperature is 80° F or above, swab your horse with a washcloth drenched in cool water, concentrating on the areas behind and between his ears, on his forehead, on the underside of his neck where the jugular vein is, in his armpits, and in his groin and underbelly. Place him in the shade where there's a natural breeze or position him in front of a fan to encourage evaporation. Rewet him every 5 minutes or whenever he dries off.

Did You Know

Your senior horse's temperature is slightly lower at dawn than it is at dusk—as much as 2 degrees different. This is normal, and it's important for you to know what his morning temperature usually is, compared to his evening temperature. For example, if it's normally 99.5° in the morning and 101° at night, a reading of 101° in the morning could mean he has a fever, even though it's technically within normal range. Get to know your senior horse's normal range, so you can better determine when his temperature is abnormal.

➤

· Reading the Heat ·

A fever occurs when your senior horse's hypothalamus, which regulates his body temperature, adjusts his "thermostat" such that he'll tolerate higher temperatures before cooling mechanisms kick in. This allows his body to battle invading organisms, by creating a hot, unfriendly environment for them—his body is literally trying to burn them out. His temperature also is a good indicator of his health. When you think something's wrong with your senior horse, one of the first questions your veterinarian is likely to ask is, "What's the horse's temperature?"

It's not uncommon for the thermostat, which is located adjacent to the pituitary gland, to malfunction in an older horse when the pituitary gland enlarges with advancing age. So, it's important for you to monitor your senior horse's "normal" temperature range at least once a month, so you can better gauge when it's abnormal.

Here's what those degrees can mean.

TEMPERATURE	POSSIBLE CAUSES
105° F or higher	Serious viral infection; heat stroke; pneumonia[G]
102° F to 104.5° F	Postexercise heat; at rest, pain, inflammation, or mild infection
99.5° F to 101.5° F	Normal
97.5° F to 99° F	Mild to moderate shock[G]; hypothermia[G]
97° F or below	Severe shock[G]

Colic

SENIOR SIGNPOST: Any of the signs outlined on the colic symptom checklist, next page.

What this might mean: "Colic" is a collection of signs that usually mean "bellyache"—it's not actually a diagnosis. Although colic pain usually means there's a problem in your senior horse's intestinal tract, it can mean other problems too, such as internal hemorrhaging, hepatitis^G, ulcers^G, peritonitis^G, and heavy tumors that are tugging on or compressing organs or their supportive tissues. A colic's severity isn't always indicated by the pain level you're observing. A horse showing Level 3 discomfort might be about to pass a harmless gas bubble and be fine. A horse showing Level 1 discomfort might be on his way to higher levels of pain or endotoxic shock^G. Right now you have no way of knowing which road he's going to take.

ACTION PLAN:

Are your horse's current symptoms limited to Level 1? **YES** ▸ Call your veterinarian *NOW*—it could be early stages of colic, or later stages involving the large intestine, which often causes milder signs (though it's not necessarily less serious). Go to **While You Wait**, page 223.

 NO

Are your horse's current symptoms no higher than Level 2? **YES** ▸ Call your veterinarian *NOW*—fast treatment could halt absorbtion of endotoxins^G through the lining of the affected intestines. Go to **While You Wait**.

 NO

Have your horse's current symptoms reached Level 3? **YES** ▸ Call your veterinarian *NOW*—your horse may be showing early signs of poisoning from absorbtion of endotoxins^G. Go to **While You Wait**.

 NO

Have your horse's current symptoms reached Level 4? **YES** ▸ Call your veterinarian *NOW*—signs could indicate circulatory shutdown from endotoxic shock^G. Go to **While You Wait**.

 NO

Have your horse's current symptoms reached Level 5? **YES** ▸ Call your veterinarian *NOW*—it'll take fast, aggressive, intensive care to save your horse's life.

NO

Call your veterinarian *NOW*.

➤

Colic Symptom Checklist

What you see	Level 1 Colic Pain (mild)	Level 2 Colic Pain (moderate)	Level 3 Colic Pain (severe, early)	Level 4 Colic Pain (severe, advanced)	Level 5 Colic Pain (severe, grave)
Attitude	Sleepy; behaves almost normally if stimulated.	Preoccupied; pays attention if interrupted but slips back into preoccupied state if left alone.	Anxious, pays attention only briefly if interrupted.	Consumed with pain; oblivious to surroundings.	Stuporous; unresponsive.
Up or down?	Stands or lies down quietly.	Repeatedly lies down and gets up.	Occasionally lies down and rolls.	Crashes to the ground without warning.	Down; won't get up.
Possible signs of pain	May yawn frequently.	Swishes or wrings tail; stretches neck; turns to look at flanks; paws; stomps hind feet.	Sweats; kicks at belly; bites at flanks.	Violent thrashing.	No apparent pain connection; "beyond pain."
Heart rate	45 to 50 beats per minute.	50 to 55 beats per minute.	55 to 65 beats per minute.	65 to 100 beats per minute.	Over 100 or irregular.
Gum color	Normal to slightly pale.	Normal to bright pink.	Reddish or bluish.	Muddy colored.	White to muddy.
Capillary refill time	Normal (1 to 1 1/2 seconds).	1 1/2 to 2 seconds.	2 to 3 seconds.	3 seconds or longer.	Over 3 seconds.
Gut sounds	Variable; gas "ping" sounds mean trouble!	Variable; gas "ping" sounds mean trouble!	Variable; gas "ping" sounds mean trouble!	Usually quiet; short blurps and/or pings might be heard.	Usually quiet; short blurps and/or pings might be heard.

[Note: There may be some overlap between signs shown at the various levels.]

To walk...Or not to walk?

In a mild to moderate colic, walking your senior horse might help move bubbles of gas and/or jostle loops of bowel back into their correct positions. But if your horse is intent on lying down, you're not going to be helping the situation by slapping, whipping, kicking, or shouting at him to get up and keep moving. You'll only be adding stress on an already stressful situation, and forcing him to expend energy he'll need to get well.

If walking seems to help your senior horse feel better, walk on. If it's a struggle to keep him on his feet, let him lie down. If he'll lie quietly, all the better. If he's intent on thrashing, no amount of physical abuse is going to stop him, and you might get yourself hurt trying. Instead, do what you can to protect him (without getting hurt yourself):

Go to **While You Wait**, below.

WHILE YOU WAIT

LEVEL 1. *Remove all feed*. Remove grain and hay from stall feeders; remove bedding if your horse eats it. (It's not unusual for a horse with mild intestinal upset to eat straw or shavings.) Leave his water.

LEVEL 2 TO 5. *If your senior horse wants to roll or thrash, protect him (and his human attendants)*.

• To keep your horse from hurting himself, and to make it easier for human attendants to stay out of harm's way: Re-bed his stall with extra-deep bedding; line stall walls with 1 or 2 layers of hay or straw bales; and remove all movable protrusions (feeders, buckets, etc.).

• Or, remove him to an arena or paddock with obstacles removed.

• Replace his standard halter with a padded one (such as a fleece-lined travel halter), so the halter's hardware won't damage facial nerves if he falls.

• Unless your senior horse is thrashing (which would make this too dangerous for you), apply padded shipping bandages to his legs.

• If it can be done safely, check/record vital signs every 5 minutes and provide the data to your veterinarian.

• If your horse is insured (mortality or major medical), call your insurance agent and report that he's colicking. Be sure to familiarize yourself with the policy before a crisis, so you know what's required to comply.

THE AGE EVENTS

1 Arthritis

What it is: Also known as degenerative joint disease (DJD), it's progressive joint inflammation due to trauma or wear and tear, leading to erosion of articular joint cartilage, which becomes frayed and thinned, causing pain and loss of function. Arthritis mainly affects your horse's weight-bearing joints.

Why your senior horse is at risk: Regardless of how good his conformation is, his risk of arthritis increases with every passing year. That's because the longer he lives, the bigger a target he becomes for injuries and wear and tear that lead to joint degeneration. His joints almost never get a break. Even standing at rest they're bearing his weight on tiny patches of cartilage.

Plus, there's a metabolic shift that occurs around age 15 (see "The Rise and Fall," page 239), leading to an escalation of cell death within bone, cartilage, and fibrous tissue. Tendons and ligaments become less elastic, more easily torn. Cartilage thins, absorbing less shock. Its shape changes, too, due to a lifetime of pressure and torque, causing joint bones to be less aligned and the cartilage, ligaments, and tendons more susceptible to strain. And, your horse's reactions slow down with age—especially if he's retired to an inactive lifestyle—making him more prone to a misstep.

Early Arthritis Signposts

The faster you identify arthritis in your horse, the quicker you can attack it. There are two kinds of equine arthritis: the sneaky kind and the obvious kind. In the obvious kind, the joint's been traumatized or infected, so is sore enough to cause lameness. Your horse is lame—you call the vet. In the sneaky kind, the joint isn't sore at first, so there's little or no ➤

Arthritis & Back Pain

Your horse can get arthritis in the joints between the vertebrae in his spine. There are numerous reasons for this, with ill-fitting tack one culprit. Other causes can include taking a misstep while carrying you or another rider; hard work without adequate conditioning; lack of flexibility; strenuous work without adequate warm-up; and advancing age. For more information about back problems in horses, see "Senior Back Check," page 314.

lameness. But that doesn't mean that arthritis isn't marching forward. The first signpost will be a little joint puffiness. If you don't look for it, you'll likely miss it—and miss out on your chance to help minimize future joint damage. Watch for these subtle but telltale signposts:

- Slight puffiness in lower-leg joints.
- Stiff, choppy gait when you first begin work, which improves when he warms up.
- Reluctance and/or resistance to perform maneuvers that previously came easily for him, such as stops and collection. He may raise his head and hollow his back.

How to Identify the Signposts

1. **Inspect your senior horse's joints every day:** Visually inspect and feel each leg joint, preferably an hour after mild exercise (such as hand-walking or at-liberty grazing), which will minimize any puffiness (such as stocking up[G]) resulting from inactivity. Press your fingers gently over each joint, feeling for smooth, well-defined "peaks" (bones) and fluid-free "valleys" (soft-tissue areas). As a joint becomes puffy, you'll feel bone edges become obscured, and valleys begin to fill, like a springy water balloon. If you're unsure, look for asymmetry. Compare the left leg to the right leg, or compare a suspicious joint to the same joint on a young, sound horse.

Synovial Fluid: Joints' Life Blood

Your senior horse's joints are full of synovial fluid[G]—a clear, pale-yellow lubricant that's normally very viscous (thick, almost syrupy). A droplet from the tip of a needle should stretch to over an inch in length before breaking. Here's what it does—and why it's important.

- It bathes the joint's parts, keeping them wet and slippery, just as motor oil protects and lubricates engine parts.
- It nourishes and cleans cartilage, which has no direct blood supply of its own.
- It also helps cartilage heal when damaged (which seems at a snail's pace under the best of circumstances).
- The fluid's thick composition acts as a barrier to inflammatory cells that are ready to invade the joint from nearby blood vessels. As long as synovial fluid is thick and healthy, invading it would be like trying to swim upstream through a river of Jell-O®.
- When your senior horse's joint is inflamed, its synovial fluid breaks down, becoming thin, watery, and clouded with debris. In response, serum and blood leak into the joint from adjacent blood vessels, further diluting the synovial fluid and causing his joint to appear puffy. The fluid becomes less effective as a cartilage cleanser and joint lubricant, setting the scene for further joint degeneration and inflammation.

Find a puffy joint? Then do the soundness check, below. If the lower joints of all four legs are swollen, and the cannon bone (shin) areas are swollen too, the swelling is more likely to be edema^G due to an underlying health problem, such as poor circulation or hypoproteinemia^G. Call your vet TODAY. (See "Swollen Leg(s)," page 146.)

2. **Perform a soundness check.** Use the guidelines below. If your horse is lame, call your veterinarian TODAY—synovitis^G in that affected joint may be escalating, resulting in joint degeneration.

• If he's not obviously limping, check his soundness. (See "How Lame is Your Horse?" page 145.) If you find he's unsound, or if you're just not sure, call your vet TODAY. While you wait, apply "Arthritis Home Treatment," page 233.
• If there's no hint of lameness, gently probe the joint with your fingers, including the puffy part, while watching your senior horse for signs of pain, such as a wringing tail, flinch, or snatching the leg away from you. If you find any sign of tenderness, call your veterinarian TODAY— your horse's synovitis is on the move. While you wait, apply "Arthritis Home Treatment," page 233.
• If there's no sign of lameness or tenderness, start "Arthritis Home Treatment" as your primary treatment—you won't need to call your veterinarian unless you want to. If the swelling fails to improve within an hour after your home treatment, the synovitis is not responding. Call your veterinarian.

Arthritis Artillery

Use these steps to help battle degenerative joint disease in your senior horse.

STEP 1: TAKE HIM OUT OF RETIREMENT.

Why it helps. Regular exercise, tailored to your senior horse's condition, increases circulation of nutrients into, and wastes out of, his joints while strengthening muscles that protect them from stress. A well-conditioned horse generally has significantly thicker and healthier cartilage than does an unfit horse of any age. Plus, fitness enhances stamina and athletic ability, which helps protect your horse from the most common 3-part cause of joint injury: FATIGUE, which leads to POOR FORM, which leads to a MISSTEP. Finally, regular exercise works wonders for a horse's attitude, appetite, digestion, and overall sense of well-being.

How to do it. Turn your horse out, and/or put him to work—carefully. (For how to start or maintain your senior on an exercise program, see "Age-Adjusted Exercise," page 340.) Pasture living is ideal; paddock turnout is better than ➤

a stall. Your senior horse evolved to graze and step—with each step, he gently compresses and releases the spongelike cartilage in his joints, promoting joint-fluid circulation that helps keep his cartilage as healthy as possible. Grazing on pasture also is best for his mental outlook and digestion.

Avoid stall confinement unless advised by your vet for a specific condition. Horses weren't designed to stand still in a "cave." Doing so freezes up joints already compromised by years of weight-bearing and wear and tear. You'll be doing your senior a big favor if you allow him, and encourage him, to move within his capabilities.

STEP 2: MAKE HIS DIET JOINT-FRIENDLY.

Why it helps. Specific nutrients can have a significant impact on joint health. There's evidence that adding the dietary supplements at right can help your senior horse avoid serious arthritis and/or live more comfortably with it. They're rated according to how well they've been studied and supported by well-designed research. (See "Credibility Scale," below). Don't assume, though, that a 2-star rating means there's no risk—always consult with your veterinarian before changing your senior horse's diet or medications.

Credibility Scale

★★ Determined effective and probably safe in limited clinical studies, not necessarily using equine subjects. And/or, equine studies are conflicting or relatively new and yet to be corroborated.

★ Probably safe and possibly effective in limited and/or poorly designed research that may or may not have used equine subjects, or may be based on longtime cultural use and folklore with few reports of adverse effects.

How to do it. Work with your veterinarian to select one or more of the joint-friendly supplements in the chart at right for your senior horse.

STEP 3: WORK THE AFFECTED JOINT PASSIVELY.

Why it helps. Passive range-of-motionᴳ exercises are well documented to encourage cartilage and soft-tissue healing in inflamed joints while decreasing scar-tissue formation (which causes a loss of range of motion).

How to do it. Pick up the affected leg. Gently bend and straighten the affected joint(s), repeating about 10 times per joint. (Also see "Senior Stretches," page 348.) Perform the exercise 3 or 4 times a day, if possible—the more you do it, the better.

(Continued on page 232)

JOINT-FRIENDLY SUPPLEMENTS

OPTIONS	RATING	WHY IT WORKS	HOW TO ADD IT	MISCELLANEOUS NOTES
FAT	★ ★	Can decrease inflammation.	1 cup a day of a mixture of 6 parts soybean or corn oil to 1 part flaxseed oil. (See "Stay-Young Diet Solutions," page 376.)	Choose raw, cold-pressed oils (available at health-food stores and fine grocers); read the label; use only food-grade flaxseed oil; consult vet if your horse is overweight.
VITAMIN E	★ ★	Believed to be an effective natural antioxidant, potentially critical for blocking degenerative conditions, including arthritis.	Give 2000 IU vitamin E daily, as d-alpha tocopherol, divided into 2 meals.	The easiest form is 1000-IU soft capsules (at drug and grocery stores); prick and squeeze the oil onto your horse's concentrate.
VITAMIN C	★ ★	A powerful antioxidant, vitamin C is believed to be important in supporting collagen maintenance and protecting joints from degenerative disease.	Give your horse 5 to 20 grams supplemental vitamin C per day, divided into at least 2 meals, as ascorbic acid or ascorbyl palmitate. (For how to add vitamin C to the diet safely, go to "Stay-Young Diet Solutions," page 376.)	As your horse ages, his liver's ability to produce his own vitamin C declines. And, his ability to eat and digest forages high in vitamin C declines as well.
CHONDRO-PROTECTIVE NUTRACEU-TICALS	★	Though controversial, some people believe providing glucosamine and chondroitin sulfate, which in part make up healthy joint material, can help maintain healthy joint cartilage and fluid.	Add a chondroprotective nutraceutical product to your horse's diet that contains glucosamine plus chondroitin sulfate (such as Cosequin® by Nutramax).	Evidence supporting their use in injectable form is compelling, with joint injections showing the highest degree of effectiveness, and injection into vein or muscle coming in second and third, respectively; oral administration is a relatively untested extrapolation from human studies.
COPPER & ZINC	★	Copper and zinc have been shown to be important minerals in the growth and maintenance of collagen, which is needed for healthy joints.	Feed a concentrate product that's labeled to contain 30 to 50 ppm (parts per million) copper and 50 to 80 ppm zinc.	Avoid mare-and-foal concentrate, even if it's labeled "okay" for seniors, because it contains too much iron for older horses.

➤

Arthritis Artillery, continued from page 230

STEP 4: IMPROVE YOUR SENIOR HORSE'S FLEXIBILITY.

Why it helps: Stretching breaks down adhesions, improves circulation, warms and limbers muscles and ligaments, improves range of motion, and helps prevent injury.

How to do it: Perform prework stretching exercises with your horse, along with a warm-up session before each day's exercise. For a stretching how-to, go to "Senior Stretches," page 348. For how to warm up your horse properly, go to "Age-Adjusted Exercise," page 340.

STEP 5: KEEP HIM COMFORTABLE—SAFELY.

Why it helps. Breaking the pain cycle can help break the inflammation cycle and speed healing.

How to do it. Talk to your veterinarian about a treatment that not only relieves your senior horse's joint pain but also is in his best interest as an individual. There are side effects to consider, which can become more of a problem with increasing dosage and duration. In many cases, your senior may benefit from a combination of conventional medications with alternative therapies. (See "Alternative Medicine," page 388.) The most common conventional pain-relieving options are explained below.

Pain-Relief Options

TREATMENT	WHEN APPROPRIATE	HOW IT WORKS
Joint injection with sodium hyaluronateG (a.k.a. hyaluronic acid, or "acid shot," such as Hylartin-V® or Legend®).	When joint puffiness is accompanied by lameness and/or tenderness, indicating that synovial fluid has broken down, which thins it and makes it a poor lubricant, a poor provider of nutrients, and an inadequate barrier to inflammatory invasion.	Restores joint lubrication; reerects the biological barrier to inflammatory cells; and helps protect cartilage from friction and chemical damage.
Intravenous injection with sodium hyaluronateG (using the proprietary product Legend®).	When more than one joint is puffy, lame, and/or tender, or when risk of joint infection is unacceptable.	Travels through the blood circulation to the joint, then works the same as joint injection.

Arthritis Home Treatment

1. **Confine your horse** to a box stall or small paddock for 24 hours (or longer, as prescribed by your veterinarian). If necessary, place a familiar companion nearby, to keep your horse from fretting and pacing.

2. **Ice the swollen joint.** Using a flexible ice pack (such as a bag of frozen corn or peas) inserted between the folds of a clean cloth (a hand towel works great), hold ICE ON for 5 min-

(Continued on page 238)

Why Cartilage Counts

Here's why cartilage is critical to your senior horse's joints. The weight-bearing surfaces of bone in his joints are coated with a smooth "hard hat" of protective cartilage. It absorbs and dissipates some of the joint's weight-bearing forces, minimizes friction, and provides a surface over which joint parts slide.

When the joint is inflamed, its lubricating synovial fluid breaks down (see "Synovial Fluid: Joints' Life Blood," page 228), accelerating cartilage wear and tear. Inflammatory chemicals eventually burn pits and furrows into it. Over time—weeks to months, depending on the severity of the problem and on how you manage your horse—the formerly thick cushion of cartilage thins, resulting in joint instability and decreased shock absorption. This increases the risk of joint injury. If further cartilage degeneration occurs, bone-against-bone contact will occur, leading to severe crippling or joint fusion.

WHAT IT DOESN'T DO	TREATMENT SPECIFICS	COSTS	RISKS
If cartilage is already damaged, this treatment can do little to directly stimulate healing of defects.	Follow with "Arthritis Home Treatment," above and 1 week layoff from work (but with controlled, mild exercise as prescribed by vet); relief can last several weeks or be permanent, depending on management, severity of problem, and quality of product used. (Higher-quality products have a higher molecular weight and generally provide longer-lasting results.) Single treatment may be sufficient; if a second treatment is needed, symptoms will return within about 4 weeks.	About $60 per dose, plus joint-injection costs.	Joint infection.
Less effective than targeted joint injection.	See joint injection, above.	About $60 per dose.	N/A.

➤

Pain-Relief Options *(continued)*

TREATMENT	WHEN APPROPRIATE	HOW IT WORKS
PSGAGᴳ (polysulfated gly-cosaminoglycan) injection, either directly into the joint or intramuscularly, using the pro-prietary product Adequan®.	When synovitisᴳ has esca-lated, with or without car-tilage damage.	Provides quick relief from heat, swelling, and pain by suppressing inflammatory cells, enzymes, and erosive chemicals that promote/sustain the inflammatory process. For longer-term benefits, protects cartilage against continued damage; improves joint lubrication by stimulating joint to manufacture hyaluronic acid; and binds to areas of cartilage that have suffered damage, stimulating the healing process. It's the only therapy that appears to promote cartilage heal-ing while also addressing the painful symptoms.
NSAIDᴳs (nonsteroidal anti-inflammatory drugs) including "bute" (phenylbutazoneᴳ), Banamine® (Schering Plough) and its generics (flunixin meg-lumine), Ketofen® (Rhone-Merieux), Arquel® (Parke Davis), and Equiproxen® (Syntex), as well as aspirin (which works poorly in horses and lasts only about 2 hours).	When pain persists, and therapy aimed at resolving the underlying problem is underway.	Blocks inflammatory response, including heat, swelling, and pain, bringing relief within less than an hour in many cases.
Joint injection with corticosteroidsᴳ ("steroids," including prednisone, dexa-methasone, hydrocortisone, betamethasone, and triam-cinolone).	When there's no joint infection or structural damage to the cartilage.	Single injection quickly diminishes pain, swelling, and heat of joint inflammation, and suppresses the action/release of harsh chemicals associated with inflamed joint.
Surgical nerve resectionᴳ (a.k.a. "denerving").	When in spite of other treatments, pain is relent-less. Most often used for joint pain in foot, such as founder, navicular, pedal-bone fracture.	Severs appropriate nerve(s) that transmit pain from the joint to your horse's brain, relieving his discomfort.

WHAT IT DOESN'T DO	TREATMENT SPECIFICS	COSTS	RISKS
Replace missing cartilage; can encourage existing cartilage to heal, but if it's worn through, won't replace it.	A series of 5-7 weekly shots is advised for IM dosing; with joint injections a single treatment may be sufficient; if a second treatment is needed, symptoms will return within about 4 weeks. For either treatment, follow with "Arthritis Home Treatment" and 1 week layoff from work (but with controlled, mild exercise as prescribed by vet).	About $60 per dose, plus veterinary costs for joint injection.	Joint infection, if given in the joint.
Promote repair or healing of cartilage, or restore lost viscosity and lubricating properties of thinned joint fluid.	May accelerate joint damage if pain is relieved without measures taken to reverse or halt the degenerative process, thereby encouraging the horse to use the joint when it's in trouble. Use only under the guidance and supervision of your veterinarian, and only when your horse's appetite is normal (unless directed otherwise by your veterinarian).	Depending on product, cost ranges from about $1 to $15 per dose—ask your veterinarian for an estimate for the product he or she is recommending.	A common toxic side effect is stomach ulcers and colon inflammation, or ulcerative colitisG. Old horses are particularly at risk due to high incidence of arthritisG and because of a tendency to be more sensitive to side effects, thanks to dehydration, decreased feed intake, and preexisting digestive problems. Ask your veterinarian about giving antiulcer medication.
Whether it promotes repair or healing is an ongoing controversy; most reports indicate that it does not. When more than one joint is involved, or when the risk of joint infection is unacceptable, this treatment may be inappropriate.	Restrict to one or two treatments per year, followed by "Arthritis Home Treatment" with at least 3 weeks layoff from work (but with controlled, mild exercise as prescribed by vet).	About $60 per joint treated.	Risk of laminitis and decreased resistance to disease increases with increasing dose and duration; laminitis risk escalates in horses over 15 years of age and/or who have had laminitis previously; diets that include iron supplementation may further increase the risk of immune system depression. Repeated steroid injections into the joint can make cartilage even slower to repair itself.
Doesn't contribute to healing in any way.	In some cases can be done under local anesthesia, but usually horse is placed under general anesthetic at an equine surgical facility; lay-up and rehab vary with surgery location.	Up to $1,000— or more.	Lack of pain can lead to increased use/degeneration of affected joint; numbed area increases chance of misstep, so denerved horses should be evaluated for safety before riding. ➤

Pain-Relief Options *(continued)*		
TREATMENT	**WHEN APPROPRIATE**	**HOW IT WORKS**
Topical DMSO[G] (dimethylsulfoxide).	To relieve minor arthritis pain and/or swelling; sometimes used as an adjunct to prescription medication/treatment.	A powerful, over-the-counter anti-inflammatory that's absorbed quickly through skin; also a scavenger of toxic free radicals, although it's unclear whether this property has any clinical significance.
Hydrotherapy[G].	For all arthritic joints.	Stimulates circulation in inflamed joints, relaxes your horse, so distracts from pain.
Capsaicin[G] **.075% cream.**	When pain is relentless in spite of other treatments.	Blocks uptake of *substance p*, a chemical involved in sending a "pain" message from the joint to the brain. With regular use over weeks to months, the nerves in the treated area begin to shrink, resulting in a gradual, chemical "denerving" effect.
Joint fusion[G] (surgical or chemical).	When affected joint normally has very little movement (the proximal pastern joint[G], the proximal and distal intertarsal joints[G], or the tarsometatarsal joint[G]).	Arthritis joint pain usually occurs only with motion; fusing the joint (causing the 2 movable parts to fuse together) can bring profound relief.

WHAT IT DOESN'T DO	TREATMENT SPECIFICS	COSTS	RISKS
Does not provide significant relief in moderate to severe cases, and does not resolve the underlying problem.	Using rubber gloves, a clean 4 x 4 gauze sponge or cotton makeup pad, and medical-grade DMSO, apply to skin over affected joint once or twice daily.	A pint bottle of medical grade DMSO costs about $15.	DMSO generates heat and a "prickly sensation" when combined with moisture—your horse may scratch, bite, or rub at a recently treated area. Next time, try diluting the DMSO with a small amount of water to allow heat to dissipate (about 10 minutes) before applying. If he still reacts, he probably isn't a good candidate for DMSO.
Does not provide significant relief in moderate to severe cases, and does not resolve the underlying problem.	Use whirlpool boots that are tall enough to immerse affected joints if you have them; otherwise use a hose outfitted with a massage nozzle; apply daily for a minimum of 10 minutes per joint. Towel-dry the area and apply a standing wrap, if applicable, to discourage swelling.	Free, unless you buy whirlpool boots, which run about $300.	N/A.
Does not resolve the underlying problem.	Cream, which contains agent that makes hot peppers hot, is available over the counter with both human and equine labels. Slather it over the joint, cover with Saran Wrap or its equivalent, and hold in place with a self-adhesive bandage such as Vetrap®. Remove bandage in 1 hour. Apply this treatment up to 4 times daily until relief occurs (may take several weeks), then maintain on once or twice daily treatments.	About $3 per tube (1.5 oz.).	The joint might degenerate faster due to removal of pain, which serves to limit usage; loss of nerve function also increases risk of a misstep because joint and adjacent muscles are numb.
Does not restore the joint; rather, it obliterates it.	It's done either by scraping apposing bone surfaces, or by injecting joint space with a caustic chemical; may take weeks for fusion to occur, but once it's complete, the pain is gone, permanently.	About $300 per joint.	N/A.

> ## Did You Know?
>
> When your horse's joints "click," that's the sound of gas bubbles popping within them. Unless accompanied by lameness and/or tenderness, the clicking is not clinically significant.

PROTECT YOURSELF: The Potential Danger of "Bute"

Several years ago, "bute"G (phenylbutazone) was available for prescription-only use in humans. It's been removed from the market because of an unpredictable—and fatal—toxic reaction.

WHAT IT IS: It's called aplastic anemiaG—your bone marrow stops producing red blood cells. Unless you can find a compatible bone marrow donor, there's no cure.

ARE YOU AT RISK? You can become sensitized from such exposure as crushing bute tablets and inhaling the resulting dust, or spilling bute on your skin.

WHAT TO DO: Ask your veterinarian for alternate NSAIDs. Be prepared to pay a little more. If bute is elected, for therapeutic and/or financial reasons, handle it with care.

- Wear rubber or latex gloves when handling it.
- Instead of crushing tablets (which creates dust), melt them slowly by letting them sit in a teaspoon of water per 1-gram tablet (it'll take about 2 minutes).
- Better yet, use a commercial, pre-mixed paste or gel with flavoring added to mask the drug's bitter taste, so you don't have to mix it yourself.

Arthritis Home Treatment, continued from page 233

utes; ICE OFF 15 minutes. Repeat 3 times in a row.

3. **Apply a standing bandage.** If the joint is wrappable, apply a standing banding to help reduce swelling and inflammation. (If you're unsure about how to wrap your horse's legs, see our previous book, *HANDS-ON HORSE CARE*, page 265 or consult your veterinarian.)

4. **Hand-walk your horse.** Twice a day remove your senior horse's bandage, hand-walk him for 15 minutes, then rewrap and return him to his stall. Gradually increase his exercise. After the prescribed period of confinement, leave the bandage off but keep your senior horse confined for half the original length of time. (If he was to be confined for 24 hours, confine him now for 12 more.) Provide 15 minutes of mild controlled exercise 4 times a day. Examples of controlled exercise: hand-walking, ponying at the walk and/or trot, or riding at the walk and trot, depending on your senior horse's condition before the problem appeared, and on how he's responded to treatment. If swelling, tenderness, and/or pain persist or return, you're going too fast.

5. **Follow up.** Check for return of swelling 1 hour after final exercise session. If it hasn't returned, go to Step 6. If it has, call your veterinarian for a re-evaluation, and keep your horse confined.

6. **Turn him out.** If he's symptom free, he can be turned out and resume a gradual return to work, if applicable. If not, call your vet. There may be a more severe problem than was originally thought.

The Rise and Fall

Aging is hard on your horse's body (and on yours). Here's why. When your horse was under 2 years of age, tissue growth in most of his musculoskeletal system, including his joints, was greater than tissue breakdown from "normal use," so there was a net gain of tissues such as bone, muscles, and joint cartilage. This is called an *anabolic state*G.

From year 2 to about 15, his tissue replacement is roughly equivalent to tissue breakdown from normal use—no net gain, no net loss. But from year 15 and up, the general trend is reversed to overall tissue breakdown—it's called a *catabolic state*G, and it's accelerated by:

- A decrease in his ability to digest and assimilate nutrients.
- Changes in his dietary needs that may or may not get heeded.
- A deteriorating maintenance/feedback system associated with thyroid and pituitary gland dysfunction.

Can you stop this natural decline? No. But you can slow it down and help protect your horse against its effects on his joints, if you know what to watch for and arm yourself with our "Arthritis Artillery," page 229.

Did You Know?

For both horses and humans, back problems are partly a result of weak or "lazy" abdominal muscles, which are supposed to remain engaged in order to support the spinal column from the inside. If you're skeptical, try this the next time you're driving in your car or sitting at your computer and your back or neck aches: Concentrate on compressing your abdominal muscles, and visualize them holding your spine from the inside. Odds are, if you can maintain this tight-tummy posture for a minute or more, your pain will go away.

To learn how to strengthen your horse's abdominal muscles, see "Senior Back Check," page 314.

NOTES

THE AGE EVENT

2 Cancer

What it is. A tumor of potentially unlimited growth that expands locally by invasion, and systemically by metastasis[G].

Why your senior horse is at risk. Because he's lived longer than horses did in the past, and because he's potentially exposed to more stress, parasites, chemicals, and pollutants in his air, water, forage, and concentrates than he would be in his natural state. Here are some equine cancer facts:

• On average, 5% of all horses (of all ages) presented to a veterinarian for examination are found to have tumors.

• Among seniors, that percentage is likely to be significantly higher.

• Roughly half of the tumors that senior horses develop start in the skin.

• The other half start in the internal soft tissues and organs, in the blood and lymphatic systems, and in the bones.

• About a third of the tumors found are malignant[G].

Cancer Signposts

As with most diseases, your horse's best bet for surviving cancer and emerging unscathed is early diagnosis and treatment, before it has grown, spread, and/or done irreparable damage. Use this chart to help familiarize yourself with common equine cancers, so you can identify the early signs. And call your vet *NOW* if you spot any of them.

The Ten Most Common Senior-Horse Cancers

Tumor Type	Where it Attacks	Signposts	Common Treatment	Life Threatening?	How to Detect
Cholangiocellular carcinoma	Liver bile duct.	Jaundice[G], weight loss, intermittent colic.	Inoperable; chemotherapy[G] usually not feasible.	Yes.	Include blood test for elevated liver enzymes at "Senior Vet Check," (see page 386) to detect evidence of liver degeneration; perform monthly checks of the whites of your senior horse's eyes, for yellow discoloration. ➤

241

The Ten Most Common Senior-Horse Cancers *(continued)*

Tumor Type	Where it Attacks	Signposts	Common Treatment	Life Threatening?	How to Detect
Granulosa cell tumor	Ovary.	Stallionlike behavior or nympho-mania^G.	Surgical removal.	Usually doesn't spread to other internal organs.	Ask vet to do rectal palpation for ovarian masses at "Senior Vet Check" (see page 386).
Lipoma	Omentum^G and/or mesentery^G in horses that are (or once were) obese.	None, or colic if these fatty tumors get wrapped around a loop of bowel.	Surgical removal.	If it interferes with gut function.	Ask vet to do rectal palpation for abdominal masses at "Senior Vet Check" (see page 386). Not all abdominal masses are within reach, though.
Lymphosarcoma	Intestines.	Weight loss, muscle loss, intermittent colic.	Usually inoperable; usually too far advanced for chemotherapy to be feasible.	Yes.	Ask vet to do rectal palpation for abdominal masses at "Senior Vet Check" (see page 386).
Melanoma	Hairless skin or dark skin of gray or light-colored horses; found in 80% of all "at risk due to color" horses over 15 years.	Visible dark, smooth, or broken lump(s) or clusters of lumps at root of tail, peri-neal^G area, vulva, and on the side of the face beneath the ears.	"Watchful waiting"; surgical removal; cryosurgery^G; intraslesional chemotherapy^G; oral cimeti-dine^G.	Usually not, but longstanding skin tumors can spread internally without warning; may become aggressive if not completely removed.	Monthly skin examinations, especially in locations described.
Pituitary Adenoma	Pituitary gland at base of brain.	See "The Age Event: Cushing's Disease" (page 257).	Symptomatic.	Treatment may restore comfort and function in roughly 50% of cases and can help keep the tumor from growing.	Learn the symptoms of ECD (see page 257) and ask vet to do diagnostic blood test with any suspicious signs.
Sarcoid	Trunk, extremities.	Visible lump(s) in skin.	Remove or obliterate by surgery, immunotherapy, topical chemotherapy.	Tends to recur but rarely spreads to internal organs; may become aggressive if not completely removed.	Monthly whole-body skin examinations.

The Ten Most Common Senior-Horse Cancers *(continued)*

Tumor Type	Where it Attacks	Signposts	Common Treatment	Life Threatening?	How to Detect
Squamous cell carcinoma	Skin of head, face, eyes, eyelids, sheath, and penis.	Wartlike growths; raw, open wound(s) that won't heal; irritation of affected tissues (such as the eyes).	Remove or obliterate by surgery, cryosurgery^G, hyperthermia^G, radiation.	More often not; tends to be locally invasive but in 10% to 20% of cases there is spreading to internal organs.	Monthly skin examination, especially in the locations described.
Squamous cell carcinoma	Stomach, esophagus, tongue, mouth, throat.	Acts hungry or thirsty, but stops eating or drinking abruptly before sated; choke^G, drooling, difficulty swallowing, weight loss.	Inoperable.	Yes.	Ask vet to check oral cavity and tongue during dental checkups; have esophagus examined by fiberoptic scope if your horse chokes^G or exhibits drooling or difficulty swallowing.
Thyroid adenoma	Thyroid gland; upper neck.	Visible or palpable lump in front, upper neck area.	"Watchful waiting;" surgical removal.	Usually not.	Ask vet to check twice a year manually (for evidence of enlargement) and/or show you how to do it.

Cancer Hot Spots

Is your senior horse at risk for cancer? Answer the following questions, then use our cancer-finder tips on a weekly basis, to help you detect it early, should it strike. Look for any lumps, bumps, or sores that won't heal. Then call your veterinarian if you find any.

1. *Is your horse gray, white, or partially white with black skin?* If so, he's at increased risk for melanoma, due to increased melanin in his skin. Melanoma tumors usually are black, covered by skin (but the skin may tear away as the melanoma grows), and often multiple. By the time your gray, white, or partially white horse is 15 years of age, his odds of having a melanoma are a sobering 80%. Although you'll see them in his skin, they can spread internally. A "benign" melanoma can become malignant over time. Be sure to check for black masses in the following locations, where melanoma is most commonly found:

➤

• The parotid area^G at the flat sides of his face, just behind the jawbone and beneath the base of his ears.
• The base of his tail.
• The perineal area^G (the hairless area under his tail, around and beneath his anus).
• The genital area (vulvar lips, penis, and sheath opening).
• The iris of his eyes (the colored part). Check to see if the choroid body^G (the normal nubbin at the upper border of his pupil) is enlarged—this is a popular spot for melanoma formation.
• Eyelids and tissues around the eyeball.

2. *Do you live more than 500 feet above sea level, or close enough to the equator to have very mild winters? Does your senior horse have little or no shelter from the sun? Does it snow there in the winter? Does your horse have pink-skinned areas on his body? Are there bald, grassless areas in his pasture?* If you answered yes to one or more queries, your horse has higher-than-average exposure to the sun's ultraviolet rays, so is at increased risk for squamous cell carcinoma (SCC), the most common, potentially malignant equine tumor. Be sure to check these locations:
• The mucocutaneous junctions (where dry skin meets moist tissue), especially where skin color is light and/or pink: lips, nostrils, vulva, eyelids, and coronary bands of light-colored legs.
• Also check the outside of the eyeball, where the "white" of the eye meets the cornea (clear part), and the tissues around the eyeball.

3. *Is your senior horse a gelding? Is his penis and/or prepuce pink, or pink-mottled in color? Do you clean his sheath less often than once per year? Does the material on and around his penis have a strong odor?* If you answered yes to one or more of these queries, he's at increased risk of SCC on the skin of his penis and sheath, due to irritation by accumulated smegma^G. Be sure to check the pink skin of your gelding's penis and sheath.

4. *Within the past 10 years, has your senior horse sustained any major skin wounds that involved stitches, proud flesh^G, infection, or burns? Has he had a skin infestation with the parasite Habronema^G?* The site of such lesion(s) is at increased risk for SCC, years after the initial insult. Be sure to check anywhere there's been a significant flesh wound, especially one with a long healing time or one involving an allergic-type nodular skin reaction.

5. *Has your senior horse ever been overweight? Have you ever found confirmed tumors under his tail or around his anus, in the groin areas, or anywhere on the hind legs? Is your senior horse a mare?* If the answer is yes to one or more of these queries, there's an increased risk for internal tumors in the pelvic or abdominal cavities. Be sure to request the following:

• Every 6 to 12 months, depending on your senior horse's age and medical history, ask your veterinarian to perform a rectal palpation, with or without ultrasound, to check for internal tumors, such as on the ovaries, mesenteric[G] fat, and intestinal lymph nodes.

Cancer Prevention

Though there's no way to banish cancer from this world—yet!—here are 5 of the best-supported equine cancer-fighting strategies.

1. Nix the Sun. Limit your horse's exposure to ultraviolet rays. Squamous cell carcinoma[G] (SCC) has been linked to sun exposure. Horses with little or no sun protection have a significantly higher incidence of SCC, especially if they have any light-colored hair and/or pink skin.

• Apply sun block or mechanical protection (fly masks, fly sheets labeled to provide UV protection). Do so daily during warm months, when the sun is closest to the earth—even on overcast days. If you live near the equator, where weather is warm most of the time, do it year-round.

• Keep your horse indoors during peak UV times. (From 10 a.m. to 3 p.m. in most areas.) Turn him out only when the sun's rays are less direct. Or, provide sun shelter, such as a walk-in shed, making it appealing by keeping a salt lick and water inside.

• Reseed and water grassless areas. The sun's rays are absorbed by live forage, but reflected by bald ground, giving your horse a double dose of UV. If he lives on a dry lot, arrange alternate living quarters.

2. Minimize Skin Irritation

• Treat flesh wounds promptly. If skin becomes infected, invaded by proud flesh[G], needs stitches but doesn't get them, gets fly strike[G], or otherwise takes a long time to heal, it's a target for squamous cell carcinoma (SCC) months or even years after the initial wound occurred.

• Treat chronic skin irritation, allergic-type skin reactions, and burns (thermal as well as chemical) promptly, for the reasons outlined above. If your horse's skin is invaded by internal parasites that cause skin nodules (such as habronemiasis[G]), get it diagnosed and treated ASAP.

➤

• Protect him against insects, such as mosquitoes and flies that cause skin irritation and carry cancer-promoting viruses and parasites.

• If your senior horse is a gelding, clean his sheath once or twice a year. SCC is commonly found in the sheath and/or penis. Studies have shown that smegma^G, that waxy, skin-irritating accumulation found there, may be responsible. For how to, see "Down & Dirty Maintenance...," page 360.

3. Avoid Carcinogens

Three common equine carcinogens are listed below. Avoid them whenever possible.

A. Insecticides: Absorption of insecticide chemicals over time is believed to increase the risk of cancer of the liver, the body's "toxic waste dump." When possible, replace or augment chemical pest control with nonchemical methods, such as by:

• Keeping premises and horses clean of pest-attracting smells, such as sweat, blood, manure, and urine-soaked bedding. *(Continued on opposite page)*

Recipe for Relief:
Homemade Fly Repellent

Experiment with skin-friendly, antibug ingredients to make your own fly repellent. If your horse is sensitive to certain substances (such as pine tar), avoid similar ingredients. Below are some examples. You'll need each of the following ingredients—and a spray-bottle—to make your homemade repellent.

Carrier liquids: Choose one or more of the following (or add to the list with your own ideas):
   Witch hazel
   Water
   White vinegar
   Aloe vera juice

Emollients: Choose one or more of the following:
   Avon's Skin-So-Soft® bath oil
   Sweet almond oil

Active ingredients: Choose one or more of the following:
   Essential oils: (available at health food stores); choose 6

and add 3 drops of each to your carrier liquid: citronella, pennyroyal, spearmint, marigold, sweet orange, lemongrass, ginger, cedar, pine needle, eucalyptus, tea tree, and lavender

Emulsifier:
   Pinch of dry mustard powder

Sample recipe:
   1. Combine 4 ounces water, 2 ounces witch hazel, and 1 ounce each white vinegar and aloe vera juice.
   2. Add 1 ounce sweet almond

oil and 3 drops each of citronella, marigold, spearmint, ginger, cedar, and lavender essential oils.
   3. Add a pinch of dry mustard powder. Blend (shake in a covered jar, whisk, or blend with a stick blender).
   4. Pour into a trigger-type spray bottle and apply in a fine mist while brushing the coat up, against the grain. Then spray again, while brushing the coat down smoothly. This coats the hairs on both sides and provides longer-lasting protection.
   5. Repeat as needed, up to 6 times per day.

• Eliminating free-standing, stagnant water, trash piles, and other breeding grounds.

• Encouraging beneficial bugs that feed on pests. Fly predators are available through Spalding Laboratories, 760 Printz Road, Arroyo Grande, CA 93420; 800.845.2847. Note: Pesticides kill not only pests but also their predators, which reproduce much more slowly. So, if you have an automatic fly system, you'll kill off the predators and possibly give surviving pests an advantage.

• Masking your horse's natural fly-attracting odors with such nontoxic camouflage as a misted 1:1 dilution of Avon Skin-So-Soft® bath oil, or a pesticide-free commercial product containing essential oils, such as Clac-86 (available through Whitman Saddle Company, 5272 West Michigan Avenue, Kalamazoo, MI 49006; 800.253.0852, stay on the line for an attendant). Or, make your own fly repellent spray. (See "Recipe for Relief," at left).

B. Herbicides: If your senior horse grazes in a pasture that's treated with herbicides, eats hay that was treated before it was harvested, lives downwind of farms, roadsides, and/or manicured lawns that use them, and/or drinks water that contains herbicide-tainted runoff, he may be at increasing risk for a variety of cancers including liver cancer, leukemia, and ovarian cancer (mares).

• When shopping for hay, consider an organic grower, or ask your grower for the names of the chemicals he uses and when he uses them relative to harvest time. Then call the Animal Poison Control Center (900.680.0000; cost $45) and ask about short-term and long-term toxicity studies.

• If you grow your own hay, avoid using herbicides. Consider hiring high school students to pull weeds by hand and stuff them in a plastic sack for ➤

Did You Know?

Although it's been accepted for generations that horse's can't burp, most veterinarians will tell you that horses can and do burp, they just don't do it as well as humans do, because horses have a more effective one-way valve at the entrance to the stomach. The most common time for a horse to burp is while he's eating a fed meal and swallowing larger amounts, more often, and in a higher head position, than would be the case if he were grazing. His stomach becomes fuller, faster, and accumulated air manages to escape upward when he swallows, while the stomach's one-way valve is open.

decomposition and disposal. For about the same amount of money you'd spend on chemicals, you'll produce hay with fewer weeds, provide gainful employment, and provide your horse with far healthier forage. Or buy or lease goats—they'll eat the weeds and leave the grass.

C. **Synthetic fertilizers:** Chemicals in fertilizer irritate the cells lining your horse's stomach and esophagus. The most common cancer in the stomach of horses is squamous cell carcinoma (SCC), which is known to occur in response to chronic irritation (as in colic) and often spreads to the esophagus, causing chronic choke^G in older horses. Use sustainable agricultural methods and organic fertilizers, keep horses away from fields and products on which synthetic fertilizers have been used, avoid overgrazing, and accept lower yields from hay fields, so you can help reduce your horse's risk of stomach cancer.

4. Limit your horse's exposure to toxic free radicals

Toxic free radicals^G are the by-products of living. They're like the exhaust from a car tailpipe—it won't run without producing them, but they're potentially deadly. In the body, toxic free radicals damage cell membranes, causing cells to die prematurely. This accelerates the aging process and encourages functional breakdown, as well as increases susceptibility to disease, including cancer.

Your senior horse's body is equipped with a system for scavenging and eliminating free radicals before they cause too much damage. Trouble is, some factors can produce such a heavy load of free radicals that his system gets overwhelmed. As he gets older, his protection diminishes, leaving him more vulnerable to free radical damage. Here's how you can help protect him:

• Avoid prolonged, strenuous, extreme activities. Any exercise that's severe enough to cause soreness (tissue breakdown) is producing an excessive load of free radicals. Help protect your horse by supplementing his pre- and post-event meals with antioxidents. See "Stay-Young Diet Solutions," page 376.

• Avoid feeding free radicals. This includes supplements, concentrates^G, or other feed products that have an "off" odor or are rancid. Spoilage chemically morphs nutrients—especially unsaturated fats—into free radicals. Particularly vulnerable are oils and oil-containing foods, such as:

- vegetable and seed oils (corn oil, soybean oil, flaxseed oil, cottonseed oil, etc.);

- seeds with a high oil content (oats, corn, flaxseeds, etc.);

- and seed meals (corn meal, flaxseed meal, etc.).

• To prevent oxidation^G, store all concentrates, seed meals, and oily supplements out of direct sunlight, in a consistently cool place. Don't buy feed that's stored by a sunny window or doorway in a hot warehouse. And, when opening a sack of feed, sniff it before you dump it in your feed bin. If it smells rancid, it's less tasty, less nutritious, and potential cancer food.

5. Search and Destroy

Check your horse's skin regularly and alert your veterinarian if you find any lumps, bumps, or sores that won't heal. Your vet will need to biopsy the suspicious area. Whenever possible, request a total excision biopsy, meaning the entire lump is removed, rather than just a piece of it. If it turns out to be cancer, often the biopsy also is the cure.

• At least once a month, combine whole-body grooming with a skin-cancer spot check.

- Start in an area of your horse's body that's not touchy or ticklish—for most horses, this would be the withers.

- Using a rubber curry in a brisk, circular motion, rough up the hair down to his armpit area. Work your way along his torso, from top to bottom, to his croup and groin area, being sure to include his belly.

- With your bare fingers, give him a fingertip massage in the same pattern, from withers and armpits all the way back to croup and groin, feeling for scabs, bumps, or anything out of the ordinary.

- Move on to his hindquarters with the same routine, being sure to inspect every area, including the root of the tail, the perineal region, the anus, the inner thighs, the genitals (vulva, penis, sheath), the hind legs, and the coronary bands.

- Then move to his forequarters, neck, head, and face.

- If you find anything, part the hair and take a good look. If it's not easily explained, describe its location, appearance, and size in writing so you can compare your findings on subsequent days.

- Be sure to note its width, length, and depth, and number and location of similar lesions. Also note whether, over the next several days, there's any change in appearance such as ulceration of the skin, or evidence of rubbing, which would suggest that it itches or hurts.

- Any lesion that hasn't resolved within 3 weeks should be biopsied.

NOTES

3Colic

THE AGE EVENT

What it is: The leading killer of senior horses. Though the term colic really means any form of abdominal pain rather than a specific condition, anything that causes such pain can quickly escalate into a serious problem.

Why your senior horse is at risk. We don't know the whole story, but we do know some age-related changes can contribute to your senior horse's higher colic risk.

• **Decreased parasite resistance.** This can lead to an increased intestinal parasite load. Damage from the parasitic burden can trigger colic.

• **Reduced water consumption.** Joint pain, mouth pain, and a reduced sensitivity to thirst can combine to reduce your horse's water intake (getting to a water source may simply seem like too much work or pain), increasing his risk of impaction colicᴳ.

• **A decline in digestive efficiency.** This can cause his intestines to have trouble moving feed through his system, and/or contribute to incomplete breakdown of feeds, resulting in a possible impaction and/or gas colic.

• **Increased stress.** Pain from arthritisᴳ and other age-related problems, coupled with a loss in social status, can combine to increase your senior horse's stress. This can lead to gas colic, constipation, impaction, and a number of other intestinal problems.

• **A sedentary lifestyle.** If your horse's aches and pains keep him from moving much, and/or his activities are restricted by his living arrangements (say, he's kept in a stall), his gut's motilityᴳ (the action that moves digested food through it) will be impaired, increasing his impaction colic risk.

• **Drug side effects.** NSAIDᴳ's, such as phenylbutazoneᴳ ("bute") can cause digestive upset and ulcers, leading to colic. Such drugs are commonly used to treat age-related inflammatory conditions, such as arthritisᴳ.

• **Tooth trouble.** An impaired ability to completely chew his feed, and perhaps a reluctance to drink water, can occur due to mouth pain. Swallowing incompletely chewed feed and dehydration can lead to impaction or other intestinal maladies.

Colic Signposts

To determine if your horse is showing signs of colic, see "Colic Symptom Checklist," page 222.

➤

Colic Prevention

Following are 12 steps you can take to help reduce your senior horse's colic risk.

1. ATTACK TAPEWORMS.

Why: Tapeworms^G cause colic in close to 10% of infested horses. Plus, the kind of colic caused by tapeworms is likely to be severe, requiring surgery. Violent colic in senior horses can end in euthanasia^G, due to expense and poor prognosis. At present, there is no reliable tapeworm test. However, research indicates that up to 80% of horses over age 15 are infested due to high exposure and declining immunity.

How: See "Senior Deworming & Vaccination Program," page 322.

2. REGULARLY DEWORM HIM—AND AVOID OVERGRAZED AND HIGH-HORSE-TRAFFIC AREAS.

Why: An age-related decline in immunity makes all-out war against parasites a must in your elder horse. Couple that immunity loss with grazing in highly contaminated areas, and your senior horse is at risk of picking up enough eggs and larvae in 30 minutes to cause colic within the following 2 weeks. All those parasites can become active and migrate through his body at the same time. Years of manure accumulation can result in heavy premises contamination with long-lived parasite eggs and larvae. (Some can persist in the field for 30 years.)

How: Go to "Senior Deworming & Vaccination Program," page 322. Avoid public fairgrounds, roadside rest stops with corrals, and crowded boarding stable pastures. If providing healthier grazing isn't possible, consider switching your senior horse to a daily dewormer^G, such as Strongid C® (Pfizer), which will kill parasite larvae before they begin migrating.

3. INCREASE YOUR SENIOR HORSE'S WATER INTAKE.

Why: He may drink less due to an age-related decreased sensitivity to thirst; decreased motivation to go to water due to pain, energy loss, and/or conflict with other horses; and/or dental pain.

How:

• Provide more than one salt source, including plain, loose salt and plain salt blocks in various locations in his living area. (If you use salt that's mixed with iodine or trace minerals, he might limit his intake due to the taste of one or more of those minerals.)

• Plus, toss 2 tablespoons of loose salt onto his hay at every feeding—most of it will spill through, but some will get on his lips and stimulate thirst.

• Provide easy access to clean, fresh water. Be alert to herd conflicts that could prevent getting to or away from the water source. (See "The Age Event: Loss of Social Status," page 279.)

• Keep footing around any troughs easy to negotiate for an older horse, by making sure it isn't slippery, rocky, or knee-deep in snow or mud.

• If the water source is electrically heated, have it inspected by a licensed electrician to be sure it's properly grounded and not giving drinkers a shock.

• In cold weather, provide a slightly warmed water source (body temperature water; ~100° F) along with the usual, room-temperature variety. Although horses often choose unwarmed water, when they do choose warmed water they tend to drink a larger volume.

• Have your horse's teeth checked by a licensed veterinarian every 6 months or whenever any signs of discomfort arise, whichever comes first. (For more on dental problems, go to "Top Priority—Tooth Care," page 332.)

4. PROVIDE A HIGH-FIBER DIET.

Why: It takes a steady stream of fiber to keep your horse's gut functioning normally. Plus, forage^G takes more chewing than concentrates do, so his salivary glands will produce more bicarbonate-rich saliva. This helps to neutralize stomach acid when he swallows, which in turn can help reduce ulcer formation. Feed in his stomach helps protect the stomach's lining, too, also reducing his risk of stomach ulcers.

How:

• If your senior horse is still capable of chewing and digesting pasture and/or hay, make sure he gets 1% to 2% of his body weight per day. (Commercial chopped hay, which is easier to chew than regular hay, is an option for a senior with dental problems.) This not only helps keep his gut moving, but also gives him plenty of chew time, allowing him to generate saliva. Caveat: During springtime, pasture grass may not have adequate fiber. Keep your senior horse locked out of pasture each morning until he eats at least 1/2% of his body weight in hay.

• If he's getting a complete feed due to dental problems, offer at least 1/2% of his body weight per day in good-quality grass pasture or hay (chopped or regular) for the chew-time benefit. Give him the hay after he's finished his complete-feed meal.

• If you stall your horse, help mimic a natural feed routine, by feeding him small amounts of roughage throughout the day.

5. AVOID FEEDING HIM IN SANDY AREAS.

Why: Nibbling feed remnants can cause sand ingestion. The older horse is more likely to go after those small, savory leaves because he may be having trouble chewing the tougher stuff. Sand can settle in his intestines, accumulating over time   ➤

and eventually causing sand colicᴳ. With increasing age, the rate at which partially digested feed passes through your senior horse's gut, known as motilityᴳ, tends to slow down. Researchers believe slower gut motility may cause a higher incidence of sand colic in older horses. That's because the slower things move through the gut, the greater the chance that heavier particles such as sand settle out and lag behind. (To check your horse's sand load, see "Nitty Gritty Sand Test," page 177.)

How: Provide feed only in areas with concrete and rubber mats, portable feeders on grassy areas (moving them to a new spot before the grass is worn away), or special feeding areas with clay footing. Note: Recent research suggests that the old standby for "sweeping" sand from the gut—psyllium-husk laxatives—doesn't work reliably. Currently there are no alternatives known to work better except eliminating the possibility of ingesting more sand, so the sand that naturally comes out in manure isn't replaced.

6. MAKE FEED CHANGES GRADUALLY.

Why: So your horse's intestinal floraᴳ (friendly, digestion-helping bacteria) have a chance to adjust to the change in their diet and don't have to resort to less efficient, gas-producing digestive techniques to deal with new feed. Otherwise, you risk gas colic, impaction colic, and laminitisᴳ.

How: See "Stay-Young Diet Solutions," page 376.

7. BEWARE ALFALFA AND WHEAT BRAN.

Why: Both have been linked to enterolith formation, especially in California and Florida, where enteroliths are most common compared to other states.

How: Make 50% or more of the forage portion of your horse's diet grass or grass hay. Add a cup of vinegar to your horse's daily ration, which may help to prevent/dissolve the stones. Feed wheat bran no more than once a week.

8. LOCK THE FEED ROOM (OR WHEREVER YOU KEEP GRAIN).

Why: A grain-bag raid can result in toxins in your senior horse's gut, which can cause a fatal colic—or laminitisᴳ.

How: Keep grain out of reach of horses, period, idiotproofing your setup to prevent human error. Use horseproof bolts on feed-room doors, chains and snaps on trash-can lids, and the like. And, call your vet NOW if your horse does manage to find—and feast on—unsecured grain.

9. CONTROL YOUR SENIOR'S STRESS.

Why: Stress decreases blood flow to your horse's gut, further slows his already aging motility, decreases digestive enzyme output, dehydrates manure, and thereby increases his risk of colic in a multitude of ways, including constipation, impaction, indigestion, and gas.

How: See "The Age Event: Loss of Social Status," page 279. If your senior horse is being picked on by other horses, move him to a less stressful environment. Talk to your vet to see whether your horse should be examined and treated for ulcers. And, if he's suffering from chronic pain, talk to your veterinarian about finding conventional or alternative ways to make him more comfortable—pain is a significant stress.

10. TAKE HIM OUT OF RETIREMENT.

Why: Physical activity, even the very mild variety of walking in a pasture, helps stimulate gut motility^G, which helps offset age-related gut slow-down.

How: See "Age-Adjusted Exercise," page 340.

11. TAKE IT EASY ON THE BUTE.

Why: Bute, Banamine®, ibuprofen, aspirin, Naprosyn® and other NSAID^Gs (nonsteroidal anti-inflammatory drugs) commonly used for equine aches, pains, and arthritis^G can damage your horse's large intestine. This can cause stomach ulcers and a condition called colitis^G, either of which can cause colic.

How: If your senior horse has a condition associated with chronic pain, talk to ➤

Did You Know?

Your horse doesn't have a gall bladder. That's because he was designed to be a "trickle feeder," meaning he eats 24/7, only taking time off to rest. So bile juices, which are produced by his liver to help him digest his feed, trickle directly, and constantly, from the liver onto partially digested feed as it moves through his intestines. Humans, on the other hand, were designed to eat discreet meals with periods of "fasting" in between, so our livers developed a handy sac, called the gall bladder, to accumulate digestive bile juices in preparation for the next meal. With this in mind, don't expect your horse to do well on one or two meals a day. Unless he's on pasture, take his daily ration and divide it into as many smaller meals as you can.

your vet about ways to manage his discomfort that are gentler on his gut. And never give an NSAID if your senior horse is off feed, dehydrated, or not drinking his usual volume of water, unless your veterinarian advises it—the toxic effects will be magnified.

12. AVOID RECENTLY FERTILIZED FIELDS.

Why: Chemical pasture fertilizer contains a high percentage of nitrogen, phosphorus, and/or ammonia, which can irritate your senior's stomach and is a common cause of colic in the springtime, when pastures and hay fields routinely are fertilized. (It also can aggravate existing ulcers.) Stricken horses appear depressed, have a decreased appetite, and may be observed to "burp." (Despite the old wives' tale, horses do have the ability to burp. They're just not very good at it: For more information, see "Did You Know" page 247.)

How: Ask to be notified when fertilizer will be spread in pastures on and around your facility. Keep your horse in an area where he can't reach grass from fertilized fields until fertilizer granules are completely gone (a month, with at least 7 days of soaking rainfall) and grass has grown at least 6 inches tall. And, don't allow him to drink from surface water that's downhill from the fertilized field during this period. Runoff is likely to contain hazardous chemical levels. This isn't that hard—if you've got only one field, divide it in half with temporary fencing, preferably electrified so he respects it. Fertilize one half, while you allow your horse to graze the other half. When it's safe, switch sides. Simple! (*Note:* Consult your vet before using "horse safe" weed-and-feed products, whose labels require little or no restriction to grazing after application.)

Did You Know?

Some vets speculate that changes in weather can spark a colic crisis, linking it to a change in barometric pressure. Such changes can occur when a calm morning evolves into a violent afternoon of thunderstorms. While such evidence is unsupported with research, there could be a connection.

THE AGE EVENT
4 Cushing's Disease

What it is: Equine Cushing's Disease (ECD), also called pituitary adenoma. It's caused by pituitary gland malfunction.

Why your senior horse is at risk. If one condition seems synonymous with old age in horses, this is it. In one study, 10 of 13 horses over the age of 20 showed at least subclinical Cushing's-type signs.

Research indicates that as your horse ages, his brain produces less dopamine, a neurotransmitter. This leads to an upset in pituitary gland function, which causes the gland to grow. Controversy exists over whether this growth is a benign glandular tumor, called an adenoma, or purely a matter of function.

Along with that growth comes hormonal imbalance. Dopamine controls the pituitary gland's output of ACTH (Adrenal CorticoTropic Hormone), a hormone that stimulates the adrenal glands to produce cortisol^G, a steroidal hormone. When dopamine levels decline, ACTH levels rise. The adrenal gland responds by producing more cortisol than your senior horse needs. The result? A cortisol overdose. (See, "Why Cortisol Counts," next page.)

ECD Signposts

The following signposts could mean your senior horse is suffering from Cushing's disease. Your ability to identify these signs early—and take immediate action—could greatly affect his ability to live with this chronic condition (there currently is no cure). Familiarize yourself with them, then go to the "ECD Action Plan," page 259.

• **Failure to shed.** This is the classic Cushing's signpost—it can occur in more than 85% of ECD cases. Your horse's coat becomes long, wavy, and/or shaggy looking, possibly with patches missing, despite longer days, warm weather, and the fact that other horses around him have already shed.

• **Laminitis.** One of the most serious symptoms of ECD is laminitis^G. For signposts, see "The Age Event: Laminitis (Founder)," page 273. ➤

• **Increased water consumption.** One of the first and earliest symptoms to appear is excessive thirst—your horse drinks noticeably more water than normal, twice his usual amount, or even more. If he lives outside and drinks from a tub, or has an automatic waterer, this may go unnoticed unless you make a point of studying his drinking habits.

WHY CORTISOL COUNTS

Here's a look at the key role cortisol plays in your horse's health—when it's released at normal levels.

• Helps maintain cardiac function and blood pressure.
• Helps regulate muscle tone, connective tissue repair, and nerve-tissue function.
• Helps reduce the immune system's inflammatory response.
• Helps balance the role of insulin in breaking down sugar for energy.
• Helps to regulate fat, protein, and carbohydrate metabolism.
• Contributes to the body's response to stress.

It's normally produced in a rhythm, with higher levels released in the morning and lower levels released at night. (Unless your horse is stressed, in which case a surge will be released immediately, regardless of time.)

Equine Cushing's Disease upsets that rhythm, causing a constant and increased cortisol release. Too much of a good thing is hazardous to your horse's health, as evidenced by the classic ECD symptoms. You can see from cortisol's normal role how an excess can produce those signs. See "ECD Signposts," page 257.

• **Increased urine output.** You notice his stall or paddock is more urine-soaked than usual. Or, you see him urinating large volumes, more often.

• **Increased or decreased sweating.** You notice that your horse sweats more or less than he typically does, and more or less than his neighbors do.

• **Muscle wasting.** Your horse's muscles seem to waste away, particularly over his topline; he may also have a potbellied appearance.

• **Weight loss or gain.** He loses weight without any change in his ration or food intake; his appetite may increase, but without a resultant weight gain; or, he may gain weight/develop fat deposits without a ration increase.

• **Energy loss.** Your senior horse tires more easily than normal, and lacks his usual brightness. This can be due to anemia[G], a blood change that can accompany ECD.

• **Chronic infections.** A suppressed immune system leaves your horse prone to infections, including respiratory, dental, and skin infections. Sole abscesses may also increase in frequency. And, wounds can be slower to heal.

• **Increased parasite load.** His suppressed immune system can also leave your horse more prone to parasite invasions, including those from pinworms[G] (*Oxyuris equi*), as evidenced by chronic tail rubbing, and roundworms (ascarids^G). Ascarids are common in young foals, but they're rare in adult horses because of top-notch mature immune systems. This changes when your horse succumbs to ECD.

• **Suppressed or abnormal estrous cycles.** Your senior mare may quit cycling, or may cycle in a way that's abnormal for her. And, she might produce milk without being pregnant.

ECD Action Plan

DIAGNOSIS: If you notice one or more of the symptoms above, call your veterinarian TODAY. (If any sign of laminitis^G is present, call the vet NOW!) He or she will make a diagnosis based on characteristic signs and blood tests. Early diagnosis—before symptoms become extreme—is key. The symptoms themselves (particularly laminitis) can be life-threatening.

TREATMENT:

1. DRUGS.

At present, two prescription medications are generally used to manage Cushing's symptoms, with varying degrees of success:

• *Pergolide mesylate* (trade name Permax), is a dopamine agonist (mimics dopamine's action) and recently has become a viable treatment option. The drug originally was used to treat Parkinson's disease in humans. In Cushing's horses, it can provide some symptomatic relief, such as encouraging shedding and increasing energy. The downside is that it can be expensive—up to around $90 per month or more. However, once a maintenance dose is established, that cost could drop to around $1/day.

• *Cyproheptadine* is a serotonin blocker that's thought to control excess pituitary secretion and has been used to treat Cushing's disease in horses for a number of years. It's fairly inexpensive—about $40 for 1,000 tablets—and many horses respond favorably to it.

2. MANAGEMENT.

• **Help regulate his temperature.** Since Cushing's adversely affects your horse's ability to stay cool in warm weather, and warm in cool weather, blanket him in the winter as necessary and body-clip him in the summer, if he's unable to stay cool. Be sure he has shade, shelter, and access to clean, fresh water.

• **Limit grass exposure.** Because ECD increases your horse's chance of laminitis, limit or stop his exposure to lush spring grass, which can trigger laminitic changes. This is especially important if he's shown any evidence, or history, of ➤

Cushing's
Fast Facts

• ECD can occur in horses as young as 7, but usually affects those in their late teens or 20s.

• It's twice as common in mares as it is in stallions and geldings.

• Similar symptoms can be caused by thyroid tumors, which are much less common in horses than Cushing's, and by diabetes mellitus^G, which is quite rare in horses but can occur as a symptom of ECD. Reliable diagnostics can help differentiate and properly treat these diseases.

• The disease is named for a turn-of-the-century American surgeon, Dr. Harvey Cushing, who studied the human brain and pituitary gland.

• Humans and dogs also are affected by Cushing's disease. However, in those species, the disease is usually associated with tumors on different areas of the pituitary gland than with equine Cushings, or with an adrenal-gland tumor. Horses don't seem to suffer from adrenal-gland tumors.

• In dogs and humans, pituitary tumors can sometimes be removed. With horses, surgery isn't an option due to the pituitary gland's lack of accessibility, and the fact that most ECD sufferers are over 20, have compromised immune systems, and therefore have low survival odds if put under general anesthetic.

• Cushing's Disease and all its effects can be triggered by excess steroid medication, which results in excess cortisol^G in the system.

• Advanced stages of ECD can lead to blindness, head-tilt, and/or dementia^G, due to growth of the overstimulated pituitary gland, which begins to press upon adjacent brain structures.

• With excellent care and medication, it's possible for a horse with ECD to live comfortably. Each case will have its own unique characteristics and response to therapy.

laminitisᴳ—once he has "foundered," he's significantly more apt to be stricken with laminitis again. (For more information on founder, see page 273.)

• **Get prompt medical attention.** If your horse suffers from any type of infection, get veterinary attention fast, because he'll be less able to cope with it by himself, thanks to decreased immunity. To help you identify such a problem, go to the appropriate symptom in the "Senior Signposts, Action Plans, Section 1."

• **Keep him vaccinated and dewormed.** Help boost his sagging immune system with a deworming and shots program suited to his lifestyle. See "Senior Deworming & Vaccination Program," page 322.

• **Keep up the dental work.** Help minimize the chance of mouth infections and decreased condition with regular dental work. See "Top Priority—Tooth Care," page 332.

• **Get him good foot care.** Have him shod or trimmed every 5 to 6 weeks, keep his feet clean, and provide him with horse-friendly footing (soft, level ground free of rocks and holes) to help minimize hoof abscesses. If he's suffered from laminitis, work with your vet and farrier to shoe him in a way that keeps him as comfortable as possible.

• **Adjust his diet.** Your ECD horse has difficulty digesting carbohydrates. In fact, he shares many of the same metabolic problems as individuals with diabetes mellitusᴳ. Use a top-quality feed, formulated by a reputable company specifically for senior horses. It'll be suitably low in carbs and high in fats, which will support his nutritional needs without adding to his risk of carbohydrate-induced health problems, such as colicᴳ and laminitis. For more information, see "Stay-Young Diet Solutions," page 376.

Herbal Helper

Human herbal lore credits the chaste berry (*Vitex agnus-castus*) with medicinal benefits, including stimulation of the brain's secretion of dopamine (declining levels of which initiate Equine Cushing's Disease). With this in mind, the herbal product Hormonise (www.emeraldvalleybotanical.com; 888.638.8262) was produced for the equine Cushing's patient. Does it work? We don't know; there've been no scientific studies. Is it safe? Probably, although in humans it can cause an upset stomach, so if you decide to try it for your horse, keep a close eye on him for colic symptoms. (See Colic Symptom Checklist, page 222.) Is it appropriate for your Cushing's horse? Maybe. Talk to your vet.

NOTES

THE AGE EVENT

5 Declining Fertility
(in mares)

What it is: Your mare's fertility has been reduced. She's failing to get pregnant, or to hold a pregnancy. (For information on reduced stallion fertility, see "Senior Stallion: Declining Pregnancy Rate" and "Senior Stallion: Trouble in the Breeding Shed," pages 213 and 208 respectively.)

Why your senior horse is at increased risk:

• When your mare turns 16, she's roughly the equivalent of 54 in human years. (For how to calculate your senior horse's equivalent human age, see "Atlas of Aging," page 286.) She's less efficient reproductively, so will be harder to get in foal than a younger mare. Studies show that at age 3, pregnancy rate can be around 85%, compared to around 45% at age 17. This can add up to time—and money.

• The odds of her maintaining a pregnancy and delivering a live, healthy foal are also less than those of a younger mare. Studies show that after age 15, your senior mare's risk of resorbing or miscarrying is about double the risk before she crossed the "senior line." This is due to age-related scarring in the cervix, uterus, and/or oviducts (regardless of whether she's had a foal or not); an increased susceptibility to uterine infection; and older (possibly genetically damaged) eggs exposed to a lifetime of stress, illness, and pollutants.

• Older mares that have had at least one foal or a history of previous uterine infections are likely to have some uterine scar tissue. In one study, all but 6 of 45 mares under age 6 had scar-free uterine biopsies, while 49 of 51 mares aged 20 to 25 had moderate to severe scarring. Widespread scarring can cause abortion in the 3rd trimester—there won't be enough glandular tissue to keep the fetus alive.

• Your older mare is at increased risk of exhaustion and uterine inertia[G] during foaling, due to decreased muscle strength, decreased stamina, and less efficient metabolism, all of which adversely affect her ability to sustain contractions. She's much more likely than a younger mare to need help during the foaling process, even if the foal's positioned perfectly.

➤

263

• She's also at increased risk of rupture of the uterine artery (and fatal internal hemorrhage) within 24 hours after foaling, due to loss of elasticity of those arteries.

• Although the reason is unknown, studies show that foals born of mares over 16 perform less well as adults on the racetrack.

• Because of increased uterine scarring and declining muscle tone in the mare, foals born to aged mares are at increased risk of perinatal asphyxia^G. They may appear normal at birth, but within 6 to 24 hours after foaling develop signs of abnormal mental functioning—jerky movements, loss of suckle reflex, blindness, aimless wandering, and coma. In severe cases, they're abnormal at birth or stillborn.

• Due to decreasing immunity and anatomic changes in the perineal^G area, senior mares are at increased risk of acute endometritis^G and toxemia^G within 24 hours after foaling—a serious infection similar to toxic shock syndrome in women, requiring emergency treatment. And, for the same reasons, the aged mare is at increased risk of developing pyometra^G, which usually ruins her for future reproduction and, in rare cases, can rupture and cause a fatal peritonitis^G.

• Due to declining gut function as well as decreased resistance to parasites and other conditions, senior mares are at increased risk of surgical colic^G within the first few months after foaling, resulting from aberrant gut motility^G in an abdominal cavity that suddenly has lots of room for a loop of bowel to twist itself into a knot.

• Due to age-related thinning and weakening of muscles, senior mares are at increased risk of developing an abdominal hernia^G or ruptured prepubic tendon^G as the pregnancy becomes heavier.

Infertility Signposts

See "Changes in Reproductive Performance," page 203.

How to Reduce that Risk

You can't always prevent the adverse affects of aging on your mare's fertility. However, if you opt to breed her, you can use these tips to help maximize your chance of success.

• **Feed her right.** Feed your senior mare a diet that's balanced and contains at least 6% to 7% supplementary fat. (For more information, go to "Stay-Young Diet Solutions," page 376.) Studies show that mares receiving at least this level of supplementary fat have healthier levels of the reproductive hormone progesterone^G, which is necessary to maintain pregnancy. And, make sure her diet contains adequate copper levels. (When in doubt, consult your vet or an equine nutritionist.) Copper deficiency has been associated with increased incidence of uterine artery rupture^G in aged foaling mares.

Did You Know**?**

If your mare passes the placenta more quickly than usual after foaling, it's a clue that her placenta may have started detaching from the uterus before she delivered her foal, depriving him of oxygen and causing brain damage. Alert your veterinarian immediately. The foal may need treatment, including supplemental oxygen and medications to control brain swelling.

• **Use ultrasound.** Have your senior mare's estrous cycles closely monitored by ultrasound, so you and your vet know how long her cycles are, what size follicle she ovulates, and whether there's any indication of uterine infection or susceptibility to it. If she's cycling normally and her uterus is clean, have her bred by a minimum contamination technique[G]: time it right, so she'll only need to be bred once in the cycle; use a stallion that's fertile and clean; and consider using artificial insemination to minimize the amount of fluid deposited in her reproductive tract.

• **Provide diligent prenatal care:** Make sure your pregnant senior mare lives in a stress-free environment where she has access to feed, water, and shelter without fear of harassment by aggressive herd members. (For more information, go to "The Age Event: Loss of Social Status," page 279.)

• **Keep her fit.** Work with your veterinarian to develop a safe exercise program suited to your pregnant mare's age and condition. That way, she'll have a leg up on the strength and stamina needed for foaling, decreasing her risk of uterine inertia[G] and endometritis[G] and improving overall circulation for more normal cycles and milk production. For more information, see "Age-Adjusted Exercise," page 340.

• **Keep up with vaccinations.** Make sure your mare gets the vaccinations your veterinarian recommends throughout her pregnancy (no more, no less).

• **Be a good groom.** Daily grooming enables you to observe your senior mare closely for signs of problems; stimulates circulation in her skin; and helps protect her against edema due to age- and pregnancy-related declines in venous elasticity, activity, and blood flow.

• **Be a careful observer.** Watch for swelling in the lower belly wall and/or legs, and/or a painful reaction when grooming or touching her abdomen. These signs could indicate that your senior mare is developing an abdominal hernia[G] or ruptured prepubic tendon[G]. Call your veterinarian if you see either. ➤

• **Bend over.** As your mare enters the third trimester, get into the habit of bending over to check her udder, even if she's several weeks from her expected due date—premature milk production usually signals placentitis^G and impending abortion. If you catch it early and alert your veterinarian, the cause may be identifiable. A possible solution, before the fetus is damaged, may be within reach.

• **Be there when she foals.** And have a willing veterinarian on call. Any equine birth can quickly turn from normal to trouble. The increased risk of age-related problems makes skilled help a must for your senior mare.

• **Be assertive.** Ask your veterinarian to carry portable oxygen, or to give you a prescription to have it on hand for his or her use on your foal, if need be. (Remember, your aged mare is at increased risk of delivering a foal with perinatal asphyxia^G.) Oxygen therapy and specific medications such as medical-grade DMSO^G and dexamethasone^G can help reverse brain swelling due to oxygen deprivation before it results in irreversible brain damage.

• **Have a contingency plan.** If your senior mare dies or is unable to care for her foal, be prepared. For example, have 32 ounces of good-quality colostrum in the freezer, which you can get from a fellow horse breeder. (There are sources available on the Internet, too—do a search using the key words "equine colostrum.") If you don't use your colostrum within 24 hours of foaling, consider yourself blessed and spread the word that it's available for anybody else who might need it—colostrum loses quality after a year in a deep freeze; in 6 months if it's in a freezer that automatically defrosts itself. Have foal-milk replacer on hand, along with a means to give it (a bottle and a rubber sheep's nipple, and/or a bucket so you can switch from the bottle to bucket-feeding). Introduce your foal to creep feed when he's 3 or 4 days of age. The sooner he's able to feed himself, the better his chances of survival should he become orphaned.

6 THE AGE EVENT
Heaves

What it is: An acquired chronic allergic response that eventually diminishes your senior horse's ability to breathe, much as asthma does in humans. When a horse's ability to breathe is impaired, his ability to do much of anything else is, too.

Why your senior horse is at risk. He's suffered a lifelong, chronic buildup of exposure to allergens in his environment, such as dust, smoke, and pollution that he'd be unlikely to encounter in the wild. The bad news is that heaves tends to worsen every year. You can help manage it—but we can't cure it—yet.

Heaves Signposts

You'll typically observe a gradual progression of respiratory distress, usually without evidence of ongoing infection (no fever, none of the other horses in the barn is sick). It may take weeks or years for the symptoms to interfere with your horse's ability to function. Here's a look at its typical progression.

• Your horse shows signs of being easily winded.

• A dry cough shows up later, and eventually becomes "juicier."

• A thick nasal discharge may then appear, as evidenced by mucus on stall walls and/or in the feed bucket.

• As the condition progresses, your horse's "air hunger" begins to preoccupy him. He's reluctant to do anything that might interfere with satisfying it, or that might make him feel more winded.

• Breathing out becomes even more difficult than breathing in. (We'll explain why in a minute.)

• His abdominal muscles become overdeveloped from helping to aid his breathing efforts, forming a curved indentation—called a heave line—along the side of his body.

• For most horses, symptoms lessen or disappear in pasture, but return with a vengeance in a stall.

• If you suspect heaves in your horse, your veterinarian can perform a respiratory challenge test. In that test, a single dose of a caffeine-related medication ➤

is administered. It'll cause a dramatic but short-lived improvement if—and only if—heaves is the problem. Treatment with bronchodilating medication such as clenbuterol^G (Ventipulmin®) and anti-inflammatory medication can bring amazing relief in many cases; antihistamines rarely are effective. But lung damage will continue unless you cut down on the allergens that are choking him.

Heaves Helpers

The following are both preventive and therapeutic management steps you can take. Use them to prevent heaves in a healthy senior horse—or to reduce its impact in a victim. Tailor your clean-up program to match your particular environment.

• **Get him out.** If possible, move your stable-bound senior horse to a grassy pasture. (Work with your veterinarian to introduce your horse gradually to grass, to avoid the risk of laminitis^G.) Doing so will eliminate dust inhaled from bedding and other barn sources. If you can only manage part-time turnout, that's better than nothing—at the very least you've reduced his exposure to some allergens.

A.K.A.
A LOOK AT THE MANY ALIASES OF HEAVES

Heaves
Broken wind
Small airway disease
Chronic airway disease
Equine asthma
Winter barn syndrome
Chronic obstructive
pulmonary disease (COPD)
Haysickness
Bronchiolitis
Allergic bronchiolitis
Emphysema
Chronic alveolar emphysema
Summer pasture-associated
obstructive pulmonary
disease (SPAOPD)

• **Or, bring him in.** If, on the other hand, your senior horse suffers from the less common summer pasture-associated obstructive pulmonary disease^G (SPAOPD; see "A Less Common Form of Heaves," page 270), take him off grass to help alleviate his respiratory distress.

• **Location, location, location.** If your horse must reside in a stall at times, make it one at the end of the barn. That way he only has one neighbor kicking up dust instead of two. And, make sure his stall is nowhere near the arena, hay storage area, or bedding storage, so blowing dust/allergens are minimized.

• **Cut down on dust.** Set up a temporary outdoor holding area for your stabled horse and move him there before cleaning stalls or dragging the indoor arena, so he won't breathe dust kicked up during those efforts.

• **Use a better bedding.** Replace dusty bedding in his stall and his neighbors' stalls with cleaner materials. (See "Senior's Best Bedding Bets," page 370).

• **Help with hay.** Replace dusty/moldy hay with cleaner forage, and wet it down before feeding. Some amateur-produced hays are baled while the forage's moisture content is too high, leading to heavy molding.

Clean, fresh hay that's been dampened with water just before feeding will help minimize dust. Also try changing to a different variety; a horse sensitive to alfalfa might improve on timothy. Processed hay cubes or complete feed pellets can be a viable alternative if they're made of top-quality, dust-free ingredients.

• **Concentrate on concentrates.** Replace dusty/moldy concentrates wit products. Some grains, especially oats, can be very dusty, depending on the ➤

An Inside Look at Heaves

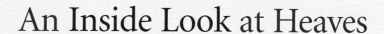

Researchers are generally agreed that heaves is an acquired allergy to the stuff of domestic equine life: allergenic dusts, molds, smoke, pollutants, ammonia fumes, and mutating respiratory viruses. Inhaling irritants sets off a self-defeating immune response, causing tissues lining the bronchiole walls (the smallest branches of the respiratory tree) to swell, ooze, and spasm, a reaction called bronchoconstriction[G]. Just as water runs more turbulently through a narrow stream than a wide riverbed, there's more air turbulence in constricted bronchioles, resulting in more inflammation, more swelling—and more bronchoconstriction.

Constant bronchoconstriction traps used air in the lungs' tiny gas-exchange chambers (called alveoli), causing them to bulge and stretch. Instead of air being expelled from your horse's lungs by elasticized alveoli, it has to be forced out by his abdominal muscles. Suddenly he has to think about exhaling and work at it, instead of just allowing it to happen automatically.

Unless your horse is removed from the triggers in his allergenic environment, respiratory insults will continue and compound themselves. Respiratory-tree tissues will become hypersensitized, reacting to every potential irritant, from a spritz of fly spray to a puff of smoke, with fits of coughing and heavy breathing with flared nostrils. This is called airway hyperresponsiveness[G].

The most common heaves triggers are:
• Poor-quality hay (dusty, moldy).
• Dusty/moldy bedding (see "Senior Bedding," page 370).
• Respiratory viruses.
• Dusty arenas and racetracks.
• Old wooden barns, which can be impregnated with molds that remain as long as the walls are standing. Metal or cement block barns can be more lung-friendly, but only if they're kept clean.
• Insect sprays.
• Smog, especially in metropolitan areas where automobile traffic is heavy, or in rural valleys where air inversions cause car exhaust from neighboring towns to drift and hover.
• Smoke.
• Noxious volatile fumes, such as from paints and solvents.

For more information on living with a heave-y horse, see "Heaves Helpers," at left.

growing, harvesting, and storage conditions. Other grains, especially corn, are prone to mold growth. Most top-quality senior horse concentrates contain oil, which virtually eliminates dust. Choose only premium-quality products, and check them for dustiness. Or feed beet pulp. Because it must be soaked in water before being fed, it's a no-dust option.

• **Try a high-fat diet.** It's been shown that some horses with heaves benefit from a ration high in fat. Add 1 to 2 cups of vegetable oil or a rice bran supplement to your senior horse's diet. (As with any diet change, introduce the fat gradually to avoid digestive upset; for how to, see page 379.) Bonus—his coat will glow!

• **Go for gravity.** The most important method for keeping your horse's respiratory tree clean is drainage. For that, use gravity. Feed your senior horse on a low, dust-free platform or a clean, bedding-free section of floor. Better yet, let him graze in a clean pasture—it's not only the pasture that's helping his respiratory tract, it's also the grazing posture.

• **Hit the trail.** Avoid dusty arena work, opting instead for trails (nondusty trails). If that's not possible, spray the arena to hold down dust (or ask the barn manager to do so), or move to a barn that practices dust control.

A Less Common Form of Heaves

While a vast majority of stall-confined horses with heaves show improvement when turned out, some horses gasp for breath while in pasture, only to breathe a sigh of relief when brought in. The latter condition is called summer pasture-associated obstructive pulmonary disease, or SPAOPD. Scientists believe it's the same allergy-connection scheme with slightly different characters: The horse is sensitized to something present in the pasture instead of allergens in his stall, and is managed accordingly.

• **Keep it clean.** Keep your horse's stall free of urine spots, and use a stall freshener (such as Sweet PDZ, by Steelhead Specialties in Spokane, Washington; 800.367.1534) to deactivate ammonia after each cleaning. It's best to stay away from lime—inhaled lime dust can severely burn your horse's respiratory tract.

• **Avoid old wive's tales.** For instance, it's doubtful that vinegar in your horse's drinking water will help to clear out respiratory gunk. What it might do is dehydrate your horse when he turns up his nose at the taste. Another old wive's tale, that of swabbing Vicks Vaporub® in your senior horse's nostrils to open his respiratory passages, also can cause problems. It'll quash his sense of smell and impair his taste, thereby contributing to inappetance. Instead of trying gimmicks, work with your

> ## Did You Know?
>
> Studies have connected heaves with exposure to chickens. The exact cause has yet to be identified, but a good guess would be feathers. If your horse has heaves and you also have chickens, consider finding a foster home for the birds.

veterinarian to develop a viable treatment/management/prevention program for your horse.

• **Reach for the petroleum jelly.** Swab a light coating of plain Vaseline® just inside your senior horse's nostrils, to help catch inhaled dust and mold particles before they get deeper. Wipe it out every day, replacing it with a fresh coat.

• **Avoid cough suppressants.** Your senior horse is coughing for a reason. Suppressing the cough will encourage mucus and debris to remain in his airways instead of coming out. Expectorants, which are supposed to help moisten the respiratory tree and loosen debris for easier cough-up, can be somewhat irritating to both your horse's respiratory tract and his stomach. Consult your veterinarian before using expectorants in your horse.

• **Let him recover.** If your horse is diagnosed with a viral respiratory infection such as influenzaG, and begins to improve, don't return him to work too soon. The viral-induced hypersensitized state (see "An Inside Look at Heaves," page 269) of his small airways will persist for several weeks after he appears fully recovered. Keep him quiet and his respiratory tract clean, to better the chances his hypersensitized state will abate. Otherwise, he may be at risk for developing heaves, or worsening it if he's already heave-y.

• **Travel smart.** Horse trailers, especially fully enclosed ones, are pods filled with molds and spores that can wreak havoc on your horse's lungs. Haul him in an open, stock-type or modified stock-type trailer, so he gets maximum ventilation. (You need to be more concerned about your horse getting fresh air than about keeping him warm—you can use sheets or blankets to accomplish that, if need be.) If you have to use an enclosed trailer, keep all the windows open to encourage maximum ventilation.

NOTES

7 Laminitis
(Founder)

What it is: An inflammatory reaction in your horse's foot or feet (generally the front ones) that alters blood supply to its laminae, the pleated, accordionlike junctions that bind his coffin bone to the inner hoof wall. It's one of the most serious health threats to your aging horse.

Why your senior horse is at risk. Many age-related factors raise the risk of laminitis in your oldster, including weight gain, hormone imbalances, and a body that's simply wearing out. Here's a look at some factors that increase his risk:

- Obesity.
- Body weight over 1,200 pounds (even if he's not obese).
- Being a pony.
- Feet that are in poor condition, such as cracked, shelly, and/or with long toes.
- Liver or kidney disease, and/or a hormone imbalance associated with Equine Cushing's Disease (ECD; see page 257).
- Stress, such as from travel, surgery, or emotional upset.
- Severe colicᴳ, diarrheaᴳ, and other serious general illnesses.
- Grazing freely on spring grass.
- Grain overload.
- Shavings or sawdust of unknown origins.
- Corticosteroid medication, such as prednisoneᴳ or dexamethasoneᴳ given for allergy and skin conditions.
- Foot concussion.
- Chronic overload on one or more feet (from compensating for lameness in another leg, say from arthritisᴳ).

Laminitis Signposts

Call your vet NOW if you spot any of these signs, then go to While You Wait, page 275. The faster you get the jump on laminitis, the more positive your horse's prognosis. If you miss the "Mild" signs, your horse's chances of recovery diminish.   ➤

MILD LAMINITIS

• Your horse walks readily and seems sound unless he's walking on a hard surface and/or when turned in a circle. Then, his gait is stiff, stilted, and hesitant.

• When standing at rest he acts restless, shifting weight from foot to foot every few seconds.

• He's lethargic and preoccupied.

• He's eating less.

• He has a weak, but definite, digital pulse in the affected foot/feet. (See page 295 for how to check your horse's digital pulse.)

• His hooves are slightly warm to the touch, or stone cold.

Laminitis: An Inside Look

The condition typically occurs as a consequence of other diseases or conditions (such as colic^G, colitis^G, acute diarrhea^G, gram-negative pneumonia^G, uterine infection, or hormone imbalances). Clinical signs usually don't appear until approximately 48 hours after the initial problem strikes. By that time, there's commonly irreparable damage to the laminae, weakening the coffin bone's attachment to its hoof wall.

Still, when you recognize and treat early-stage (acute) laminitis—and the underlying cause is resolved—your horse's recovery rate can come close to 100%. In such a case, "recovery" would be defined as a return to comfort and life as usual, at least from all outward appearances. There still will be irreparable damage inside the affected feet, making him more susceptible to future bouts of laminitis.

However, if you fail to recognize early signs, a greater proportion of laminae will weaken and eventually die. This erodes the coffin-bone attachment, causing the bone to drop and rotate away from its inner hoof wall. When this occurs, the condition switches from acute to chronic and is called *founder*. Its treatment success rate drops, though new treatments offer hope for management—and survival. In severe cases, the coffin bone can rotate down and pierce the horse's sole. A horse with this condition is called a "sinker^G." His odds of survival are slim to none.

Well-funded molecular biology studies are ongoing through such research groups as the Morris Animal Foundation, as investigators attempt to identify what initial processes produce laminitis, so they can hopefully block them. Until then, your best bet is prevention—and early detection.

MODERATE LAMINITIS

• He's reluctant to move.

• When standing at rest, he bears more weight than usual on his hindquarters and holds his front feet farther forward than usual.

• When moving, he limps and/or rocks back on his hindquarters to spare his front feet.

• His attitude is depressed.

• He's off his feed.

• If you try to lift one foot, he resists because added weight on the other foot magnifies his pain.

• He flinches or reacts when you apply pressure to the toe area of sole on his affected foot/feet. (This is easier to detect if you're using hoof testers.)

• His hooves are warm.

• He has a steady, consistent digital pulse in the affected foot/feet.

SEVERE LAMINITIS

• He refuses to move, possibly lying down and refusing to get up unless forced.

• He's deeply depressed and preoccupied with pain, likely refusing to eat.

• His heart and respiratory rates are elevated (heart rate over 50 beats per minute; respiratory rate over 20 breaths per minute), due to pain and possibly toxins (depending on the underlying cause).

• He grinds his teeth, a sign of pain.

• The digital pulse is strong and easy to find.

• His hoof walls are obviously warm.

While You Wait

1. CONFINE YOUR HORSE. Confine your horse to a small (12 x 12) stall or paddock with soft footing. If he moves stiffly, is reluctant to move, rocks back on his legs, or has an exaggerated digital pulse (see page 293), don't move him. Rather, confine him where he stands, using portable corral panels or a makeshift enclosure. Or, simply stay with him until your vet arrives.

2. DON'T FEED HIM. Offer water only. Your horse should have no feed of any kind until your vet's ruled out laminitis, which might be the result of, or be worsened by, certain kinds of feeds.

Prevention Pointers

Use these guidelines to help minimize those risks.

• **Keep him trim.** If your horse is overweight, get veterinary help: he must lose that extra weight, but he has to do it safely without creating deficiencies of any important nutrients. To determine if he's overweight, see "Senior Condition Check," page 300.

• **Watch for fat deposits.** Even if your senior horse isn't overweight, watch for ➤

fat deposits at his tail base, the crest of his neck, or within his sheath. They could indicate an underlying illness that would predispose him for laminitis, such as a thyroid disorder^G, Equine Cushing's Disease^G, or diabetes mellitus^G. If you see them, call your veterinarian.

• **Watch that pony.** Researchers aren't sure why ponies are at higher risk, but they are predisposed to founder. Possible reasons include a tendency toward obesity and long life—both risk factors. To minimize the risk, control as many other factors as you can.

• **Keep his feet fit.** Make sure his feet are trimmed at least every 6 weeks. Have your farrier evaluate him for long-toe/low-heel syndrome, which increases torque and encourages laminitic separation, then have him remedy the situation if it exists. Finally, supplement your horse's ration with methionine and biotin, to improve hoof condition.

• **Get your senior an annual exam.** An annual physical, complete with blood work, can help uncover such insidious chronic problems as liver and kidney dysfunction, and hormonal imbalances. (See "Senior Vet Checks," page 386.) Work with your vet to control such conditions through medication, management, and diet.

• **Minimize stress—and stay alert.** Laminitis is a common byproduct of any equine stress, be it from a change in environment, companionship, or illness/injury. Closely monitor your stressed/injured/sick horse for signs of laminitis. Call your vet NOW if you see any such signs.

• **Be wary of spring grass.** Recent studies have shown it can lead to carbohydrate overload, thus laminitis. Here's why: If nighttime temperatures are too cool for grass growth, extra energy absorbed from daytime sun is sent to the stem's base in the form of a sugar called fructan, to be used for growth the next cloudy day. Too much fructan can lead to carbohydrate overload. Because it's stored at the grass blades' base, pasture mowing doesn't help. Here's what does:

  - If your senior horse has had laminitis or has any of the risk factors listed above, avoid spring pasture entirely. Allow him to graze only after nights are consistently warm and grass has started to build seed heads (so fructan storage is less likely). Then introduce him to pasture gradually, an hour or two each day, after first filling his belly with hay.

  - If he doesn't have any risk factors, avoid grass founder by feeding him hay before turnout and limiting his grazing time. Introduce him gradually to pasture, starting with an hour a day and building by a half hour each subsequent day. Or, supplement his grazing with fresh hay every day, and allow him 24-hour grazing before spring grass starts to grow, so he keeps it nibbled down and never gets an overload. That way, his total intake will be low and he'll have to cover a lot of ground to get much grass.

• **Don't supplement iron.** Excess iron can increase your senior horse's odds of catching an infectious disease, putting him at risk of laminitis as a side effect of that infection. Avoid iron supplements unless prescribed by your vet. If you think your horse needs an iron supplement, consult your vet.

• **Lock the grain room.** A grain-room binge results in carbohydrate overload, which generates toxins in your horse's gut. This almost certainly will cause laminitis if not treated before your horse shows signs of trouble. Develop horse-proof—and human-error-proof—methods for keeping feed out of reach. And call your vet NOW if your horse raids the pantry despite your efforts.

• **Select bedding carefully.** Avoid stall bedding that includes sawdust, wood shavings, or wood chips made from black-walnut trees. A toxic ingredient in the wood oil has been proven to cause laminitis on contact. To be safe, stick with 100% pine products. If you're not sure of the source of a particular load, send it back—it's not worth the risk.

• **Synchronize the steroids.** If your senior horse is being medicated with a corticosteroidG (such as dexamethasone, prednisone, or triamcinolone), try to give it to him in the morning. While these medications can increase his laminitis risk if given in high doses or for extended time periods, that risk is somewhat decreased if the drug is given in the morning, when his body naturally has a higher level of steroids.

• **Don't work him on hard ground.** Foot trauma can cause inflammation in the laminae, precipitating "road founder." Work on soft, level footing; shoe him, if he's not shod, to help prevent concussion; keep him fit for the level of work you're requiring; and toughen his soles, by painting them with "sole paints," available through your vet or veterinary supply catalogs.

• **Manage any unsoundess.** Work with your vet to aggressively treat and manage any unsoundness, be it acute (such as from a recent injury) or chronic (such as from arthritisG). Doing so can help prevent overburdening a sound or less-lame limb, and thus help reduce risk of laminitis. ➤

Is it Founder— or Laminitis?

When laminitis becomes founder is open to debate. The most common definition of founder is any case of laminitis in which the symptoms (primarily pain) persist for more than 2 weeks despite treatment, or recur. Another commonly used definition relates to coffin-bone rotation. If radiographs (x-rays) indicate there's rotation, it's founder. Whether or not it's founder does not relate to the level of pain.

Treatment Tips

Use these tips to fight laminitis, should your horse be diagnosed with the condition.

1. LEARN THE LAMINITIS SIGNPOSTS. Call your veterinarian NOW if your senior horse shows any of those signs. (See "Laminitis Signposts," page 273.) And, go to "While You Wait," page 275.

2. SEARCH FOR THE CAUSE. If your senior horse is diagnosed with laminitis, help your veterinarian search for the underlying cause so it can be resolved. Consider the possibility of grain overload, check bedding for walnut shavings or sawdust, check feed tags for iron content, and describe any symptoms that could be indicative of ECD^G or diabetes^G, such as increased water consumption, increased urination, delayed shedding, or a change in your senior horse's sweating (more than usual, less than usual). If he's on corticosteroid medication, put that high on your list.

3. BLOOD TESTS can help determine whether your horse has a thyroid disorder^G or ECD. Depending on the individual case, the human drugs pergolide, cyproheptadine, insulin (in some cases), and/or thyroid hormone have been used successfully in resolving underlying hormone imbalances, thereby decreasing the likelihood of recurring or chronic laminitis.

4. ASK ABOUT EXPERIMENTAL DRUGS. Nitroglycerine cream or skin patches (used in human heart patients for chest pain) have shown promise. They're applied to your horse's coronary bands and/or the blood vessels at the back of the affected leg's pastern, and the active ingredient is rapidly absorbed through the skin, resulting in relaxation of spasming blood vessels in the stricken foot. The drug pentoxyphyline has also shown promise in enhancing blood flow through capillary beds in the laminitic foot. Some studies show it works better than the old standby, acepromazine, for this effect.

5. LISTEN TO YOUR VET. Follow your veterinarian's management instructions to the letter. If you have doubts, talk to him or her about them, and/or seek a second opinion. There are many old wives' tales about founder that might tempt you to do things differently. Your horse might suffer as a result.

8 Loss of Social Status

What it is: Loss of social status^G within his domestic "herd," which hampers your horse's ability to thrive—and survive. (Such a status loss will affect any horse that's turned out with other horses.)

Why your senior horse is at risk. As he ages, a number of possible changes in his body and mind can adversely affect his herd social standing. His vision may dim, his hearing may dull, and declining strength and encroaching stiffness can slow him. Plus, mental dulling and age-associated aches and pains may distract him from his usual self-protective vigilance.

With these strikes against him, he's more apt to allow a social underling to invade his personal space, shoulder in on feeding rights, and generally get away with insubordination. Do that once, and you ask for it to happen again. Do it twice, and you've just dropped a rung on the social ladder. It may be cruel, but it's Nature's way of letting the strong survive and the weak get weaker. As a result, few wild horses live much past their 18th birthday.

In domestic life, however, it's not uncommon for horses to live well into their 20s and 30s. In a sense, we've created a new species with a new set of problems. This elderly herd member is an aberration—in the natural setting, he'd be long gone. To care for him, you may need to step in and provide some "assisted living." The "Status-Loss Signposts," below, and the "Safe Senior Living" guidelines that follow, will help you.

Status-Loss Signposts

Just as you watch out for your aging parents, you need to watch out for your aging horse. That way, you'll know when he needs to graduate from "independent living" to "assisted living," or even a "nursing home." Use this series of questions to check your senior horse's social status.

• **Can he get to feed and water without being hassled?** That is, can he get there easily, select what he wants, and eat/drink his fill without danger of being harassed ➤

or hurt? If not, he's at risk of weight and condition loss at best—and colic^G and other life-threatening conditions at worst.

• **Does he demonstrate normal mental alertness and arousal?** When he's approached by a herd member, is he alert to that approach and responding appropriately (pinning his ears or moving out of the way)? If he's frequently caught off guard, due to eye or hearing problems or mental preoccupation with aches, pains, or illness, he's at risk of injury.

• **Can he move independently, with no apparent loss of balance?** That means he can get out of harm's way without stumbling or hesitating. If he can't, he'll look like the herd weakling, which can invite conflict from other herd members.

If you're unable to answer "yes" to all 3 questions, avoid waiting until your senior horse loses weight or gets injured before you move him to an environment where he can eat, drink, and move about without risk of conflict. The time is now. Here's what you can do.

Safe Senior Living

1. FEED WISELY. Horse-to-horse aggression almost always centers around food, particularly when everybody's hungry. So your senior horse can safely satisfy his hunger:

• Provide plenty of feed, per your veterinarian's guidelines.
• Provide at least one feeding station per horse.
• Space feeding stations at least 20 feet apart.

If your senior still can't eat without risk of conflict, move him to a separate area for feeding. This not only will protect him from aggressive attacks, it'll also help him to maintain his weight by allowing him to satisfy his hunger completely, at his leisure.

2. MONITOR CONFLICT. If conflict exists outside feeding time (look for bite marks on your senior horse's rump or torso, a reluctance to approach other horses, and/or the appearance of resentment such as ear-pinning, squealing and/or tail swishing), move him permanently. If possible, arrange for him to share a separate pasture with lower-ranking or socially benign herd mates, so he can have the physical benefits of grazing at will, plus the emotional benefits of a comfortable social group.

3. HANDLE WITH CARE. A socially deposed senior can be agitated and defensive, so might jump or bolt when startled. (If his vision and/or hearing are impaired, he'll be easily startled. For more information, see "Senior Hearing Check" and "Senior Vision Check," pages 310 and 306, respectively.) Be careful around him, making sure he's aware of your presence before you approach. And, leave yourself plenty of escape room, should he spook or bolt.

NATURE'S WAY

Most of the time, a horse whose position has slipped seems to resign himself rather quickly. He quietly defers to his newly promoted superiors when it comes to food, water, and shelter. In the wild, such deference can ultimately lead to weakness, illness, and death. That's why you need to monitor your domestic senior's condition, to see if his lowered status is costing him food, water, shelter—and his health.

Even worse, some senior horses seem unwilling or unable to accept lowered social status, resulting in frequent altercations with the young upstart(s) who now outranks him. Most of the time, it's the old horse that'll lose—and could suffer injury. Like the deferential one, he's also likely to go hungry, as he can't bully his way successfully to the feed bin.

The risk of injury is exacerbated by Nature. Until a newly "promoted" younger horse gets 100% cooperation and respect for his new position, he'll defend it vigorously, like a big bully, making injury more likely. In the wild, it was in a herd's best interest to get social matters settled quickly so everyone could get back to watching out for each other and for predators. Ongoing conflict is a distraction, which is bad for overall group survival. Domestication hasn't altered those instincts.

So, if a senior citizen fails to back down, other herd members could begin challenging him, too, perhaps to achieve quicker closure. Life can get miserable for him—he'll be stressed, hungry, thirsty, beaten up, and possibly injured. In the wild, this would be the beginning of the end. That end likely would come during the next harsh weather season, either summer or winter, when food is scarce.

HANDS-ON SENIOR HORSEKEEPING

CHAPTER 1

ATLAS
OF AGING

285

Atlas of Aging

Human Age	Horse Age
Toddler to preschooler: up to 6 years old	**Foalhood to 1 year old**

CAPPY JACKSON

- Abundant energy (when not sleeping!)
- Rapid gain of weight and muscle
- Needs a diet rich in fats and high-quality protein to support growth, but low in carbs to avoid too-rapid growth
- Feed must be soft or liquid (few teeth!), and easily digested
- Vision and hearing are sharpening
- Thin skin is becoming well padded with subcutaneous fat
- A weak, immature immune system is vulnerable to infection
- Sensitive to weather changes
- Needs social skills, relies on strong, tolerant herd members for protection
- Needs exercise to form strong bones and muscles, with care to avoid injury/overstress
- Needs diligent farriery to shape hoof development

Human Age	Horse Age
Adolescent/ pubescent: 7 to 14 years old	**Adolescent/ pubescent: 1 to 2 years old**

SUE M. COPELAND

- Becoming less wasteful of energy
- Weight gain is leveling off
- Teeth are continuing to come in; can handle adult feeds
- Vision and hearing are at their peak
- Puberty arrives
- Immunity is improving
- Becoming hardier to weather changes
- Herd is becoming less tolerant and indulgent; rules must be followed
- Still needs careful exercise to grow thick, strong bones

You've heard the old adage, "once an adult, twice a child"—it's true of horses as well as humans. Many of your senior horse's needs are strikingly similar to those he had when he was a foal. The better you understand this, the better you'll be able to care for him in the later stages of his life. To help, study the information on these two pages. For fun, we added a comparison in human years.

Human Age	Horse Age
Late teens to prime adulthood: 15 to 48 years old	Prime adulthood: 3 to 14 years old

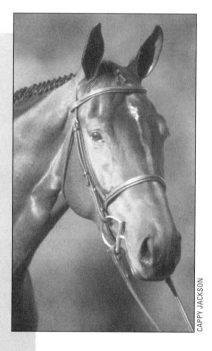

CAPPY JACKSON

- Practices energy economy
- Physically matured and muscles bulked up and defined with use
- Dietary needs depend on lifestyle
- Digestive efficiency is at its peak
- Teeth are narrowing; increased risk of gum disease
- Hearing and vision may decline depending on environment/experience
- Immunity is at its peak
- Physically tolerant of weather changes
- Herd position is defined; maintained by vigilance and social know-how
- Exercise needed to maintain condition

Human Age	Horse Age
Middle age to senior citizen: 49 to 96 years old	Middle age to senior citizen: 15 to 30+ years old

KEVIN MCGOWAN

- Energy levels and stamina are decreasing
- Declining weight/muscle mass
- Needs more quantity/quality feed rich in fats and protein to hold weight and condition, but low in carbs to avoid metabolic upset and laminitis[G]
- Needs easily chewed/digested feed for declining dental/digestive health
- Risk of vision/hearing difficulties increases
- Skin is thinning, losing its fat padding
- Declining immunity increases vulnerability to disease, internal/external parasites, insects
- Lung capacity is decreasing
- Susceptibility to allergies is increasing
- Sensitive to weather changes
- Herd members increasingly challenge, deny access to feed, and cause general increase in personal and physical stress
- Needs cautious and regular exercise to reduce stiffness/stocking up ➤

VIRTUAL BIRTHDAY TEST

For an estimate of how old (or young!) your senior horse *really* is—despite his actual years—take the following test. (*Note:* For questions you can't answer, give a "0" score.)

1) In the past year, how much of each 24-hour day has your senior spent in a stall?

a) On average, more than 16 hours ..+5
b) 12 to 16 hours ....+4
c) 8 to 12 hours ....+3
d) less than 8 hours ....- 2

2) In the past year, how much of each 24-hour day has he spent on pasture?

a) On average, more than 16 hours ..-4
b) 12 to 16 hours ....- 3
c) 8 to 12 hours ....- 1
d) less than 8 hours ....+4

3) Has his back begun to sink ("swayback")?

a) Yes ....+1
b) No ....- 1

4) To your knowledge, has he ever been diagnosed with laminitisᴳ?

a) Yes ....+3
b) No ....- 1

5) Has he ever had colic surgery?

a) Yes ....+3
b) No 0

6) In the past year, did he receive treatment to eliminate tapeworms?

a) Yes ....- 2
b) No ....+1

7) In the past 5 years, has he had pneumonia?

a) Yes ....+1
b) No 0

8) Has he ever had a flesh wound that took longer than 3 months to heal?

a) Yes ....+1
b) No 0

9) In the past 5 years, has he had mild to moderate exercise 3 days per week?

a) Yes ....- 2
b) No ....+1

10) Is your senior horse a pregnant mare?

a) Yes ....+2
b) No 0

11) Is your senior horse overweight or underweight?

a) Yes ....+2
b) No ....- 1

12) Has he had a dental checkup and treatment within the past 6 months?

a) Yes ....- 1
b) No ....+1

13) Is he being fed an age-adjusted diet formulated for seniors?

a) Yes ....-3
b) No ....+2

14) Did (or does) your senior horse have a strenuous, athletic career?

a) Yes ....+2
b) No 0

15) Has your senior horse ever been diagnosed with sarcoid(s)ᴳ?

a) Yes ....+1
b) No 0

16) Is he gray, and/or has he ever been diagnosed with melanomaᴳ?

a) Yes ....+2
b) No 0

17) In the past year, has your senior horse had more than one episode of chokeᴳ?

a) Yes ....+2
b) No ....-1

18) In the past year, are horses that used to be respectful now pushing him around?

a) Yes ....-1
b) No 0

19) Has he ever been diagnosed and/or treated for recurrent colicᴳ or ulcersᴳ?

a) Yes ....+1
b) No 0

20) Has he had a CBC (complete blood count) and chemistry panel including liver, kidney, and muscle screening, yielding a clean bill of health within the past year?

a) Yes ....-1
b) No 0

Add up your scores, being sure to pay attention to the minus signs. Divide the total by 4, and add the result to your horse's chronological age. This is his virtual age. Is it lower than his chronological age? Congratulations! You're managing for longevity in your senior horse. Is it higher? Consider adjusting management factors (such as decreasing stall time, scheduling a dental exam, etc.), and do what you can to lower his virtual age.

How old in human years?
Use this equation to calculate your senior horse's age in human years, based on his chronological or virtual age. (This equation works only for horses over 3 years of age.)

3 X (AGE IN YEARS - 3) + 15 = YOUR HORSE'S AGE IN HUMAN YEARS

Examples:
• A 12-year-old horse is 42 human years old. [3 x (12-3) + 15]
• A 20-year old horse is 66 human years old [3 x (20-3) + 15]
• A 30-year-old horse is 96 human years old [3 x (30-3) + 15]
• A 30-year-old horse whose virtual age is 18 is 60 in virtual human years [3 x (18-3) + 15]

CHAPTER 2

BASELINE SENIOR BEHAVIOR

2 How to Establish your Senior's Baseline Behavior

Knowing what's normal for your aged horse can help you quickly detect what's not. Here's a chart of typical behaviors for the average senior horse. Fill in your horse's personalized behavior, then take a mental inventory every time you see him. If you notice abnormal behavior, turn to "Senior Vital Signs" (page 291). If your findings tell you there's a problem—or you suspect something's amiss—refer to your horse's symptoms in Section 1.

		BASELINE BEHAVIOR	
SETTING	**AVERAGE SENIOR HORSE**	**SAMPLE ENTRIES**	**YOUR HORSE**
Stall or paddock	8-12 bowel movements per day	*5 piles at night; 5-6 during daytime*	
Stall or paddock	Dozes quietly or watches activity through window or over fence	*Stall walks and paces fenceline*	
Idle time	Takes naps, either standing or lying down, when the midday-to-noon-time sun shines, and late at night when feeding is finished	*Lies down in pasture between 11 a.m. and noon, flat out on his side; lies down in stall after dark but stays on his sternum*	
Stall, pasture, or paddock	Lies down to nap and sleep	*Usually sleeps on his feet (getting up and down is too hard for him)*	
Pasture	Grazes and sticks with herd	*Grazes/stays on outskirts of herd*	
Paddock/ pasture	Rolls daily; shakes off immediately afterward	*Rarely rolls; always shakes off*	
Pasture	More active in cool/cold, or breezy weather; will stand and hang head when it's pouring rain; will stand with butt to the wind if it's very windy	*Plays like a youngster when the wind blows!*	
Feed time	Cleans up all feed	*A slow—but steady—eater*	
Group feeding	Feeds according to social position	*Bottom of the pecking order; generally last to eat*	
Water source	Usually drinks after eating and exercise	*Drinks after eating hay and grazing*	
Water source	Drinks 10-15 gallons/day	*Drinks around 12 gallons/day*	

CHAPTER 3

SENIOR
VITAL SIGNS

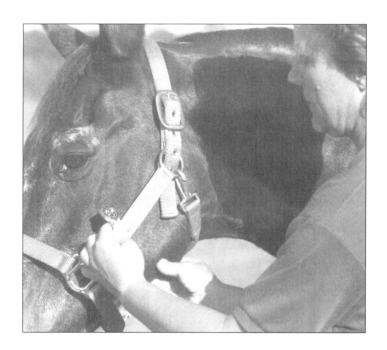

Senior Vital Signs

Step-by-step instructions for how to take your horse's vital signs are provided in this section. Compare your findings to the chart on the opposite page. Be ready to relay abnormal readings if you call your veterinarian to report a suspected problem. Your knowledge of both current and baseline readings can help him or her determine how quickly he/she needs to see your horse.

How to Take your Horse's Temperature

Shake down a glass thermometer or activate an electronic one. Lubricate the tip with a dab of K-Y® or petroleum jelly. Lift your horse's tail and gently insert the thermometer into his anus, to a depth of 2 inches. With the heel of your hand resting against his buttock for stability, hold the thermometer in place. Release his tail if he fusses (shifts his weight, clamps or swishes his tail). Some horses will tolerate a thermometer better if their tails are free. It takes about 2 minutes for a glass thermometer to register; about 30 seconds for an electronic one (listen for the beep).

Tip #1: Your horse's normal temperature will be lowest in early morning, and up to 2° F higher in late afternoon. It's unaffected by weather unless he's shivering or sweating. To establish a baseline, record his morning, midday, and late afternoon temperatures daily for 1 week, then average the readings for each time of day.

Tip #2: Exercise causes a normal rise in your horse's temperature—to as high as 106° F. It can take up to 2 hours to return to normal. To determine whether an elevated temperature is due to illness or exercise, check at 15-minute intervals. If it declines to normal, exercise was likely the cause.

Tip #3: Keep an extra thermometer. If you get an abnormal reading, check again with the backup thermometer to confirm the reading and rule out technical error.

(Continued on page 294)

SENIOR VITAL SIGNS

VITAL SIGN	NORMAL RANGE	ABNORMALS & POSSIBLE CAUSE	YOUR HORSE
Temperature	99-101.5°F	*Below normal:* hypothermia; shock. *Above normal:* infection; heat exhaustion; exercise/muscle exertion.	6 a.m.: Noon: 6 p.m.:
Heart Rate	30-44 beats per minute	*Below normal:* good athletic condition; heart problem; poisoning; hypothermia; shock. *Above normal:* exercise; pain; fever; heat exhaustion; shock; heart problem; anxiety.	
Respiratory Rate	10-15 breaths per minute	*Below normal:* athletic condition, hypothermia; shock; drug effect. *Above normal:* exercise; fear; pain; fever; heat exhaustion; electrolyte imbalance; shock; respiratory infection.	
Gut Sounds	Long rolling rumbles interspersed with shorter gurgles; quiet periods no longer than 2 minutes	*Quieter than normal:* gut motility^G slowed or stopped, often associated with illness or colic. *Noisier than normal:* hunger, digestion of a meal; nervousness; or gut inflammation. *High-pitched pings interspersed with periods of quiet:* accumulated gas (often a sign of colic^G).	
Digital Pulse	Subtle and difficult to feel	*No pulse:* could be normal or it could indicate poor circulation. *An obvious or strong pulse:* could indicate a variety of foot problems, including laminitis^G (founder) or an abscess^G.	
Gum Color	Pale to bubble-gum pink	*Whitish gums:* could indicate anemia or shock. *Bright pink gums:* could indicate illness; poisoning; shock^G or could be normal if the horse has just been excercising. *Brick-red, blue, or muddy-colored gums:* could indicate poisoning or shock^G.	
Capillary Refill Time (CRT)	1-2 seconds	*Faster-than-usual CRT:* means your horse's blood pressure is elevated, probably due to recent exercise, excitement, or anxiety. *Slow CRT:* can indicate illness; poisoning; or shock^G.	
Skin Pinch Test	Less than 1 second	*1 second or longer:* your horse may be dehydrated.	

How to Take your Horse's Heart Rate

Grab a watch with a second hand or digital timer. Stand by your horse's left side, facing his left elbow, as shown (right). Place the bell of the stethoscope behind the point of his elbow and press it gently into his armpit. His heart beat should have both a lub and a dub component—count the two together as one beat. Count the number of beats in a 15-second period and multiply by 4 for beats-per-minute.

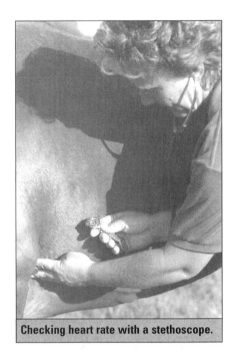

Checking heart rate with a stethoscope.

How to Take your Horse's Heart Rate Digitally

While holding your horse's halter with one hand, place the fingertips of your other hand on the underside of the jawbone beneath his cheek, to locate the facial artery which crosses under the jaw (right). (*Tip:* The artery is firm and about half the diameter of a pencil. If you move your fingers forward and back along the jawbone, you'll feel the artery slip back and forth.)

Once you've found it, gently feel for the nudge of your horse's pulse through the artery, and count the number of beats in 15 seconds. Multiply by 4 for beats-per-minute.

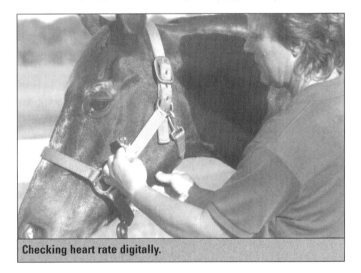

Checking heart rate digitally.

How to Take your Horse's Respiratory Rate

Place the bell of the stethoscope in the center of your horse's throat, approximately 6 to 8 inches below his throatlatch (opposite page). Listen to the air rush by as he inhales and exhales. Count the number of breaths taken in a 15-second period and multiply by 4 for breaths-per-minute.

Tip: If you don't have a stethoscope, you can take your horse's respiratory rate by:
• Watching the rise and fall of his chest wall or flanks with each breath. In a

healthy horse at rest, there should be little external movement with each breath.

• Watching for nostril movement with each breath, or holding a mirror in front of his nostril and watching for fogging with each breath. In a healthy horse at rest, there should be little nostril flair. (*Note:* Your horse might sniff at the mirror and give a falsely elevated reading.)

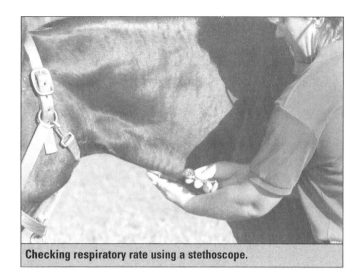
Checking respiratory rate using a stethoscope.

How to Listen to your Horse's Gut Sounds

Divide each side of your horse's abdomen into five sections: high flank; low flank; high belly (between flank and ribs); low belly; and ventral midline (just to one side of the seam that divides his lower belly into left and right sides). Press the stethoscope firmly into each section and listen for a minimum of 30 seconds, the longer the better. (It can be normal for there to be up to a 2-minute interval of quiet between prolonged rumbles. If you don't listen long enough, you might mistakenly think there are no sounds.)

How to Check your Horse's Digtal Pulse

Squat facing the side of your horse's front leg. Using the thumb and middle fingers of your right hand, feel behind and on either side of his lower fetlock (above the sesamoid^G area), as shown. Apply very slight fingertip pressure, adjusting your fingers' position and their pressure until you feel a faint pulse.

Tip #1: You're feeling for a difference in the pulse's strength—not the number of beats. This increase is often indicative of inflammation in the ➤

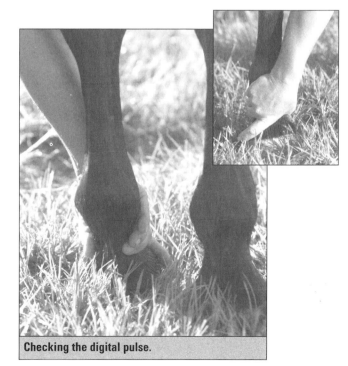
Checking the digital pulse.

foot. Vessels dilate to allow more blood into the damaged area, but flow through that area may be impeded due to the inflammation. This causes a sort of backup, which you can feel in your fingertips as a "bounding" pulse.

Tip #2: If you can't detect a pulse, that could be normal for your horse, he could have a circulation problem—or you may be feeling the wrong spot. The next time your veterinarian is out, ask him or her to check your horse's digital pulse, and to show you how to do the same. Be patient—it can take practice!

Tip #3: Always check both front legs, so you can compare digital

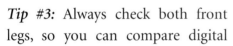

Optional, 2-handed method for checking digital pulse.

pulses. A bounding digital pulse in both front legs could indicate a problem in both front feet, such as laminitis[G].

Tip #4: A difference in digital pulses between the front legs will generally support other signs you're seeing (e.g., your horse is lame on the leg with the stronger pulse). However, in cases of chronic lameness in one leg, the harder-working good leg may be getting a slightly larger volume of blood due to the demands on it, so may have a slightly stronger digital pulse.

Tip #5: Make sure your horse has been at rest when you check the digital pulse. Exercise within the past hour—enough exertion to cause an elevation in respiratory rate—can change the character of your horse's digital pulse, making it seem stronger or weaker, depending on what's going on in nearby tissues, and result in confusion.

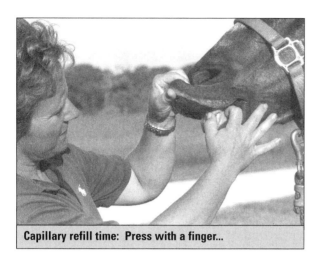
Capillary refill time: Press with a finger...

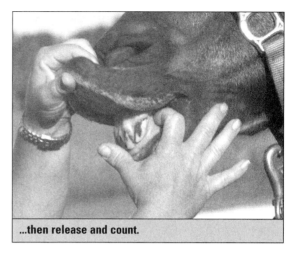
...then release and count.

How to Check your Horse's Mucous Membrane Color and Capillary Refill Time (CRT)

Lift your horse's upper lip and look at the color of his gums. Are they a normal pale to bubble-gum pink? Or are they a warning-sign pale pink, dark red, blue-tinged, or muddy-colored? Now check his capillary refill time. Press on the upper gum with a finger to blanch out the color (see photos above), then count how many seconds it takes to resume its original color. Normal is 1 to 2 seconds. (See chart, page 293.)

Skin-Pinch Test

Pinch a "tent" of skin at the lower end of your horse's neck on one side, just where it joins the shoulder. Watch the tent when you release the skin. If it takes a second (long enough for you to cite, "one-thousand-one") or longer to spring back flat, your horse may be dehydrated. Practice this daily, so you know what "normal" looks like for your horse's pinch test. Call your veterinarian if you suspect the horse may be dehydrated.

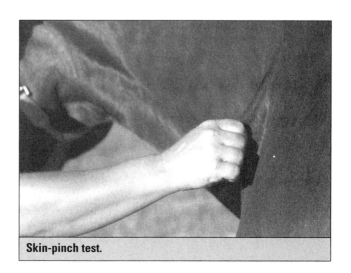
Skin-pinch test.

NOTES

CHAPTER 4

SENIOR CONDITION CHECK

KAREN E.N. HAYES DVM, MS

Senior Condition Check

4

Is your aging horse too fat or too thin? Use the following chart to see how he measures up. (Don't just trust your eyes—take a hands-on approach and feel for fat deposits, or a lack of them.) Then read on to see what action plan you should take as a result of your findings.

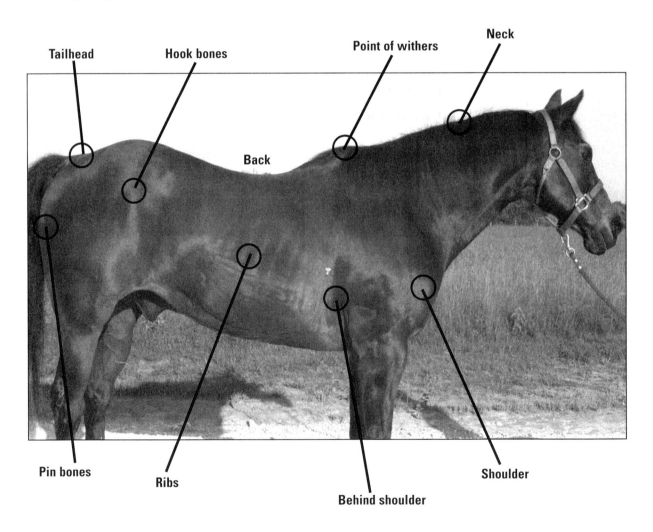

1—POOR (Extremely emaciated; no fatty tissue can be felt)					
NECK	**WITHERS**	**BACK**	**HINDQUARTERS**	**RIBS**	**SHOULDER**
Bone structure easily noticeable	Bone structure easily noticeable	Spinous processes (tops of vertebrae) project prominently	Tailhead, pin bones (back of pelvis), and hook bones (front of pelvis) project prominently	Ribs project prominently	Bone structure easily noticeable
2—VERY THIN (Emaciated)					
Bone structure faintly discernible	Bone structure faintly discernible	Slight fat covering over base of spinous processes; transverse processes of lumbar vertebrae (bones that stick out to the side of each vertebrae) feel rounded; spinous processes are prominent	Tailhead prominent	Ribs prominent	Bone structure faintly discernible
3—THIN					
Neck accentuated (obviously thin)	Withers accentuated (very prominent)	Fat buildup halfway on spinous processes, but easily discernible; transverse processes cannot be felt	Tailhead prominent, but individual vertebrae cannot be visually identified; hook bones appear rounded, but are still easily discernible; pin bones not distinguishable	Slight fat cover over ribs; ribs easily discernible	Shoulder bone structure accentuated
4—MODERATELY THIN					
Neck not obviously thin	Withers not obviously thin	Backbone sticks up above muscles	Tailhead prominence depends on conformation; fat can be felt around it; hook bones not discernible	Slight fat cover over ribs; ribs easily discernible	Shoulder bone structure accentuated

➤

5—MODERATE					
NECK	**WITHERS**	**BACK**	**HINDQUARTERS**	**RIBS**	**SHOULDER**
Neck blends smoothly into body	Withers rounded over spinous processes	Back level	Fat around tailhead beginning to feel spongy	Ribs cannot be visually distinguished, but can be easily felt	Shoulder blends smoothly into body
6—MODERATELY FLESHY					
Fat beginning to be deposited along crest	Fat beginning to fill in around both sides of withers	May have slight crease down back	Fat around tailhead feels soft	Fat over ribs feels spongy	Fat beginning to be deposited in area behind shoulder
7—FLESHY					
Fat deposited along crest and below it	Fat deposited along both sides of withers	May have crease down back	Fat around tailhead is soft	Individual ribs can be felt, but you also feel noticeable filling between ribs with fat	Fat deposited behind shoulder
8—FAT					
Noticeable thickening of neck	Area along withers filled with fat	Crease down back	Tailhead fat—very soft; fat deposited along inner buttocks	Difficult to feel ribs	Area behind shoulder filled in flush with body
9—EXTREMELY FAT					
Bulging fat	Bulging fat	Obvious crease down back	Bulging fat around tailhead; fat along inner buttocks may rub together; flanks filled flush with body	Patchy fat appearing over ribs	Bulging fat

Source: Don R. Henneke, PhD, Director of Equine Science Program at Tarleton State Texas University in Stephenville, Texas. Dr. Henneke's grading system has been accepted as the standard in the horse industry, and in the court system for helping to determine neglect or abuse.

Did Your Horse Make the Grade?

Here's what action you'll need to take, based on your horse's grade.

GRADE 1 TO 3: Call your veterinarian NOW! Your horse is dangerously thin, suggesting he may have a serious underlying health and/or management problem. This will make him susceptible to further problems as well as to disease.

GRADE 4: Your moderately thin senior horse may need to pack on some pounds—especially if you're heading into winter. As temperatures fall, he'll start to burn more calories just to

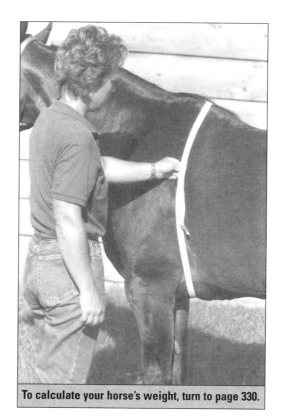

To calculate your horse's weight, turn to page 330.

stay warm. That means he'll lose more weight. If he has a full winter coat you may not notice. Consult your veterinarian about a safe, moderate weight-gain plan for your horse. While you're at it, schedule a check-up for him. That way, you can determine if his almost-too-thin condition is natural for him, or due to disease.

GRADE 5 TO 7: Congratulations! Your horse is in great shape. To keep him that way, regularly check (at least every 30 days) his condition. If your horse scored a 7, keep an eye on his weight, to be sure he doesn't tip the scales into a fatter grade. If he starts to pack on pounds, work with your vet to craft a safe weight-loss ➤

Did You Know?

The older your senior horse gets, the more difficult it will be to restore declining condition—it's much easier to maintain good condition. So, the sooner you can get his condition into the grade 5-to-7 range, the better for you both.

program for him that may include eliminating grain from his ration, reducing his forage intake, and adding a moderate exercise program, if the horse is sound. (See "Age-Adjusted Exercise," page 339.)

GRADE 8 TO 9: Fat alert! If your horse's grade is a 9, he's dangerously obese, putting him at risk for laminitis^G, joint stress, fatty internal tumors, and other problems. If he's a grade 8, he remains at risk for these problems, but to a slightly lesser degree. Consult with your veterinarian immediately to have your senior checked for health problems that could account for his obesity (such as a thyroid^G problem or Equine Cushing's Disease^G), and/or that could stand in the way of an exercise program (such as lameness or a cardiovascular problem). And get him on a vet-approved diet—NOW!

Did You Know?

A winter coat can hide weight loss. Begin a monthly check by running your hands over your horse's condition checkpoints. If his ribs become more prominent than normal, adjust his ration accordingly. For many horses, the seasonal transition from fresh grass to hay (which varies in nutritional quality) can trigger weight loss. Consult your vet if your horse suddenly loses weight with no apparent cause.

CHAPTER 5

SENIOR
VISION CHECK

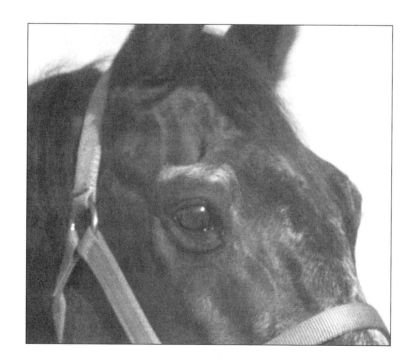

5 Senior Vision Check

Is your senior citizen losing his eyesight? Unlike elderly people and dogs, who suffer age-related vision changes that can lead to blindness, it's rare for a horse's aging eyes to go blind. In fact, since significant vision loss is rare in horses, many veterinarians don't consider eye exams a must for older equines except as part of a general "physical." But there are good reasons to specifically request an eye exam, including the following age-related changes that can spark problems in your horse's eyes:

• *Weakening Immune System:* As your horse ages, his immune system weakens. This can increase his susceptibility to eye maladies, such as corneal ulcers^G and moon blindness^G. Cataracts^G, common in other species, do occur in horses but less often. Observed as an opacity of the eye's lens, they will impair the horse's ability to see straight ahead, while his peripheral vision may remain relatively unaffected.

• *Ability to mask vision loss:* Horses with compromised vision can conceal their condition in familiar environments by adhering to familiar routes and routines. In fact, they'll attempt to conceal the problem in unfamiliar surroundings, too. Horses are prey animals. In the wild, predators are likely to single out the herd member that looks most "impaired." A sight-challenged wild horse has the best survival chance if he keeps his secret to himself. Your domestic horse instinctively knows this.

So, your senior's ability to navigate with his peripheral vision—and adhere to his normal routine—can make detection of a vision problem difficult. However, if he begins spooking, tripping, having trouble negotiating different elevations, or knocking into objects, his vision could be the culprit. Perform the "Quick Vision Test" at right, then report your results to your veterinarian. (Be sure to test both eyes.)

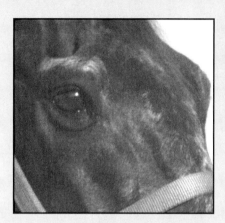

Quick Vision Test

What you'll need:
- Halter and lead rope
- A disposable diaper or clean dish towel
- Tape, such as duct or electrical
- A handful of cotton balls
- Hay or straw bale

1. Halter your horse. Blindfold one eye by laying a lightweight, thick pad, such as a disposable diaper folded in half, or a dish towel folded in thirds, across the eye. (If using a diaper, place the absorbent side against his skin.) Tape it to your horse's halter.

2. Wear clothing that doesn't "swish." In a well-lit area with minimal distractions, have a helper loosely hold your horse. Stand 3 feet away, to the side of the uncovered eye, where the opposite eye is completely concealed. Lob 3 cotton balls toward him, one after the other, so they bounce gently off the side of his face between his eye and muzzle.

3. Observe his reactions. Did he flinch when the first one approached, before it touched him? Did he try to avoid the second? Did he watch the third one? If your answers are no, no, and no, he probably can't see out of that eye. Repeat with the other eye.

4. If you're still unsure, move him to a well-lit area. With one of his eyes covered, lead your horse on a loose lead rope toward a bale of hay set 15 feet ahead. Walk purposefully—don't go so slowly that he has time to lower his head and smell it.

5. Observe his reactions. Does he try to avoid hitting the bale? If not, he probably can't see it. Cover the other eye, and repeat.

NOTES

CHAPTER 6

SENIOR
HEARING CHECK

Senior Hearing Check

Like you, your horse can lose his ability to detect sound as he ages. Age-related hearing loss in humans begins at about age 20 (roughly the same point as age 5 for a horse), starting with the higher frequency sounds and working down the scale. High-frequency hearing loss isn't generally obvious in humans until it's accumulated to the degree that it affects day-to-day functioning, usually sometime after the age of 50 (roughly equivalent to 15 years old for a horse). Because your horse has a wider range of high-frequency hearing than you do (normal human range is 100 hertz to 15,000 Hz; normal horse range exceeds 25,000 Hz), he can lose more of it before you notice a lack of response to sounds you can hear.

If you suspect a hearing loss in your horse (he's unusually slow to respond to your voice or standard barn sounds, and/or he's become easy to startle because he doesn't appear to hear your approach), administer the "Quick Hearing Test," at right. Consult your veterinarian with your results. Though currently the veterinary community lacks a way to compensate for age-related hearing loss in horses, your vet might find a simple (and simple-to-fix) cause, such as tick infestation, ear mites, and ear infections, all of which can be treated quite successfully.

THE PRYER REFLEX

Your horse's ears signal where his attention is directed. By watching them when on the ground or in the saddle, you can help avoid a possible spook. For instance, if you see a piece of plastic blowing to the left and you're wondering whether he sees it, look at his left ear. If the open part of that ear swivels toward the bag—a movement called the *Pryer Reflex*—he's tuning into it. If he's afraid of bags, picking up on that ear movement gives you time to direct his attention elsewhere and maybe avert a spook.

Whatever the cause, if your horse has a hearing loss, you'll need to make some management changes for safety. Even if his hearing is fine, these practices are a good idea:
• Always speak to him or otherwise get his attention before you approach, so you don't startle him.
• Be sure he hears your alert, by monitoring the direction of his ears—one or both should flick toward you.
• Check his ears regularly for signs of insect infestation or infection. Look for redness, scratching, and/or hair loss on or around the ear that could indicate rubbing.

(Continued on page 312)

Quick Hearing Test

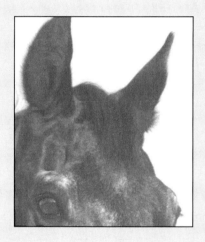

If your horse has perfect hearing, he probably can perceive all the same sounds you can (if your hearing is normal), plus higher-frequency (ultrasonic) sounds that to the human ear are imperceptible, such as some of the highest wavelengths of an urgent whinny.

If your senior horse is hearing-impaired, his ability to hear high-frequency sounds will be the first to suffer, particularly if they're soft. Here's a test you can use to screen your horse for high-frequency, low-amplitude hearing loss.

What you'll need:
• A variety of noisemakers: a plastic grocery bag, several twigs to snap, and a "silent" (to you) dog-training whistle. The bag and breaking twigs will emit a wide range of sounds, including high-frequency ones. The dog whistle emits high-frequency sounds that you can't hear.
• A familiar-to-your-horse stall, or other small enclosure, that's free of wind noise, traffic noise, and other such audio distractions. Remove any feed—chewing hay or grain will adversely affect your horse's ability to hear. (Just as chewing potato chips affects yours.)

1. Put your horse in the stall or enclosure. Stand at least 10 feet behind him (out of kicking range). Remain there until he ignores you. Then, with minimal movement (so you don't evoke a visual response instead of an auditory one), make some soft stimulus sounds: Crinkle the bag, snap the twigs, blow several blasts on the dog whistle. Wait a minute or so between each, so he won't figure out the sounds are coming from you and ignore them.

2. Evaluate your horse's reactions. You'll know he's heard a sound if he flicks an ear toward you (or spooks). If he fails to react to the bags and twigs, he could have a profound hearing loss. (Or, he may have chosen to ignore the noise!) If he doesn't react to the dog whistle, he could have some high-frequency hearing loss. Consult your vet if you suspect any degree of hearing loss.

Equine Ear Insights

Here are some fun facts about the way your horse hears:

• Like you and other animals, he has *binaural* hearing, meaning his ears can hear sound concurrently.

• His external ears, known as pinnae, act like satellite dishes to capture sound waves and funnel them to his inner ears. Because of the large, cuplike shape of his pinnae—especially when compared to your small, flat ones—very little sound spills out, so he can capture noises you might miss.

• His ability to hear a wider range of high-frequency tones, such as the ultrasonic squeak of a bat, enables him to detect sounds you can't hear. For a prey animal, this hearing acuity makes sense. Your horse is hard-wired to listen for the high-frequency sounds of stealth—the snap, crackle, and pop of grass, dried leaves, and twigs, say under a mountain lion's paws.

• Your horse uses those high-frequency sounds to locate the direction from which they came. He does this by gauging which ear hears them first, and at what intensity. Unlike animals that can hone in on a precise location, your horse needs only an approximate indication of where the sound erupted—so he can prepare to flee in another direction.

• If the sound tells him action may be warranted, he'll follow with eye movement, then finally raise and turn his head so he can better focus, freezing his body so as not to give away his position. (You've probably seen grazing horses do this. You'll notice they also quit chewing—the better to hear.)

• If he perceives danger, he'll likely spook—and run.

Did You Know?

Some horses are more "emotional" or reactive toward sound than others. Male horses may react more strongly to sound simply because they're traditionally the herd watchdogs. They don't necessarily hear any better than females do, but they feel a need to alert their "herd" to perceived danger. That's why some horses suffer more anxiety than others in a new environment. A strange place can put your horse on "high alert" for danger, causing him to be emotionally aroused and making his reaction to noise even stronger than it would be in a familiar environment.

You can help reduce your horse's reactivity in stressful situations (such as at a show, while riding in a new place, or on the road in a horse trailer) by blocking out a majority of noise with earplugs. Tack stores and tack-supply catalogs carry equine models. Or, you can make your own using thick wads of cotton, or 1-inch black yarn balls (nearly invisible in the ear), available at art-supply stores. Be sure to remove the plugs immediately after each class or event.

CHAPTER 7

SENIOR
BACK CHECK

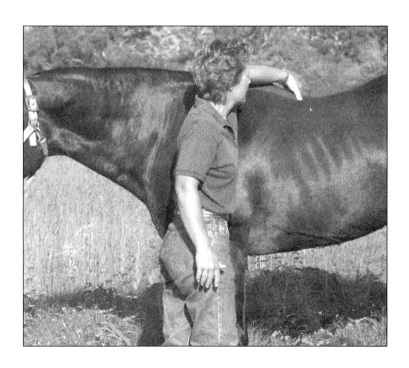

7 Senior Back Check

Just as with your back, years of wear and tear can take their toll on your horse. Use the following info to understand, identify—and help prevent—back problems in your horse. The earlier you detect such problems, the more quickly you can treat them and help avoid compensatory damage.

The Mechanics of Muscle-Related Back Pain

Muscle-related back pain can result from exertion, compensatory strain (due to pain elsewhere in the body), and/or poor management skills. (See "Man-Made Back Problems," page 319.) The pain involves spasms of the large supportive muscles alongside your horse's spine. These spasms trigger a vicious cycle (right).

THE BACK-PAIN CYCLE

INJURY → MUSCLE PAIN/INFLAMMATION → MUSCLES CONTRACT (spasm), to protect area → SPASMS cause more pain → This triggers ADDITIONAL PAIN → Nerve endings can become INFLAMED, contributing to pain

Any back injury can produce spasms, and such injuries may not be clearly evident. Pain onset may be immediate, or occur several hours later. As with you, the most common area affected is your horse's lower back, over his loins. Whenever he attempts to protect his sore back, by hollowing it when you groom, saddle, mount up, and ride, he strains his already-injured muscles. This causes additional injury and pain, perpetuating the cycle.

Age-Related Back Pain

Contrary to popular belief, your senior horse's back muscles don't do most of the work supporting his back. The lion's share of that load is borne by his abdominal muscles, which are thick and hammocklike. As those muscles weaken with advancing age and/or lack of exercise, more of the supporting role falls to your senior horse's back muscles. Oddly enough, these were designed only to flex, extend, and laterally bend his back when he's in motion—they aren't intended to support all that weight. The result can be the spasm cycle outlined at left. Also, while it's common to think of a swaybacked old horse as having a weak back, his back condition may have started with weak abdominal muscles. Some of the most effective movements for strengthening your horse's abdominal muscles include hill work (especially uphill), trotting on the flat, and lope/canter departures. For other back strengtheners, see "Senior Stretches," page 354.

Is Your Senior Horse at Risk for Back Pain?

He is, if he falls into one of the two following categories:

1. He participates in a high-level performance event. These include jumping, eventing, speed events, cattle events (cutting, team penning, working cow horse, roping), Western pleasure, and dressage. Each requires a level of performance that can lead to muscle sprain and strain in the back or elsewhere, which can trigger back pain. (See "Did You Know" page 318.)

How to minimize that risk: Work with your vet to design a management and training program that minimizes back problems in your senior horse. And turn to "Age-Adjusted Exercise," page 339.

2. He has one or more of the following conformation faults:

• *Small and/or poorly shaped hooves:* Too-small feet, contracted heels[G], and long-toe, low-heel syndrome (a tendency to grow more toe than heel), all can contribute to navicular syndrome[G]. In an effort to protect his painful front feet, your horse may sore his back.

• *Short, steep pasterns:* Such pasterns can't absorb shock as well as long, sloping ones, so contribute to concussive injuries of the feet and legs.

• *Post-legged:* A lack of sufficient hock angulation (which makes the hind legs appear straight up-and-down, or postlike), can increase hind-leg concussion.

• *Sickle or cow hocks:* Too much hock angulation, called "sickle hocks," or hocks that point or angle toward each other, called "cow hocks," can result in hock strain and pain, and thus back pain.

• *Weak loins:* A dip over the loins can indicate a lack of muscling, making him prone to injury at that site.

• *Croup higher than withers:* In a mature horse, such a fault makes it difficult for the horse to shift his weight rearward, over his hindquarters, for collection. To compensate, he'll tend to hollow his back, resulting in hyperextension of the muscles there.

• *High tailset:* This indicates weakness through the hip, which can lead to hind-leg problems, which can result in back pain.

• *Neck ties too deep into chest:* Such a horse will naturally be high-headed, ➤

preventing him from achieving a balanced, collected frame from which he can safely perform maneuvers. This can result in back muscle strain.

How to minimize the risk: Avoid buying a senior horse that exhibits these faults. If you already have one, work with your vet to minimize the risk through careful training and management programs.

Hands-On Back Check

Is your horse's back sore? Use this six-step program to detect telltale signs of back pain. If your horse tests positive for any sign, call your vet for an appointment.

1. OBSERVE HIM IN HIS STALL, PADDOCK, OR PASTURE. LOOK FOR:

• *A reluctance to raise or lower his head.* His neck muscles tie into his back muscles, so moving his neck up and down can aggravate back pain.

• *Hock sores.* Some experts believe hock abrasions can be due to a sore-backed or -limbed horse's struggle to rise, even in a deeply bedded stall.

• *Weathervane movement.* Watch for a reluctance to bend his neck or back laterally, in order to turn around. Such a straight-spine body configuration resembles a weathervane turning in the wind.

• *Reluctance to stretch.* If your senior normally gets up from a nap, then stretches by extending a front and hind leg, a failure to do so could signal pain.

• *Reluctance to lie down, and/or roll.* If your senior horse typically lies down to nap, or likes a roll in the dirt, and suddenly fails to do either, it could signal back or leg pain.

2. PERFORM A TACTILE TEST.

To check for muscle soreness in your senior horse's neck and back, palpate the muscles on either side of his spine. Press with flat fingertips, beginning at the top of

Tactile test: Press at the top of your horse's neck...

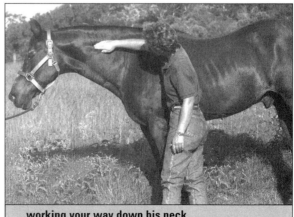

...working your way down his neck...

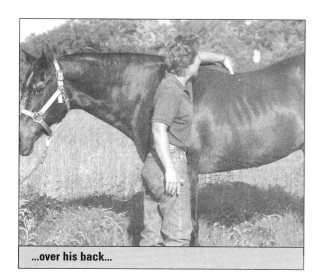

...over his back...

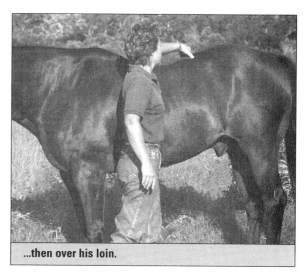

...then over his loin.

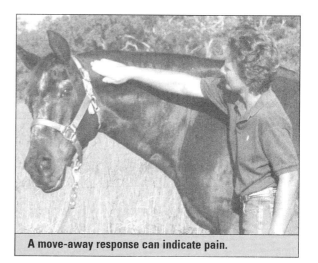

A move-away response can indicate pain.

his neck as shown (opposite page), working your way back. Use the same amount of pressure as you'd need to feel your femur (thigh bone) through the muscle on your thigh. Work your way down your horse's neck, then down his back, and finally over his loin.

If your horse raises his head, swishes his tail, and/or tries to move away (right), reevaluate the area several times to test his response. He may be sore, or he simply may be sensitive. Pay particular attention to the area over his loins, where soreness is commonly located. Any hollow-backed, move-away response as you palpate this area is a strong sign of soreness. Mark that spot with tape or livestock chalk.

3. PERFORM A BACK LIFT.

Perform the back lifts described on page 354. These not only will provide you with information, they're an effective way for your horse to strengthen the muscles of his abdomen, which support his back. If you're unable to elicit the "lift" described in that exercise, it's possible your horse is protecting a back that's painful when it bows up, or he has pain elsewhere that makes it difficult for him to engage his abdominal muscles.

4. OBSERVE HIS BEHAVIOR AS YOU GROOM AND TACK UP. WATCH FOR:

Raised head, hollowed back, and swishing tail. These signs signal pain; a swishing ➤

tail signals irritation and pain. (*Note:* Some horses are naturally thin-skinned or demonstrate these behaviors due to an old injury. If your horse normally behaves in this manner, look for an increase in the degree of his behavior.)

5. OBSERVE HIM AS YOU RIDE. FEEL FOR:
• *Hollowed back as you mount,* as he attempts to protect sore back muscles.
• *Stiffness at onset of work.* If your senior horse starts out stiff and resistant, with reluctance or refusal to lengthen his stride, he's in pain.
• *Resistance to perform normal maneuvers.* Your senior loosens up a bit after the warm-up. But he greets cues for maneuvers requiring a rounded back (stops, back-ups, collection, etc.) with stiff-jawed, hollow-backed, tail-swishing resistance.

6. WATCH SOMEONE ELSE LEAD/RIDE YOUR HORSE. LOOK FOR:
• *Signs of lameness.* See page 142 for signposts of lameness.
• *Signs of resistance.* See Step 5, above.

Did You Know?

Back pain can result from a problem elsewhere in your horse's body. (It also can trigger problems elsewhere.) Common contributing factors include navicular syndrome[G] or other pain in your senior horse's front feet, and/or hock or stifle pain in his hind legs. As he attempts to shift his weight off the sore feet or limbs, he uses his back muscles differently. This initiates the pain and inflammation that ignite the spasm cycle. Until the primary problem is identified and treated, such back pain will recur, despite any efforts to alleviate it.

Man-Made Back Problems

You could be contributing to—or even causing—your senior horse's back pain if you're guilty of any of the following practices:

• **Putting cold water on a hot back.** This can lead to muscle contraction or spasms. Use tepid or sun-warmed water instead.

• **Inadequate warm-up/cool-down.** Cold muscles aren't as elastic and supple as warmed up ones, so can be more easily injured; improper cool-down can lead to muscle damage and stiffness. See "Age-Adjusted Exercise," page 340.

• **Poorly fitting saddle and/or inadequate or dirty padding.** A poor-fitting saddle applies pressure points along your horse's back; inadequate or dirty padding can irritate those points and/or cause sores. Use adequate padding (wool is a natural shock-absorber, breathes well, and wicks away moisture), and wash pads weekly.

• **Leaving a too-tight cinch/girth on too long.** The unending pressure can sore your horse's back, especially when you add your weight. This is a particular problem on mutton- or flat-withered horses, on whom the cinch/girth needs to be snugged down. When on long rides, periodically dismount and loosen the cinch/girth, to give your horse's back a break. (Don't forget to tighten it before remounting!)

• **Poor grooming habits.** A dirty horse provides a breeding ground for bacteria and fungus, and acts as a magnet for biting insects. Compromised skin can lead to back irritation and pain. Pads pick up dirt and can cause/irritate pressure points. Groom your horse daily, paying particular attention to his saddle and girth/cinch areas before and after you ride.

• **Poor shoeing.** Improper front-foot angles can result in such problems as navicular area soreness; improper sole protection; and general foot soreness. Too low a heel angle in the

hind feet can lead to hock problems; unbalanced feet can cause hock and stifle pain. Any and all will be exacerbated by the wear and tear of age. And all can eventually cause compensatory back problems. Choose a top-quality farrier and vet who will work together to determine the best shoeing approach.

• **Unbalanced diet.** Vitamin E and/or selenium deficiencies can contribute to muscle soreness. A diet too high in protein and/or carbohydrates also can adversely affect muscle function. Have your vet evaluate your horse's ration—based on his age and your region—to be sure it suits his specific needs.

• **Turning out a fresh horse.** If you keep your senior stalled, and turn him out when he's fresh, his stiff muscles could be subject to sprains and strains from sudden movements such as stops and bucks. Instead, turn him out after you've ridden or longed him, so his muscles are supple and warm before he plays.

• **Inadequate dental care and/or bitting problems.** Mouth pain and irritation will cause your senior citizen to tense his jaw, which in turn causes him to stiffen his neck and back muscles, increasing the likelihood of injury. Schedule regular dental care (see "Top Priority—Tooth Care," page 332) and work with your vet, equine dentist, or a reputable trainer to be sure your bit suits your horse's mouth conformation.

• **Improper training/riding techniques.** If your senior has made it to his twilight years without having learned the basics of yielding to the bit or collection—and you still ride him—he'll be unbalanced under saddle, and resistant, putting him at risk for injury. Incorporate suppling, flexion, and collection into your senior horse's work routine, and invest in lessons with a reputable trainer. You could lengthen your oldster's productive years by doing so.

Resource: Tim Bartlett, DVM.

NOTES

CHAPTER 8

SENIOR DEWORMING & VACCINATION PROGRAM

Senior Deworming & Vaccination Program

As your horse ages, his immune system gradually weakens. In most healthy horses, immunity decline begins between ages 18 and 22. That leaves your senior more susceptible to disease and less resistant to parasites. The following deworming and vaccination programs are samples you can use to craft the right program for your horse's needs. (When in doubt, consult your vet.)

Senior Vaccinations & Deworming Schedule at-a-glance

The schedule at right contains recommended vaccinations and purge deworming^G schedules based on your horse's lifestyle. If you use a daily dewormer^G, ignore the deworming notes here and go to "Sample Daily Dewormer Program," page 324. (For more information on individual vaccinations, see "The What's and Why's of Senior Vaccinations," page 325.) Footnotes can be found below the chart. Please note that we advocate rotating deworming classes—not just products. No single dewormer can protect your horse 100 percent. Please read the labels on any product you buy, to be sure you're providing sufficient rotation.

how to Get a Fecal Egg Count

To make sure your deworming program is effective for your horse, schedule twice yearly fecal egg counts^G, one in the spring, after your ground thaws, and the other in the fall, after the first killing frost. Your veterinarian can recommend any changes to your program based on the results.

Seal two fresh (preferably still warm) manure "muffins" in a Zip-lock® plastic bag and submit within 1 hour to a laboratory-equipped veterinary facility for a fecal egg count.

Tip: Take the sample directly to the clinic, rather than handing it to your on-the-road veterinarian, who might not get back to the lab for several hours. The test likely will be run by a technician at the facility right away. Results will be given in "eggs per gram" (epg). On an effective purge program, your horse's count should be below 100 epg. On a daily program, his count should be 0 to 50.

Tip: For best accuracy, have your horse's fecal egg count done daily for 3 to 5 days and average the results.

SENIOR VACCINATIONS & PURGE DEWORMING^G SCHEDULE

	OPEN HERD*		SEMI-OPEN HERD**		CLOSED HERD***	
	Dewormer	**Vaccines**	**Dewormer**	**Vaccines**	**Dewormer**	**Vaccines**
JANUARY	5 days fenbendazole *(to kill encysted small strongyles; see "Daily Dewormer" chart January 1 entry)*	Tetanus, Rabies, Botulism[++], Flu/Rhino[+]	Ivermectin/moxidectin[+++]	Tetanus, Rabies, Botulism[++], Flu/Rhino[+]	Ivermectin/moxidectin[+++]	Tetanus, Rabies, Botulism[++], Flu/Rhino
FEBRUARY	Pyrantel pamoate *(double dose for tapeworms; see "Daily Dewormer" chart, June 1 entry)*					
MARCH	Pyrantel pamoate	Flu/Rhino[+] Encephalomyelitis, Potomac Horse Fever[++]	Pyrantel pamoate	Encephalomyelitis, Potomac Horse Fever[++]	Ivermectin/moxidectin[+++]	Encephalomyelitis, Potomac Horse Fever[++]
APRIL	Ivermectin/moxidectin[+++]				Pyrantel pamoate *(double dose for tapeworms)*	
MAY	Ivermectin	Flu/Rhino[+]	Ivermectin	Flu/Rhino[+]		
JUNE	Ivermectin				Pyrantel pamoate	
JULY	Oxfendazole or oxibendazole or pyrantel pamoate	Flu/Rhino[+]	Pyrantel pamoate			
AUGUST	Oxfendazole or oxibendazole or pyrantel pamoate					
SEPTEMBER	Pyrantel pamoate *(double dose for tapeworms)*	Flu/Rhino[+], Encephalomyelitis, Potomac Horse Fever[++]	Pyrantel pamoate *(double dose for tapeworms)*	Flu/Rhino[+], Encephalomyelitis, Potomac Horse Fever[++]	Pyrantel pamoate *(double dose for tapeworms)*	Encephalomyclitis, Potomac Horse Fever[++]
OCTOBER	Ivermectin					
NOVEMBER	Ivermectin	Flu/Rhino	Ivermectin			
DECEMBER	Ivermectin				Ivermectin	

+ If showing, give flu/rhino every 2 months   ++Give only in areas where disease occurs   +++Give only under veterinary supervision
* **Open herd:** Your horse is hauled regularly to events, and/or you keep him at a place with a transient horse population. Frequent exposure to unfamiliar horses (whose vaccination and deworming schedules are unknown) increases his exposure to pathogens and parasites. For maximum protection against both, deworm him monthly.
** **Semi-open herd:** Your horse and his mates are on a regular vaccination and deworming program. New arrivals are immediately dewormed, with fecal egg counts monitored. There's plenty of pasture, so it's not overgrazed (which helps limit parasite exposure).
*** **Closed herd:** Your senior is rarely exposed to horses other than his vaccinated and dewormed herd mates. Pasture is extensive. His protection needs are relatively low since his exposure is low.

Resource: Midge Leitch, VMD and Practical Horseman Magazine.

Sample Daily Dewormer Program

If you have your horse on a daily deworming^G product (such as Pfizer's Strongid C®), use the vaccination program on page 323, ignoring the purge deworming^G guidelines. The following schedule will help you kill parasites that a daily dewormer might not attack. Dewormers mentioned are to be administered in addition to daily dewormer. (Unsure about the pros and cons of a daily dewormer? Consult your veterinarian.)

DAILY DEWORMER^G: sample program	
January 1	Attack encysted cyathostomes^G (small strongyles). These monsters burrow into your horse's intestinal lining at a certain stage of development before they emerge and wreak havoc on his intestines. Potential damage includes colic, diarrhea, bleeding, and weight loss. You have two options: • Administer fenbendazole (such as Panacur or Safe-Guard by Hoechst Roussel Vet) at a larvicidal^G dose. The larvicidal dose for a 1,100- to 1,200-pound horse is 60 cc of 100 mg/ml concentration given daily for 5 days in a row. That dose is also now marketed in paste form. Or— • Use moxidectin under veterinary supervision, as it's labeled as effective against encysted small strongyles. *Caveat:* Moxidectin may be unsafe for very young or very old horses, and for debilitated or very thin horses of any age. For that reason, we recommend veterinary guidance—especially on senior horses.
March 1 (spring thaw)	Attack bots. Administer ivermectin or moxidectin (see caveat, above) paste or gel per manufacturers' instructions, or arrange for your vet to administer liquid dewormer and boticide via nasogastric tube, to kill bots in your horse's stomach as well as any adult (and some immature) stages of intestinal parasites. • Have your vet lab perform a fecal egg count; there should be fewer than 50 eggs per gram. (If the sample contains more than 50 epg, consult your vet—your horse might have a heavy load of adult and/or encysted parasites.)
March 2-May 31	Administer daily dewormer. Scrape bot eggs from your horse's legs daily.
June 1	Attack tapeworms. If tapeworms are a problem in your area (ask your vet), administer a double dose of pyrantel pamoate paste (such as Strongid-P), or arrange for your vet to give a double dose of liquid pyrantel pamoate via nasogastric tube, to kill tapeworms as well as intestinal parasites that may have reached adulthood. If you see tapeworms (they look like flat noodles) in your horse's manure the day after the double dose, repeat it in a week. And schedule double doses every 6 months thereafter.
June 2 until 1 month after first killing frost	Administer daily dewormer. Scrape bot eggs from your horse's legs daily.
1 month after first killing frost	Have your vet lab perform a fecal egg count; there should be fewer than 50 epg. (If the sample contains more than 50 epg, consult your vet—your horse might have a heavy load of adult and/or encysted parasites.) Adult botflies should be dead, and your horse's legs should be free of eggs. Administer ivermectin or moxidectin (see caveat, above) to kill bots in the stomach, as well as adult intestinal parasites.
From above treatment through January 1	Administer daily dewormer.

The What's and Why's of Senior Vaccinations

What vaccinations does—and doesn't—your senior horse need? That depends—on his lifestyle and your region of the country. In the chart on page 323, we gave you recommendations based on lifestyle. Below, we'll further break down vaccine options, describing the disease you'll be protecting your horse against, plus notes on why—and when—your horse might need the vaccine.

The What's and Why's of Senior Vaccinations				
DISEASE	WHAT IT IS	FREQUENCY & TIME OF YEAR TO VACCINATE	DOES YOUR HORSE NEED IT?	
Equine Protozoal Encephalomyelitis (EPM)	Potentially debilitating disease of spinal cord and brain caused by a protozoal[G] organism carried by opossums, armadillos, and possibly others.	*Note:* The authors believe that as of publication, available vaccine(s) are too experimental to recommend; FDA approval is safety approval only.	Consult your veterinarian.	?
Eastern Equine Encephalomyelitis and Western Equine Encephalomyelitis (EEE/WEE; also known as sleeping sickness)	Potentially deadly viral diseases of the central nervous system. There is no treatment. Survivors often have residual brain damage.	In regions with cold winters, vaccinate 1x per year, in the spring, just before mosquitoes emerge. If winters are warm enough for year-round mosquitoes, vaccinate 2x a year, in spring and fall.	Yes.	✔
Venezuelan Equine Encephalomyelitis (VEE—the other sleeping sickness)	Similar to EEE/WEE. There is no treatment. Survivors often have residual brain damage.	Government restricts use to areas where the disease has been reported; usually near Mexico-USA border. Give 2x a year, in spring and fall.	If reported in your area, yes.	?
Influenza (Flu)	A viral infection that leaves your horse's respiratory tract irritable and prone to cough for weeks after recovery.	1x per year, in the spring, if your horse lives alone and stays home, or if he lives in a closed herd of flu-vaccinated horses. Every 2 months if your horse travels or commingles with other horses of unknown vaccination history.	Yes.*	✔ ➤

	The What's and Why's of Senior Vaccinations, *continued*		
DISEASE	**WHAT IT IS**	**FREQUENCY & TIME OF YEAR TO VACCINATE**	**DOES YOUR HORSE NEED IT?**
Tetanus (Lockjaw)	Usually fatal disease caused by bacteria common in your horse's environment. Risk is high in horses that aren't vaccinated.	*Tetanus toxoid:* 1x per year, in early spring or at the time of a broken-skin injury if it occurs 12 months or more after the last tetanus toxoid vaccination. *Tetanus antitoxin:* To be used only if a broken-skin injury occurs in a horse with no known history of tetanus toxoid vaccination.	Yes. ✔
Equine viral rhinopneumonitis (equine herpes-virus or rhino)	Same as for flu.	Due to short-lived protection from vaccine and questionable efficacy^G, consult your vet for recommendations for your horse.	Consult your vet. ?
Strangles	A bacterial respiratory disease that can make your horse a carrier for years afterward if the bacteria manage to conceal themselves in his guttural pouches^G.	Routine use of this vaccination has become controversial and is not generally recommended, due to the incidence of tissue reaction at the injection site and questionable efficacy^G.	If strangles is endemic^G in your area, discuss the pros and cons with your veterinarian.** ?
Rabies	Fatal viral disease spread by the bite or saliva of infected mammals; all other animals (including humans) that come into contact with an affected horse are at risk.	1x per year, in early spring. Must be given by licensed veterinarian.	Yes. ✔

The What's and Why's of Senior Vaccinations, *continued*				
DISEASE	**WHAT IT IS**	**FREQUENCY & TIME OF YEAR TO VACCINATE**	**DOES YOUR HORSE NEED IT?**	
Potomac Horse Fever (PHF)	Potentially deadly protozoal^G disease, believed to be transmitted by ticks, that can cause severe diarrhea and laminitis.	1 to 2x per year: In spring, before disease-carrying ticks become active, and again in fall if PHF is endemic^G in your area.	If PHF is endemic^G in your area, discuss the pros and cons of this vaccine with your vet.	**?**
Botulism	Often fatal paralysis caused by bacterial toxins present in contaminated feed or soil.	1x per year in the spring in endemic^G areas.	Yes, if botulism is endemic^G in your area. Otherwise, no.	**?**
Equine Viral Arteritis (EVA)	A viral disease, spread by sexual contact or by coughing or sneezing, that causes flu-like respiratory disease, leg swelling, and can cause abortion. Vaccine must be purchased and given by state-approved veterinarian. Exposed stallions not vaccinated prior to sexual maturity can become carriers.	One lifetime vaccination, given 1 month prior to breeding season.	Yes, if your mare has never been diagnosed with EVA and is booked to a stallion with positive or unknown EVA history. Otherwise, no.	**?**

*Intranasal flu vaccine (Flu Avert®, from Heska), provides protection at the virus's point of entry: your horse's nasal passages. Research has shown good immune response and longer-lasting, better protection than from injectable flu shots; must be administered by a veterinarian.

**Intranasal strangles vaccine (Pinnacle®, from Fort Dodge), may be more effective than the IM form as it provides protection at a point of entry. Also has a decreased risk of localized reactions.

Deworming Product Samples

The charts on pages 323 and 324 provided you with sample deworming schedules for your horse, based on your choice of purge dewormers^G or a daily deworming^G program. Below you'll find additional information on the dewormers mentioned, as well as others, plus notes on what parasites they attack, and their safety margins.

DEWORMING PRODUCT SAMPLES
(Note: This chart is not meant to represent a complete listing of available deworming products.)

Category	Active ingredient	Brand names	Comments
Avermectin	Ivermectin	• Eqvalan (Merial) • Zimecterin (Farnam) • Equimectrin (Horse Health) • Rotectin-1 (Farnam)	Highly effective against a broad spectrum of equine parasites, including bots^G, with a wide safety margin^G.
Milbemycin	Moxidectin	Quest (Fort Dodge)	Kills some of the encysted larval forms of small strongyles and has extended control over this specific parasite; its effectiveness against other parasites is similar to ivermectin. Narrower safety margins, not recommended for very young, elderly, thin, or ill horses.
Benzimidazole	Febantel	Cutter Paste (Bayer)	Effective against roundworms, large and small strongyles, and pinworms^G; not bots. Wide safety margin.
	Fenbendazole	• Panacur (Hoechst Roussel Vet) • Safe-Guard (Hoechst Roussel Vet)	Effective against roundworms, large and small strongyles, and pinworms; not bots. Wide safety margin.
	Oxfendazole	Benzelmin (Syntex)	Effective against roundworms, large and small strongyles, and pinworms; not bots. Wide safety margin.

DEWORMING PRODUCT SAMPLES
(continued)

Category	Active ingredient	Brand names	Comments
Benzimidazole	Oxibendazole	Anthelcide EQ (SmithKline Beecham)	Effective against roundworms, large and small strongyles, and pinworms[G]; not bots[G]. Wide safety margin[G].
Organo-phosphates	Dichlorvos	Cutter Dichlorvos Wormer (Bayer)	Effective against roundworms, large and small strongyles, pinworms, and bots. Narrow safety margin; to be used in adult horses only.
Piperazine	Piperazine	Alfalfa Pellet Wormer (Farnam)	Mild dewormer, variably effective against roundworms, large and small strongyles, and pinworms; not bots. Wide safety margin. Good choice as a first dewormer for foals or any horse suspected of having a heavy worm infestation, when a massive kill-off of worms might be injurious to his health.
Pyrimidine	Pyrantel pamoate	• Strongid Paste (Pfizer) • Strongid Liquid (Pfizer) • Rotectin-2 (Farnam)	Effective against roundworms, large and small strongyles, and pinworms; not bots. Wide safety margin. Not to be used with piperazine (antagonistic). When purge-dose is doubled, effective against equine tapeworms.
	Pyrantel tartrate	• Strongid C (Pfizer) • Strongid C2x (Pfizer) • Equine Wormer Pellets (Kaeco) • Foal & Horse Pelleted Wormer (Manna Pro)	When given as a daily dewormer (Strongid C and C2x), effective against larval forms of parasites picked up in the environment; not bots. When given as a purge-dewormer (Equine Wormer and Foal & Horse Pelleted Dewormer), effectiveness equivalent to pyrantel pamoate. Wide safety margin. ➤

How Do You Know How Much Dewormer to Give?

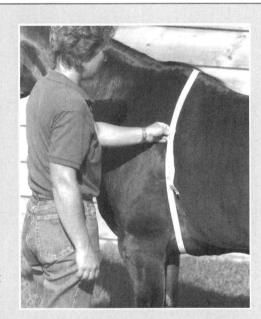

Follow the manufacturer's instructions, based on your horse's body weight. Use this method for an estimate that's usually more accurate than what you'll get from a standard commercial weight tape.

Step 1: Using a flexible (but not stretchy) tailor's measuring tape, measure the circumference of your horse's girth, in inches, running the tape just behind the elbow on both sides and straight over his withers. (See photo above.) Write this number down.

Step 2: Using a rigid carpenter's measuring tape or a 6-foot folding ruler, measure the length of your horse's torso on one side, in inches, from the point of his shoulder to the point of his hip. Write this number down.

Step 3: Apply your measurements to the following formula:

$$\frac{[(\text{Girth})^2 \times \text{Length}]}{330} = \text{Body weight}$$

Example: Say your horse has a girth of 66 inches and a body length of 62 inches. His body weight would be:

$$\frac{66^2 \times 62}{330} = 818.4 \text{ pounds}$$

Do NOT give your horse a purge dewormer if he hasn't received any dewormer for more than a year. The massive kill-off of a heavy parasite load could make him sick or cause an intestinal blockage. Ask your vet to recommend a mild dewormer for his first treatment.

CHAPTER 9

TOP PRIORITY— TOOTH CARE

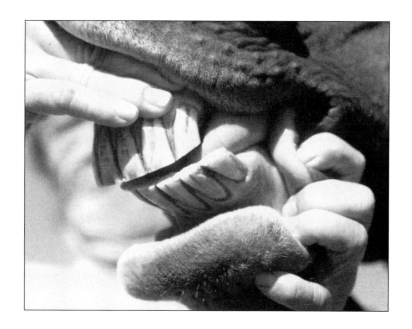

9 Top Priority— Tooth Care

Your horse is "long in the tooth." He's a grazer, designed to chew all day, every day. Grinding up forage wears the teeth down, so each tooth is equipped with a long root. As the tooth wears down, its root "feeds" more grinding surface into his mouth—much like a Pez® dispenser.

Here's how age can affect that process.

Gum disease: Because the cheek teeth taper from crown (wider) to root (narrower), and because more of the tooth is pushed out as your horse ages, his teeth will become narrower. Gaps develop between them—places where food can accumulate, to cause gum disease.

Tooth loss: Horses over the age of 20 can literally run out of root/tooth, and be left with tender gums exposed. If the opposite tooth (the upper or lower "partner" tooth) hasn't yet fallen out, this can be the source of significant mouth pain—the grinding surface of the "partner" tooth can dig into the toothless gum across from it.

Broken teeth: By the simple law of averages, the longer your horse lives, the greater the chance that a tooth will be cracked or knocked out.

How this could affect your horse:

Mouth pain: Your horse's mouth will be uncomfortable. Sharp edges on his molars, or sharp canine teeth[G], can cut his cheeks and gums, triggering pain. He'll be less inclined to eat, or to properly chew what he does eat, than if he weren't hurting. He'll also toss his head in response to bit pressure. Severe cuts can become infected, or cause abscesses or ulcers.

Ineffective chewing. Your horse's upper and lower molars must smoothly contact one another to allow for proper food grinding. (See illustration, page 336.) If these rows of teeth, called *molar arcades*, are uneven or misaligned, your horse won't be able to chew effectively. Incisors can also affect your horse's ability to grind food and rip off grass while grazing—if they grow too long or uneven, they'll affect his whole bite, possibly preventing his molars from contacting one another properly.

Increased risk of colic[G] and choke[G]: When your horse can't chew properly, he ends up swallowing partially chewed food, which is more difficult to digest than chewed food, increasing his risk of colic. It's also more difficult to swallow, which can lead to choke.

Neck/back pain: When your horse's mouth is out of balance, it can stress his *temporo-mandibular joint* (TMJ), which connects his lower jaw to his skull. Similar to TMJ syndrome in humans, this can lead to pain and/or stiffness in your horse's neck and back.

Additional dental problems: By not chewing on the sore side of his mouth, he'll experience a lack of wear on that side, which will result in excess tooth growth, with the points cutting into cheek and gum. His lack of chewing also could result in loosened tooth attachments on that side, leading to premature tooth loss.

Loss of condition: His inability to chew and digest his food will lead to weight loss. That, in turn, could weaken him—and his immune system—making him more susceptible to viral and bacterial invaders.

Signposts of Dental Problems

Call your veterinarian if you observe any of the following signposts.

• Changes in eating/drinking habits: Watch for "quidding" (dropping of partially chewed food), tossing feed on the ground, passing unchewed grains in manure, swishing his mouth in water, dunking his muzzle in water, refusing feed after appearing hungry, or jerking away from water after appearing thirsty.

• Foul-smelling nasal discharge: This could indicate the root of a cheek tooth has abscessed G, and that the discharge has leaked into the nasal sinuses.

• A swelling, or foul-smelling drainage on face: A wound on your horse's face—usually beneath an eye, that has a foul-smelling drainage and/or is swollen, can also indicate an abscessed tooth root.

• Foul breath: Bad equine breath, often smelling strongly of mothballs, can indicate retained food and gum disease.

How to Delay Problems

Dental exams. Have your horse's teeth checked and floated G (if necessary) by a veterinarian who practices equine dentistry, at least once a year until the age of 15, then at least twice a year after that. (If your veterinarian doesn't do teeth, ask him or her for a referral to one who does.) Between checkups, watch for problems and schedule an early exam if you see signposts of dental problems—don't wait until the next scheduled exam to have your vet treat them.

MANAGEMENT TIPS:
Utilize feeds specially designed for older horses, such as Purina's Equine   ➤

Senior. These are "prechewed"—processed so that complete chewing isn't necessary. Even toothless horses can be maintained on pelleted complete feeds (designed to be given without hay), soaked in water to make gruel. (*Tip:* Use a half-gallon of water per pound of feed.)

Note: When feeding a complete feed designed to be given without hay, continue to provide some hay or forage, after the complete feed has been eaten. For more on how and why, go to "Stay-Young Diet Solutions," page 376.

A Virtual Float

Here's a quick tour of your horse's mouth during an equine dentistry float[G].

1. A speculum holds open the mouth of a sedated late-teens Thoroughbred mare. Equine dentist Buff Hildreth, DVM, of Richmond, Texas, uses molar cutters to remove a large hook[G].

2. And here's the hook. Removing these helps to realign the jaws and allows for freer jaw movement.

3. Once major problems are resolved, Dr. Hildreth uses a hand file to smooth out rough edges, or "float" the teeth. (*Note:* some vets use power tools instead of hand files. It's a matter of the dentist's personal preference.)

4. After floating the molars, Dr. Hildreth evaluates the incisors. (See illustration, page 336.) This horse appears to have an offset bite,

meaning the upper incisors on one side are very long, and the lower incisors on the opposite side are very long, causing them to meet on a diagonal rather than a straight line.

5. Dr. Hildreth uses a hand file to smooth out the incisors.

6. An equine dental technician demonstrates use of a Dremel tool to even out wear on the incisors, which helps ensure proper molar function.

7. Good dental work results in good occlusion^G in the aged Thoroughbred mare's mouth. The incisor gap is created because the molars come into contact as the jaws move from side to side.

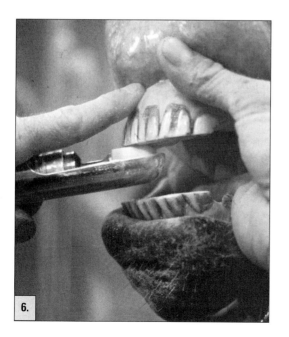

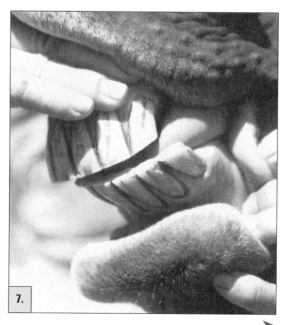

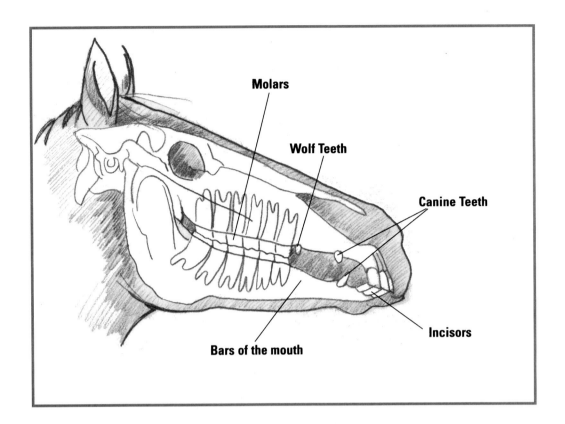

Molars

Wolf Teeth

Canine Teeth

Incisors

Bars of the mouth

HOW TO FIND AN EQUINE DENTIST OR DENTAL TECHNICIAN

Ask your vet if she has taken continuing education in equine dentistry. If she hasn't, ask her to refer you to a veterinarian who's made a commitment to a high-quality dental practice, or to a certified dental technician who works under the auspices of a licensed equine veterinarian who can sedate your horse if need be, perform invasive procedures such as tooth extractions, and provide general oversight of the dental care with your horse's overall health in mind.

Here's an organization that certifies dental technicians: International Association of Equine Dentistry, c/o Janice Holm, secretary, P.O. Box 2458, Brevard, NC 28712; phone 877.642.1931 (toll free) or 828.883.2230; fax 828.883.4610; or go to www.iaeqd.org.

• Geldings and stallions have 44 permanent teeth; mares have 36 to 40.

• Your horse has six upper and six lower front teeth, called incisors. These are designed to tear off grass and other forage.

• Your horse has 12 upper and 12 lower molars, or back teeth. These are designed to grind food into a digestible form.

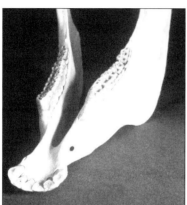

• Molars continue to erupt throughout your horse's lifetime, to ensure he continues to have the ability to grind food as he ages. This continuous growth, however, can exacerbate problems if his mouth is out of balance—which is why regular dental care is key to good tooth health in your horse's senior years.

• Incisors also continue to grow throughout your horse's life. If he lives in a natural grazing environment (on pasture 24 hours a day), they'll naturally wear down somewhat from tearing off grass. (But if they're not perfectly symmetrical, some of that wear will be uneven and will require preventive maintenance.)

Tooth Trivia

• A stall-kept horse lacks natural incisor wear, which can hasten overgrowth of those teeth. When his incisors become too long, they can prevent his molars from contacting one another, reducing his ability to properly grind food.

• Geldings and stallions have 2 upper and 2 lower canine teeth (see illustration at left), which are remnants of fighting teeth once used by their ancestors. They sit in the gap between the horse's incisors and molars, known as the bars of his mouth. Mares rarely have canine teeth.

• Wolf teethᴳ are remnants of molars that no longer serve a useful function. They're located just in front of the molars on the upper jaw, and very rarely, in front of molars on the lower jaw.

CHAPTER 10

AGE-ADJUSTED EXERCISE

10 Age-Adjusted Exercise

Your horse can remain active—even highly competitive—until his late teens and beyond. In fact, even if your senior citizen is somewhat unsound, he'll likely benefit from regular work (adjusted to suit his age and fitness level, and to accommodate his limitations and unsoundness). With exercise, he's more likely to maintain better mental and physical health than a horse that's totally retired from work.

In this chapter, we'll focus mainly on the senior horse who, aside from a few minor aches and pains that resolve once he's warmed up, is basically sound. If your horse has more than minor discomfort, join forces with your veterinarian to formulate an individualized exercise program that can give your senior the benefits without exacerbating his problem, based on the guidelines below. That could include hand-walking or swimming, if you have a facility in your area. No matter what level of work you and your senior horse engage in, the interaction you'll get from working him will provide a great way to monitor his well-being.

Benefits of Senior Exercise

Here's a sampling of the benefits of working your senior.

- **Keeps 'em young.** Just as in humans, exercise can prevent or even reverse age-related changes in strength and muscle mass.
- **Improves metabolism.** It affects hormone levels, helping to make the metabolic state of a working senior's muscle more like that of a young horse's. And, by keeping muscles "on duty," it helps prevent atrophy from lack of use, another avenue to keeping the metabolism awake and active.
- **Improves circulation.** Regular exercise helps get your aging horse's blood moving, improving circulation to his entire body. This, in turn, can help resolve such problems as "stocking up" and improve age-related decreases in balance and sure-footedness by improving circulation to, and nerve sensitivity in, his legs and feet. It also improves circulation to the brain, which helps him correctly identify his position and orientation with respect to the ground.

- **Improves digestion.** Horses evolved to move across open plains—nibble, step, nibble, step—not to stand still in a stall or paddock. The more your horse moves, the better his digestive system works. Specifically, exercise helps his gut motility[G], which helps food pass through his digestive tract. Slowed motility can increase his risk of colic.

- **Improves soft-tissue elasticity.** As with humans, the more your horse works his muscles, tendons and ligaments, the more limber and elastic they'll be, helping to improve his joints' range-of-motion with less risk of injury.

- **Improves overall joint health.** A joint's cartilage acts like a sponge. When it bears weight, joint fluid it has absorbed is squeezed into the joint. When weight is lifted, it absorbs more joint fluid. That's how nutrients are delivered to cartilage and other parts, and waste materials are pulled away. Exercise enhances this process, keeping the joint's inner components clean, nourished, and well-lubricated, thereby maintaining optimal joint health as well as providing relief from minor arthritis discomfort.

- **Likely helps aerobic capacity.** In humans, regular exercise through the 30s, 40s, and 50s will limit the expected decrease in aerobic capacity with increasing age. Even humans in their 70s and 80s can benefit from physical conditioning, by gaining aerobic capacity, muscle strength—and an overall improvement in quality of life. A similar effect might occur in horses that are in training throughout their teen years and beyond, enabling them to stay competitive—and likely healthier —in that period.

Caveats for Senior Exercise

HE'LL BE STIFFER, LONGER. Age makes it harder to warm up, so your senior horse will take longer to limber. This is the result of natural wear and tear that can make your horse's joints and muscles stiffer than a younger horse's will be. That means he needs more warm-up time before you begin a work session. Walk at least 10 minutes before you increase speed. Use suppling exercises and lateral movements, if you can, to help stretch your horse's muscles. You'll feel that he's ready to move on when he begins to lengthen his stride and move in relaxed, cadenced steps.

HE'LL GET HOTTER, FASTER. Advanced age makes it harder to cool off. Studies have shown that age affects a horse's cooling capabilities during exercise. To cool himself, your horse must transport heat from his body's core to the skin surface and blood vessels. Aged horses' hearts have to work harder to pump blood for heat dissipation through narrowed and less elastic blood vessels and capillaries in the skin; the body's natural "priority list" tells your senior horse to focus blood flow ➤

on vital organ function first, and the extremities (including legs, joints, and skin) last. And, age can reduce sweat-gland function. Less sweat means less evaporative cooling. All of this means your oldster can't handle the combination of heat and exercise as well as he could when he was younger. During hot weather, taper his exercise, and/or ride in the early morning or evening, when temperatures have cooled. Help him cool off afterward with at least 10 minutes of walking, a cool rinse, a nice breeze (not a draft!), and access to cool, clean drinking water.

HE'LL HAVE LESS AEROBIC CAPACITY—thus less speed, less strength, and less endurance. In studies that allow measurement of VO_2max (oxygen saturation and lung capacity) and endurance, it was revealed that, as in older humans, it's likely equine aerobic capacity declines in advancing years. That means for any given running speed, an older horse (even though he's fit) will be working at a much higher percentage of his aerobic capacity than a similarly fit younger horse will, meaning he'll be working harder—and will tire sooner. Start any senior exercise program gradually, and monitor your horse carefully for signs of fatigue (such as increased heart rate and respiration without evidence of his usual quick recovery, excessive or less-than-usual sweating, lowered head, lack of interest in water and hay, and lack of interest in his surroundings). If your senior horse seems to tire more quickly than normal (for him), and/or if you see any of the above signs of fatigue, cut back his work and consult your veterinarian. In addition to normal age-related changes in exercise tolerance, he could have an underlying condition that's compromising his work capacity.

DON'T FORGET TO "LISTEN." There's no blanket recommendation for a senior conditioning program, though we'll give you some guidelines, below. No matter what your program consists of, start slowly, and vigilantly monitor your horse for signs you may be overworking him, such as fatigue (described above), heat, swelling, and pain in his lower limbs, lameness, stiffness, or unusual resistance (pinned ears, swishing tail), which could indicate pain. If you observe any of those signs, ease up and consult your veterinarian.

Exercise Guidelines for Out-of-Shape Seniors

If your senior citizen is already enjoying the benefits of a conditioning program, hats off to you! Keep in mind the caveats listed above, check out "Your Aging Athlete," page 344, and keep on working him. If, however, he's been idle for a while, use these steps to help safely start an exercise program.

Step 1. Schedule a veterinary examination. Years of wear and tear likely have taken their toll in one way or another. There may be a foot-related lameness, for example, such as navicular syndrome^G, which may not be evident in the idle horse, and which may require medication as well as special shoeing, to keep your senior as comfortable as possible when he works. Degenerative joint disease (arthritis^G) is also a common age-related ailment. Any chronically painful condition must be addressed, and the discomfort dealt with—the sooner the better. Otherwise, pain can negate any exercise-related benefits and can, according to several studies, accelerate aging. Your vet can help you identify problems and recommend pain relief, shoeing, and exercise programs.

Step 2. Study the "Caveats For Senior Exercise" on page 341. Commit them to memory. With them in mind, monitor your horse as you work him. Remember, your goal is to make your senior horse happier, healthier, and more comfortable, with your own pleasure, enjoyment, and ambitions taking a back seat.

Step 3. Work in good footing. Aged muscles, tendons, and ligaments are less resilient than young ones. Help avoid injury by not asking your senior to work on hard, slick, uneven, or deep surfaces.

Step 4. Start slowly and warm up well. For instance, when you start, limit work sessions to 10 or 15 minutes on the longe line or under saddle, three times a week. If your senior horse has joint problems, ask your veterinarian whether

(Continued on page 345)

Should You Retire Your Horse?

Here are signs that he's ready to cut back—or perhaps stop entirely.
- A pattern of reduced vitality, such as a consistent series of "off" days.
- Chronic lameness that worsens with work.
- Lack of enthusiasm for work and activities that formerly interested him.
- Swaying as you mount, indicating weakness and/or loss of balance.
- Stumbling on smooth footing, or other signs of reduced coordination.

When and if the time comes, arrange to turn him out with one or two friendly companions in a pasture featuring reasonable forage, shelter, and a clean water supply. That way, he can exercise himself, but won't push himself beyond his capacity.

If he's a people-oriented horse who doesn't do well without work or attention, and your vet okays the decision based on your horse's condition, consider donating him to a reputable handicapped riding program. The work will be light—with a heavy dose of supervised attention.

YOUR AGING ATHLETE

Do you have a senior athlete? A horse that seems to keep on ticking, either at home, on the trail, or on the circuit? Lucky you. While you need to manage him as an individual (a program that works for one horse can wear out another), here are some global tips that can help you keep your aged equine active for years to come:

SCHOOL LESS. Chances are your horse knows his job. That means your job is to keep him fit—not keep drilling him. A good rule of thumb is to concentrate on conditioning as your priority, focusing on specific skills on an as-needed basis. That could be once or twice a show season (if he shows, he gets regular tune-ups at competitions)—or less.

FOCUS ON FITNESS. The way to keep him fit is with moderate but consistent exercise—*little* and *often* being the keys. For instance, hack, do hill work, and/or trail ride 5 days a week in the summer. Avoid the temptation to completely let down your senior in the winter. The more you let an older horse down, the longer it takes to bring him back. Instead, cut him back to a walk, trot, and canter just two or three days a week during your "off" months. Then, when show or riding season hits, you can increase the number of times you ride, and gradually increase the intensity of those rides.

TAKE IT EASY. Choose work that keeps your horse in good shape without pounding his joints and muscles. For instance, plan on easy cross-country hacks and 3- to 5-minute canter intervals, with plenty of long walks in between to allow his breathing and heart rate to recover.

BE CONSISTENT. Ride lightly every day or every other day. If you try to "save" your horse for weekend events (such as shows or clinics), he'll get stiff and out of shape during the week. (The same holds true, though to a slightly lesser degree, for his younger cousins.) This will make him more prone to injury when you do ride. Develop a plan, be it 15 minutes a day—or 45. Let your horse's condition be your guide.

PICK YOUR EVENTS. While a heavy competitive schedule will stress any horse, your oldster will feel that stress sooner than a young horse will, and suffer longer from it. Be selective about when and in what events you show your horse. Keep in mind that his ability to regulate body temperature may be compromised, making weather an issue. Avoid choosing too many shows per year, or too many classes per day, or trailer trips that are too long and stressful in hot or otherwise challenging weather. When in doubt, consult your veterinarian.

CREATE A DREAM TEAM. It's rare for an older horse not to show some signs of stiffness and soreness. Recruit your farrier and veterinarian as partners in seeing that your horse gets what he needs before minor problems balloon into major ones. Solutions could include bar shoes to help foot soreness, more turnout to relieve stiffness, and a joint supplement (see "The Age Event: Arthritis," page 227) and/or an NSAID[G] such as phenylbutazone[G] as needed to keep him comfortable.

STAY ALERT. Your horse will tell you when it's time to cut back on his work level. Even with terrific care, his athletic ability will begin to decline. This generally happens somewhere in the late teens. One of the first symptoms you might feel is a reduction in stride length—you just can't get your horse to open his stride as you once could. When you try, his attitude might change to a resistant one (pinned ears, swishing tail), because he simply can't comply. When that happens, taper his workload a bit and accommodate his new limitations: show him in a less-stressful division of your chosen event. For instance, if he's a 3'6" hunter, drop him back to a 3' division. Use common sense. He can have a lot of good miles left, if you're tuned in and willing to let them be lower-impact miles.

Hand-walking can provide low-impact exercise, as well as a great way for you to monitor your senior's well-being.

the constant turning involved with longeing will stress already compromised joints. If so, ask him or her if using an extra-long longe line (say, one that's closer to 60 feet) to widen the circle will help. If not, replace longeing with long-lining, in which you use two longe lines as "reins" as you walk behind the horse. (Consult a reputable trainer for how to long-line, if you've not done it before.)

When you initiate your work sessions, walk your horse for a majority of the time, to help his joints limber up (just as you'd stretch before jogging). This is especially ➤

true in cold weather, when his muscles and joints will be extra tight. When you trot him, do so on a loose rein or line until you feel or see him moving forward freely, a sign he's limbering up. As he gains strength, gradually introduce the canter. Finish with at least 10 minutes of walking, to allow your senior citizen to cool off. As a rule of thumb, don't increase your weekly training time or distance by more than 5 percent per week.

Step 5. **Change things up.** The more you vary your horse's exercise, the more muscle groups you'll work—and the more you both will reap the mental and physical benefits of a well-conceived and varied exercise program. For instance, as your horse's condition improves, incorporate hill work if possible, to help build muscles—and change the scenery. Do arena work in one session, then trail ride or hack cross-country the next. If your senior horse knows how to drive, hook him up to a light 2-wheel cart and go for a leisurely spin once a week, for another flavor of exercise. If he doesn't drive, consider getting a trainer to help you teach him—it's a great way to exercise his brain and engage new muscles, without making him carry weight on his back. Consider ponying him one day, riding bareback another day, and taking new trails. Be creative—and have fun.

Step 6. **Be realistic.** While a horse in his mid-teens with a history of performance training may someday be capable of competitive work (depending on the demands of your chosen sport, and his condition and soundness), making that the goal for a formerly idle 20-year-old may be less realistic. When in doubt, err to the side of conservative. And, consult your vet.

CHAPTER 11

SENIOR
STRETCHES

11

Senior Stretches

Y ou've heard of physical therapy for people, but for horses? You bet. While standard equine physical therapy includes hand-walking and swimming (in specially designed equine pools), range-of-motion stretching exercises and passive joint work are also included in this category. Both have proven to benefit joints compromised by age-related wear and tear, and inflammation. Best of all, you can do these at home—and don't need a pool!

Below is passive joint work, as well as some time-honored general stretching exercises. If you're interested in having other physical therapies performed on your horse by a trained professional, ask your veterinarian for a referral and for collaboration.

Passive Joint Work

Why you'll do it: You've been advised by your vet to confine your horse to keep him from further injuring an inflamed or injured joint while it heals. (And your vet approves passive joint work.)

What it does: Encourages healing of cartilage and other soft tissues within the joint, while decreasing scar-tissue formation (which can cause joint stiffening and range-of-motion loss).

How to do it:
1. Pick up the affected limb.

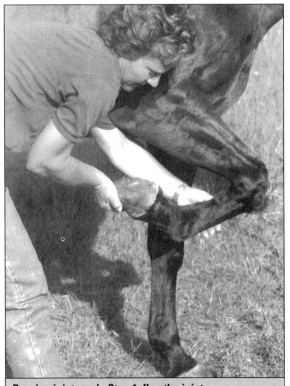

Passive joint work: Step 1, flex the joint.

Alternately flex (bend)...

2. ...and extend the affected joint(s).

Perform 3 or 4 times a day, or more, for a minute at a time. The more you do it, the better.

Stretches 101

Now for the general stretches. Think of them as yoga for your horse, and perform them daily, or as often as your schedule allows. Not only will they benefit him physically, the feel-good aspect—plus positive interaction with you—will boost his mental fitness. Here are some stretch basics:

• Consult your veterinarian if your horse has an acute or chronic injury or condition that could be

Passive joint work: Step 2, extend the joint.

adversely affected by stretching, such as a torn tendon, ligament, or cartilage, or any severe lameness that makes it painful for him to lift a leg.

• Work in a quiet, spacious area with minimal disturbances, to reduce the risk of your horse being spooked, to give you plenty of room to stretch him—and to escape trouble, if necessary.

• You'll be in vulnerable positions. Stay alert and be prepared to move quickly out of harm's way, if necessary.

• Have a horse-savvy and attentive helper hold your horse while you work. Such a person is invaluable for protecting your safety if your horse should start to lose his balance or otherwise move.

• At first, your senior horse may resist out of anxiety or confusion. As he relaxes, you'll be able to feel how far he's able to stretch. If he has trouble reaching as far as you've asked him to, or holding that position, start with a lesser degree until he becomes more flexible. Proper stretching should never hurt!

• When you achieve optimal stretch for each exercise as described (or your horse's max), hold it for a count of 10 to 15 seconds. Then SLOWLY release. Repeat each stretch three times.

➤

• Your horse may enjoy his stretches so much that he begins to anticipate—shooting a front leg forward or a hind leg backward, catching you off guard. Be prepared for quick or unexpected movements on his part, so you can retain your hold on the leg, continuing your stretch maneuvers once he's finished his.

• If, during or after any stretch, your horse seems distressed or uncomfortable, back off and go on to the next one. Make a veterinary appointment to investigate the reason for his discomfort.

The Stretches

#1: FORELIMB STRETCH

Why you'll do it: For general maintenance, to warm, limber, and stretch soft tissue in your senior horse's front legs, and to improve/increase the range of motion in his front-leg joints.

How to do it:

A. Stand at your horse's right shoulder, facing his hindquarters.

B. Pick up his right front leg, bending it as you would to clean the hoof.

C. While supporting the leg between your knees (farrier-style), grasp the hoof in both hands and rotate it gently counterclockwise, then clockwise, to limber the pastern joints. (The joints below the fetlock.)

D. Without setting the leg down, turn around so you're facing the same

1-C: Pick up his right front leg as you would to clean the hoof, rotating the hoof gently.

1-D: Without setting the leg down, turn and face forward.

1-E: Then lift the knee and move the bent leg in a small circle.

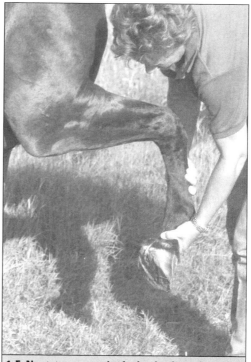

1-F: Next, turn so you're facing backward, and unfold the leg...

direction as your horse. Then bend his knee so his leg is folded as much as possible (the fetlock joint is not bent), with one hand supporting the cannon (shin) bone and the other cupping the bent knee.

E. Now lift the knee slightly against the flesh of his chest, moving the whole bent leg as a unit in a small circle. (Think of drawing a circle in the air with his knee joint.) Rotate the leg to the right, then the left, to limber his shoulder joint. (*Caveat:* Avoid rotating his elbow joint. It's a hinge-type joint, so wasn't meant to rotate.)

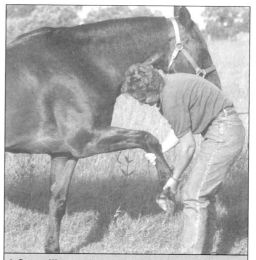

1-G: ...pulling on the pastern and cannon bone as you slowly step backward, lifting the bent leg such that the forearm is parallel to the ground.

F. Now turn so you're facing backward again. Unfold the leg slightly and switch your grip. Support the leg with one hand on the pastern area and one at mid-cannon bone, as you slowly step backward (in the direction your horse is facing). ➤

G. As you do, gently lift the bent leg toward a position in which the forearm bone (above the knee) is parallel to the ground, with the leg bent to 90°.

H. Release partially, then slowly pull the pastern forward, straightening the leg. (It'll naturally drop down, so that it's no longer parallel to the ground.) Hold.

I. Release the foot to the ground slowly. Repeat the entire sequence twice more, then stretch the other foreleg.

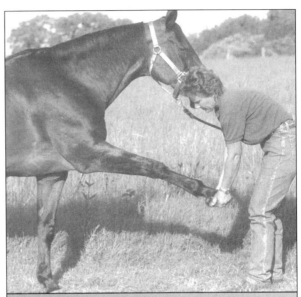

1-H: Slowly pull the pastern forward, straightening the leg.

#2: HIND-LIMB STRETCH

Why you'll do it: To help loosen stiff/sore hips, lower back, and/or stifles. Stretching these areas can be hard on your own back, so don't hesitate to ask a strong-backed friend to help, or hire a trained equine physical therapy specialist (your veterinarian should be able to refer you to one).

2-C: Catch the fetlock joint on your thigh, farrier-style.

2-D: Taking baby steps, gently stretch the leg back, directly away from your horse's body.

How to do it:

A. Stand at your horse's right hip, facing rearward.

B. Pick up his hind foot as though to clean the hoof.

C. Catch the front of his bent fetlock joint on the inner thigh of your right leg, farrier-style.

D. Take baby-steps carefully to the rear, taking the leg with you to stretch it back, directly away from the body, until it no longer extends easily. Hold for a few seconds, to make sure he's not going to snatch the foot away from you.

E. Support the leg in both hands at the fetlock joint. Turn to face the front and inch

2-E: Turn to face frontward and inch back a bit farther, if possible.

your way backward a little farther, if possible, to increase the stretch. If he resists, hold that position until he relaxes, then try to go a little farther. Watch for the large muscles of his rump and his "quads" (quadriceps muscle) to relax. They'll change from being visibly bunched up, to being elongated and smooth. (You'll feel it happen, too—suddenly there'll be no resistance.) When this happens, his hip, stifle, and hock joints will achieve maximal stretch, comfortably. Take your time. Hold, then gently release the leg down. Repeat twice more, then stretch the other hind limb.

F. Pick up the leg again, as though you're going to clean out the hoof. Supporting the fetlock, inch your way backward (toward your horse's head), pulling his ➤

2-F: Supporting the fetlock, inch backward...

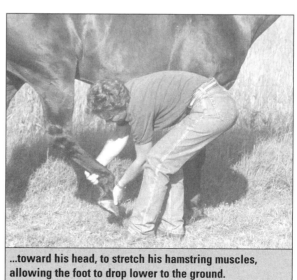

...toward his head, to stretch his hamstring muscles, allowing the foot to drop lower to the ground.

leg gently toward his head to stretch his hamstring muscles. Keep inching backward, waiting for him to relax (you'll feel his muscles suddenly stop resisting), allowing the foot to drop lower to the ground as you get closer to his forehand.

G. When your horse is just about to set the foot on the ground, gently go with it and place it there in the giant-step-forward position you've pulled it to. Repeat twice more, then do the other hind limb.

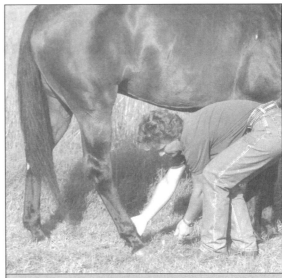

2-G: When your horse is about to set his foot down, lower it for him, in its stretched position.

#3: BACK LIFT (a.k.a. "AB" CRUNCHES)

Why you'll do it: To help relieve—and prevent—back pain, by asking your horse to "hunch" his back upward, much like a cat stretches. This requires him to contract— and thus strengthen—his abdominal muscles. Your horse doesn't naturally round his back when he stretches, as cats and dogs do. Indeed, most of the force in his

3-A: Work your fingertips into the muscles around his withers, to relax him. (Note the slight back sag on this 29-year-old mare.)

back is concave. As he ages, his abdominal weight pulls it downward, and the natural weakening of his abdominal muscles allows this. When you ride, you sit on the middle of his back's weakest point.

Downward pull and pressure cause his back to sink, compressing the bony fingers of his spinous processes (upward bony projections on the vertebrae). Over time they can touch each other, causing a painful condition called "kissing spines." This stretch reverses that bend, spreading the spinous processes apart. It can also help reduce age-related back sag, by strengthening the abdominal muscles.

TIP

For proper stretching, patience and repetition are key.
Remember the physical therapists' mantra: The first time you ask a body part to stretch, it says "no." The second time, it says, "huh?" The third time, it says "OK!"

How to do it:

A. Stand just behind your horse's shoulder. Work your fingertips vigorously into the muscles around his withers to relax him. (No long fingernails, please—this is supposed to be pleasant for your horse.)

B. Gradually and gently, work your fingers down to the middle of his under-   ➤

3-C and D: Gradually work your way to his belly, pressing your fingertips into the muscles there. (Note how this mare has contracted her abdominal muscles in response to that pressure, lifting her back. Compare to Photo 3-A at left.)

belly. If he's touchy about his underbelly, go slow. It may take minutes—or days—to accustom him to the sensation.

C. Starting just to your side of the midline, about 2 hand-breadths behind where a saddle girth/cinch would be, press your fingertips into the muscles there, as though probing for a marble under his skin. With your fingertips planted in this way, move them in small circles. (*Tip:* Don't slide them across his skin. Rather, move the skin with them.)

D. Watch his topline to see if he bows up his back. (If you're short, and/or your horse is tall, ask a friend to watch for you.)

E. If there's no response, move your fingertips to a new spot about an inch toward his hindquarters and repeat, until you get a back rise. Hold that position, while he holds his abdominal crunch, for a count of 10. Release, wait a few seconds, then repeat for a total of 6 reps. Repeat on the opposite side.

#4: CARROT NECK STRETCH

Why you'll do it: To increase the flexibility and range of motion in your horse's neck and back, by stretching muscles and soft tissues in those areas, and opening up the spaces between the spinous processes.

4-A: Show your horse the treat.

How to do it:

A. Gather some of your horse's favorite treats, such as carrots or hay/grass. Offer him a bite to get his attention. (Watch your fingers!)

B. Standing by his shoulder, bring the treat to the brisket area of his chest, so he has to tuck his chin in order to reach it, spreading the tops of the vertebrae in his upper neck.

C. Next, slowly lower the treat between his knees, baiting him to follow and stretching the vertebrae of his lower neck and withers.

D. Ask him to bring his nose around to the girth area of his right side, just behind his right elbow, to stretch the ligaments at the left side of the neck vertebrae. Repeat on the other side. (Continued on page 358)

4-B: Bring the treat to his chest.

4-C: Next, bring the treat to his knees, baiting him to follow.

4-D: Now ask him to follow the treat toward his girth area.

4-E: Finally, ask him to reach down to his fetlocks, if he can. (Our aged model had trouble doing so at first, but did limber with repeated stretching.)

Carrot Neck Stretch, continued

E. Finally, stand next to your horse's front leg. Hold a piece of treat between his front legs, asking him to reach down to his fetlocks to fetch it, opening up the spinous processes of his back and neck. (If he tries to back up in order to snag the treat, place him in front of a wall, to block that evasion.)

Carrot Stretch Tips

• Hold each position for 10 to 15 seconds, then feed your horse and release him.

• If he steps away from you with his hind legs, he's trying to get the treat without bending his body. That's because he's stiff and the stretch is hard for him. Position him next to a stall or barn-aisle wall, to block that evasion.

• If your horse has trouble reaching as far as you've asked him to, or holding that position, start with a lesser degree of stretch until his muscles relax and become more flexible. Remember, stretching shouldn't hurt, if you're doing it right, which means gently and gradually.

• Look for differences in the angle of your horse's head as he reaches for the treat on his right and left sides. He might tilt his head one way on his left side, and another on his right side. That means he's stiffer on one side than the other. Move the carrot or other treat around and up and down, getting him to chase the morsel until he bends evenly on both sides.

• Be sure to make him hold the stretch for the described amount of time. If you were to let him simply reach around and snatch the treat, you'd be negating the flexibility benefits of the exercise. (Waiting will also make him less pushy about treats.)

12

CHAPTER 12

DOWN & DIRTY MAINTENANCE
Sheath & Udder Cleaning

12 Down & Dirty Maintenance: Sheath & Udder Cleaning

Y ou've heard the saying, "It's a dirty job, but somebody has to do it." Well— that somebody is you when it comes to cleaning your senior horse's sheath or udder. That's because neglecting this little bit of dirty work can be hazardous to his or her health. Here's why:

Smegma: Male horses secrete a lubricant from their sheaths, which combines with dirt and other secretions to form a waxy substance called smegma[G] (the consistency of half-dried hand cream). Stallions naturally clean the smegma from their penises and sheaths if and when they're breeding, and/or when they extrude the penis all the way during normal daily erections. Geldings don't have that form of natural cleaning and rarely extrude the penis all the way, which encourages normal debris and smegma to accumulate—and irritate.

Cancer. Smegma is a cause of squamous cell carcinoma[G]—it's as much a cancer stimulant as sunlight is. That means the more smegma your gelding carries around, the higher his risk for this form of cancer.

Don't forget the mares. Mares experience the same accumulation of waxy debris between the two halves of their udders.

Beans. In geldings, smegma can collect and get trapped in the groove around the urethra. When this happens, a "bean" is formed—a lump of grayish-white, claylike smegma the shape and size of a pinto bean, or larger. Beans can cause extreme discomfort, and even block the urethra.

Check time. Injuries, infections, and/or parasite infestations can go unnoticed in your horse's sheath or udders. By the time a problem is severe enough to reveal itself, it might be advanced—and difficult to resolve. Sheath or udder cleaning gives you a great opportunity to closely inspect those areas.

Time-to-Clean (or past time) Signposts

Crust on penis. You see large crusts on the surface of your gelding's penis when he drops it to urinate.

Unpleasant odor. You notice a nasty odor coming from your gelding's sheath or your mare's udder.

Tail rubbing: If you deworm your horse regularly, and have ruled out parasites such as lice, a dirty udder or sheath could be the culprit. Since your horse can't easily scratch the affected area, he or she may settle for a scratching session in an adjacent one.

Problems urinating. If a bean is pinching your gelding's urethra (the opening at the end of his penis), he may stretch his body and drop his penis, but have trouble passing urine, or urinate frequently, in small amounts. Or, he may assume the position and pass urine in a weak or split stream, as though something were impeding the flow. If you see any of these signposts, call your veterinarian immediately. If a bean is the problem, your sheath-cleaning schedule should be adjusted to prevent future bean formation.

Swollen sheath or udder. Smegma and dirt accumulation can lead to inflammation or infection, which can lead to swelling. If you see this signpost, call your vet—the infection will require prescription treatment. Then, follow up with regular sheath cleaning as recommended by your vet.

Resistance or change in performance: If your normally compliant horse becomes resistant to a certain maneuver (say, a lead change) that involves come-from-behind movement, and your vet has ruled out lameness or soreness, check your horse's sheath or udder. A bean can create resistance in geldings due to pain.

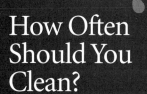

How Often Should You Clean?

For the average gelding, the answer is once or twice a year. Cleaning more often can irritate the skin, rob it of needed moisture, and disrupt the normal population of bacteria living there, leaving it susceptible to bacterial or fungal infection. ("Friendly flora" create a healthy environment within the sheath.) This same schedule also applies to the udder area of the average mare.

Sheath-Cleaning 101

What You'll Need:
- Hose. (If you have a way to warm the water, your horse will appreciate it.)
- Bucket of warm water.
- Latex or rubber gloves. Trust us, you'll want to use them as the residual smell from a dirty sheath can stick with you. (*Tip:* Ask your vet for a pair of long, disposable obstetrical sleeves—they work great!)
- Roll of paper towels. (Tear off 20 to 30 single sheets and submerge them in your bucket of warm water. You'll use these to rinse and remove loosened grime as you clean.)

➤

• Optional: Instead of paper towels, use a tube sock, which you can slip over your gloved hand to gently scrub your horse's penis and sheath (below). Toss it when finished.

• Lubricating cleanser designed for the job, such as Excalibur, by Bee Smart. (*Note:* Some people use mineral oil, which softens and helps ease removal of smegma. But, it also leaves a residue that can attract dirt.)

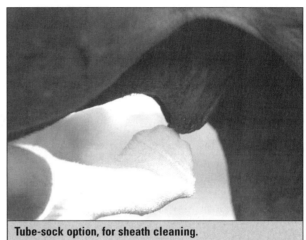

Tube-sock option, for sheath cleaning.

• Twitch.

• Trimmed fingernails. (Need we say more?)

• Halter, lead rope—and a "horse-wise" helper. (While cleaning your horse's sheath, you're in too vulnerable a position to be caught unawares if your horse should spook. A good handler at the end of the lead rope can help you and your horse stay safe.)

• Lots of patience!

Step 1. Halter your horse and have your helper hold him. Avoid tying him—unless he's used to having his sheath cleaned, he may object to your handling of this sensitive area and move around. Tying him could trigger a panic response. (*Tip:* As with any procedure, your horse will likely be more cooperative after turnout or exercise than he would be when fresh.)

Step 2. If your horse isn't used to having his sheath and penis handled, gradually accustom him to the sensation. (This could take days.) Stand on his left side, facing his rear, just ahead of his left flank. Keep your body close to his, so you're less likely to get kicked and less likely to be hurt if he does manage to kick you. Place your left arm over your horse's back, so you'll feel slight movements that indicate a kick could be coming your way. (If you're left-handed, reverse these directions to clean him from the right side.) Gently run your hands over his belly and inside his hind legs. If he lifts his tail (a kick precursor), moves away, or tries to kick, retreat your hand to an area of comfort (say, his hip) until he relaxes, then try again. Use this advance-retreat method until you can consistently touch his sheath. Now, you're ready to clean him. (*Caveat:* If your horse continues to vigorously object to your touch, twitch him. Many horses will stand quietly when twitched. If he continues to object or you're not comfortable applying a twitch, call your vet. He or she can come out and lightly sedate the horse, making your job safer and easier. Some vets will perform the sheath cleaning for you, for a fee.)

Step 3. Put on your glove. Generously lube the gloved hand with your cleanser of choice; don't forget the back of your hand. (If you're using a tube sock, slip it on now, and cover it with cleanser.)

Step 3. Lube gloved hand with cleanser.

Step 4. Clean his sheath. Give your horse a heads-up, by resting your hand against his belly, then sliding it back until you've reached his sheath. (If you were to grab for the sheath, you could startle him and invite a kick.) First, lube up the inside of his sheath with cleanser. Then feel around for small clods of smegma, peeling them and removing them as you do. Add more cleanser as needed. Continue until the sheath feels smooth and clean.

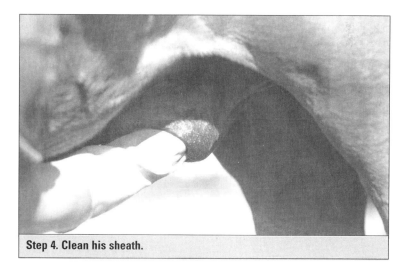

Step 5. Clean his penis. If your horse has dropped

Step 4. Clean his sheath.

(if he hasn't, skip to Step 6), lube the entire penis, paying close attention to the top (the area nearest his belly), where crusts and smegma are thickest. Use two or three paper towels from your bucket of warm water to rinse and remove loosened material from his penis and sheath. Repeat the lube-and-rinse process several times, until the sheath's inner surface and the penis feel smooth to your touch. Rinse with paper towels until they appear clean. ➤

Step 6. If your horse hasn't dropped his penis, your mission now is to go after it. Be brave. With a well-lubed glove, insert your hand deeper into your horse's sheath—keeping a close eye on his reaction. Grasp the end of his penis and gently pull downward. If he still won't drop, work "blind" inside the

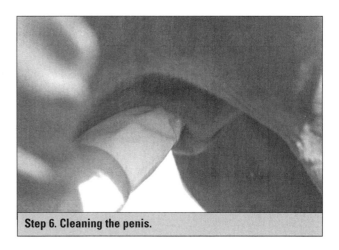
Step 6. Cleaning the penis.

sheath. Slide a lubed, gloved hand all the way up to the top of the penis. Use more cleanser as necessary to keep the area lubricated. Use the lube-and-rinse process outlined in Step 5.

Step 7. Check for beans. Grasp the end of your horse's penis with your left hand, firmly but gently squeezing it to expose the tip. Gently run your index finger around the small pocket at the tip of his penis, working out the whitish, clay-like bean material. (You may have to repeat several times to get it all.) *Caveat:* This may be uncomfortable for your horse, so be extra careful—he's most likely to kick during this step. If your horse vigorously objects, quit and consult your vet. Your safety is a key priority.

Step 7. A bean.

Step 8. Using low-pressure hose water or clean bucket water and paper towels, thoroughly rinse your horse's sheath and penis. You may want to start with this step first, to be sure your horse doesn't object. If he does, use your advance-retreat technique to acclimate him to the rinse sensation. It's worth it. Since many horses tolerate rinsing well, you can use this rinsing technique every week or two in warm-weather months to flush out foreign material. Because you're using only water, you won't disrupt the natural microorganism balance.

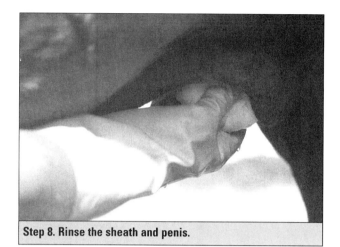

Step 8. Rinse the sheath and penis.

Step 9. Congratulations! You're finished! Now, make the next time even easier by handling your horse's sheath each time you groom him. With time and repetition, you both will come to accept such contact as a part of his everyday care.

Udder-ly Clean

What You'll Need:

• Hose (warm water will be better accepted by your mare than cold water).

• Bucket of clean, warm water.

• Latex or rubber gloves.

• Optional: a tube sock (slipped over your gloved hand, it acts as a washcloth to gently scrub your mare's udders).

• Paper towels (peel off about 20 to 30 and soak them in the bucket of water).

• Lubricating cleanser, such as Excalibur, by Bee Smart.

• Twitch.

• Trimmed fingernails.

• Halter, lead rope—and a skilled helper.

• Lots of patience!

Step 1. See Step 1 under "Sheath Cleaning 101," page 362.

Step 2. Follow the guidelines under Step 2 in "Sheath Cleaning 101," to desensitize both sides of your mare's udder to your touch.

Step 3. Put on your glove (and tube sock, if you're using one). Generously lube the gloved hand with your cleanser of choice; don't forget the back of your hand. Standing on your mare's left side, just ahead of her left flank (as outlined in ➤

Step 2 under "Sheath Cleaning 101")...

Step 4. ...clean her udder. Gently reach between her teats, using your fingers to pick and peel away debris. Use more cleanser as necessary to keep the area lubricated. Then rinse with the wet paper towels. Continue your lube-and-rinse process until the skin feels smooth and clean. (*Caveat:* If your mare objects vigorously to your cleansing attempts, apply the twitch. If she still objects or you're not comfortable applying a twitch, consult your veterinarian. It might be necessary for him to lightly sedate her for the procedure, making it less stressful for you both.)

Step 3. Lube gloved hand with cleanser.

Step 5. Repeat your gentle cleansing on the outside of her udder.

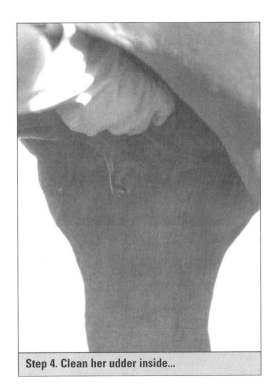

Step 4. Clean her udder inside...

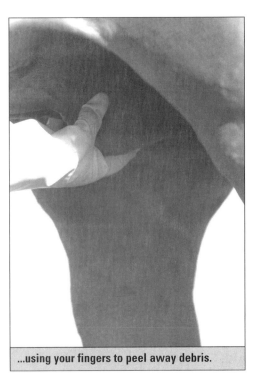

...using your fingers to peel away debris.

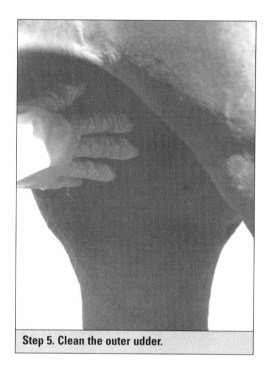

Step 5. Clean the outer udder.

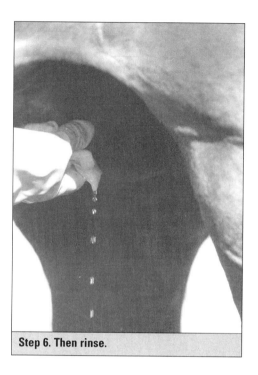

Step 6. Then rinse.

Step 6. Final rinse. Using the hose or a fresh bucket of clean, warm water, rinse your mare's udder thoroughly, being sure to rinse the area between her teats. You may want to start with this step first, to be sure your horse doesn't object. If she does, use your advance-retreat technique to acclimate her to the rinse sensation. Since many horses tolerate rinsing well, you can use this rinsing technique every week or two in warm-weather months to flush out foreign material. Because you're using only water, you won't disrupt the natural microorganism balance.

Step 7. That's it! Continue handling your mare's udders every time you groom her, so the sensation becomes familiar and comfortable to her. That'll make the next cleaning session easier for you both.

NOTES

CHAPTER 13

SENIOR BEDDING

13 Senior Bedding

Two of your senior horse's biggest age-related health threats—arthritis[G] and heaves[G]—can be affected by bedding. Your choice can predispose him for either condition, or make them worse if he's already got them.

The best stall bedding for your senior horse will have many of the same sort of attributes as does his "natural" bed—a grassy meadow. That means it'll:

- Be clean to begin with—and easy to keep clean.
- Cushion old bones and joints.
- Provide traction, rather than a slick surface, to help prevent slipping and make it easier (and safer) to get up.
- Have minimal dust, and/or be hypoallergenic.
- Be highly moisture absorbent (absorb more than twice its weight in moisture).
- Absorb or neutralize odors.
- Be safe if eaten.
- Have low flammability.
- Be easy to store.
- Be affordable.

See our chart at right comparing common bedding materials, using a thumbs-up or -down ranking. The more thumbs up, the better the bedding.

Caveat: Beware the Cabinetmaker's Sawdust & Shavings

Shop carefully for bedding. Small, local, specialty mills that make cabinets, furniture, molding, and trim may be a willing source for sawdust and shavings, but there's a risk: They often use potentially horse-toxic, oily hardwoods such as black walnut and mahogany. They might also use myriad other "exotic" woods that could be harmful to your horse's health. Even brief contact with toxic shavings and sawdust can cause laminitis (see "The Age Event: Laminitis," page 273). If you choose to bed your senior horse on shavings or sawdust, buy from sources that specialize in "horse safe" material made from pine.

YOUR SENIOR BEDDING CHOICES

BEDDING	👍👍👍 TO 👎👎👎	PROS	CONS
Hay	👎👎👎	Good-quality hay is safe if eaten; gives you something to do with the hay that's not good enough to feed; doesn't pose a new storage dilemma; widely available; biodegradable; affordable.	Not particularly easy to keep clean; lacks good cushioning qualities; slick; extremely dusty and allergenic; absorbs urine and odors poorly; highly flammable; slow to compost.
Straw	👎👎	Good-quality straw is safe if eaten; absorbs moisture very well; biodegradable; affordable.	Not particularly easy to keep clean; lacks good cushioning qualities; slick; only slightly less dusty and allergenic than hay; absorbs odors poorly; not easily found in all areas of the country; requires lots of storage space; highly flammable; slow to compost.
Shavings	👍	Moderately easy to keep clean; moderately moisture absorbent; absorbs odors moderately well; safe if eaten (but not recommended); biodegradable; affordable.	Not a great cushion but better than hay and straw; somewhat slick (but less so than hay and straw); dusty and allergenic; requires lots of storage space; becoming less available as more timber mills sell by-products to fiber product manufacturers; slow to compost.
Sawdust	👍	Easy to keep clean; moderate cushion; not slick; highly moisture absorbent; absorbs odors moderately well; safe if eaten (but not recommended); lower flammability than shavings; biodegradable; affordable.	Extremely dusty and allergenic; requires lots of storage space; becoming less available as more timber mills sell by-products to fiber product manufacturers; slow to compost.

➤

YOUR SENIOR BEDDING CHOICES *(continued)*

BEDDING	👍👍👍 TO 👎👎👎	PROS	CONS
Shredded paper	👍	Not dusty; hypoallergenic; moderately moisture absorbent; absorbs odors well; safe if eaten (but not recommended); easy to store (in plastic trash bags); affordable.	Not particularly easy to clean; lacks good cushion; slick; flammable; availability varies depending on the businesses in your area (newspaper publishers, hospitals, accountants, and other companies with large bookkeeping departments are good sources); slow to compost.
Screened topsoil	👍👍	Initial cleanliness varies with shipment, but it's easy to keep clean if well maintained; when rototilled daily, good cushion; good traction; low dust and hypoallergenic if kept moist; highly moisture-absorbent; highly odor absorbent if rototilled daily or every other day; safe if eaten (but not recommended); not flammable; no storage required (delivery required once yearly); initial cost (about $80 for a 12 x 12 foot stall) quickly offset by the fact that it's easy to keep clean with very little soil wasted; speeds composting of manure—garden-ready in 1 month.	Maintenance requires daily or every-other-day rototilling; can get very hard if not rototilled daily or every other day; can be dusty and allergenic if not kept moistened; not particularly odor absorbent if not rototilled daily or every other day.
Peat moss	👍👍👍	Easy to keep clean; good cushion; good traction; good peat is relatively low in dust; hypoallergenic; extremely absorbent of both moisture and odors; safe if eaten (but not recommended); low flammability; easy to store (plastic-covered bales can be stacked outside); available at garden and home-improvement stores as well as feed stores; initial cost (about $50 for a 12 x 12 foot stall) quickly offset by the fact that it's easy to keep clean with very little peat wasted; fastest composting of all bedding materials except soil—garden-ready in 1 month (other bedding materials take up to a year).	Poor-quality peat can be dusty and allergenic (this is easily resolved by keeping it moist).

A Bedding Secret: PEAT MOSS

What makes peat moss such a good bedding for seniors? Lots of things! Here are the high points, and the how-to's.

Baled peat moss.

High Points from the senior point of view:

• **Good for Lungs:** It's the most absorbent bedding available, by far, absorbing 10 times its weight or more in moisture (urine), and unsurpassed in its ability to absorb odors (ammonia).

• **Good for Bones/Joints:** It's soft, cushion-y, and nonslick if bedded deeply enough (minimum 6 inches, preferably 8 to 12 inches—the deeper it is, the easier it is to keep clean and fresh).

• **Good for Hygiene:** It's clean, and easy to keep clean. See how-to's, below.

Here's How To Put Down The Peat
Step 1. Shop around. Prices vary widely. They're likely to be lowest toward the end of gardening season. (A good time to stock up.) Good sources include garden, home improvement, and feed stores. Plan on paying between $4 and $11 for a compressed, 4.4-cubic-foot bale (roughly the size of a standard hay bale). For a 12 by 12-foot stall, you'll need about 12 bales to net a 6- to 8-inch depth, depending on how much it fluffs when you open the bales. Check the advertising pages in your favorite horse magazines for bulk sources that'll deliver peat moss by truckload, instead of bales. It's likely to be significantly cheaper, depending on delivery charges.

Step 2. Make it deep. In a clean, stripped stall, add enough peat for a minimum 6-inch depth; 12 inches is better, so there's plenty of peat to absorb urine. Otherwise the urine may flood through to the stall base and puddle, causing ammonia fumes to build.

Step 3. Pick out manure daily. Use a basket-type manure fork to sift out manure. Pick out soaking-wet urine spots (if you happen to be nearby when your senior horse urinates), or stir them with a rake if they've ➤

PEAT MOSS *(continued)*

already been absorbed. (There's no need for a rototiller if you're using peat moss without topsoil, as it naturally retains its loftiness.)

Step 4. Keep it moist. Keep the peat moist enough to hold together briefly if you squeeze a handful, but not so moist as to stick to your hand. It absorbs urine better this way, and isn't as dusty. With practice, you can toss leftover drinking water from your horse's bucket in an even spray. Or, keep a watering can outside his stall and dump leftover water in it; sprinkle the peat's surface. Work any water in with a pitchfork or garden rake after you've picked out manure.

Step 5. Consider adding topsoil and getting a rototiller. Here's why:

• The peat moss, and the fresh, ammonia-free smell of your horse's stall, will last a lot longer—6 months or more—if you mix it with an equal amount of screened topsoil. That's because topsoil contains beneficial organisms that "sweeten" urine-soaked bedding by breaking down ammonia, rather than just absorbing it.

• You can have topsoil hauled in from landscape suppliers; for a 12 by 12-foot stall you'd need about 3 yards of topsoil for a 12-inch deep,

50-50 topsoil/peat moss bed. Cost for the topsoil: about $50 to $100, depending on delivery charges.

• A rototiller helps spread urine and oxygen around, so organisms can work efficiently and aerobically. It also keeps bedding fluffy (otherwise, the topsoil tends to compact). A lightweight (about 20 pounds) tiller is ideal for small stalls because it's easy to maneuver. Such models are available at garden and home-improvement stores for $200 to $300.

A bigger tiller, which can double as a serious gardener's tool, costs from $400 to $1,000, depending on size/model. These monsters make quick work of a big stall or run-in shed, but they're too hard to maneuver in an enclosure that's not at least 15 feet in one dimension. (The bigger the stall, the more sense a big rototiller makes.)

• Daily or every-other-day tilling may sound like a lot of work, but actually it takes no more than 2 or 3 minutes to do a 15 by 15-foot stall—we defy you to dig out and haul away pee spots, and re-bed that same stall faster than that! The paybacks are many, including the fact that the entire barn will smell like a freshly tilled garden, instead of ammonia.

CHAPTER 14

STAY-YOUNG
DIET SOLUTIONS

14 Stay-Young Diet Solutions

You want your horse to stay young forever, right? That's not possible. But with proper nutrition, you help give him his best shot at a long, quality life. Several changes have—or will—occur on some level in your aging horse's body. (More about those in a minute.) In most cases, they won't be supported by the standard hay-and-grain ration that may have maintained him through his prime.

If your horse's diet isn't upgraded to meet his changing needs, you'll see associated changes in his body, subtle and insidious at first, but cumulative and potentially devastating. These changes can be the result of malnutrition, which is shockingly common in senior horses. It can cause serious health problems, accelerate your senior horse's aging process, bring on degenerative diseases sooner rather than later, impair his ability to ward off infections, and downgrade not only the length of his life but also its quality.

IRON: JUST SAY NO!

There's a prevailing belief that senior horses need iron supplements to retain vigor. (Think "Geritol.") Not so. Unless he's chronically bleeding (iron helps rebuild red blood cells), your senior horse's body recycles its own iron. In fact, an iron-supplemented senior is at risk for serious health problems, such as liver disease and a potentially fatal blood disorder called hemochromatosis. The most common result of even moderate iron overload is decreased resistance to bacterial infection. Bacteria thrive and multiply in iron-rich environments. The body's natural tendency to lock up its iron stores when threatened by bacterial infection is overridden when supplemental iron is present. Unless your vet prescribes such supplementation for a specific problem—don't do it.

Following is a rundown on the 4 most common age-related changes that affect a senior horse's nutritional needs, and what'll happen if his changing needs in each area aren't met. With this information, you can work with your vet to decide whether your horse's current ration merely needs a little tweak, or a complete overhaul. Then, turn to the "Stay-Young Diet Solutions" chart on page 380. Think of it as a menu for your senior horse, from which you can work with your vet to choose one or more upgrades to match your horse's changing needs, whether it's a mainstay, such as a senior-formulated feed, or a supplement.

The Big Four

We'll discuss only age-related issues here, not specific diseases and/or disabilities, which carry their own dietary requirements. If your senior horse has been diagnosed with a disorder such as kidney or liver disease, consult your vet for help in designing a ration that's right for the condition.

Give it a Soak

If your senior has difficulty picking up, chewing, or swallowing his feed, if his manure appears dry, and/or if he has a chronic respiratory condition such as heaves[G], he may benefit from having his feed soaked or wet down just prior to feeding. Water added to your senior horse's pelleted or extruded feed (concentrate or complete feed), and/or to his hay cubes, can soften the food and start the breakdown process. Soaking his long-stemmed hay just prior to feeding will cut down on dust.

PROBLEM #1: LONG IN THE TOOTH

What's Happening: Aging teeth are interfering with your senior horse's ability to glean the nutrition he needs from his ration. (For more information on senior dental care, see "Top Priority—Tooth Care," page 332.)

Why: The root ends of every horse's teeth are narrower than the crown ends. So, as your senior horse's back teeth (his molars) grow out with age, he develops ever-widening gaps between them. This, coupled with the fact that each tooth in an old horse's mouth eventually runs out of root, means that his future can hold such problems as impacted feed, periodontal disease[G], pain, loose teeth, lost teeth, and teeth that no longer meet and grind properly. Plus, if any of his front teeth (incisors) are damaged, diseased, or missing, he'll be unable to graze efficiently.

PROBLEM #2: WEIGHT LOSS

What's Happening: Even though your senior horse is getting his usual amount of feed and appears to be chewing adequately, he's losing weight.

Why: The aging horse's digestive tract loses its ability to digest feed and ➤

assimilate nutrients, due to several age-related changes in the gut, including a lifetime of parasite-inflicted damage, slowed gut motility[G], decreased production of digestive enzymes, and decreased water intake.

PROBLEM #3: MUSCLE LOSS

What's Happening: Your senior horse's blood protein levels are dropping, resulting in a loss of muscle.

Why: With age, he's losing his ability to digest dietary protein efficiently. So, much of the protein he eats is being wasted, especially if his regular feed is on the lower end of the quality scale (and therefore not very easily digested). On top of the downturn in protein intake, he's also losing increasing amounts of protein he'd already assimilated and stored as muscle tissue, via a natural breakdown process called catabolism[G].

MAKE ALL DIETARY CHANGES SLOWLY

Whenever making a change to your horse's diet, do it gradually, so his gut bacteria can adjust without causing intestinal upset. This applies whether you're adding oil, switching to a new concentrate, adding a new supplement, or going to a complete feed. The rule of thumb: Give him 25% of your target daily amount of the new product for 1 week, reducing his old product accordingly. Increase the amount of new product to 50% the 2nd week, 75% the 3rd, and replace the old product by 100% in week 4.

• Fantastic Fiber •

Regardless of age and dental health, horses require 1% to 2% of their body weight per day in forage, for optimal digestive function. By fiber[G], we mean mature pasture or hay (long-stemmed or processed). Without that minimum, your senior horse is at risk for:

Stomach ulcers[G]. Without adequate chew time, there won't be enough bicarbonate-rich saliva entering his stomach to neutralize acid.

Laminitis[G]. Without roughage to dilute them, carbohydrates may cause a more profound—and toxin-producing—shift in his gut bacteria, as well as a spike in his blood-insulin levels.

Colic[G]. Without roughage to stimulate his gut's muscles, partially digested feed will move more slowly through his intestines, get too dry, and result in increased risk of impaction.

If your senior horse has dental problems, he may do well with chopped hay, hay cubes, or hay pellets. Another choice is a complete pelleted or extruded feed formulated for senior horses. When in doubt, consult your veterinarian.

Adding Oil

Fat, in the form of food-grade vegetable oil, is a safe, effective way to increase energy in your senior horse's ration. It's up to 90% digestible, reduces feed dust, which is important for older horses suffering from heaves[G] (a.k.a. COPD), and requires no chewing, making it a great choice for tooth-impaired seniors. And, because fat increases your horse's total and HDL cholesterol levels, it can augment his ability to manufacture, metabolize, and utilize the cholesterol-based hormones his body needs to stay vital.

How Much & What Kind ?

You can feed up to 2 cups of oil per day. As with any change, start gradually and build over the course of at least a week. (Start with 1/4 cup or less, morning and evening, building slowly from there.) Any food-grade oil will help your senior horse gain weight. The ideal is a mix of 6 parts soybean or corn oil to 1 part flaxseed oil. This approximates the oil mix your horse would get if he were in his prime, living wild on the prairie, nibbling fresh forage, seeds, and grains. Choose liquid oils that have been:

• Processed without heat (a.k.a. "cold-pressed," which rules out major brands such as Mazola, Wesson, and Crisco);
• Have never been used in cooking;
• And have been properly stored in a cool location away from sunlight.

To ensure it's cold-pressed, read the label. Before each use, sniff the oil. If it smells sharp or otherwise "off," toss it.

PROBLEM #4: DRY, HARD, SMALL, AND/OR TACKY MANURE BALLS

What's Happening: Partially digested feed is moving more slowly through your senior horse's gut than it did when he was younger.

Why: One reason is age-related loss of gut-muscle response to fiber and water, which used to stimulate greater motility[G]. Another reason is a decline in your senior horse's intake of these agents, due to dental problems, competition from herd mates, and general aches and pains that decrease his incentive to seek feed and water. A third reason is a decline in your senior horse's overall activity level. Research has shown that physical activity stimulates gut activity, so a sedentary lifestyle results in a sluggish gut. There also is evidence that decreased intake of key minerals can result in muscle dysfunction, including slowed and/or inefficient gut motility. This can lead not only to impaction colic[G] but also to other types of colic, including torsion and gut displacement (in which a loop of bowel travels out of its proper position and becomes entrapped).

➤

Stay-Young Diet Solutions

DIET MAINSTAYS				

SENIOR-FORMULATED CONCENTRATE

WHAT IT IS	WHY IT WORKS	PROLEMS IT CAN SOLVE	HOW TO FEED IT	COMMENTS
Reputable, commercially prepared grain concentrate, formulated specifically for senior horses. Includes appropriate mineral balance, protein and fat levels, decreased carbohydrates, and fiber, all in an easy-to-chew form that's already partially "digested."	Palatable and easy to digest; can provide good nutrition for the average senior with adequate dental ability.	#1, #2, and #3.	Per manufacturer's or your vet's instructions.	Appropriate for a senior horse that's still able to chew 2% of his ideal body weight in forage[G].

GOOD-QUALITY HAY

WHAT IT IS	WHY IT WORKS	PROLEMS IT CAN SOLVE	HOW TO FEED IT	COMMENTS
Long-stemmed, baled hay of superior quality that's fresh, not moldy, dusty, or caked with dirt, mildew, or conditioners, nor does it contain toxic weeds or foreign material. Leaves are firmly attached to stems and are green. Blossoms and/or seed heads are partially budded or emerged, not mature, and not shedding petals or seeds. It has been protected from moisture, dust, sunlight, and wind.	Most nutrition is contained in hay leaves, not stems. Nutritional content is at its peak when seed heads/blossoms are beginning to emerge—leaves are tightly attached to stems. Hay cut/baled after that point suffers nutrition declines, which are accelerated by sunlight, moisture, and wind; moisture also increases odds of mold growth.	#2, #3, and #4.	Offer an amount equivalent to 2% of his ideal body weight per day, divided into 2 or more meals.	Appropriate if your senior horse's teeth are still in good enough condition to chew long-stemmed forage.

CHOPPED HAY

WHAT IT IS	WHY IT WORKS	PROLEMS IT CAN SOLVE	HOW TO FEED IT	COMMENTS
Commercial hay (loose, or in cubes) made of superior quality forage that's chopped, therefore easier to chew and digest, and contains consistent (certified) nutrition.	Ensures quality and digestibility. Local hay quality can vary with weather, cultivation, equipment, baling, and storage. Reputable companies that sell chopped/cubed hay use high-quality hay that's date stamped for freshness. Your senior horse gets better nutrition with less chewing/digesting effort.	#1, #2, and #3.	Offer an amount equivalent to 2% of his ideal body weight per day, divided into 2 or more meals.	Good if he can chew chopped forage, but is having trouble with long-stemmed forage.

DIET MAINSTAYS, *continued*

SENIOR COMPLETE FEED

WHAT IT IS	WHY IT WORKS	PROLEMS IT CAN SOLVE	HOW TO FEED IT	COMMENTS
Reputable, commercially prepared concentrate plus fiber^G, to take the place of hay and grain, formulated specifically for seniors. Includes appropriate mineral balance, protein and fat levels, decreased carbohydrates, and fiber in an easy-to-chew form that's already partially "digested."	Palatable and easy to digest, even if swallowed without chewing; can provide a good nutritional foundation, including fiber, for the dentally challenged senior.	#1, #2, and #3.	Per manufacturer's or your vet's instructions.	Each meal should be followed with supplemental hay or pasture, at a daily rate of 1/2% of your senior's ideal body weight. See "Supplemental Forage," below.

PROBLEM-SOLVING SUPPLEMENTS

SUPPLEMENTAL FORAGE

WHAT IT IS	WHY IT WORKS	PROLEMS IT CAN SOLVE	HOW TO FEED IT	COMMENTS
Superior quality forage^G in the form of long-stemmed or chopped hay, or pasture, supplied to a horse that's being fed a complete-feed ration (see "Senior Complete Feed," above).	Boosts fiber intake beyond that provided in complete feed, for improved gut motility^G and protection against such disorders as impaction colic^G; added chew time increases saliva output, helping neutralize stomach acid and protect against ulcers^G; directs energy away from sterotypies^G and stress- or boredom-associated disorders such as wood chewing.	#4.	Feed 1/2% of your senior horse's ideal body weight per day. (5 pounds of hay or pasture per day for a 1,000-pound horse.)	Feed it after he's eaten his complete feed.

FAT

Food-grade vegetable oil added to a concentrate or complete feed.	A highly digestible way to boost caloric intake without increasing carbohydrate load (and therefore risk of carbohydrate-linked disorders such as laminitis^G and certain kinds of colic).	#1 and #2.	See "Adding Oil," page 379.	Requires no chewing. Bonus: His coat will gleam.

PROTEIN

Protein powder made of casein or whey (milk protein) or albumin (from egg whites).	Milk and egg proteins are rich sources of the amino acid lysine^G, which your senior horse needs to utilize dietary protein.	#3.	We like MLO's Milk And Egg Protein powder (http://www. mlo products.com) at 1 to 4 heaping tablespoons a day, divided into 2 or more feedings.	Consult your veterinarian before adding protein. ➤

PROBLEM-SOLVING SUPPLEMENTS, *continued*

FLAX

WHAT IT IS	WHY IT WORKS	PROLEMS IT CAN SOLVE	HOW TO FEED IT	COMMENTS
Whole flax seeds (a.k.a. linseeds) or stabilized flax meal (a.k.a. linseed meal).	It can help lubricate your senior horse's gut, stimulate gut motility[G] and soften manure; can improve skin and coat health, and combat allergies and conditions such as arthritis[G]; can help with weight gain.	#2 and #4.	Up to 2 cups per day, divided into 2 or more feedings, added to your senior horse's feed. Available in most feed stores. (You may have to ask them to order it for you.)	For weight gain, choose vegetable oil—it's more economical. If your horse also needs help with gut motility, allergies, and/or chronic inflammatory conditions, choose flax.

VITAMIN C

WHAT IT IS	WHY IT WORKS	PROLEMS IT CAN SOLVE	HOW TO FEED IT	COMMENTS
Vitamin C in the form of ascorbyl palmitate or ascorbic acid.	While few controlled equine studies exist, evidence shows it stimulates a stronger immune response to vaccinations. It's also a well-known antioxidant and promoter of soft-tissue healing.	#1.	20 grams of vitamin C per day, divided into 2 or more feedings. We like ascorbyl palmitate, which is absorbed three times better than ascorbic acid. One source is Roche Vitamins' "Stay-C 35;" 800.526.0189.	Great for the senior who can't chew vitamin C-rich fresh forage. Vitamin C may also be warranted for seniors susceptible to colds or other infections, and those diagnosed with, or at risk for, cancer.

VITAMIN E

WHAT IT IS	WHY IT WORKS	PROLEMS IT CAN SOLVE	HOW TO FEED IT	COMMENTS
Vitamin E, as d-alpha tocopherol.	It's an effective natural antioxidant that's poorly stored in the body, especially over winter months when only dried and aging feeds are fed.	#1 and #2.	Choose a commercial equine supplement or buy 1,000 IU soft capsules at your drug store. At each of 2 daily meals, prick one with a pin and squeeze the oil onto his feed.	He'll also likely benefit if he's suffering from a chronic disease, under stress, has neurological problems, and/or he has cancer.

SALT & MINERALS

WHAT IT IS	WHY IT WORKS	PROLEMS IT CAN SOLVE	HOW TO FEED IT	COMMENTS
Plain salt in block and loose form, plus equine commercial mineral mix in pelleted form or incorporated into a senior-formulated concentrate or complete feed.	Making salt in both forms available to your horse will likely encourage increased water intake. Trace-mineral (not salt) needs are better met in a well-balanced vitamin-mineral supplement than in a block.	#1, #2, #3, and #4.	Provide loose table or livestock salt in a separate container, plus block salt. Feed a mineralized commercial feed, or a pelleted mineral supplement.	Free access to plain salt, plus a measured/balanced mineral supplement, is especially important if his manure balls are small, hard, dry, and/or tacky, indicating slow gut motility and/or decreased water intake.

Selenium: Lifesaving Poison

Selenium is a powerful antioxidant mineral that works with Vitamin E to combat toxic free radicals^G in your senior horse's body. Most unsupplemented horses get all the selenium they need in pasture and hay. However, many regions—especially those with pine-type (needle-bearing) trees, indicating acidic soil—are selenium-deficient. Horses that eat selenium-deficient forage are at increased risk for a variety of health problems, mostly degenerative ones and cancers from an overload of toxic free radicals.

Trouble is, there's a fine line between getting enough selenium and getting too much. An excess causes problems including dry, brittle coat and hooves, loss of tail hairs, birth defects, and sudden death. Some regions contain soil with toxic selenium levels, which can produce toxic forage. Even without selenium supplements, these horses are at risk for selenium poisoning.

Does your senior horse need a selenium supplement? Ask your veterinarian to submit a blood sample to a state or commercial laboratory to test your oldster's selenium levels. If the report indicates he needs supplementation, proceed with your veterinarian's guidance. For added safety, use oral supplements, not injectable ones. They're less likely to result in overdose. To help ensure your horse gets precisely what he needs, mineralwise, try to find a locally formulated feed designed by equine nutrition experts to complement your regional soil content.

NOTES

CHAPTER 15

SENIOR VET CHECKS

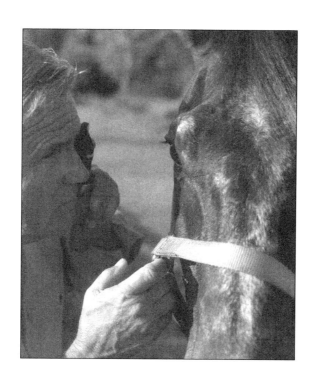

15 Senior Vet Checks

Taking optimal care of your senior horse includes regular veterinary check-ups and maintenance. By taking a proactive approach to his care with your vet—rather than having a knee-jerk reaction to problems that arise—you'll be able to head off many problems at the pass, or at least discover them early, when they're easiest to resolve.

Following is a good baseline program. If your senior horse has been diagnosed with a condition that requires alterations, consult your vet to organize an amended schedule.

SERVICE	HOW OFTEN	COMMENTS
General physical examination with internal eye, oral, external urogenital, rectal palpation, and soundness evaluation.	Every 6 to 12 months, depending on your senior horse's condition.	Vet will generally look for changes in condition, hydration, eye structure, urogenital cancers, and developing musculoskeletal problems. Rectal palpation provides monitoring of pelvic and caudal (rearward) abdominal cavity for abnormal growths, thickenings, fat deposits, herniation, or internal reproductive tract abnormalities.
Dental exam and treatment.	At least every 6 months, depending on your horse's mouth condition.	Adjust for dental changes that occur with age, so your horse will be less likely to lose condition, develop a sinus infection, or suffer pain as a result of a dental problem.
Blood tests: CBC (complete blood count) and general chemistry screen.	Every 6 to 12 months, depending on your senior horse's condition.	To screen for insidious health problems such as anemia^G, leukemia^G, hypoproteinemia^G, internal bleeding, systemic infection, liver disease, kidney disease, myositis^G, and electrolyte imbalance.
Fecal exam for parasites.	At least every 6 months, depending on your senior horse's condition.	To monitor the effectiveness of your senior horse's deworming program and adjust it if necessary to avoid (or respond to) parasite resistance and to prevent unnecessary dewormings.

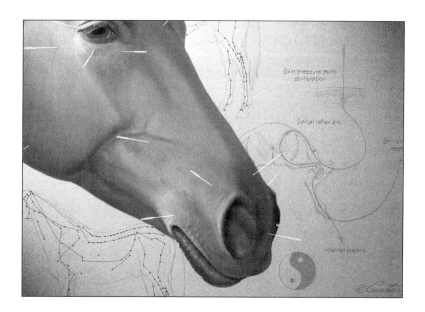

CHAPTER 16

ALTERNATIVE MEDICINE

16 Alternative Medicine

How do you feel about alternative medicine for your senior horse?

Many horse owners feel caught in the middle—between by-the-book veterinarians who scorn any therapy not backed by science, and those who embrace anything alternative while rejecting skills and precepts learned in veterinary school. Each side has compelling arguments. Who's the better guardian of your horse's health?

Neither. Anyone who shuns alternative medicine may shun a therapy that could help your horse. Anyone who hangs all his or her hopes on alternative medicine may overlook a proven conventional therapy. Keep an open mind, and use this rule of thumb: If, based on your veterinarian's opinion, an alternative treatment won't hurt your horse, there may be nothing to lose in trying it. And your horse could benefit.

Caveat: By law, anyone who administers treatment to your horse for a fee must be a licensed veterinarian. Alternative treatments—including acupuncture, herbology, homeopathy, physical therapy, chiropractic, magnet therapy, cold laser therapy, and so on—aren't standardized, centralized, or even recognized in many regions, though some have certification programs. It may be up to you to decide whether someone offering such services has the experience and insight to advise you and safely treat your horse. For these reasons, we recommend that you choose veterinarians with specialty training and experience in your chosen alternative treatment, rather than a layperson. For information on alternative veterinary medicine associations, see page 394.

Following are examples of alternative therapies that have earned acclaim from certified conventional veterinarians in practice and in veterinary schools. If you feel your senior horse may benefit from these or other alternative therapies in conjunction with conventional treatment, talk to your veterinarian, and/or ask for a referral to an equine practitioner who has experience and success in using alternative methods.

Acupuncture

WHAT IT IS: The stimulation of certain key points on energy channels running through your horse's body, known as "meridians."

HOW IT WORKS: According to Traditional Chinese Medicine (TCM), living organisms are a road map of energy conduits, called meridians. These carry life-giving energy to and from every body system. Any interference or interruption in that energy flow can disrupt normal function, leading to disease.

Acupuncture in the treatment of disease reopens "blocked" energy flow in targeted meridians and reestablishes normal function. Diagnostic acupuncture uses these same meridians to detect an energy blockage. Precision in selecting the proper points, inserting needles (if used) to the proper depth, and maintaining treatment for the proper length of time are critical for successful acupuncture. Experience and expertise are key.

There are several types of acupuncture commonly used in equine medicine:
• **Simple needling (AP):** This involves the insertion of fine, solid-metal needles, leaving them in place while occasionally twirling them, for a total of about 20 to 30 minutes. Most horses are tolerant of AP; some even seem to look forward to the relief it provides.
• **Electroacupuncture (EAP):** After insertion, acupuncture needles are connected to an electrical stimulator that delivers electrical impulses to the points for 20 to 30 minutes. Most horses tolerate EAP well.
• **Moxibustion (moxa):** A smoldering, punklike "cigar" of rolled herb is held above the acupuncture point until the heat becomes uncomfortable; the heat is withdrawn for a few seconds, then reapplied. This cycle is repeated 15 to 20 times for each point. Alternatively, the moxa is used to heat an inserted acupuncture needle.
• **Laser stimulation:** A painless beam of laser light is used to stimulate acupuncture points. Reports indicate that the more powerful the laser, the more effective the treatment (approaching the effectiveness of simple AP).
• **Point injection:** A liquid (vitamin B_{12} is commonly used) is injected into the acupuncture point for prolonged stimulation that lasts as much as an hour after injection.

WHEN IT MIGHT HELP:
• Chronic pain, as in founder[G], arthritis[G], or back pain. Scientific studies are being conducted by the Morris Animal Foundation on the effects of acupuncture on equine pain.
• Anhidrosis[G] (inability to sweat)
• Laminitis[G]
• Peripheral nerve paralysis[G]
• Allergy
• Navicular disease[G]
• Nervousness, cribbing

➤

RULES OF THUMB:

• Seek conventional treatment first. Where appropriate, augment it with acupuncture, or;

• Try acupuncture after conventional treatment has produced less-than-satisfying results.

• If your horse has a condition for which lapsed time means more tissue damage and a worsening prognosis (such as laminitisᴳ, severe colicᴳ, bowed tendon, navicular diseaseᴳ), seek proven conventional care immediately as his primary treatment. You can then use acupuncture to augment that protocol.

HOW TO FIND AN EQUINE ACUPUNCTURIST:

To find a certified veterinary acupuncturist near you, contact the International Veterinary Acupuncture Society (IVAS): P.O. Box 271395, Fort Collins, CO 80527; 970.266.0666 phone; 970.266.0777 fax; or e-mail at **IVASoffice@aol.com**. They'll provide you with the closest IVAS-certified veterinarian in your area.

Note: You may find, via word of mouth, a non-IVAS-certified vet who's had more hands-on equine acupuncture experience than some IVAS acupuncturists. A veterinarian can become certified by IVAS after 4 weekends of class work and a 3-month internship. Relatively speaking, this is not much training. Legally, IVAS certification isn't required for a veterinarian to perform acupuncture on your horse. However, anyone who treats your horse with acupuncture must be a licensed veterinarian.

Once you locate an acupuncturist, ask him or her for references. If possible, find an acupuncturist—certified or not—who's recommended by other equine veterinarians.

Chiropractic

WHAT IT IS: A system of therapy whose premise is that disease results from a lack of normal nerve function, which is rooted in misalignment of bones in the spine. The practice of manipulating and/or adjusting the spinal column is therefore employed, to maintain nerve health, and thus that of organs and connective tissues.

HOW IT WORKS: According to chiropractic theory, when bones in the spine aren't moving correctly relative to each other, they interfere with nerves, which are thought to be the body's master controller. This neural interference, in turn, can affect bones, muscles, or nerves elsewhere in the body. Manipulation of the misaligned bones helps restore the body to health.

Specific to horses, here's the deal. Your horse's spine is naturally quite flexible. (You've likely seen him reach his nose back to his hip to scratch an itch.)

However, when injury, a poor-fitting saddle, or other occurrence restricts spinal-column mobility, it triggers a cascade of events. Joints between vertebrae become inflamed; muscles spasm; nerve signals can be blocked; and the health of those joints begins to decline due to lack of nourishment to their cartilage. (For more information on degenerative joint disease, see "The Age Event: Arthritis," page 227.)

Chiropractic appears to restore normal range of motion (or as much as possible), which helps prevent further damage and might even help reverse minor damage. It also can help your horse feel better if he's in pain.

What it doesn't appear to do is cure infectious neurological conditions, including EPM, and degenerative conditions, such as osteoarthritis, although some equine chiropractors claim to benefit internal medical problems as well as musculoskeletal ones. While treatment can improve nerve supply to organs (and perhaps make your horse feel better), in general it's not a replacement for traditional therapy.

WHEN IT MIGHT HELP:
• Problems of the neck, back, and pelvis. (For signs that your horse might have back pain, see "Senior Back Check," page 314.)
• A horse on stall rest, who will stiffen from lack of exercise. Chiropractic may be able to help him stay limber.
• Some chiropractors help restore range of motion to leg joints, particularly hips, shoulders, and knees.

CAVEATS: AVOID CHIROPRACTIC TREATMENT IF:
• There's any chance of a fracture. Movement will exacerbate the injury.
• Your horse has suffered a fresh injury, especially one with a wound. Bruising and muscle/tissue damage can make it too painful.

HOW TO FIND AN EQUINE CHIROPRACTOR:
Not all equine chiropractors are equally qualified. With the increased popularity and acceptance of this treatment, many practitioners have entered the field. Choose one that's certified by the American Veterinary Chiropractic Association, P.O. Box 563, Port Byron, IL 61275; 309.658.2958; e-mail AmVetChiro@aol.com; **www.animal-chiropractic.org**. Also select someone licensed to practice in your state and recommended by people who have used him or her. Ask your vet, trainer, and respected friends for recommendations. To be safe, always consult your regular veterinarian first and ask for his/her input regarding the use of chiropractic on a particular condition in your senior horse. That way, you can take a team approach to maximizing benefit—and avoiding risk.   ➤

Herbology

WHAT IT IS: The use of herbs to help treat and/or prevent equine health problems.

HOW IT WORKS: As with conventional medications, herbs have the potential to create powerful effects in your senior horse's body, both to prevent illness and to promote healing. They're similar to conventional medications in that they can have side effects and interactions (some dangerous) with other medications. In some instances, they may be better than modern medicines in that they might be gentler, have fewer side effects, not require a prescription, and possibly cost less.

What makes them different from modern medicines—and potentially more dangerous—is that most herbal remedies used on horses haven't been tested for safety and efficacy. That means a particular herb may not work on your horse—or could make his condition worse. And natural therapies, which in this country cannot be sold with medical information or label warnings, are often administered without professional advice. This increases the risk you might give your horse the wrong herb or one that interacts with medicines he's already taking.

WHEN IT MIGHT HELP:

- Respiratory problems
- Anhidrosis^G
- Anxiety/stress reduction
- To improve energy
- Minor digestive disorders
- Minor skin conditions
- Pain relief and wound healing
- Minor arthritis^G
- Some reproductive problems

Caveat: Natural therapies can be inconsistent in quality, purity, and potency. This gives them a greater potential for not only producing less than the desired effect, but also a host of untoward side effects, including allergic and toxic reactions. When in doubt, consult your veterinarian.

HOW TO FIND AN EQUINE HERBOLOGIST:

First, ask your veterinarian for a referral, if he/she knows of a reputable veterinary herbologist. Failing that, contact: The Veterinary Botanical Medicine Association, Dr. Kimberly Stagmeier, secretary, 1506 Shadow Ridge Circle, Woodstock, GA 30189; **ksdvm@bellsouth.net.**

Homeopathy

WHAT IT IS: A system of medicine developed by German physician Dr. Samuel Hahnemann in the early 19th Century. Its theory is that medicines causing symptoms in healthy patients will cure those same symptoms in sick patients. Hence Dr. Hahnemann's central observation, "like cures like."

HOW IT WORKS. It's said to stimulate your horse's own healing abilities, thus strengthen him. Symptoms, as signposts of a treatable internal imbalance, are important guides to proper treatment. That said, homeopathic therapies aren't necessarily harmless, though they are said to generally have no side effects and a wide safety margin. The active ingredients in these therapies can be toxic (such as poison ivy and arsenic). They're generally diluted to such an extent that the toxins are said to be harmless.

While treatments often can be purchased at your local health-food store, homeopathy is not a substitute for conventional veterinary care, and could actually hinder it (and your horse's functioning) through drug interactions. That's why it's important to work with your veterinarian on this and any alternative therapy.

WHEN IT MIGHT HELP:

- Bruising and soreness
- Fever and inflammation
- Respiratory problems
- Digestive problems
- AbscessesG
- As a calming agent
- Wound care

HOW TO FIND AN EQUINE HOMEOPATHIC VETERINARIAN:

First, ask your veterinarian for a referral, if he/she knows of a reputable vet who practices homeopathy. Failing that, contact: Academy of Veterinary Homeopathy (AVH), 6400 Independence Blvd, Charlotte, NC 28212; 866.652.1590 phone; 704.535.6669 fax; office@theAVH.org; **www.theavh.org**.

➤

Alternative Medicine Contact Information

Here's a sampling of some alternative medicine associations.

• American Holistic Veterinary Medical Association (AHVMA)
2218 Old Emmorton Road
Bel Air, MD 21015
Ph: 410.569.0795
Fax: 410.569.2346
Email: AHVMA@compuserve.com
web site: www.altvetmed.com

• International Veterinary Acupuncture Society (IVAS)
P. O. Box 271395
Fort Collins, CO 80527
Ph: 970.266.0666
Fax: 970.266.0777
Email: IVASOffice@aol.com
web site: www.ivas.org

• American Veterinary Chiropractic Association
P. O. Box 563
Port Byron, IL 61275
Ph/fax: 309.658.2958

Email: AmVetChiro@aol.com
web site: www.animalchiropractic.org

• Veterinary Botanical Medicine Association
Dr. Kimberly Stagmeier, secretary
1506 Shadow Ridge Circle
Woodstock, GA 30189
Email: ksdvm@bellsouth.net.

• Academy of Veterinary Homeopathy (AVH)
6400 East Independence Blvd
Charlotte, NC 28212
Ph: 866.652.1590
Fax: 704.535.6669
Email: office@theAVH.org
web site: www.theavh.org

CHAPTER 17

EUTHANASIA

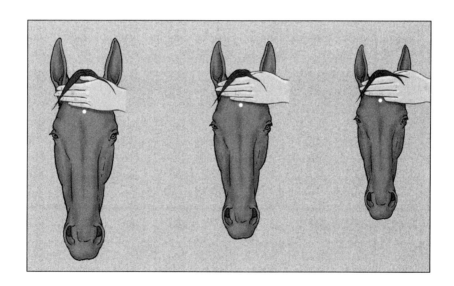

17 Euthanasia

I f you're caring for a senior horse, the inevitable thought has crossed your mind: Might you someday have to make a decision to euthanize him? If so, how will you know it's time?

Fortunately, if you know what to look for, it'll be fairly obvious. Unfortunately, emotions may creep in, causing you to second-guess yourself. Complicating the issue is the fact that, as much as you've relied on your veterinarian's guidance through your horse's life, this choice ultimately will be yours.

An Agonizing Decision

The decision to euthanize may be obvious if your horse has a fatal injury or disease and/or a condition that renders him incapable of comfort. The signposts below, as well as input from your veterinarian, will help you identify those situations.

It's when it's not so obvious that things get murky. Say your senior has a progressively worsening skin condition that's driving him crazy, and the only treatment will put him at risk for laminitis. What then? Or, he has a chronic foot lameness and the only hope of pain relief is denervationᴳ—which may render your horse pain-free, but could accelerate the breakdown process in his feet, speeding his demise? These are not easy decisions.

Your veterinarian can help you determine whether your senior horse's condition has a reasonable chance of improvement. If so, you might postpone your decision. Otherwise, set aside your emotions and try objectively to ascertain whether the balance of each day is positive or negative for him. The following guidelines will help you.

IT'S LIKELY TIME IF YOUR HORSE SUFFERS FROM THE OBVIOUS—

• An obvious fracture of a weight-bearing long bone. Even under ideal conditions most adult horses with a broken leg are euthanized, even if the owner has limitless funds and access to a top-notch veterinary orthopedic surgical team. If internal bone/joint components are exposed (and therefore contaminated), even immediate expert care usually is unsuccessful.

• An obvious breakdown of supporting soft tissue in a long bone, such as a laminitis "sinkerᴳ," or a ruptured ligament in a horse with degenerative desmitisᴳ.

• Violent, self-destructive thrashing due to relentless pain, mental disorder, or severe loss of equilibrium due to a condition for which treatment is unknown, unreliable, unavailable, or likely to be associated with a long, painful recovery.

• External evidence of shock: Muddy-colored, brick-red, gray-blue, or ghostly white gums, prolonged capillary refill time (4-6 seconds), heart rate at rest consistently over 80 beats/minute, ice-cold extremities, and deepening mental depression. For more information, go to "Senior Vital Signs," page 292.

• Abdominal contents exposed and/or contaminated due to rupture or laceration of a body wall, or breaking-through at a recent surgery incision.

AND IT COULD BE TIME IF HE SUFFERS FROM THE NOT-SO-OBVIOUS—

• Any chronic condition that fails to respond to veterinary and supportive care, resulting in relentless discomfort and loss of ability to maintain self-care skills such as eating (a priority to your horse), drinking, urinating, and defecating.

• Any chronic condition that fails to respond to treatment and interferes with your horse's ability to stand, move without excess pain, and defend himself.

• Any chronic condition that fails to respond to treatment and interferes with his ability to share/enjoy the companionship of other horses, a priority that to him may be second only to eating.

Merciful Methods

Veterinarians generally choose lethal injection or gunshot for euthanasia. In Europe, gunshot is the preferred method; in the U.S., lethal injection is more popular, likened to the emotional ideal of dying in one's sleep.

METHOD: LETHAL INJECTION

Pros: If done properly, is less violent in appearance; bloodless; quiet; and humane.

Cons:

• Only one type of drug—barbiturates—shuts down the brain first, before shutting down other bodily functions. Other products (such as T61 and succinylcholine) cause a heart attack or paralysis and suffocation, so are meant to be used on a horse under anesthesia.

• Some vets don't have the license to carry barbiturates, which are classified as ➤

controlled substances. The other drugs are cheaper and safer to carry. (The licensee is responsible in case of theft or misuse.)

• Regardless of drug, administration requires expertise: it must be given via vein or heart injection, either of which requires skill. If the needle misses the mark, the drug won't work and can cause a violent and painful reaction.

• Prompt and proper disposal of the body is critical, either by deep burial, cremation, or a renderer. House pets and wildlife can sink into a coma after consuming relatively small amounts of tissue or blood from a barbiturate-injected body. *Note:* Regardless of euthanasia method, local ordinances and sanitary district laws must be consulted before burying a horse.

METHOD: GUNSHOT

Pros:

• If done properly, it's reliable, instantaneous, externally bloodless, and humane.

• Body disposal is somewhat less complicated than with lethal injection since no chemicals were used that could sicken or kill scavengers. However, if the horse was on any medications, care must still be taken.

Cons:

• Emotional/social stigma can make this method upsetting for witnesses.

• In inexperienced hands, it can be unreliable, inhumane, and unsafe.

X-Marks the Spot? **Pure Fiction**

You've probably seen it in the movies. To euthanize a horse via gunshot, the cowboy draws a line from the left ear to the inner corner of the horse's right eye, and from the right ear to the inner corner of the left eye, making an "X." He then places his gun barrel at the X's center and pulls the trigger. That's the wrong placement. A bullet entering at that spot will most likely penetrate the ethmoid turbinates, part of the nasal cavity beneath the brain. There, it'll cause horrific bleeding but not the intended quick death. The X-myth is why you'll often hear stories of people shooting their horses at the chosen spot, only to have the horse remain standing after the shot is fired. Avoid that nightmare by using the guidelines outlined on page 400.

Act of Mercy

Warning: This section may upset you—it's about how to put your senior horse out of his misery if he's in agony and you can't find a vet in a hurry. Despite the discomfort it may cause now, there's information here you may want to learn, in the best interest of your horse. If he were in agony due to a mortal injury or illness, and no vet could get to you—what would you do?

This isn't paranoia. It's responsibility. So your horse doesn't suffer, take the time to formulate a plan for an emergency euthanasia. Since only veterinarians can legally possess euthanasia drugs, many veterinary experts suggest that the best way to carry out that plan is with a well-placed bullet. It's a practice regularly used on farms and ranches across America, and widely used in Europe as the euthanasia of choice. (If you don't have a gun, try to recruit a policeman.)

WHY A GUN?

The emotional and social baggage of firearms on this continent may make it difficult for you to accept that a violent weapon can be used for a humane purpose. But in Europe, learning how to perform euthanasia via gunshot is part of the official veterinary curriculum—veterinarians there are exempted from gun-control restrictions.

When proper technique is employed, many veterinarians report having fewer problems with this method than with lethal injection. They say it's faster, with none of the lingering that's often evident with injected agents.

HERE'S HOW IT'S DONE.
EQUIPMENT
• **The firearm:** A handgun is preferred because there's no need for other personnel beside the person pulling the trigger. The shooter can hold the horse's lead rope in one hand and the pistol in the other. (If a rifle is the only firearm you have access to, the shooter will need to recruit someone to hold the horse on a loose lead. The holder should stand behind the shooter.)

• **The ammunition:** Most experts agree a .22 caliber, .32 caliber (common in Europe), 9 mm, or .38 caliber can generally be used for safe, sure euthanasia of a horse. Some say the .22 might not have sufficient velocity and mass to penetrate the skull in a very large, draft-type horse. If you have any doubt, firearms experts generally suggest a .38. To help ensure swift and certain euthanasia, and for decreased risk that the bullet will pass through the horse with sufficient energy to injure the shooter or bystander, experts recommend using a bullet that's soft-nosed (also known as a "dum-dum" bullet), hard-cast of lead, or hollow-point, rather than one encased in a full metal jacket. Most everybody who owns firearms (including a passing highway patrolman) will have one of these types of ammunition on hand. ➤

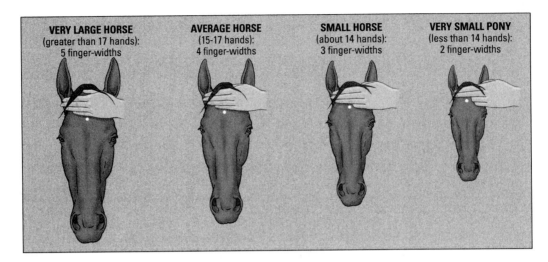

- **Placement and aim:** The bullet's entry site should be the exact midline of the horse's forehead, the following distance down from the base of the forelock:

Very large horse (greater than 17 hands): 5 finger-widths.

Average horse (15-17 hands): 4 finger-widths.

Small horse (about 14-hands): 3 finger-widths.

Very small pony (less than 14 hands): 2 finger-widths.

Aim should be at a point perpendicular to the skull at the entry site. Or, if the horse is in an unnatural position, such as twisted or entrapped, direct the aim down the neck. This will help ensure a safe knockdown and help keep the bullet from injuring a bystander.

Unless the gun is designed specifically for livestock euthanasia (common in Europe), experts say the muzzle should not be placed directly against the horse's head. This could confine the explosion of gunpowder and gas within the gun, resulting in an explosion in the shooter's hand. Instead, it's recommended that the muzzle be held 1 to 12 inches away. (The farther distance permits the bullet to gain greater velocity before encountering bone, which is advisable if using a .22.)

OTHER SAFETY ISSUES

Keep these guidelines in mind when performing or directing an emergency euthanasia.

- **Ricochet:** When performed properly, with the correct equipment and aim, there should be very little risk of ricochet. However, any witnesses should stand behind the shooter. If possible, the procedure should be done outside, away from solid surfaces that could bounce a bullet.

- **Unexpected direction of fall:** On rare occasions (particularly if the bullet isn't directed down the neck), a horse will lunge forward rather than fall straight down, potentially injuring the shooter. To avoid injury, perform the euthanasia in an area where there's room to maneuver. Have the shooter aim carefully and stand off to the side. (If possible, stand uphill from the horse.)

• **Anxiety:** So the horse won't spook at a hand raised in front of his face, apply a blindfold. (This may also make the act easier, as the shooter won't have to look the horse in the eye.)

• **Logistics:** Choose a location where the body can be easily reached by equipment so it can be removed or buried. Rigor mortis can set in within an hour, making it next to impossible to maneuver a body through a 4-foot stall door. *Tip:* Positioning your horse by the shavings pile, if you have one, will provide a cushioned place for his final fall, and easy access with equipment.

• **Insurance:** If your horse is covered by mortality insurance, contact your insurance company before acting. Without their authorization to euthanize, the claim may be denied.

A Witness's Guide to Euthanasia

Will you opt to be with your horse when he's put down? That's a big decision, one that you'll want to think hard about (if given time), and discuss with friends and family. There is no right answer except that which works for you.

If you do choose to stay with your horse, here is what you'll likely see.

Gunshot: When properly used, you'll witness an instantaneous, painless death. The shooter will position himself in front and to the side of your horse, as outlined under "Other Safety Issues," on page 400. Once he's determined proper placement of the gun barrel, he'll pull the trigger. The horse will collapse immediately, dead. You'll see minimal blood.

Lethal injection: Your veterinarian may shave the area above the jugular vein, most likely on your horse's left side. This will allow easier access to the vein, especially if your horse's coat is long. She may then inject a local anesthetic, numbing the area so she can insert a large-bore catheter. Once she's determined she's safely in the vein, she'll inject the first of one to three drugs, which will rapidly render the horse unconscious. When euthanized while standing, horses become unconscious so quickly they're not aware they're sinking to the ground. (If a horse falls heavily or flips over backward, rest assured he's not aware of it.)

The medication quickly suppresses nerve function; after one or two delayed breaths, breathing stops. The heart slows and stops beating a few minutes later. Your horse may slightly paddle his legs. His eyes will likely stay open. Once your vet begins injecting drugs, the entire painless procedure generally takes around 15 to 20 seconds.

REFERENCE INFORMATION

Glossary

Abdominal hernia, See Hernia, abdominal.

Abscess, also: abscessed 66, 80, 110, 189, 293, 333, 393 A local infection that has become enclosed by fibrous tissue—the body's attempt to protect itself by walling off the infection.

Acute cataract, see Cataract, acute.

Acute endometritis, see Endometritis, acute.

Acute myositis, see Myositis, acute.

Airway hyperresponsiveness 61, 62, 189, 269 An asthmalike, overreactive state of the respiratory tract (often seen in the recovery phase after an upper respiratory infection such as influenza[G]) in which dust, smoke, chemical fumes, pollens, and/or heavy breathing induce airway spasm and cough.

Alar fold, excessive 67 The fold of skin on the outer edge of the nostrils which, when thickened, enlarged, or improperly situated, can interfere with breathing, cause a snoring noise, and possibly impair performance due to inefficient air intake.

Alkali disease, see Selenium toxicosis.

Ampullitis 208 Inflammation and/or infection of the stallion's ampullae (paired accessory sex glands that secrete part of the seminal fluid). Can interfere with ejaculation.

Anabolism, also: anabolic, anabolic state 239 A metabolic state in which the body is growing or bulking up, so that the total amount of tissue gained exceeds the amount lost. For more information on condition, weight loss, and muscle loss in the senior horse, see "Senior Condition Check," page 300.

Anaphylaxis, also: anaphylactic reaction 33, 35, 37, 63, 110, 174 A term most often used to describe a severe, life-threatening allergic-type reaction to a substance to which the horse has previously been exposed or "sensitized." Penicillin reactions and beesting reactions are common examples. Symptoms in the horse may include hives, skin swelling, sweating, weak or thready pulse, labored breathing, anxiety, and collapse, and death from suffocation (due to swelling of respiratory tissues), shock, or cardiac arrest. For best chance of recovery, anaphylaxis must be recognized and treated early with high volume fluid therapy, oxygen, and selected drugs as appropriate.

Anemia, aplastic 46, 151, 238 An anemia in humans that can be caused by exposure to phenylbutazone[G] (bute). It's characterized by defective function of blood-forming organs such as bone marrow.

Anemia, also: hemolytic anemia 68, 103, 188, 197, 258, 386 Abnormally low red blood cell count in the circulating blood. Can be caused by bleeding, by damage to and/or premature destruction of red blood cells (hemolytic anemia) because of illness or poisoning, or by a decrease in red blood cell production by the body because of illness.

Anhidrosis 37, 40, 63, 64, 65, 68, 188, 189, 190, 197, 198, 218, 389, 392 Failure of the sweat glands, resulting in abnormally low production of sweat. In the horse, for which sweating is the primary mode of body cooling, it can cause a dangerous increase in body temperature.

Anovulatory follicle, see Follicle, anovulatory.

Antioxidant 248, 382 Chemical substances which block the oxidation[G] of cells in the body. When oxidation occurs, natural toxic byproducts called free radicals[G] are produced, which have been linked with premature cell death, disease, cancer, and the aging process. With aging, the body loses more and more of its ability to protect itself against oxidative breakdown and free radical damage. For more information on cancer in the senior horse, see "The Age Event: Cancer," page 241.

Arrhythmia, cardiac 139, 188 A heart condition that results in an irregular heart beat.

Arthritis, also: degenerative joint disease, DJD 45, 49, 143, 150, 208, 227, 235, 251, 255, 273, 277, 343, 370, 382, 389, 392 Joint inflammation, characterized by thinning joint lubrication, decreased cartilage nutrition, increased accumulation of waste material and debris in the joint fluid, swelling of the joint, heat, and pain. May or may not include cartilage damage. Can become a chronic, self-perpetuating condition known as degenerative joint disease, or DJD. For more information on arthritis in the senior horse, see "The Age Event: Arthritis," page 227.

Ascarids, roundworms 259, 328, 329 A term usually used to refer to a particular type of parasite named *Parascaris equorum* that resides in the small intestine of horses. Mature ascarids can reach lengths of 20 inches. The shape of the worm is round, like spaghetti. Symptoms of infestation usually apply to foals, which cough when immature larvae migrate through the lungs, up to the throat, and are swallowed into the digestive system. Most adult horses are relatively unaffected by ascarids unless they have a very heavy infestation which suggests a weak immune system. Pinworms and strongyles are other types of equine intestinal roundworms. *Habronema* is an example of an equine skin roundworm, causing "summer sores." For more information on parasite control in the senior horse, see "Senior

Deworming & Vaccination Program," page 322 .

Aspiration pneumonia, see Pneumonia, aspiration.

Atrophy 18 Decrease in size or wasting away of body tissue, due to lack of use.

Aural plaques 120, 121 Flat, raised, chalky lesions on the inner, upright surface of the horse's external ear. Caused by a virus and believed to be spread by biting insects. There is no known treatment.

Autoimmune disease 31 A disease in which the immune system targets "friendly" cells, attacking the victim's own tissues. Examples are pemphigus foliaceus[G] and lupus erythematosus[G].

Babesiosis, also: piroplasmosis 103 An infection of the blood by one or both of the organisms *Babesia caballi* and *Babesia equi*, which are found in areas with a year-round warm climate. Symptoms include fever, labored breathing, jaundice[G], colic[G], and dependent edema[G], and over time victims develop anemia[G] and diarrhea[G]. Prognosis for recovery depends on which organism is causing the infection—horses infected with *B. equi* often die within 2 days of showing signs, while those infected with *B. caballi* are more likely to recover. Prompt medical treatment improves the odds of full and faster recovery.

Bean 166, 183, 191, 360, 362 A lay term for smegmolith, a smooth, rounded structure often formed in the recessed area around the tip of the urethra in male horses, mostly geldings. For more information on beans, smegma[G], and sheath cleaning, see "Down & Dirty Maintenance: Sheath & Udder Cleaning," page 360.

Boticide 75, 324 A deworming agent that will kill *Gasterophilus* stomach worms, also known as bots[G]. Ivermectin and moxidectin are approved boticides.

Bots, also: bot eggs, *Gasterophilus* species 324, 328, 329 A stomach parasite of the horse. Resembling a plump grubworm, the mature bot measures about 1/2 to 1 inch long and roughly half as wide. Spread by botflies, which resemble a honeybee with a turned-under tail end, they deposit small yellowish eggs on the hairs of the horse's lower legs. The eggs stick to the horse's lips when he rubs his face there or bites at an itchy leg. Once in the warm, moist environment of the lips, the eggs hatch and the larvae make their way to the stomach, where they attach to the lining and feed on blood. Bot infestation can cause stomach irritation and ulcers, and in severe cases, stomach rupture. For more information on controlling bots and other parasites, see "Senior Deworming & Vaccination Program," page 322.

Botulism, forage poisoning 67, 159, 323, 327 A neurologic disease caused most often by ingesting the toxin of *Clostridium botulinum*, a bacterium present in soil and decaying vegetable matter and animal tissue. One source is carcasses of small wild animals accidentally killed and baled into hay. Another is rotting hay, as is found on the ground when feeding horses from a large livestock bale. In areas where the toxin is present in the soil, placing horse feed on the ground can cause botulism outbreaks. Foals, aged horses, horses with ulcers[G], and horses that are in poor health are especially vulnerable. Symptoms range from tongue lolling, drooping eyelids, loss of tail tone, and slobbering, to generalized muscle weakness, difficulty rising, and paralysis. Mental functioning remains normal. Vaccination can help prevent outbreaks in endemic[G] areas. Treatment with botulism antitoxin has improved the survival rate from 10% to more than 70%.

Bowel disease, chronic inflammatory 146, 175 One of several conditions of the large intestine that cause chronic inflammation of its lining, thereby interfering with nutrient and water absorption. Depending on the specific disease, symptoms can include weight loss, muscle loss, intermittent colic[G], impaction, or diarrhea[G].

Bronchitis, also: bronchiolitis, bronchopneumonia 60 Respiratory tract inflammation caused by viral or bacterial infection, parasite damage (e.g., lungworm infestation), or direct lung damage due to smoke or toxic gas inhalation. The main symptom is cough, with fever if the lungs are involved (bronchopneumonia). Chronic bronchitis is one facet of heaves[G] (chronic obstructive pulmonary disease, or COPD).

Bronchoconstriction 269 Spasm of the bronchioles (small branches of the lung's airways), usually due to irritation or allergic-type reaction, resulting in coughing and labored breathing.

Bute, see Phenylbutazone.

Canine teeth 332 Saber-shaped teeth (2 upper, 2 lower) that sit in the gap between the incisors ("front") teeth and the molars ("grinders") of geldings and stallions. Rarely found in females. For more information on dental care in the senior horse, see "Top Priority—Tooth Care," page 332.

Cannon keratosis 26 A poorly understood skin condition with scurf, crust, and hair loss on the anterior (front) surfaces of the hind limb cannon (shin) bone areas. There is no cure, but symptoms can be managed by regular bathing of affected areas with shampoos made for treating seborrhea[G].

Capsaicin 236 A chemical present in hot peppers which, when applied topically on a regular basis, can alter nerve function and relieve some forms of chronic pain in what has been termed "chemical denerving."

Catabolism, also: catabolic, catabolic state 38, 239, 378 A metabolic state in which overall tissue breakdown exceeds tissue growth, resulting in visible loss of weight and muscle mass. Most horses enter a catabolic state naturally around age 15, making it somewhat more difficult to maintain condition ➤

unless dietary adjustments are made. In addition to being a "normal" part of aging, the catabolic state can be caused by certain disease processes, such as malignant cancers and chronic digestive disorders, and long-term use of corticosteroid medications. For more information on condition, weight loss, and muscle loss in the senior horse, see "Senior Condition Check," page 300.

Cataract 100, 101, 113, 306 An abnormal condition in which the clear lens of the affected eye becomes opaque, resulting in permanent vision impairment. There is no known treatment to prevent or reverse cataract formation, but use of eye drops to dilate the pupil can improve vision. Surgery to remove the affected lens can help restore vision.

Cataract, acute 100 Sudden onset of cataract[G]. Occurs in the aftermath of uveitis[G] in roughly 50% of cases. Also can occur after serious generalized illness or injury to the eye. Surgical removal is not recommended in an eye that has a history of uveitis because of increased risk of postoperative complications.

Cataract, senile 101, 113 Gradual cataract[G] formation, associated with advanced age. When compared to acute cataracts, senile cataracts are less opaque, cause less vision impairment, and are less likely to cause dramatic adjustment difficulties for the horse because of their gradual onset.

Cellulitis 146, 147 Infection or inflammation within cells or connective tissue, often caused by invasion of the tissues by an insect or spider bite, beesting, or snakebite. Also can be caused by generalized illness, such as Equine Viral Arteritis[G]. Symptoms include swelling, heat, redness and tenderness of affected tissues.

Cellulitis, orbital 110 Inflammation of tissues behind the eyeball, causing the eye to appear to bulge.

Cervicitis 164, 207 Infection of the cervix, usually associated with vaginal and/or uterine infection. Can also result from direct trauma to the cervix, such as during foaling.

Cervicosympathetic trunk 41 The main nerve trunks of specific nerves as they branch from the spinal cord in the neck region.

Chemotherapy, also: intralesional chemotherapy 241, 242 A term usually used for medical treatment of cancer with certain chemicals. In intralesional chemotherapy, the chemicals are injected directly into the tumor.

Chemotherapy, topical 242 Localized application of a chemotherapy[G] drug directly to a skin lesion, such as a sarcoid[G].

Choke 60, 63, 77, 78, 134, 135, 136, 243, 248, 288, 332 A blockage of the esophagus in which swallowed feed cannot pass through to the stomach. As a result, saliva, chewed feed, and swallowed water spill out through one or both nostrils. There may or may not be a visible, palpable lump in the neck,

depending on the location of the blockage—if it's in the lower portion of the esophagus, it will be out of view, in the chest cavity. Can be caused by feed that has been inadequately chewed and moistened with saliva, or from direct injury to the delicate esophageal tissue by rough feed, stomach tubing, or leakage of caustic medications from jugular vein injections.

Cholangitis, also: cholangiohepatitis 33, 103 A type of liver disease in which the ducts that carry bile (the liver's primary product) become inflamed, narrowed, and blocked. Can result from infection, abscesses, parasites, tumors, ingestion of moldy feed, poisons, ulcers, scarring, bile stones, and inflammation or obstruction of the upper digestive tract. Symptoms depend on (and may be overshadowed by) the underlying cause and can include colic[G], weight loss, jaundice[G], and signs of abnormal mental functioning.

Cholangiocellular carcinoma 241 Cancer of the cells lining the bile ducts in the liver.

Cholelithiasis 95, 103 The formation of bile stones. Because horses do not have gall bladders, the stones are present within the bile duct network within the liver. Depending on the location, size, and number of stones present, symptoms can range from no clinical signs to chronic skin pruritus (itchiness), intermittent fever, recurrent colic[G], jaundice[G], and weight loss.

Chorea 123 Involuntary spasmodic muscle movements due to neurological tissue damage.

Choroid body 244 A normal, bulbous structure on the upper margin of the pupil of the horse's eye, about the size of a peppercorn and the same color as the iris.

Chronic obstructive pulmonary disease, also: COPD, heaves, broken wind 40, 60, 64, 68, 189, 193, 198, 267, 268, 271, 370, 377, 379 A chronic, often seasonal respiratory disease of the horse in which structures within the lungs lose their normal elasticity, making it difficult for inhaled air to be expelled and interfering with transfer of oxygen from lungs to bloodstream. Symptoms generally are induced by exposure to seasonal allergens such as hay dust and dusty stall bedding. Signs may include reduced performance, labored breathing, nostril flare, cough, nasal discharge, and the appearance of a muscular ridge known as a heave line running diagonally between the ribs and the flank on both sides. For more information, see "The Age Event: Heaves," page 267.

Cimetidine 242 Antacid medication first available for human use under the trade name Tagamet®. Has proved useful in equine medicine as a form of chemotherapy for the treatment of melanoma[G].

Clenbuterol 268 A medication first available for equine use under the trade name Ventipulmin®. Has proved useful in relaxing the respiratory tree in horses suffering from bronchconstriction[G], as in heaves[G].

Clostridial myositis 137 Infection of muscle tissue due to invasion by *Clostridium* bacteria which are carried from the skin into deeper tissues, most often during intramuscular injection. It has been estimated that 1 in 100,000 intramuscular injections results in clostridial myositis, not necessarily linked with errors in injection technique. Symptoms, including localized swelling, heat and pain at the injection site along with high fever and signs of general malaise, appear within 24 hours of the injection and can quickly progress to shock and death. With prompt medical treatment, including appropriate antibiotics and anti-inflammatory medications, the prognosis for swift and complete recovery is good. Without treatment, the condition usually is fatal.

Coital exanthema 162 A venereal disease of the stallion, due to spread of equine herpesvirus[G] type 3 from the mare, causing fever, depression, and blisters, pustules, and ulcerated lesions on the penis of the stallion. With sexual rest, symptoms often subside.

Colic 23, 40, 55, 79, 153, 170, 172, 173, 175, 190, 251, 254, 261, 264, 273, 274, 280, 288, 293, 324, 332, 378, 390 One or more of a collection of symptoms indicating "bellyache" (abdominal pain), including repeated yawning, depression, loss of appetite, turning to look at flanks, lying down, rolling, and violent thrashing. Most commonly results from gas accumulation in the intestines (due to excess gas production, as in gas colic, or a physical blockage with dry manure, as in impaction colic[G], or a functional blockage, as in gut displacement, twist, or torsion), but also can indicate stomach pain, pain involving kidney, liver, or muscle tissue, or labor pain. Determining the underlying cause, the severity, appropriate treatment, and prognosis often requires a skilled diagnostic workup. For more information on colic in the senior horse, see "The Age Event: Colic," page 251 and "Colic Symptom Checklist," page 222.

Colic, impaction, also: blockage, intestinal blockage 79, 179, 184, 251, 254, 379, 381 Blockage in the intestinal tract due to accumulation of semi-formed manure that has become lodged. Usually occurs in the cecum (the horse's vatlike counterpart to our appendix) or colon, where manure becomes increasingly dry and less likely to move because its water is reabsorbed by the bowel wall. The blockage causes abdominal pain, usually because of trapped gas. If caught early, veterinary treatment with stool softeners and/or laxatives, and rehydration with oral (via stomach tube) or intravenous fluids, often is successful. Otherwise, abdominal surgery is needed. For more information on colic in the senior horse, see "The Age Event: Colic," page 251.

Colic, sand 177, 254 Colic resulting from accumulated sand in your horse's intestines, due to being fed on sandy soil, or from eating dirt in grassless pastures. Sand can irritate the intestines, resulting in enteritis[G] or diarrhea[G], or can build up to the point of impaction[G]. Treatment usually consists of pain medications, antispasmodics to soothe the gut, and mineral oil, to help aid passage of sand. Surgery may be necessary. Prevention is key.

Colitis, also: ulcerative colitis, right dorsal colitis 14, 44, 46, 86, 149, 151, 235, 255, 274 Inflammation of the colon due to infection, as a side effect of certain antibiotics, or from the high dose and/or long-term use of NSAID[G]s.

Collagenolytic granuloma, also: nodular necrobiosis, equine eosinophilic granuloma with collagen degeneration 97 A common skin disease of the horse, causing the formation of nodules, either singly or in groups, ranging from the size of a poppy seed to 5 inches in diameter. In some cases no underlying cause is determined, but most cases are associated with a local hypersensitivity or allergic-type reaction to insect bites. Some cases are believed to be due to skin trauma from poorly fitting tack. The nodules are not itchy or painful. Some regress if treated with corticosteroids[G]; others must be removed surgically.

Collapsed pharynx 67 Collapse of a horse's pharynx, which can be triggered by intense exercise and flexion at the poll. The pharynx isn't a rigid chamber. Rather, it has soft walls and is kept open mainly by muscles. When a horse breathes in, air rushing through pulls on the walls; weakened muscles can allow the pharynx to collapse inward. The stronger the airflow (as a result of deep breathing due, say, to intense exercise, which also fatigues throat muscles), the more likely a collapse. The resulting noise is like heavy breathing or intake of a snore.

Concentrate 248 Any feed that provides nutrients in a low-fiber, nutrient-dense form, such as whole or processed grains and supplements. For more information on the use of concentrates in the senior horse's diet, see "Stay-Young Diet Solutions," page 376.

Congestive heart failure, also: CHF 60, 63, 68, 198 A progressive condition in which one or more valves of the heart fails to completely seal, allowing backwash of blood into the blood vessels of the lungs with every beat, requiring the heart to work harder to pump blood through the body. The cardiac muscle enlarges in order to do the work, the valvular leakage worsens, and the backwash increases, eventually leading to leakage of serum into the lung tissue, interfering with breathing and causing a moist cough. Medical treatment to enhance cardiac performance and clear excess fluid from the lungs can improve the patient's stamina and reduce or eliminate the cough until the condition worsens enough to require a dosage increase.

Contact dermatitis 34 Allergiclike skin sensitivity to physical contact with certain substances.

Contracted heels 315 An abnormal hoof conformation characterized by the heel and quarters of the hoof being narrower (from side to side) than the toe area. Often attributed to hoof wear, trimming, and/or shoeing techniques that favor a long toe or otherwise limit the normal expansion that occurs in the heel area when the foot bears weight.

Cornea 105, 106 The smooth, clear, transparent globe covering approximately the anterior 1/3 of the horse's eyeball. ➤

Though it may look like curved glass, the cornea actually consists of many layers, like an onion.

Corneal abscess 100 An infection buried between the onion-like layers of the cornea[G].

Corneal ulcer 100, 102, 306 A lesion on the cornea[G] that has caused some of its onionlike layers to degenerate or erode. Most often due to an eye injury that has become infected. Without proper treatment, a corneal ulcer can spread and threaten permanent vision loss, possibly even loss of the eyeball.

Corticosteroids 234, 257, 260, 266, 273, 277 A family of medications related to the substance cortisol which is produced naturally by the adrenal glands in response to stress. Hydrocortisone, dexamethasone, prednisone, and triamcinolone are examples of corticosteroids used in the horse to alleviate certain kinds of pain, manage the symptoms of certain allergies, and as a form of chemotherapy for certain cancers. Laminitis[G] and a type of Cushing's disease[G] can occur as adverse side effects of corticosteroid use, particularly with high dosages and/or long-term use.

Cortisol 258, see also Corticosteroids.

Cribbing 90 A stereotypy[G] in which a horse braces his upper teeth on a solid surface such as the top of a gate or fence board, presses down by tensing his neck muscles, and gulps air, making a grunting sound. Believed to begin in boredom and develop into a form of addiction due to opiate chemicals released by the brain while cribbing.

Cryosurgery 242, 243 A means of obliterating a lesion such as a tumor, a wart, or a sarcoid, by freezing, usually with liquid nitrogen or carbon dioxide.

Culicoides **gnat, also: midges, no-see-ums, 34** Biting insects, about the size of a dash (-) on this page, *Culicoides* gnats attack the topline (mane, back, and tail bed) or underpinnings of horses, either during the heat of the day or at dusk, depending on the variety of gnat. See *Culicoides* hypersensitivity.

Culicoides **hypersensitivity, also: sweet itch, Queensland itch 34, 164** A seasonal allergic-type dermatitis triggered by *Culicoides* gnats[G], causing the afflicted horse to damage his skin and/or rub out his mane and tail by excessive rubbing. The allergic response worsens with every year of exposure to the gnat, as does unaffected horses' odds of developing the allergy, due to cumulative effects.

Cushing's disease, see Equine Cushing's Disease.

Cutaneous lymphoma 97 A type of cancer in the horse, characterized by single or multiple lumps under the skin, 1/2 to 1 inch in diameter, which tend to fluctuate in size over time. Affected mares may go into remission during pregnancy, then relapse after foaling. Remission also has occurred with corticosteroid[G] therapy, but standard chemotherapy[G] is considered too expensive and generally is not used in the horse. In most cases, no other symptoms accompany the skin lesions until associated tumors of the internal organs become extensive enough to cause illness, which takes an average of 6 years to occur. For more information on cancer in the senior horse, see "The Age Event: Cancer," page 241.

Cyathostomes, also: small strongyles, strongyles, encysted larval strongyles 79, 324 Slender parasites, 1/4 inch to 3/4 inch long, that inhabit the large intestine of the horse and feed on blood. The larvae are acquired by eating infested forage or soil. They mature while burrowing into the walls of the cecum (the horse's vatlike "appendix") and colon, in the connective tissue lining the abdominal cavity, or within internal organs such as the liver and pancreas, where they can remain for months or even years as "encysted" cyathostomes. To complete their maturation, they return to the lumen of the large intestine. Significant tissue damage occurs during migration of these parasites through the tissues—concomitant migration of large numbers of these parasites can cause symptoms such as colic[G] or diarrhea[G]. Over time, the cumulative damage to the digestive system can contribute to age-related malnutrition. For more information on control of strongyles and other parasites in the senior horse, see "Senior Deworming & Vaccination Program," page 322.

Cyathostomiasis 175 Clinically evident illness due to mobilization of a heavy infestation of cyathostomes[G], with symptoms of colic[G], decreased appetite, and/or diarrhea[G]. Three typical scenarios lead to cyathostomiasis: (1) a historically inadequate deworming program coupled with low individual immunity and/or high exposure to parasite larvae; (2) atypical exposure to an unusually high number of parasites, for example when allowing your horse to graze where heavy accumulations of parasite eggs and larvae are present, followed by signs of cyathostomiasis within the following 3 weeks when consumed larvae migrate through the victim's digestive tract; and (3) deworming a heavily infested horse with an agent that kills or disturbs massive numbers of encysted cyathostomes at once, resulting in an unusual amount of tissue damage in the gastrointestinal tract. Currently the most effective way to avoid cyathostomiasis is to avoid grazing areas that are suspected or known to have had years of heavy equine traffic, and/or to adminster daily deworming[G] with pyrantel tartrate.

Cyst 66, 189 An abnormal, fluid-filled structure formed by the body in response to chronic irritation. Typically lined by specialized cells that secrete its fluid contents, which is why cysts tend to refill after being drained. Surgical removal of the sac and its secretory lining usually is necessary to eliminate the structure permanently.

Daily deworming 15, 23, 322, 324, 328 A parasite control program in which the chemical pyrantel tartrate (Strongid C® and

Strongid C-2X®, and generic preparations) is given daily in a low dose, usually as a top-dressed pellet. When given in this way, it kills parasite larvae (most significantly large and small strongyles[G]) before they begin their destructive migration through the body, and before they encyst in tissues. For more information on control of strongyles and other parasites in the senior horse, see "Senior Deworming & Vaccination Program," page 322.

DDSP, also: dorsal displacement of soft palate, laryngopalatal displacement 66, 67 An abnormal position of the rear portion of the soft palate, usually temporary and usually occurring during heavy exercise such as racing, in which the palate's tissues lift up and become trapped above the epiglottis, causing a sudden snoring or gurgling noise with respiration and a functional blockage of the respiratory tract, also known as "choking down." In most cases when exercise is stopped, which usually occurs abruptly because the horse suddenly can't breathe, the displacement resolves itself. A variety of surgical procedures are employed to prevent the displacement, often successfully unless the underlying cause is damage to an associated nerve.

Degenerative eye disorder, see Eye disorder, degenerative.

Dementia 260 A state of mental dysfunction which may include such symptoms as disorientation, depression, aimless wandering, and illogical behavior.

Denerving, see Nerve resection.

Dermatitis 26, 37, 88 Inflammation of the skin, due to infection, acute or chronic irritation, and/or allergy. Symptoms may include redness, heat, swelling, pain and/or itching, with or without scaling, crusting, oozing, and hair loss.

Dermatophilosis, see Rainrot.

Dermatophytosis, also: ringworm 26, 30 A skin disorder caused by proliferation of one or more common environmental fungi that can invade the skin when its natural immunity has been compromised, for example when waterlogged from prolonged wet environmental conditions without the opportunity to dry and without direct sunlight. Once established, this type of skin infection becomes more virulent[G] and can be contagious and able to cross to other species, including humans and house pets. Symptoms include single or multiple areas of hair loss, sometimes with reddening, usually without evidence of discomfort or itching. Treatment includes shaving, cleaning, and drying of affected areas, topical antifungals, and/or oral antifungals in severe cases.

Desmitis, degenerative, also: degenerative suspensory ligament desmitis, DSLD 147, 159 A chronic and progressive breakdown of the suspensory ligament[G], usually in both hind limbs, resulting in pain, heat, and swelling. Affected horses show progressive sinking of the fetlock joint as the ligament

weakens and tears. A definitive cause has not been identified, but it has been associated with aging, obesity, pregnancy, and repetitive injuries as well as possible familial heritability.

Detached retina, see Retina, detached.

Dew poisoning, also: scratches 27, 28, 31 A skin condition characterized by raw, crusted, scaly lesions at the backs of the pasterns. Believed to be initiated by moist, unhygienic footing compromising the skin's local immunity and allowing common skin bacteria to invade the hair follicles; can become chronic.

Dexamethasone, see Corticosteroids.

Diabetes, also: diabetes mellitus 72, 184, 260, 261, 276, 278 An abnormal metabolic condition, uncommon in the horse but sometimes seen as an accompaniment to a more pervasive metabolic disorder known as Equine Cushing's Disease[G]. More common in ponies than in horses. Symptoms include excessive water intake, excessive urine output, and laminitis[G]. Treatment of the underlying cause generally resolves the diabetes.

Diaphragm, ruptured 188 A tear in the muscular sheet that separates your horse's chest from his abdomen. It usually is the result of severe blunt trauma to the chest or abdomen, as from a kick or from being hit by a vehicle. Signs can include: signs of colic; labored breathing; decreased exercise tolerance; and resentment (and sometimes collapse) when a girth is tightened. Treatment generally is surgical repair; prognosis is guarded.

Diaphragmatic hernia, see Hernia, diaphragmatic.

Diarrhea 44, 149, 174, 176, 273, 274, 324, 327 Abnormally wet, unformed, more frequently passed stool, resulting from abnormally rapid movement through the intestinal tract and/or impairment of the large intestine's ability to absorb water. Can cause life-threatening dehydration and electrolyte imbalance. Treatment depends on the underlying cause.

Dictyocaulus, see Lungworms.

Dislocated lens, see Lens, dislocated.

DMSO, also: dimethylsulfoxide 34, 236, 266 An industrial solvent that has medicinal properties including anti-inflammatory and anti-pain action. Due to its rapid absorption through intact skin, it has been mixed with certain topical medications to enhance their local and/or systemic effect.

Dorsal spinous process(es) 128, 199 Upright bony protrusions normally present on the spinal vertebrae. The most prominent dorsal spinous processes form the structure known as the withers.

Drug eruption 162 A variety of skin lesions that occur as an allergic-type reaction to such as medications penicillin, phenylbutazone[G] ("bute"), and others. Possible lesions ➤

include hives, reddened plaques, and swelling.

E. coli enteritis 174, 175 Intestinal infection with the bacteria *Escherichia coli*, which can be contagious to other horses as well as to humans.

Ear mites 88, 116, 117, 126 Infestation of the external ear canal with microscopic mites of the *Psoroptes* family, which feed on tissue fluid within the ear. Symptoms may include head shaking, ear rubbing, waxy ear discharge, hearing impairment, or no symptoms, depending on severity of infestation. Treatment with an ear solution containing an insecticide labeled safe for use in horses' ears is effective.

Ear ticks 88, 116, 126 Infestation of the external ear canal with the soft-shelled "spinose ear tick" *Otobius megnini*, which also can infest sheltered horse facilities. Symptoms include head shaking, ear or head rubbing, and abnormal head carriage (holding the head at a tilt, for example). Treatment with an ear solution containing a tick-killing insecticide safe for use in horses' ears must be accompanied by treatment of the infested facilities as well, or reinfestation of the horse's ear(s) is likely.

Eastern Equine Encephalomyelitis (EEE), also: sleeping sickness 67, 325 Often deadly viral infection of the brain and spinal cord of horses and humans. Spread by mosquitoes. Begins with fever and general malaise and can progress to dementia, blindness, weakness, staggering, and paralysis. Less than 25% of victims survive and usually have permanent brain damage. Vaccination is very effective as a preventive. For more information on control of this and other contagious diseases in the senior horse, see "Senior Deworming & Vaccination Program," page 322.

Edema 18, 101, 128, 146, 165, 199, 229 Swelling due to excessive accumulation of fluid in soft tissues. Can be caused by inflammation in the affected tissues, poor circulation of blood and/or lymph, fever, certain infectious diseases such as Equine Viral ArteritisG (EVA), or by abnormally low protein levels in the blood (hypoproteinemiaG). For more information on hypoproteinemia and muscle loss in the senior horse, see "Senior Condition Check," page 300, and "Stay-Young Diet Solutions," page 376.

Efficacy 326 Effectiveness, ability to produce the desired effect, usually referring to a particular treatment.

Emphysema, subcutaneous 137 Puffy-looking skin swelling that feels "bubbly" to the fingertips. Occurs when air invades space under the skin, such as when the respiratory tract and/or lungs have been punctured, allowing air to escape. Also can occur when tissues beneath the skin have become infected with an organism that produces gas.

Encephalomyelitis, also: encephalitis, encephalomyelopathy 67, 88, 92, 110, 116, 123, 193 Inflammation of the brain (encephalitis) and spinal cord (encephalomyelitis or encephalomyelopathy), also known as Sleeping Sickness. See Eastern Equine Encephalomyelitis (EEE), Western Equine Encephalomyelitis (WEE), Venezuelan Equine Encephalomyelitis (VEE). For more information on control of this and other diseases in the senior horse, see "Senior Deworming & Vaccination Program," page 322.

Endemic 326, 327 Prevailing in a particular community or region, usually referring to an infectious disease.

Endometritis, acute 22, 132, 142, 174, 218, 264, 265 A life-threatening infection of the lining of the mare's uterus, most often occurring within 3 days after the mare foals, particularly if passage of the placenta (afterbirth) was delayed or incomplete. Symptoms may include high fever, sweating, shivering, loss of appetite, and stoppage of milk production, followed in some cases by laminitisG. Prognosis for full recovery is good with prompt treatment, otherwise the condition often is fatal.

Endotoxemia, also: endotoxins, endotoxic shock 48, 95, 142, 174, 221 A form of blood poisoning (endotoxemia) due to absorption of a toxic substance (endotoxin) present in the cell wall of gram-negative bacteria in the gastrointestinal tract. Occurs most commonly in severe colicG, grain overload, and intestinal infections. Normally blocked from entering the bloodstream in a healthy horse, endotoxin may be absorbed under one of two circumstances: (1) there is an extraordinary amount of it present in the gut (usually because something has upset the bacterial flora), or; (2) the gut's lining has been damaged and is no longer able to act as an effective barrier to endotoxin. Symptoms can include rapid heart and respiratory rate, a deepening or muddying of gum color, fever, collapse, and death. Intensive and prompt care is necessary to save the horse before cardiovascular failure occurs.

Enteritis 174, 175 Inflammation of the intestines, usually due to infection.

Enteritis, granulomatous, also: enterocolitis, granulomatous 86, 97, 174, 175 A chronic inflammatory condition of the lining of the small or large intestine that interferes with normal digestion and absorption of nutrients. No consistent underlying cause has been identified. Symptoms can include changes in appetite, low-grade or recurrent colicG, diarrheaG, weight loss, ventral edemaG, and muscle loss. Treatment usually includes corticosteroidsG, to manage the inflammation; prognosis is poor for long term recovery and treatment itself can cause serious side effects.

Enteropathy, protein-losing 23, 133 Loss of protein via manure due to intestinal disorder.

Epiglottis, entrapped 67 An abnormal condition in which the epiglottis becomes caught in a nearby fold of tissue at the back of the throat. Adversely affects the horse's ability to breathe and is particularly evident during strenuous exercise. Treatment is surgical.

Epilepsy 54, 89, 94 Any of a variety of disorders caused by disturbed electrical impulses in the central nervous system. Typically marked by convulsive attacks (seizures); may include diminished or clouded consciousness.

Equine Cushing's Disease, also: Cushing's syndrome, ECD, pituitary adenoma 15, 38, 40, 48, 68, 72, 111, 117, 142, 182, 184, 195, 198, 204, 206, 242, 257, 273, 276, 278, 304 A metabolic disorder most often associated with advanced age, usually due to the enlargement of (and increased production of hormones by) a portion of the pituitary gland at the base of the brain. For more information on Cushing's disease in the senior horse, see "The Age Event: Cushing's Disease," page 257.

Equine degenerative myelopathy (EDM) 159 A common spinal cord and brain stem disease of the horse. Though the cause is unknown, a deficiency of vitamin E is suspected to play a role. Symptoms appear gradually over time, usually are symmetrical, and usually are worse in the hind limbs than in the forelimbs, which may appear to be unaffected. Affected horses appear to be clumsy and dizzy, may lift their hind limbs higher than necessary when moving, and may "dog sit" when asked to back. Supplementation of the diet with high doses of vitamin E has proved to be the most effective treatment, bringing visible improvement within a few weeks and continuing for several months.

Equine herpesvirus, also: EHV, equine viral rhinopneumonitis, EVR 326 Equine herpesvirus type 1 can cause an upper respiratory disease, late-term abortion, and neurologic disease ("paralytic rhino"). Type 4 is associated mostly with respiratory infection. Stress and a depressed immune system can increase the individual's susceptibility to one or more of the herpesvirus diseases. The respiratory form, which causes fever, runny nose, and sometimes a cough, is spread directly from horse to horse via respiratory fluids. With maturity and repeated exposure to the virus, horses show milder and milder symptoms and may eventually show no external signs at all, even when laboratory tests show that infection has in fact occurred. In other words, experienced broodmares that don't show external signs of catching "a cold" may in truth be infected with the virus, which places their pregnancies at risk. The abortive form, which starts as a respiratory infection (with or without external symptoms) in the pregnant mare, is spread to the unborn fetus via blood. Vaccination is the only available preventive method, but the immune response is weak and short-lived. For more information on prevention of equine herpesvirus infection in the senior horse, see "Senior Deworming & Vaccination Program," page 322.

Equine Infectious Anemia, also: EIA, Coggin's disease, swamp fever 53, 54, 103 Diagnosed by a blood test (Coggin's test), this is a viral disease spread by biting flies and mosquitoes. Infected horses, which are believed to serve as a reservoir of virus by which other horses can become infected, may show no symptoms or may show low grade to severe symptoms including loss of energy, lethargy, recurrent fever, decreased appetite, weight loss, and ventral edema^G. There is no treatment and no preventive vaccine; this is a "reportable" disease that requires horses testing positive be quarantined where biting/sucking insects can't get to them, or be destroyed.

Equine Protozoal Myeloencephalopathy, also: Equine Protozoal Myeloencephalitis, EPM 44, 52, 67, 88, 149, 190, 325 Inflammation of the brain and spinal cord due to infection by the protozoal organisms *Sarcocystis neurona* and *Neospora caninum/hughesi*. Horses that are under stress or aged are believed to be at increased risk due to depressed immune systems. Studies have shown the disease is transmitted to horses by ingestion of the organism in the feces of opossums and armadillos; other suspected sources such as rodents and birds have not been confirmed at the time of publication. Symptoms vary widely and may appear suddenly or gradually, including vague to profound changes in gait, unusual lameness, stiff, spastic, or extreme leg movement when in motion, staggering, slobbering or other evidence of difficulty swallowing, weakness, depression, and seizures. Diagnosis is based on symptoms, blood test, and/or analysis of spinal fluid. Treatment (one to several months of antiprotozoal medication given orally, plus supportive and anti-inflammatory medications) improves the chance of partial to complete recovery by approximately tenfold. Prevention by vaccination is under investigation. As of publication, a vaccine has been made available under preliminary FDA approval based on safety only (not efficacy).

Equine sarcoidosis, also: sarcoid, granulomatous disease 34, 162 An abnormal condition characterized by single or multiple skin lesions (sarcoids), and/or granulomatous (proud fleshlike) lesions in the internal organs. Treatment for the skin lesions only, which are believed to be viral in origin, may include surgical removal and/or immunostimulant medications injected directly into one or more of the skin nodules, which often results in regression of all nodules. Treatment of internal sarcoidosis, the cause of which is unknown, usually includes corticosteroids^G and carries a poor prognosis.

Equine Viral Arteritis, also: EVA 146, 327 A viral infection that can cause an upper respiratory disease or abortion. Symptoms of the respiratory form, which usually is spread directly from horse to horse by respiratory secretions, include fever, loss of appetite, edema of the lower legs and ventral body wall, runny eyes and nose, cough, and reddening and swelling of the tissues around the eyes. Most victims survive unless they have lowered immunity, as do young foals and aged horses. Survivors can be expected to have lifelong immunity. Venereal infection sometimes causes abortion with no other signs of general illness. Vaccination prior to exposure is an effective preventive. For more information on control of this and other contagious diseases in the senior horse, see "Senior Deworming & Vaccination Program," page 322.

Esophagus, ruptured 60 A tear in the esophagus. Can occur with rough or repeated treatment by stomach tube, or as ➤

a consequence of choke[G] or its treatment. Because esophageal tissue tends to scar and shrink during the healing phase after injury, any horse with ruptured esophagus has a poor prognosis for repeated episodes of choke.

Euthanasia 252, 395 The taking of life for humane reasons, producing a quiet, painless death.

Excessive salt consumption, see Salt, excessive consumption of.

Exertional rhabdomyolysis, see Tying-up syndrome.

Eye disorder, degenerative 100 Any abnormal condition of the eye in which there is progressive degeneration of tissues, threatening breakdown of the eyeball itself, and/or of the capacity to see.

Fecal egg count 16, 322 Laboratory examination of a measured amount of manure, in an attempt to quantify a horse's intestinal parasite load. May produce misleading results unless serial counts taken several days in a row are averaged, because adult parasites are known to pass eggs sporadically, and a single day's count may not be representative. For more information on control of parasites in the senior horse, see "Senior Deworming & Vaccination Program," page 322.

Fertilizer poisoning 79, 256 Colic[G] (abdominal discomfort) due to ingestion of fertilizer containing high concentrations of phosphorus or potassium.

Fetal hydrops, also: hydroallantois 215, 216 An abnormal condition of the heavily pregnant mare in which the volume of allantoic fluid (the fluid surrounding the fetus) becomes excessive. Symptoms can include an abnormally large pregnant belly, ventral edema[G], reluctance to move, and loss of appetite. The fetus is not likely to survive intact, and the mare also is in grave danger due to the possibility of shock[G] occurring if the fluids are expressed rapidly. The most successful treatment includes termination of the pregnancy, with or without cesarean surgery, with large volumes of IV fluids given to the mare to prevent shock.

Fiber, see forage.

Float, also: floated 333, 334 An equine dental procedure in which sharp points (edges) on the molar (grinder) teeth are filed (floated) in order to protect soft tissues of the mouth, and occlusive surfaces are shaped to optimize function. The instrument used is called a float, which can be a long-handled manual file, or a motorized rotary tool. For more information on dental care in the senior horse, see "Top Priority—Tooth Care," page 332.

Flora, also: bacterial flora, friendly flora 254 Normal population of bacteria that inhabit the digestive tract and aid in the digestion of feed. Certain conditions and treatments, such as an abrupt change in diet, grain overload, and the use of some antibiotics, can upset the flora, killing "good" bacteria or allowing a change in the population's balance, resulting in intestinal inflammation, excessive gas formation, colic[G], diarrhea[G], and potentially fatal shock[G].

Flu, see Influenza.

Fly strike 245 Oozing, bleeding wounds caused by fly bites, which attracts more flies—and bites.

Follicle, anovulatory 205 An ovarian follicle that fails to ovulate. May occur as a result of a temporary hormonal imbalance or an abnormality in that particular follicle. All mares can occasionally have an anovulatory follicle, but the incidence increases with advancing age, making it more difficult to achieve conception.

Folliculitis 49, 143, 146, 147 A common and painful skin condition of the horse that causes inflammation of the hair follicles, usually in skin that has been irritated (such as saddle or tack areas), leaving it vulnerable to invasion of the follicles by bacteria. Generally not considered to be contagious. Treatment includes medicated shampooing and appropriate antibiotics. Some cases resolve on their own.

Forage, also: fiber 253, 378, 380, 381 The predominant portion of the equine diet, which together with water is necessary for proper function of the approximately 100-foot-long digestive tract. For more information on colic and dietary fiber in the senior horse, see "The Age Event: Colic," page 251, "Colic Symptom Checklist," page 222, and "Stay-Young Diet Solutions," page 376.

Founder, see Laminitis.

Free radical, also: toxic free radical 248, 383 A natural byproduct of metabolism which has been linked with disease, cancer, and the aging process. The young, healthy body naturally can protect itself from oxidative damage and toxic free radicals, to a point. When it's overwhelmed, free radicals cause wholesale destruction of cells. With aging, the body loses more and more of its ability to protect itself against oxidative breakdown and free radical damage. For more information on cancer in the senior horse, see "The Age Event: Cancer," page 241.

Free radical scavenger 248 A substance that can bind and remove free radicals[G] from the body, to reduce their destructive effect. See also Antioxidant.

Gas colic, see Colic.

Glaucoma 101, 110 A serious abnormality of the eyeball that interferes with the circulation of fluid within the eye, resulting in a buildup of pressure and, eventually, death of internal eye structures and blindness. Previous infection, inflammation, or trauma to the eye can lead to glaucoma because of resultant internal adhesions that block the outflow portals for the eye's fluids. Glaucoma itself usually is not painful, but often the underlying cause is extremely painful. The glaucomatous eye may appear enlarged or bulging. There is no effective long-term treatment unless normal circulation within the eyeball can be restored surgically, which depends on the underlying cause.

Goiter 134, 135 Enlargement of the thyroid gland just below the horse's throatlatch. Can occur in thyroid dysfunction disorders such as hypothyroidism[G], or in cases of nutritional hyperthyroidism due to excessive iodine intake (as can occur when kelp-based supplements are fed).

Granulomatous disease, see Equine sarcoidosis.

Granulosa cell tumor, also: GCT 205, 242 A tumor of the ovary in mares. Symptoms may include aggressive, stallionlike behavior, including mounting of other mares, due to hormones that are secreted by the abnormal tissue. Usually benign; surgical removal of the affected ovary is curative in most cases. For more information on cancer in the senior horse, see "The Age Event: Cancer," page 241.

Gut motility, see Motility.

Guttural pouch, also: guttural pouch infection 75, 91, 189, 326 The paired guttural pouches are closed chambers located under the skin, one beneath each ear behind the jaw bone. Running through each pouch are several important structures, including blood vessels and nerves that serve the head and brain. One or both guttural pouches can become infected, and certain types of infections (particularly fungal ones) threaten to erode the walls of blood vessels within the pouch, which can split open and hemorrhage, sometimes fatally. Horses that show intermittent thick "snot" drainage when the head is held lowered, or intermittent nosebleed, should be checked for guttural pouch infection (usually done endoscopically). Medical treatment may include surgery to tie off at-risk blood vessels, to prevent hemorrhage.

Habronemiasis, also: *Habronema*, summer sores 26, 97, 109, 120, 162, 164, 244, 245 An allergic-type skin reaction to infestation with the larvae of equine stomach parasites, *Habronema* and/or *Draschia*. These enter the skin when houseflies and stable flies deposit their eggs on moist body parts, such as around the eyes or on open wounds. Symptoms include single or multiple, itchy, ulcerated[G] skin nodules that don't heal and often are complicated by proud flesh[G]. Treatment with ivermectin dewormer paste kills the larvae; simultaneous treatment with a corticosteroid[G] medication might be needed to calm overreactive tissue.

Head shaking 75, 88, 90 Vigorous head movements, from side to side, up and down, or rocker-fashion like a dog, often when insect pests are not apparent. May be due to inflammation of nerve tissue triggered by sunlight or wind, discomfort associated with tack; a painful tooth problem; or a behavior problem. Can result in irritating sensations on the face.

Heart arrhythmia, see Arrhythmia, cardiac.

Heat exhaustion 218 A potentially fatal rise in body heat, usually occurring with strenuous exercise during hot weather, due to dehydration and electrolyte imbalance from massive sweating. Can also result from anhidrosis[G]. Symptoms may include depression, rapid breathing, rapid and sometimes irregular heart rate, refusal to drink or eat, depression, weakness, and tremors. Intensive care, including intravenous fluids and electrolytes, may be required for best chance of recovery.

Heaves, see Chronic obstructive pulmonary disease.

Hematoma 137, 138, 189 A severe bruise, due to blunt trauma to soft tissue, resulting in a smooth swelling from accumulation of blood under intact skin. Depending on the location, size, and potential scarring of each case, treatment may range from first aid (ice, pressure, and rest) to surgical drainage of the blood after clotting has occurred.

Hemolysis 184 Rupture of red blood cells, resulting in their contents (chiefly hemoglobin) spilling out into the bloodstream or test tube. Can result from certain types of blood infections or poisonings, or when a snake or insect bite has occurred. Symptoms can include yellowish discoloration of the "whites" of the eyes and the normally pink mucous membranes such as the gums.

Hemolytic anemia, see Anemia.

Hemothorax 64 An abnormal condition in which blood has leaked into the chest. Most often due to trauma.

Hepatitis 33, 103, 146, 221 Inflammation of the liver. Can result from several causes, including infection, blockage in the bile duct, poisoning, pancreatic disease, ulcers, certain types of surgical colic[G], and as a side effect of anesthesia, medications, or tetanus antitoxin[G] use. Symptoms can include loss of appetite, depression, jaundice[G], intermittent fever, weight loss, and recurrent colic, but in many cases there is no visible abnormality because more than half the liver must be dysfunctional before symptoms appear.

Hepatoencephalopathy 52, 103, 110 Abnormal mental function resulting from buildup of natural toxins in the body when impaired liver function has failed to detoxify and/or eliminate them.

Hernia, abdominal, also: ventral hernia 22, 132, 133, 215, 264, 265 A partial rupture of the ventral (lower) abdominal wall, most common in aged pregnant broodmares during the late stages of pregnancy when weight and pressure on the body wall are greatest. The symptom is an obvious bulge or swelling in the abdomen. Surgical repair, done after foaling, often is successful. Not to be confused with ruptured prepubic tendon[G], which carries a poorer prognosis.

➤

Hernia, diaphragmatic 64, 188 An abnormal tear in the diaphragm (a muscular sheet that separates chest from abdomen). Usually the result of trauma such as a hard fall or collision. Symptoms can include colic[G] (when an abdominal structure such as a loop of bowel becomes trapped in the diaphragmatic tear) and/or respiratory distress (when abdominal contents work their way through the tear and crowd the lungs).

Hernia, inguinal 23, 133 An abnormally large opening or weakness in supportive soft tissues in the groin area, permitting abdominal structures (usually a loop of bowel) to slip through the opening and reside under the skin instead of within the abdominal cavity. Often attributed to congenital abnormality but has been related to trauma as well. Can result in colic[G] and/or damage to the displaced organ, particularly if it becomes entrapped.

Hook (dental) 334 A portion of a tooth that has become elongated due to lack of wear by an apposing tooth. For more information on teeth and dental problems in the senior horse, see "Top Priority—Tooth Care," page 332.

Hydrotherapy 236 Treatment of a tissue injury, inflammation, and/or infection by the use of warm or cold water.

Hyperthermia 218, 243 Especially high fever, particularly when induced for therapeutic purposes.

Hypoproteinemia 14, 18, 20, 22, 130, 133, 146, 147, 165, 229, 386 Abnormally low circulating protein levels in the blood. Can be due to inadequate quantity and/or quality protein intake, impaired digestion/metabolism, or excessive protein loss by the body due to disease such as kidney or liver dysfunction, chronic inflammation in the digestive tract, or cancer[G]. In addition to symptoms of the underlying cause, the affected horse will begin to lose muscle mass and, as the condition progresses, develop edema[G] of the ventral body wall and/or lower legs. For more information on hypoproteinemia and muscle loss in the senior horse, see "Senior Condition Check," page 300, and "Stay-Young Diet Solutions," page 376.

Hypothermia, also: hypothermic 56, 154, 220 Abnormally low body temperature. Can result from severe environmental conditions that overwhelm the normal warming systems of the body, or from an abnormality such as generalized illness or cardiovascular collapse that affects the body's ability to regulate heat.

Hypothyroidism, see Thyroid disease.

HYPP, also: hyperkalemic periodic paralysis 53 Usually associated with an inherited genetic abnormality tracing to the Quarter Horse sire Impressive. Symptoms include intermittent episodes of muscle spasm and weakness associated with an abnormal elevation of the electrolyte potassium, sometimes leading to collapse and death. Some cases can be managed successfully through dietary adjustments to minimize potassium levels.

Idiopathic 415, 416 Any medical condition for which the cause is unknown.

Inflammatory bowel disease, see Bowel disease, chronic inflammatory.

Influenza, also: flu 271, 325 A contagious viral respiratory infection that is spread directly from horse to horse via respiratory fluids, or indirectly by virus transfer on hands, clothing, buckets, etc. Symptoms include fever, loss of appetite, depression, runny nose, and cough, which often lingers for several weeks. The vast majority of victims recover completely, though residual cough is possible if returned to work before hypersensitive airways have fully returned to normal. Vaccination provides unreliable protection because of the variety of viral strains possible in the environment and the fact that vaccine strains may or may not be effective against the prevalent virus at the time. Many outbreaks occur at horse shows and other events in which horses are stressed and grouped together. For more information on control of this and other contagious diseases in the senior horse, see "Senior Deworming & Vaccination Program," page 322.

Inguinal hernia, see Hernia, inguinal.

Interovulatory interval, also: IOI 204, 210 The number of days between successive ovulations in a cycling mare during the breeding season, usually 20 to 21 days. When the IOI is abnormally shortened, uterine inflammation and/or infection should be considered; when abnormally long, temporary hormonal imbalance often is the cause.

Intertarsal joint, proximal and distal 236 Two of the four main subjoints within the hock.

Intralesional chemotherapy, see Chemotherapy, intralesional.

Intraluminal 210 Refers to the potential space within an enclosed structure, such as the tubular organs including the bowel and uterus.

Intraluminal fluid accumulation (uterine), also: IFA 210 A pool of liquid within the uterine lumen that usually is considered abnormal in the mare, as the health of uterine tissue is based on the organ's ability to clear itself quickly of cellular debris and breeding fluids.

Jaundice, also: icterus 33, 104, 241 Yellowish discoloration of the "whites" of the eyes and the normally pink mucous membranes, due to increased levels of a yellow pigment (bilirubin) in the circulating blood, as can occur in certain types of liver disease and hemolysis[G].

Joint fusion 236 Obliteration of joint cartilage between two apposing bones, resulting in the two bone surfaces healing together and eliminating movement between them.

Lactation tetany, also: eclampsia, hypocalcemic tetany, transport tetany, idiopathic^G **tetany 218** Rigid muscular tone resulting from abnormally low calcium and magnesium levels in the body, due to low intake and/or high usage (e.g., during heavy lactation). Symptoms, which may include a stiff, high-stepping hind limb gait, staggering, labored breathing, weakness, and coma, often are brought on by stress.

Laminitis, also: founder 15, 31, 44, 45, 46, 48, 49, 117, 142, 149, 150, 151, 156, 158, 174, 182, 190, 192, 204, 254, 257, 259, 261, 268, 273, 277, 287, 293, 296, 304, 327, 378, 381, 389, 390 A complex inflammatory disease that attacks the delicate, accordion-like folds (laminae) of the foot, resulting in altered blood flow, separation of the laminae from the hoof, and significant pain and suffering. Can be triggered by one or more of a variety of circulatory, hormonal, metabolic, dietary, toxic, and physical events that may or may not involve the feet initially but which ultimately result in an acute ("laminitis") and/or chronic ("founder") lameness of potentially devastating magnitude. For more information on laminitis in the senior horse, see "The Age Event: Laminitis (Founder)," page 273.

Larvicide 324 An agent that kills larvae.

Laryngeal hemiplegia, also: laryngeal paralysis 67, 189 Loss of normal tone in the muscles that hold one or both sides of the larynx open for breathing. Symptoms may include decreased performance and a roaring^G or snoring sound during inhalation. The cause may be injury to nerve tissue supplying the larynx, or nerve damage due to lead poisoning, but in many cases no cause is identified. Treatment is surgical.

Lead poisoning 67 A neurological disorder resulting from ingestion of peeling lead-based paint, motor oil leaked from an engine that used leaded gasoline, or other sources in junk piles and around old facilities. Symptoms may include a snoring or roaring^G sound on inhalation, drooling and dropping partially chewed feed due to impaired ability to swallow, depression, staggering, and weakness. Treatment includes an antidote, but permanent dysfunction may occur in severe or long-standing cases.

Leg mange 34 A contagious, itchy skin condition due to infestation, usually of the lower legs and occasionally the tail head, with *Chorioptes* mites, which are microscopic and feed on dead skin cells. Symptoms usually are worse in the colder months of the year and may include rubbing or biting at infested areas, resulting in broken or rubbed-out hair, abrasions, and oozing/crusting sores. More prevalent in draft horses that have long "feather" hair at the fetlock area. Treatment with ivermectin dewormer and/or topical insecticides labeled safe for use on horses usually is effective and should be done at least three times, separated by 1 or 2 weeks.

Lens, dislocated 100 An abnormal eye condition in which the lens moves out of its usual position behind the iris (the colored part within the eye) and comes to rest between the iris and the cornea^G. Can result from glaucoma^G, uveitis^G, or direct trauma to the eye.

Leukemia 386 A type of blood cancer in which abnormal white blood cells proliferate to excessive numbers in the bone marrow, other organs, and blood. For more information on cancer in the senior horse, see "The Age Event: Cancer," page 241.

Leukoencephalomalacia, also: mycotic encephalomalacia, moldy corn poisoning, blind staggers 92 An abnormal brain condition in which affected brain tissue softens and degenerates, resulting in permanent dysfunction. Caused by poisoning with the toxin from a specific mold that can infest corn. Liver damage also occurs. The mold usually is not visible to the naked eye. It can infest corn while still in the field as well as in storage. Only laboratory testing can assure that feed corn is not contaminated.

Lice 34, 35, 163 Skin parasites of the horse that are visible and can be spread to other horses. Some lice feed on skin cells and debris; others are blood suckers. Symptoms usually are worse during the colder months of the year and may include itching and patchy hair loss over the topline and trunk, or on the mane, tail, and lower legs, depending on whether the infestation involves biting or sucking lice, respectively. Severe infestation with blood-sucking lice can cause anemia^G and associated symptoms of poor performance and weakness. Topical insecticides labeled safe for use on horses are effective.

Lipoma 242 A tumor composed of fat cells. For more information on cancer in the senior horse, see "The Age Event: Cancer," page 241.

Longe, also: longeing, longe line (also lunge, lungeing, lunge line) An exercise and training drill in which the horse is connected to a line about 30 feet in length (longe line) and asked to work in a circle around the handler.

Lordosis, also: swayback 20, 21, 130, 131 An abnormal curvature of the spine that appears in the horse as swayback^G.

Lungworms 61, 62 Parasites (*Dictyocaulus arnfieldi*) that are carried without symptoms in mules, asses, and donkeys but which can spread to horses and ponies that share pasture. The symptoms are similar to those seen with COPD^G, including cough, labored exhalation, and reduced performance. Treatment with ivermectin dewormer is effective.

Lupus erythematosus 26, 31 A chronic autoimmune^G disease that can result in anemia^G, arthritis^G, and impaired kidney function.

Lyme disease 52 Infection with the spiral-shaped bacteria *Borrelia burgdorferi*, spread by the bite of an infected tick. ➤

Signs vary widely and can include: recurrent lameness that shifts from one leg to another and for which no other cause can be found; arthritis; stiffness; and reluctance to move. Treatment usually is administration of antibiotics from the penicillin or tetracycline family.

Lymphatic lacunae, also: uterine cysts 206, 210 Abnormal, fluid-filled structures in a mare's uterus that may interfere with pregnancy.

Lymphosarcoma 162, 242 Cancer of the lymph nodes. For more information on cancer in the senior horse, see "The Age Event: Cancer," page 241.

Lysine 381 An amino acid (one of the building blocks of protein) necessary for, among other things, healthy hoof horn, a healthy hair coat, and the body's ability to synthesize protein from components provided by the diet. Among all the amino acids in the common sources of protein given to horses, lysine is the indispensable one most likely to be missing, and its absence in the diet can significantly decrease a horse's ability to build and maintain blood protein and muscle. Abundant in milk products and certain grains.

Malignant 241 Usually referring to cancer that spreads from its original location to other sites in the body.

Malignant hyperthermia 218 Sudden onset of high fever and rigid muscles due to drug reaction or to abnormally low blood calcium levels.

Maple, red, poisoning by 103, 184 Hemolytic anemia[G] due to ingestion of wilted leaves of the red maple tree (*Acer rubrum*).

Medullary washout 73, 183 An abnormal kidney condition resulting from imbalance of salt and water intake (usually excessive water drinking) that impairs the kidney's ability to concentrate urine.

Melanin 98, 163 Dark brown or black pigment that colors skin, hair, and portions of the eye.

Melanoma 97, 98, 162, 163, 242, 243, 288 Cancer of the cells that form melanin[G]. In the horse melanoma usually is benign but can become malignant without warning. For more information, see "The Age Event: Cancer," page 241.

Mesentery, also: mesenteric 242, 245 A membrane that covers and encloses the abdominal organs and their blood vessels, attaching them to the body wall.

Metastasis 241 Spread of a disease process, such as a cancer, from its original site to other part(s) of the body.

Minimum contamination technique (breeding) 265 Breeding management technique by which the smallest possible volume of semen, with the optimal number of viable sperm, is deposited into the mare in a way that introduces as little contamination as possible.

Mite, mange 163 Any of numerous small to minute arachnids (same family as ticks and spiders), which include the parasitic mites responsible for mange.

Moon blindness, also: uveitis, recurrent uveitis, periodic ophthalmia 100, 101, 102, 105, 110, 112, 306 Uveitis is a painful, inflammatory disease of the iris (the colored part of the eye). Recurrent uveitis, moon blindness, and periodic ophthalmia refer to a type of uveitis that tends to occur repeatedly, at apparently random intervals. Permanent blindness can result; prompt and aggressive medical treatment is essential to prevent it. There may be several underlying causes, some of which have yet to be confirmed. Resident infection by the bacterial species *Leptospira* is suspected in some cases; other cases are considered idiopathic[G].

Motility 170, 251, 255, 264, 293, 341, 378, 379, 381, 382 The natural movement of the intestinal tract within the abdominal cavity, which serves to mix consumed feed with digestive juices and propel the resultant mixture through the tract. A sense of the gut's motility can be appreciated by listening for "gut sounds" (borborygmi) with a stethoscope placed at various locations on the abdomen—when motility ceases, as can happen in colic[G] and other forms of intestinal illness, the gut becomes ominously silent. With advancing age, gut motility tends to slow down, predisposing the older horse to excessively dry manure and impaction colic. For more information on colic in the senior horse, see "The Age Event: Colic," page 251.

Mycotoxin 103 Poisonous substance produced by mold growth.

Myoglobinuria 184 The presence of myoglobin, an oxygen-transporting muscle pigment, in urine, giving the urine a reddish-brown color.

Myositis 128, 149, 184, 190, 199, 386 A complex inflammatory disease that attacks muscle tissue. Can be caused by one or more of several factors including overexertion, electrolyte imbalance, dietary and/or metabolic factors, and possibly hereditary predisposition. Without proper treatment, severe myositis can lead to permanent scarring of affected muscle, kidney damage, and potentially fatal metabolic upset.

Myositis, acute, also: exertional rhabdomyolysis, tying-up syndrome 44, 128, 149, 184, 190, 195, 199 Severe muscle disorder causing stiffness, hardening, and breakdown of major muscle masses. There is a variety of causes and types of myositis; proper treatment and prognosis depend on accurate diagnosis.

Narcolepsy 53, 54, 89, 94 An abnormal condition characterized by sudden, brief attacks of deep sleep.

Navicular syndrome 315, 318, 343, 389, 390 A complex and potentially crippling inflammatory disease that attacks the navicular apparatus of the foot, including the navicular bone (a pulleylike bone that serves as the fulcrum for the deep digital flexor tendon), the navicular bursa (a pillowlike pad between the bone and the tendon), its supportive ligaments, and/or the flexor tendons that run over it. Can be caused by poor conformation and/or poor shoeing (such as in a long-toe, low-toe configuration). Also can be caused by infection and/or direct injury to the navicular apparatus, as in the case of a penetrating wound. Treatment can include medical intervention in the early stages, to short-circuit the chemical/circulatory changes, followed by corrective farriery and lifestyle changes to improve circulation without stressing damaged tissues.

Nerve resection, also: denerving 234 Surgical removal of a section of nerve or nerves that supply sensation to your horse's feet (commonly the palmar digital nerve, which supplies sensation to the rear third of your horse's foot). Used as a measure of last resort to relieve pain from such conditions as navicular disease^G and laminitis^G.

Neuritis 88 Inflammation or degenerative lesion of a nerve. Signs include pain, sensory disturbances, and impaired or lost reflexes.

Nigropalladial encephalomalacia, also: "chewing disease," 92 Encephalomalacia (softening) of a specific portion of the brain, caused by poisoning from ingesting yellow star thistle^G. Signs include sudden onset of paralysis of the mouth, making it impossible for the horse to hold or chew food or drink water. The upper lip is tense, the corners of his mouth held back in a grimace, and his tongue moves awkwardly in a futile attempt to hold and move food in his mouth. The horse may champ his jaw, yawn, and toss his head, and may submerge his head in water up to his eyes in order to drink. Brain damage is permanent; there is no treatment.

NSAID, also: nonsteroidal anti-inflammatory drug 174, 234, 251, 255, 345 A class of medications that can block components of inflammation, including pain, swelling, and heat. Some NSAIDs also help to reduce fever. Aspirin, "bute" (phenylbutazone^G), flunixin meglumine (Banamine® and generic products), and naproxen sodium are examples of common NSAIDs.

Nymphomania 242 Excessive sexual desire in a mare.

Occlusion 335 The bringing together of opposing tooth surfaces, such as the upper and lower molars. Proper tooth occlusion is needed for the grinding of your senior horse's food. For more information, see "Top Priority—Tooth Care," page 332.

Omentum 242 A fold of peritoneum (abdominal lining) connecting or supporting abdominal structures.

Onchocerca cervicalis, also: Onchocerciasis 34, 120 A worm that's carried to your horse in the bite of tiny *Culicoides* flies (also known as midges or no-see-ums). Adult worms live along the crest of a horse's neck in the broad, bandlike ligament called the ligamentum nuchae. The worms' tiny offspring migrate through the connective tissue to the skin of his lower chest, lower abdomen, head, neck, and withers, and also can invade his eyeballs. Signs can include itching, patchy hair loss, and crusting and scaling in the middle of the forehead. If the eye is affected, signs can include uveitis^G and conjunctivitis (pinkeye). Treatment involves killing the worms and their offspring with ivermectin or moxidectin dewormer and can cause an initial worsening of symptoms due to the presence of the dead parasites in your horse's tissues, but improvement is usually seen within a week.

Onion poisoning 103, 184 Both wild and cultivated onions, as well as their "cousin" garlic, are toxic to horses, causing hemolytic anemia^G. Signs can include icterus (jaundice), brownish-colored urine, and weakness and loss of stamina as the anemia progresses. Treatment usually is supportive. Prevention of further ingestion is key. If the anemia is severe, a transfusion may be needed.

Optic nerve, injury to 110, 112 Injury to the optic nerve—the large nerve that connects your horse's eye to his brain—can cause temporary or permanent blindness, depending on the severity of the injury. The most common cause of optic nerve injury is flipping over backward and landing on the poll: at the moment of impact, inertia jerks the brain backward, which tugs on the optic nerve.

Orbital cellulitis, see Cellulitis, orbital.

Osteomyelitis 128, 199 Inflammation and/or infection within bony tissue.

Ototoxic, also: ototoxicity 125, 126 Adverse affects on the organs or nerves involved in hearing, due to exposure to certain drug(s).

Oxidation 248 A chemical process in which a compound joins with oxygen and loses an electron, resulting in an ion with a positive charge. Similar to the process that causes iron to rust, oxidation in the body has been associated with the production of toxic free radicals^G, which are believed to be the roots of cell destruction, illness, cancer, and aging. For more information on oxidation, aging, and cancer in the senior horse, see "Stay-Young Diet Solutions," page 376, and "The Age Event: Cancer," page 241.

Paraphimosis 165 Entrapment of, and rubber-bandlike constriction on, an extended penis by the sheath's opening. The most common cause is prolonged extension of the penis, which causes it to swell (due to the effects of gravity) until the sheath's opening becomes too tight. Treatment generally focuses first on treating any external wounds on the penis, ➤

then on replacing it into the sheath so the swelling will subside. Treatment is then aimed at identifying, and resolving if possible, the underlying cause for prolonged penile extrusion. Penile paralysis^G, which often is permanent, is one cause of this problem. Depression, weakness, and long-acting sedatives can cause temporary relaxation of the penis.

Parasitic thromboembolism 52 Blockage of a blood vessel by a parasite-induced blood-clot particle that has broken away from its formation site at the wall of a parasite-infested artery.

Parotid 244 Referring to the area adjacent to the ear.

Pastern joint, proximal 236 The upper joint of the pastern area, beneath the fetlock and above the coronary band.

Pemphigus, also: pemphigus foliaceus 26, 31, 97, 120 A skin disorder caused by the body's immune system mistakenly attacking some of its own cells involved in skin production. Signs tend to wax and wane, and include the formation of blisters and pustules that break open and form crusted sores. Lesions generally start on a horse's face and limbs, eventually spreading to the rest of his body. There's no cure, but treatment can control the lesions and cause the disorder to go into remission. Some reports indicate that the younger a horse is, the greater the chance that the condition will go into long-term remission. Treatment may involve suppression of the immune system by administration of systemic corticosteroids^G (which can cause increased risk of infection and laminitis^G).

Penile paralysis 165, 166 Loss of motor control of a stallion or gelding's penis, as a result of disease, injury, or neurological disorder, or an adverse side effect of some tranquilizers.

Pericarditis 139 Inflammation of the pericardium, the membrane that encloses the heart.

Perinatal asphyxia, 264, 266 An abnormal condition of the newborn foal characterized primarily by deranged mental functioning, due to restricted oxygen supply before or during foaling. Especially common in foals born to older mares.

Perineal 242, 244, 264 Of or relating to the perineum^G.

Perineum 207 The hairless, soft tissue area between the anus and vulva in mares, and between the anus and testicles in stallions (or where the testicles were in geldings).

Periodontal disease 87, 91, 377 Disease of the gums and connective tissue around your horse's teeth. Incidence of this condition increases as your horse ages and his teeth become narrower, leaving spaces between them where food and debris can become lodged. The most common sign of periodontal disease is foul-smelling breath, most often smelling like moth balls.

Peripheral nerve paralysis 389 Any condition that causes loss

of motor function in nerves that supply external structures, such as the legs, skin, and facial features.

Peritonitis 55, 153, 168, 215, 221, 264 Inflammation of the membrane that lines your horse's abdominal cavity. Painful, and usually fatal. Can be triggered by such conditions as a ruptured uterus (as in certain difficult foalings, or in pyometra^G) or ruptured intestine.

Pharyngeal cyst 67 A fluid-filled cyst around the tissues at the back of your horse's throat. If the cyst impinges upon his airway, signs can include abnormal respiratory noise and decreased performance. Treatment usually is surgical removal by one of many available techniques.

Pharyngitis 61, 62 Inflammation of the pharynx.

Pharynx, collapsed, see Collapsed pharynx.

Phenylbutazone, also: bute 14, 46, 86, 135, 151, 234, 238, 251, 255, 345 A nonsteroidal anti-inflammatory drug (NSAID^G) that's used in the treatment of such inflammatory conditions as arthritis^G. Can be corrosive to your horse's stomach lining, resulting in ulcers^G.

Photic head shaking 90 Head shaking^G triggered by exposure to light, especially sunlight.

Photosensitization 26, 54, 97, 108 A skin disorder due to a photoactivating substance in the skin that produces skin-damaging chemicals when triggered by the absorption of ultraviolet light. The photoactivating substance can include certain toxic plants or drugs, or it can be a chemical byproduct of liver disease. Signs can include: redness; blistering; ulceration; and crusting of exposed skin that's pale-colored and not protected by hair, such as muzzle and eye tissues. (Another form of photosensitization is photoactivated vasculitis^G, for which the photoactivating substance hasn't been identified.) An effort to determine the type and source of the photoactivating substance must be made so treatment can address the underlying cause. Other preventive steps may include sunblocks, masks, or keeping the horse indoors until dusk. Skin lesions are treated as any other superficial ulceration, generally with debridement (physical scrubbing) of damaged tissue, disinfection, and protection against further irritation.

Pinworms (*Oxyuris equi*) 34, 163, 164, 258, 328, 329 A type of intestinal parasite that deposits its eggs in the tissues of the anus, causing intense anal itching. The most common external sign of pinworm infestation is a rubbed-out tail, the result of the horse's attempt to scratch his anus. Many of the commonly used deworming medications are effective in eliminating pinworms. For more information on parasite control in the senior horse, see "Senior Deworming & Vaccination Program," page 322.

Piroplasmosis, see Babesiosis.

Pituitary adenoma, see Equine Cushing's Disease.

Placentitis 266 Inflammation of the placenta (afterbirth) in a pregnant mare.

Pleuritis, also: pleuropneumonia, shipping fever 44, 47, 63, 65, 69, 149, 152 Infection involving the lungs (pneumonia^G) and/or the pleural cavity (pleuritis^G), often associated with the stress of a recent long-distance shipment. Signs can include fever; depression; lack of appetite; labored breathing; and a soft cough (which is painful because of chest movement). Treatment generally includes administration of antibiotics that the causative bacteria are sensitive to. If the pleural cavity contains accumulated pus, a drain probably will be installed to remove it.

Plugged tear duct, see Tear duct, plugged.

Pneumonia 60, 61, 63, 188, 220, 274 Infection in the lungs, sometimes occurring after a viral upper respiratory infection, due to bacteria that take advantage of your horse's weakened resistance. Other contributing factors can include: stress; aspiration; long-distance shipment; and exposure to powerful bacteria that can cause pneumonia even in horses that are otherwise healthy and unstressed. Signs may include fever; lack of appetite; cough; discharge of pus from nostrils; depression; and rapid and/or labored breathing. Treatment usually includes support and administration of appropriate antibiotics that the causative bacteria are sensitive to.

Pneumonia, aspiration 60, 63 Pneumonia^G resulting from contamination of lung tissue by foreign material such as medications intended for the stomach, or regurgitated stomach contents.

Pneumonia, gram-negative 274 Pneumonia^G due to infection with a particular type of bacteria.

Pneumothorax 64, 188 The presence of air or gas in the pleural cavity (the space between your horse's lungs and his chest wall), usually the result of a penetrating wound. Because his lungs can't expand properly, it's difficult for him to get enough oxygen. Signs usually include anxiety and preoccupation with breathing. Treatment generally is surgical repair.

Pneumovagina, also: wind sucking 164, 207, 211 Aspiration of air and/or debris into a mare's vagina.

Polydipsia 72, 73 Excessive water drinking.

Polyneuritis equi, also: cauda equina syndrome 159, 165 A disease of the nervous system. The affected horse moves stiffly, as if all joints and all four feet hurt. Although he has no fever and his appetite is unaffected, he tends to lose weight and muscle mass, especially over his shoulder blades and upper thighs. He trembles as he becomes progressively weaker, lifting his head only when alerted, then lowering it to his knees when at rest. There's no known treatment.

Porphyrins 185 Pigments widely present in nature, including certain bodily fluids and tissues.

Potomac Horse Fever, PHF 174, 327 An intestinal infection with the protozoal organism *Ehrlichia risticii*. Symptoms include diarrhea^G, fever, depression, and colic^G, often followed by laminitis^G. The organism has been found in common parasites of snails, aquatic insects (such as mayflies and dragon flies), bats, birds, and amphibians around surface freshwater, especially streams and rivers, which serve as a natural means of spreading the disease downstream. Treatment is supportive. Vaccination to prevent the disease is recommended in endemic^G areas. For more information on prevention of Potomac horse fever in the senior horse, see "Senior Deworming & Vaccination Program," page 322.

Prednisone, see Corticosteroids.

Prepubic tendon, ruptured 22, 132, 133, 215, 264, 265 Breakdown of the broad, sheetlike tendon that attaches the rectus abdominus (belly) muscles to the pelvis, usually occurring in heavily pregnant mares and resulting in catastrophic loss of belly support that is rarely reparable.

Progesterone 207, 212, 264 A hormone secreted by a mare's ovaries, adrenal cortex, and placenta. Its primary function is to prepare the uterus for pregnancy and reduce the uterine muscle reactivity that might cause pregnancy loss.

Protein-losing enteropathy, see Enteropathy, protein-losing.

Protozoa, also: protozoal, protozoan 325, 327 Potentially infectious organisms, separate from the more commonly regarded viruses and bacteria. Potomac Horse Fever^G (PHF) and Equine Protozoal Myeloencephalitis^G (EPM) are examples of protozoal diseases of the horse. For more information on prevention of EPM in the senior horse, see "Senior Deworming & Vaccination Program," page 322.

Proud flesh 244, 245 An overgrowth of pink, bubbly-looking tissue during healing of certain flesh wounds, particularly those involving the lower legs where there's no muscle beneath the skin. It can protrude from the injury site like a tumor, preventing new skin from covering the wound. Treatment depends on location and severity, and usually will include one or more of the following: topical applications of various medications designed to melt away the excessive tissue; pressure bandages; and/or surgical removal.

PSGAG; also: polysulfated glycosaminoglycan 234 An injectable drug (proprietary name, Adequan®) that can provide relief from joint heat, swelling, and pain by suppressing inflammatory cells, enzymes, and erosive chemicals that promote/sustain the inflammatory process. Also helps ➤

lubricate joints, protects cartilage, and promotes cartilage healing. Can be injected into the joint, or intramuscularly.

Psychogenic polydipsia, also: psychogenic PU/PD 72, 73, 183 Excessive water drinking (polydipsia) without thirst, such as out of stress or boredom, resulting in excessive urine output (polyuria).

Purge deworming 52, 62, 133, 175, 322, 324, 328 A parasite-control program in which an anthelmintic (deworming agent) is administered once every 6 weeks or as often as needed to keep fecal egg counts below 100 eggs per gram. Also called periodic deworming. For more information on parasite control in the senior horse, see "Senior Deworming & Vaccination Program," page 322.

Purpura, also: purpura hemorrhagica 22, 132, 146 A form of vasculitis^G that can occur several weeks after recovery from a respiratory illness such as strangles^G. The affected horse generally has severe, warm, painful edema^G at several locations on his body, including legs, lower abdomen, and muzzle. The swelling can cause his skin to stretch and split, oozing serum and blood. Edema also can affect his lungs and breathing. Treatment generally is aggressive intensive care and intravenous corticosteroids^G to reduce swelling; antibiotics if bacterial infection of damaged tissues is suspected; and nursing care as detailed in vasculitis^G. Often fatal.

Pyelonephritis 128, 199 An inflammation of kidney tissues and the surrounding pelvic lining, usually due to bacterial infection.

Pyometra 164, 167, 264 Translated, means "uterus full of pus"; a uterine infection that can't drain because the cervix has sealed itself closed, usually due to scarring. While pyometra in dogs and other species can be fatal, a protective coating in a mare's uterine lining prevents bacteria and toxins from entering her bloodstream. In almost every case, "pyo" ruins the uterus, as pus is corrosive. For more information, see "Pyo Pointers," page 168.

Rabies 52, 67, 76, 326 A fatal viral infection of the central nervous system. All warm-blooded mammals are susceptible, including horses, humans, and house pets. Usually spread by the bite of an infected animal, or by the infected animal's saliva coming into contact with an existing skin wound. Signs vary widely and can include colic^G, lameness, bizarre gait, slobbering, depression or excitability, and convulsions; death occurs within days of onset of signs. There is no treatment. Contact with a rabid or suspected horse by people or animals should be reported to a health professional for preventive treatment and/or quarantine. The only defense for horses is preventive vaccination and elimination of known carrier species (skunks, raccoons, foxes, bats, unvaccinated house pets) from the immediate environment. For more information on prevention of rabies in the senior horse, see "Senior Deworming & Vaccination Program," page 322.

Rainrot, also: dermatophilosis 26, 31 A crusting skin disorder affecting your horse's saddle area, with tufts of crusted-together hair easily pulled out, leaving a raw crater. The causative organism, which has characteristics of both bacteria and fungi, tends to thrive in wet weather when the skin is waterlogged and less capable of fighting infection. It can be spread to other horses via contaminated grooming tools.

Range of motion 230 The extent to which a joint can move in any direction. For more information on joint movement in the senior horse, see "The Age Event: Arthritis," page 227.

Retina, detached 100 An abnormal condition of the eye in which the retina (the "input" portion) begins to come apart from its attachment at the back of the eyeball. Can be due to trauma; also commonly follows severe inflammatory conditions of the eye such as uveitis^G.

Red maple, poisoning by, see Maple, red, poisoning by.

Rhino, see Equine herpesvirus.

Rhinotracheitis 60 Inflammation of the nasal cavities and trachea; upper-respiratory tract infection characterized by nasal discharge.

Ringworm, see Dermatophytosis.

Roaring 67, 415 An abnormal respiratory noise in your horse, most often noticed during exercise when breathing is heavy. Possible causes can include: laryngeal hemiplegia^G; the presence of a mass in the horse's upper respiratory tract; or abnormal position of normal tissues within the upper respiratory tract (from the nostrils to the windpipe [trachea]). Treatment generally is aimed at identifying and resolving the underlying cause.

Roundworms, see Ascarids.

Ruptured diaphragm, see Diaphragm, ruptured.

Ruptured esophagus, see Esophagus, ruptured.

Ruptured prepubic tendon, see Prepubic tendon, ruptured.

Ruptured uterine artery, see Uterine artery, ruptured.

Russian knapweed 67 Poisoning from eating fresh or baled Russian knapweed, a perennial weed that causes permanent brain damage similar to that seen with yellow star thistle^G poisoning. Signs generally include sudden onset of paralysis of the mouth, making it impossible for the horse to hold or chew food or drink water. The upper lip becomes tense, with the corners of the mouth held partially open in a grimace, and the tongue moving awkwardly in a futile attempt to hold and move food. The horse champs his jaw; yawns; tosses his head; and may submerge his head in water up to his eyes in order to drink. Brain damage is permanent; there's no treatment.

Safety margin (wide, narrow) 328, 329 A term referring to the toxic potential of a medication. When the safety margin is narrow, even a small overdose may have grave consequences. When wide, a large overdose usually causes no ill effects.

Salmonellosis, also: *Salmonella* **174, 175** A contagious intestinal infection by *Salmonella* bacteria, causing severe acute or chronic diarrhea[G]. Acute diarrhea is usually accompanied by fever and abdominal pain; horses that recover often fall victim to laminitis[G]. Treatment usually requires aggressive intensive care and quarantine.

Salt, excessive consumption of 72 Abnormal intake of salt, usually seen in idle, stall-bound horses and associated with boredom. Can result in salt poisoning[G] if adequate fresh water is not also available.

Sand colic, see Colic, sand.

Sarcoid 97, 108, 109, 242 A skin condition caused by invasion of tissues by an unidentified virus. Lesions usually are tumor-like, sometimes ulcerated, and may spread locally or to other areas of your horse's body. Typically found on the head, especially at the base of the ears, but also may be found on the belly, shoulders, torso, lower legs, or in skin lesions. Sarcoids on the lower legs usually appear at the site of cuts, bruises, or skin breaks and can resemble granulation tissue (proud flesh[G]). Can be treated surgically, with cryosurgery[G], with topical chemotherapy[G], or with immunotherapy (injection of the site with a commercial immune stimulant). Treatment may actually stimulate growth in the lesion, and/or the growth may return after removal. For more information, see "The Age Event: Cancer," page 241.

Scratches, eczematoid dermatitis, see Dew poisoning.

Seborrhea 38 A skin disorder that results in excessive scaling, crusting, and greasiness, due to abnormally increased secretion of skin oils known as sebum. Often associated with an allergy or chronic bacterial infection.

Selenium deficiency 45, 150 An insufficient dietary supply of the mineral selenium, a powerful antioxidant mineral, which can result in a variety of health problems, mostly degenerative ones, and cancers from an overload of toxic free radicals[G].

Selenium toxicosis, also: selenium poisoning, alkali disease 30, 157, 158 Poisoning from overdose of this essential mineral. Unfortunately there's a narrow margin between the amount needed for health, and the amount that can make a horse sick—or worse. When a dose is mildly toxic, chronic selenium poisoning (alkali disease) occurs. When the dose is moderately toxic, subacute selenium poisoning occurs. When the dose is

highly toxic, acute selenium poisoning occurs. Symptoms can include depression; labored breathing; diarrhea[G]; collapse; and death within 24 hours of ingestion of the mineral.

Seminal vesiculitis 208 Inflammation of a stallion's seminal vesicles, the passageways through which semen must flow during ejaculation. Can result in blockage, and failure to ejaculate. See also Ampullitis.

Senile cataract, see Cataract, senile.

Seroma 138 The result of blunt trauma causing bleeding under the skin. A seroma is a hematoma[G] in which accumulated blood has separated into serum and clotted red blood cells.

Sesamoid 295 A small pyramid-shaped bone, paired with an identical partner, located at the back of the fetlock joint on all four lower legs of the horse. This pair of bones at the fetlock joint is also called the "proximal" sesamoids, while the navicular bone at the back of the foot is the "distal" sesamoid.

Shipping fever, see Pleuropneumonia.

Shock 95, 174, 217, 293 A life-threatening shift in blood circulation and profound depression of vital processes, in response to one or more of several factors, including severe dehydration, hemorrhage, heat exhaustion, trauma, major surgery, or toxemia[G] due to poisoning or advanced disease such as colitis or severe colic[G]. Can result in weak pulse, rapid, shallow respiration, restlessness, anxiety, dullness, lowered blood pressure, and subnormal temperature. See also Endotoxic shock[G].

Sinker 274 Term for a horse with severe or advanced laminitis[G] or founder, in which the stricken laminar tissue has separated from its attachment to the hoof, allowing the coffin bone to descend ("sink") toward (and sometimes through) the sole. In most cases, this event marks a loss of hope for recovery of the laminitis victim. For more information on laminitis in the senior horse, see "The Age Event: Laminitis," page 273.

Smegma 166, 244, 246, 360 A waxy or pasty accumulation of cellular debris mixed with oil secreted by glands in the skin lining the male horse's penile sheath and between halves of a mare's udder. For more information on smegma and related topics in the senior horse, see "Down & Dirty Maintenance...," page 360.

Social status 193, 279 Your horse's standing within his herd. See "The Age Event: Loss of Social Status," page 279.

Sodium hyaluronate 232 The acid salt of hyaluronic acid, a very thick fluid that's present naturally and also can be injected directly into joints affected by such conditions as synovitis[G] and arthritis[G]. Restores joint lubrication, reerects a biological barrier to inflammatory cells, and helps protect cartilage from friction and chemical damage. Most ➤

horses experience a beneficial effect that can last for several months. Available in several viscosities (thicknesses); the higher the molecular weight, the more effective—and expensive.

Squamous cell carcinoma, SCC 97, 98, 108, 118, 162, 165, 243, 244, 245, 360 Cancer of a specific type of cells present in skin and mucous membranes lining internal organs such as the bladder, intestines, and uterus. SCC is commonly associated with ultraviolet rays on unpigmented, hairless skin adjacent to a white-coated area, which reflects sun onto the vulnerable skin for a double dose of UV rays. When lesions are few and accessible, treatment generally is removal and/or obliteration by surgery or cryosurgery[G]. When too extensive or inaccessible, often the only treatment option is chemotherapy[G]. For more information on squamous cell carcinoma and other cancers in the senior horse, see "The Age Event: Cancer," page 241.

Stereotypy 90, 381 Also called "stable vice"; a repetitive motion or behavior typically exhibited by a high-strung horse in a restricted, inactive setting. Weaving and cribbing[G] are examples of stereotypies. Can become deeply rooted, even addictive, due to opiate chemicals secreted by the brain during expression of the behavior.

Stocking up 147, 148, 156, 228 A horseman's term referring to swelling of the lower legs of the horse, usually associated with periods of confinement and inactivity and believed to be related to poor circulation of blood and/or lymph. For more information on prevention or treatment of stocking up in the senior horse, see "Age-Adjusted Exercise," page 340.

Strangles, also: bastard strangles 44, 52, 110, 149, 326 A contagious respiratory disease of the horse caused by the bacterium *Streptococcus equi*. Symptoms include fever, swelling of the lymph nodes under the jaw and in the throat region, and a thick drainage of pus and mucus from the nostrils and abscesses[G] of affected lymph nodes. In selected cases the infection can travel to, and form abscesses in, internal tissues distant from the respiratory tract—this is called bastard strangles. Treatment may include supportive care, hot packing and possibly drainage of abscessed lymph nodes, and in select cases the administration of antibiotics. Prevention by injected vaccination is controversial due to poor protection and a high incidence of vaccine reactions; a newer vaccine administered in the nostril may prove to be a safer and more effective way to protect against strangles outbreaks. For more information on control of strangles in the senior horse, see "Senior Deworming & Vaccination Program," page 322.

Strongyles, see Cyathostomes.

Subcutaneous emphysema, see Emphysema, subcutaneous.

Summer pasture-associated obstructive pulmonary disease (SPAOPD) 268, 270 A less common form of chronic obstructive pulmonary disease[G] (COPD, heaves), triggered by an allergen present in your horse's pasture rather than in his stall environment.

Summer sores, see Habronemiasis.

Suspensory ligament(s) 160 A strong, branched tendon, containing some muscle tissue, located at the back of the lower legs (roughly speaking, running from the top of the cannon bone to the prominent rearward protrusions of the fetlock joint), the main job of which is to support the fetlock joint when under load.

Swayback, see Lordosis.

Sweet itch, see *Culicoides* hypersensitivity.

Syncope 53 Temporary loss of consciousness; fainting.

Synovial fluid 228 The viscous, circulating liquid that bathes the internal structures of major joints.

Synovitis 229, 234 Inflammation of the soft, pliable membrane lining a joint. Often the first in a series of events that can lead to arthritis[G] (degenerative joint disease).

Tapeworms 252 A flat, segmented type of intestinal parasite that inhabits a specific area of the digestive tract known as the ileocecocolic junction (where the small intestine, the cecum, and the large intestine join). Once believed to cause no ill effects in the horse, studies show tapeworm infestation can predispose its victim to the type of colic[G] that's more likely to require surgery for any chance of survival. Symptoms of infestation can range from no symptoms, to mild intermittent colic, to severe surgical colic. As of this publication, treatment of tapeworm infestation in this country requires off-label use of available equine dewormers (higher than labeled dosage and frequency), or off-label use of a dewormer labeled for use in the dog. For more information on parasite control in the senior horse, see "Senior Deworming & Vaccination Program," page 322.

Tarsometatarsal joint 236 The lowest (closest to the ground, distalmost) of the hock's four subjoints, located between the hock proper and the upper surface of the cannon bone.

Tear duct, plugged 105 Blockage, either due to abnormal development or from debris, in the tubelike duct that carries tears from the eye to the nostril, resulting in tears spilling over onto the face.

Testicular degeneration 213 Breakdown of one or both testicles, often associated with earlier trauma to the tissue. The affected testicle gradually becomes visibly smaller, and sperm production and fertility are adversely affected.

Tetanus, also: lockjaw 326 A disease, often fatal, that causes painful muscle spasms. As a species, the horse is highly susceptible to tetanus, caused by the toxin of the bacterium *Clostridium tetani*, which is found normally in horse manure and is a common inhabitant of soils around horse facilities. Symptoms begin with mild stiffness and reluctance to lower the head, and progress to a rigid sawhorse stance with muscles of the face pulled back into a grimace. Jaw muscles are unable to relax for chewing. Drooling and labored breathing, as well as a tendency to overreact violently to sudden noise, touch, or movement, may also be evident. Treatment includes intensive care and intravenous tetanus antitoxin[G]; fatal outcome is common. Vaccination with tetanus toxoid[G] is quite effective as a preventive; use of tetanus antitoxin should be avoided as a preventive because of an increased risk of fatal liver disease as a side effect. For more information on prevention of tetanus in the senior horse, see "Senior Deworming & Vaccination Program," page 322.

Tetanus antitoxin 326 Antitoxin is a product made from serum containing antibodies against a specific toxin (poison). Tet-anus antitoxin is made of equine serum and contains antibodies against the tetanus toxin. To be used only if a broken-skin injury occurs in a horse with no known history of tetanus toxoid[G] vaccination.

Tetanus toxoid 326 A vaccine made of toxin (poison) that has been altered chemically so that it has no toxic effects, but is able to stimulate an immune response. Administered annually, tetanus toxoid stimulates your horse's production of antibodies against the toxins that cause tetanus[G].

Thromboembolism 52 Blockage of a blood vessel by a blood-clot particle that has broken away from its formation site.

Thyroid adenoma 243 A tumor of the thyroid gland. Can cause symptoms similar to Equine Cushing's Disease[G], but is much less common in horses than that condition.

Thyroid disease, also: thyroid disorder, hypothyroidism 31, 38, 40, 48, 111, 134, 142, 195, 204, 276, 278, 304 A metabolic disorder that occurs infrequently in the horse, characterized by decreased production of the thyroid hormone that governs metabolic rate. Most common in young horses, but can occur in the aged horse as well. Symptoms include long haircoat, increased susceptibility to heat and cold, lack of energy, lethargy or nervousness, poor performance, and reduced reproductive efficiency. In some studies, thyroid disorder has been implicated as a cause of repeated bouts of myositis[G], or tying-up syndrome. Readily and successfully treated with supplemental thyroid hormone.

Ticks, see Ear ticks.

Topical chemotherapy, see Chemotherapy, topical.

Toxemia 22, 132, 264 A general toxic (poisonous) condition due to absorption and systemic dissemination of bacterial toxins from an infection (such as peritonitis[G]), or due to dissemination of toxic substances (such as some byproducts of protein metabolism) that are inadequately metabolized because of malfunction of systems or organs (such as the kidneys).

Tracheitis 61, 62 Inflammation of the trachea (windpipe).

Tying-up syndrome, see Myositis.

Ulcerative colitis, see Colitis, ulcerative.

Ulcers, also: ulceration, ulcerated 14, 46, 75, 79, 151, 173, 221, 288, 378, 381 Surface sloughing of tissues or mucous membranes, due to a toxic or inflammatory reaction at the site. For instance, repeated use of phenylbutazone[G] ("bute") can result in ulcers in your horse's gut.

Urinary incontinence 167 Loss of urinary control, resulting in random or constant urine dribbling, due to loss of muscle tone and/or a neurological dysfunction.

Urine pooling 164, 207, 211 Accumulation of urine in a puddle on the floor of a mare's vagina, due to drooping and loss of muscle tone in the tissues there. Can set the stage for inflammation and infection in the vagina, cervix, and uterus.

Urolith 167, 183, 191 A stone, formed in the urinary tract from crystallized minerals in the urine. Usually not noticed until it has become lodged in your horse's urinary tract, resulting in symptoms of discomfort and/or changes in urinary behavior.

Uterine artery, ruptured 55, 153, 264 A catastrophic and often fatal breakdown of one of the paired uterine arteries that supply the mare's uterus, resulting in massive internal bleeding and violent coliclike pain. Usually occurs within a day or two before or after foaling.

Uterine inertia 263, 265 Insufficient uterine muscle strength and stamina to expel a foal, due to overall loss of condition.

Uveitis, acute, see Moon blindness.

Vaginal varicose veins, also: varicose veins in the vagina, vaginal varicositis 167, 185 Abnormally swollen or dilated veins of the vagina, often associated with occasional vaginal bleeding.

Vaginitis 207 Inflammation of the vaginal lining.

Vasculitis 22, 49, 132, 143, 146 Inflammation of small blood vessels and capillaries which, because of damage to their walls, leak serum into tissues and cause swelling ➤

(sometimes to the point of skin splitting), most often in the lower legs. It is a symptom of an underlying, body-wide problem, most often a viral respiratory infection. Treatment is generally directed at the underlying cause, plus supporting skin with padded compression bandages to help prevent splitting.

Vasomotor rhinitis 88, 90 An abnormal sensation in the muzzle region of a horse, possibly triggered by direct sunlight, dust, or wind on the face and often causing head-shaking[G] behavior.

Venereal disease 164 Infectious disease of the genitals, usually spread by sexual contact or through use of contaminated obstetrical instruments.

Venezuelan Equine Encephalomyelitis (VEE), also: sleeping sickness 67, 325 Often fatal viral infection of the brain and spinal cord of horses and humans. Spread by mosquitoes, the disease begins with fever and general malaise and can progress to dementia[G], blindness, weakness, staggering, and paralysis, and is fatal for many of its victims. Vaccination is an effective preventive but is recommended only in those areas where outbreaks of the disease have been reported, generally near the Mexican border. For more information on control of this and other contagious diseases in the senior horse, see "Senior Deworming & Vaccination Program," page 322.

Venous thrombosis 49, 143 Formation or presence of a blood clot within a vein.

Ventral edema 22, 132 Tissue swelling located on the underside of your horse's body (along the lower belly). See also edema.

Ventral hernia, see Hernia, abdominal.

Verminous encephalitis 52 Inflammation of brain tissue due to its invasion by parasite larvae.

Verminous thromboembolism 52 Formation of a blood clot, lodged in a blood vessel, due to presence of parasite larvae within the walls of the vessel.

Western Equine Encephalomyelitis (WEE), also: sleeping sickness 67, 325 Of the trilogy of sleeping sicknesses (EEE, WEE, and VEE), this one is the mildest and most common. Affects horses and humans and is carried by mosquitoes. Causes fever and general malaise and can progress to restlessness and excitability, depression, weakness, staggering, and paralysis, with 10 to 50% of victims dying. Permanent brain damage occurs in some, but not all, survivors. For more information on prevention of WEE in the senior horse, see "Senior Deworming & Vaccination Program," page 322.

Wind sucking 164, 211 A term used to describe a sterotypy[G] in which a horse grips an object in his teeth and forcibly swallows air (a.k.a. cribbing[G]); or, aspiration of air/debris into a mare's vagina due to an imperfect seal by the lips of the vulva.

Wolf teeth, wolf tooth 336, 337 Horseman's term for first premolar tooth, usually present only on the upper arcade on both sides, usually in stallions or geldings; seldom in mares. Each wolf tooth sits just in front of the molars, is very small, and has a short root, which makes it relatively easy to remove in the standing horse, often without sedation. Routine removal sometimes is requested, as many horsemen believe wolf teeth interfere with bitting and training. For more information on dental problems in the senior horse, see "Top Priority—Tooth Care," page 332.

Yellow star thistle 67, 92 Poisoning from eating the fresh or baled perennial weed causes permanent brain damage. A specific region of the brain becomes softened and liquefied.

References

Adair HS, Andrews FM: Diseases of the peripheral nerves. In: Kobluk CN, Ames TR, Geor RJ. *The Horse: Diseases and Clinical Management.* Philadelphia, PA: W. B. Saunders Company; 1995;482.

Airaksinen S, Heinonen-Tanski H, Heiskanen ML. Quality of different bedding materials and their influence on the compostability of horse manure. *Journal of Equine Veterinary Science.* 2001;21:125-130.

Asbury AC: The uterus. In: Kobluk CN, Ames TR, Geor RJ. *The Horse: Diseases and Clinical Management.* Philadelphia, PA: W. B. Saunders Company; 1995;990-997.

Beech J: Chronic obstructive pulmonary disease. In: *Veterinary Clinics of North America, Equine Practice.* 1991;7:79-92.

Bertone JJ: Medical Diseases of the Lower Alimentary Tract. In: Kobluk CN, Ames TR, Geor RJ. *The Horse: Diseases and Clinical Management.* Philadelphia, PA: W. B. Saunders Company; 1995;315-327.

Bistner S: Diseases of the eye. In: Kobluk CN, Ames TR, Geor RJ. *The Horse: Diseases and Clinical Management.* Philadelphia, PA: W. B. Saunders Company; 1995;1185-1205.

Boulton E: Liver and biliary system and pancreatitis. In: Kobluk CN, Ames TR, Geor RJ. *The Horse: Diseases and Clinical Management.* Philadelphia, PA: W. B. Saunders Company; 1995;363-369.

Browning AP. Polydipsia and polyurea in two horses caused by psychogenic polydipsia. *Equine Veterinary Education.* 2000; AE:231-236.

Carleton CL: Conditions of the vulva, vagina, and vestibule. In: Kobluk CN, Ames TR, Geor RJ. *The Horse: Diseases and Clinical Management.* Philadelphia, PA: W. B. Saunders Company; 1995;985-989.

Chandler K, McNeill PM, Murphy D. Small intestinal malabsorption in an aged mare. *Equine Veterinary Education.* 2000; AE:166-170.

Clark LL, Roberts MC, Argenzio RA: Feeding and digestive problems in horses. *Veterinary Clinics of North America, Equine Practice.* 1990;6:433.

Cox JH, Murray RC, DeBowes RM. Disease of the spinal cord. In: Kobluk CN, Ames TR, Geor RJ. *The Horse: Diseases and Clinical Management.* Philadelphia, PA: W. B. Saunders Company; 1995;453-466.

Derksen FJ: Chronic obstructive pulmonary disease. In: Beech J (ed.): *Equine Respiratory Disorders.* Philadelphia, PA; Lea & Febiger; 1991;223.

Divers TJ. Equine Cushing's disease and laminitis. Proceedings: *The First International Equine Conference on Laminitis and Diseases of the Foot.* 2001;77-78.

Dyson SJ, Arthur R, Palmer SE, Richardson D: Suspensory ligament desmitis. In: *Veterinary Clinics of North America, Equine Practice.* 1995;11:196.

East LM, Savage CJ: Abdominal neoplasia. In: *Veterinary Clinics of North America, Equine Practice.* 1998;3:475-494.

Else RW, Holmes JR: Cardiac pathology in the horse. *Equine Veterinary Journal;* 1972;4:195.

Embertson RM: Upper airway conditions in older horses, broodmares, and stallions. In: *Veterinary Clinics of North America, Equine Practice.* 1991;7:149-164.

Freeestone JF, Melrose PA: Endocrine diseases. In: Kobluk CN, Ames TR, Geor RJ. *The Horse: Diseases and Clinical Management.* Philadelphia, PA: W. B. Saunders Company; 1995;1137-1149.

Geor RJ: Performance-limiting conditions of the lungs. In: Kobluk CN, Ames TR, Geor RJ. *The Horse: Diseases and Clinical Management.* Philadelphia, PA: W. B. Saunders Company; 1995;263-268.

Ginther OJ. *Reproductive Biology of the Mare.* 2nd edition. Cross Plains, WI. Equiservices; 1992;111, 113, 504, 540.

Hardy J: Diseases of soft tissue. In: Kobluk CN, Ames TR, Geor RJ. *The Horse: Diseases and Clinical Management.* Philadelphia, PA: W. B. Saunders Company; 1995;797-799.

Hennig GE, Steckel RR: Disease of the oral cavity and esophagus. In: Kobluk CN, Ames TR, Geor RJ. *The Horse: Diseases and Clinical Management.* Philadelphia, PA: W. B. Saunders Company; 1995;289-296, 298-303.

Hood DM: Laminitis in the horse. In: *Veterinary Clinics of North America, Equine Practice.* 1999;2:287-294.

Johnson PJ: Dermatologic tumors. In: *Veterinary Clinics of North America, Equine Practice.* 1998;3:625-658.

Lewis LD. *Equine Clinical Nutrition: Feeding and Care.* Media, PA: Williams & Wilkins; 1995.

Little C: Diseases of joints. In: Kobluk CN, Ames TR, Geor RJ. *The Horse: Diseases and Clinical Management.* Philadelphia, PA: W. B. Saunders Company; 1995;707-719.

Martin BB, Klide AM: Physical examination of horses with back pain. In: *Veterinary Clinics of North America, Equine Practice.* 1999;15:61-70.

McGuirk SM, Muir WW: Diagnosis and treatment of cardiac arrythmias. *Veterinary Clinics of North America, Equine Practice.* 1985;1:353.

McKeever KH, Malinowski K. Endocrine responses to exercise in young and old horses. *Equine Veterinary Journal 1999;* Supplement 30; 561-566.

McKeever KH, Malinowski K. Exercise capacity in young and old mares. *American Journal of Veterinary Research.* 1997;58:1468-1472.

Meyers PJ: Ovary and oviduct. In: Kobluk CN, Ames TR, Geor RJ. *The Horse: Diseases and Clinical Management.* Philadelphia, PA: W. B. Saunders Company; 1995;1001-1008.

Paradis MR: Tumors of the central nervous system. In: *Veterinary Clinics of North America, Equine Practice.* 1998;3:554-559.

Polzer J and Slater MR. Age, breed, sex, and seasonality as risk factors for equine laminitis. *Preventative Veterinary Medicine.* 1996; 29:179-184.

Rooney JR: Internal haemorrhage related to gestation in the mare. *Cornell Veterinarian;* 1964;54:11.

Samper JC: Diseases of the male system. In: Kobluk CN, Ames TR, Geor RJ. *The Horse: Diseases and Clinical Management.* Philadelphia, PA: W. B. Saunders Company; 1995;961-968.

Sinha AK, Cox JH: Diseases of the brain. In: Kobluk CN, Ames TR, Geor RJ. *The Horse: Diseases and Clinical Management.* Philadelphia, PA: W. B. Saunders Company; 1995;413-423.

Trotter GW, Bennett DG, Behm RJ. Urethral calculi in five horses. *Veterinary Surgery.* 1981;10:159.

Turrel JM: Oncology. In: Kobluk CN, Ames TR, Geor RJ. *The Horse: Diseases and Clinical Management.* Philadelphia, PA: W. B. Saunders Company; 1995;1111-1130.

Williams MA, Angarano DQ: Diseases of the skin. In: Kobluk CN, Ames TR, Geor RJ. *The Horse: Diseases and Clinical Management.* Philadelphia, PA: W. B. Saunders Company; 1995;541-573.

Williams N. Disease conditions in geriatric horses. *Equine Practice.* 2000;22:32.

Index